Parties and Policies

DAVID R. MAYHEW

Parties and Policies

HOW THE AMERICAN
GOVERNMENT WORKS

Yale University Press
New Haven &
London

Published with assistance from the Institution for Social and Policy Studies, Yale University.

Set in Sabon type by Keystone Typesetting, Inc.
Printed in the United States of America.

Library of Congress Control Number: 2008923514
ISBN 978-0-300-13762-0 (paperback : alk. paper)

A catalogue record for this book is available from the British Library.

This paper meets the requirements of ANSI/NISO Z39.48-1992 (Permanence of Paper).
It contains 30 percent postconsumer waste (PCW) and is certified by the Forest Stewardship Council (FSC).

10 9 8 7 6 5 4 3 2 1

Contents

Introduction

Images and proper nouns arise in a jumble as we reflect on the history and underpinnings of American policy making — the New Deal era, the Bush tax cuts, gridlock, electoral realignments, the congressional pork barrel, long Senate debates, midterm earthquakes, the Reagan upsurge of 1980, the Great Society of the 1960s, the Iraq Resolution of 2002. A great deal of complicated history has taken place and continues to do so.

Scholars try to bring order to jumbles like these. That can involve *theorizing*, a term that implies a universalistic kind of explanation. "Rational actor"–type accounts are one kind of example, although there are others. The scholarly role can also involve *generalizing*, which in the study of American policy making can quickly lead backward into a search for historical patterns. In political science, probably for good reason, the line between theorizing and generalizing is often blurry or invisible.[1] Ordinarily we aim for satisfying intellectual order regardless of whether theorizing and generalizing are being emphasized or blended.

As history unfolds, *learning* is another exercise of the scholarly life. Explanatory theories are crafted or updated as new political realities kick into place. On the generalizing side, a wonderful aspect of history is that it keeps adding new material for time-series patterns. Updating can thus take place in both the theoretical and the generalizing realms. Yet such updating doesn't seem to render earlier scholarship irrelevant. Various theories of whatever vintage may offer continuing, simultaneous handholds on various surfaces of an evolving politics. Generalizing that draws on history often dwells on the political concerns of the present. Yet generalizing at a past moment that addresses the concerns of that past moment may retain a singular focus and validity. Consider V. O. Key Jr.'s *Southern Politics*.[2] Also, concerns come and go, and they may come again.

Theorizing, generalizing, and, I hope, learning are all reflected in the selection of the fourteen essays presented here as chapters. In their dates of origin, they extend across a third of a century, although they have a common objective. Directly or indirectly, all of them inquire into the roots of policy making in the American system.

Concerns of the moment as prompts to broader speculation enjoy ample representation in these essays. In the 1970s, the alleged "decomposition" of the American party system into rudderless voters and freelance politicians brought a wave of scholarship by, among others, Morris P. Fiorina and me.[3] Two of my short writings from that time appear here. In the late 1980s, the election of George H. W. Bush, apparently by driving a last nail into the idea that unified party control of the government was the "normal" state of affairs at the American national level, triggered a wave of work about divided party control by, among others, Morris P. Fiorina (again), Gary C. Jacobson, and me.[4] A few essays centering on that topic, or spurred by it, appear here. The election of 1992, which brought a new spell of Democratic power, and that of 1994, which brought the Republicans' Contract with America, tossed in the air once again the idea of decisive transformative elections as a property of the American system.[5] More essays here. Also, for me, the surprising rise and reign of Speaker Newt Gingrich in the mid-1990s induced speculation and writing about the consequential actions of individual Capitol Hill politicians. Another essay. The apparent recent stiffening of the Senate cloture pivot — the basis for successful filibustering — has brought another wave of scholarship by, among others, Keith Krehbiel, Gregory J. Wawro and Eric Schickler, and, very briefly, me.[6] Finally, the event-rich environment of the first decade of 2000 has spurred me to write about wars, and events in general, as causes of policy making.

As these fourteen essays share an objective, they also share a negative background theme. They are iconoclastic to the point of orneriness on the question of how useful political parties are as an analytic window onto American politics. They emphasize the *non*illumination supplied by various models of parties that are standard in political science.[7] For policy-making purposes, is unified party control of the government all it is often cracked up to be? Well, no. Is policy making ordinarily motored by party programs? Be careful. Can American history be helpfully sorted into a sequence of "party systems"? Probably not. Are "electoral realignments" a valid guide to the past or present? Be very careful. Do the elected politicians of a national party cohere into "teams"? Be careful of that, too. Ordinarily, my aim is not to try to stamp out understandings like these — that would be foolish — but to cut them down to a tolerable size.

That is the negative side. The positive side is more interesting — indeed, to me, a continuing source of fascination. It proceeds from a question that searches beneath and beyond the parties: On the route to American policy making, how do events, fancies, public moods, ideological animations, and the like sift themselves through an immensely complicated constitutional system in which, adding to all the rest, government officials themselves may choose to engage in autonomous action? Certainly the parties play a role along this route, but it is an intricate and qualified role. Modeled in any fashion, the party system has competitors. One is the built-in dissonance supplied by an array of elected officials — presidents, senators, and House members — heaved up by different constituencies at different dates and enjoying fixed terms and constitutional powers. Another is the complex of incentives, rewards, and penalties that attach to individual politicians as opposed to parties. Individual politicians are in certain ways the natural enemies of the parties and chronic victors over them. Another is the real evolving life of the society. In the policy-making realm, moods, tempers, and shocks — consider 9/11 — may override anything to do with the parties.

History supplies the empirical grist for all fourteen essays. The history gets deeper as the essays proceed, since I present them here in more or less the order I wrote them. Also, I have tended as a matter of evolving research inclination to cast farther and farther back for illuminating material. A time series crafted in the 1970s covers 16 years. Another crafted around 1990 covers 44 years. Others crafted more recently cover 200 and 216 years. Yet I hope that all the essays have some continuing relevance to the twenty-first century, and I make a case for that relevance as I introduce them here one by one.

As an analytic move, following the insight of Anthony Downs in *An Economic Theory of Democracy*, is it useful to characterize the American parties as unified "teams"?[8] Certainly it is, for a great many purposes, and that designation trails through these essays in many places. Yet there are limits. As it works out in practice, the American system of separation of powers can nudge members of Congress toward individualizing their behavior in ways that undermine the unity of the parties and leave certain distinctive traces in policy making. That case is made here in Chapter 1, "The Electoral Incentive," an excerpt from my *Congress: The Electoral Connection,* first published in 1974.[9] For one thing, the members may be nudged toward "credit claiming" —that is, efforts to sluice government benefits to particular states, districts, or other narrow recipients and then claim "I did it myself!" at election time. Done on a large enough scale, as in omnibus pork barrel measures, this propensity can particularize government spending, and in general government action, beyond what presidents, parties, the public, and indeed members of Congress, if they thought about it, might prefer. For another thing, the members may be nudged toward "position taking"—that is, taking public positions by way of speeches, roll-call votes, and other venues meant to please their home constituencies.[10] Of course, that happens. Why would it not? Why should it not? There are many sides to this matter. One that gives pause is that the members may get rewarded electorally for what they *stand for* as opposed to what they actually *do* in the enactment process or actually help to *cause* once policy enactments bring downstream effects through implementation.[11] The overall result can be a kind of feel-good, symbolic quality to congressional action—or at least a tendency in that direction.[12] In the American system, the presidency does offer a bundle of single-person instrumental rationality as a counter to this congressional position-taking tendency, although of course that solution has its problems, too.

As it happens, the American parties bottomed out in the 1970s as tamers of their members' individualism. In a variety of ways, the parties have grown stronger on Capitol Hill since then. Certainly roll-call voting is more party-line these days. Yet the logic and practice of member individualism have not gone away. From all reports, individual credit claiming is alive and well on Capitol Hill in the twenty-first century. The stronger, more centralized congressional parties have been using member-specific payoffs to build general coalitions.[13] "Earmarking" of local benefits has reached a new level of scandal in first decade of the 2000s.[14]

Nor has position taking by House and Senate members at the cost of party unity lost its availability or grounding. In one study employing *Congressional Quarterly*'s "key" roll calls of recent decades—no trend in the relevant respect seems to have occurred during this time—a surprising number of instances appear in which many House members seem to have gained in elections, net of all else including party affiliation, from the individual positions they took.[15] The policy consequences of non-party-line voting are not minor. Centered though it was in a Democratic-based coalition, the McCain-Feingold campaign finance reform found its way through Republican-led chambers of Congress in 2001–2 courtesy of defections by GOP "moderates." A great help to the Bush tax cut of 2001 was Senator Max Baucus of Montana, rank-

ing Democrat on the Finance Committee, who enraged his Senate party colleagues but appeased his conservative home state by going along with the White House.[16] We have seen in the 2000s, whether or not it reflected loyalty to party, the importance of position taking by senators aiming for the White House. How did Senators John Kerry, Joseph Lieberman, John Edwards, and Hillary Clinton vote on the Iraq war? That question was hard to step around in the middle of the first decade.

In the role that parties do enjoy in policy making, one key mechanism is the "net partisan seat swing" in House and Senate elections. For example, the Democratic tide in the 1932 and 1934 elections led to the New Deal. The Republican tide in the 1946 midterm helped spur the important Taft-Hartley Labor-Management Relations Act of 1947. What would happen if congressional seat swings declined in size? Would that impair the fresh initiative capacity of Congress, contribute to policy stasis in general, perhaps ramp up the initiative role of the White House? Chapter 2, a 1974 essay on the "vanishing marginals" in the House, was provoked by these questions.[17] At that time, individual politicians seemed to be scoring a historic victory over the party system — or at least over certain traditional competitive aspects of it. Incumbency advantage had found its day.[18] Incumbent House members were winning their elections by bigger and bigger margins. Challengers were falling behind.

One consequence of this rising incumbency advantage, it seems likely in retrospect, was the unbrokenness of the forty-year Democratic supremacy in the House between 1954 and 1994. Most House incumbents of that era were Democrats. They were hard to beat. Seat swings against them were dampened. It is also true that the Democrats enjoyed a sizable advantage in party identification among voters during those times, which aided the party's victories, yet one plausible statistical estimate has it that if the Republicans had competed under counterfactual pre-1960s conditions of lesser incumbency advantage during these later decades they would have captured the House at least three times — in 1966, 1968, and 1984.[19] Such victories might have brought differences in policy. In structural terms, they might have deflected the Republicans from becoming so dominantly an executive-centered party as they became under Nixon, Ford, Reagan, and the Bushes.

Granted, that was yesterday. Impressive swings in House seat holdings took place in 1994 and 2006. Many incumbents lost both times. Even so, it is well to realize that the numbers of House members actually losing their elections have kept falling to historic lows in recent times.[20] Beyond this, in terms of victory margins, recent work has shown that incumbents in a wide range of statewide elective offices — governors, U.S. senators, and the rest — have been doing better during the past half century or so than they once did.[21] It is an imperfectly understood trend.[22] In the U.S. House arena, the psychology of elections has possibly changed. Absent some catastrophe, to take over the House these days seems to promise taking it over forever. Quite different was the House electoral universe — and, I would guess, the understanding of it — during a previous time of fairly closely balanced party identification, the 1940s and 1950s, when the House shifted party control four times in ten elections.

Backstopping these concerns in the 1970s about credit claiming, position taking, and declining seat swings was a mid-twentieth-century ideal of parties as hugely important producers of public policy, at least in potential. It was a post–New Deal image and aspiration.[23] For political scientists, the idea of "party government" played a role somewhere between a Platonic form and a grail.[24] Chapter 3 addresses an especially creative statement of that view, V. O. Key's *Southern Politics,* issued in 1949. The southern states of that era offered an uncommon theoretical and empirical leverage. *Not* having competitive two-party systems, as contrasted with the northern states, they were fair game for the "so what?" question. In Key's argument, fed in part by this regional contrast, competition between well-organized parties was seen to serve not only voter choice in general, but also, distinctly, the interests of the "have-nots" of society. In effect, through the mechanism of parties, this was a blending of Downs with soft-core Marx. Key's treatment is rather scattered but it has many insights. In Chapter 3, I try to add more order to Key's argument. From his text, I tease out a list of twenty discrete theoretical claims that he made for the virtues of party competition. What does or might it accomplish? These are ideas of enduring interest. I also speculate about why he seems to have backed off the "have-nots" part of his argument in later writing.

In the canonical view of parties, single-party control of the government plays a leading role. That means, in the American national context, the same party controlling the White House and both houses of Congress. "You cannot compound a successful government out of antagonisms," wrote Woodrow Wilson.[25] If control of the branches is divided, it is said, high-stakes party programs cannot pass, and, more generally in many formulations, legislation production will be minimal at best as a deadly gridlock or stalemate sets in. Nourished by an admiration of the British parliamentary system, this line of thinking understandably rose to a status of conventional wisdom during the twentieth century thanks to the legislative production of the New Freedom under Wilson, the New Deal under Franklin D. Roosevelt, and the Great Society under Lyndon B. Johnson — all conducted under circumstances of unified party control.

Yet by the late 1980s this theorizing seemed to be taking on a horse-and-buggy aspect. That was for two reasons. First, how relevant could it be to a system where single-party control of the government was becoming less and less common? By choice or happenstance, the American voters were serving up divided party control.[26] For quite awhile, this propensity could be put down as an aberration—Eisenhower the victorious general, Nixon the Vietnam-era wild card, Reagan the charmer. But George H. W. Bush in 1988? Today, from the perspective of the 2000s, this waywardness has become ever more obvious. As a statistical matter, divided party control of the national government has become virtually normal. It has existed three-fifths of the time since World War II. Moreover, in an exercise of inventiveness, the American electorate and its politicians have been expanding the combinatorial particulars of party control.[27] If one scans beyond the yes versus no question—is party control unified or not?—eight possible triadic mixes of party control exist in principle—for example, Republican presidency, Republican Senate, and Democratic House as in 1981–82 under Reagan. In fact, *six* of those eight possible combinations have occurred since 1980.[28] In general, any theory centering on unified party control has come to look like a geometry for the wrong, or at least a rare, reality.[29]

Second, was unified party control all that exceptional an engine of legislative production anyway? That is an empirical question, and it began being asked around 1990 in a number of historical time-series studies.[30] Chapter 4, "Divided Party Control: Does It Make a Difference?," is an overview of one of those studies, my own more lengthy *Divided We Govern* (first published in 1991). Anchored in a data set of 267 arguably important laws enacted between 1947 and 1990, this research project supplied a negative answer: There hadn't been all that great a difference in legislative production, possibly close to none at all given certain controls, between conditions of unified and divided party control. Mesmerized by the Great Society and its antecedents, observers had misconstrued the record. Overlooked were such measures as the Marshall Plan in 1947, the Federal Highway Act of 1956, disability insurance in 1956, the Clean Air Act of 1970, the Campaign Finance Reform Act of 1974, the Earned Income Tax Credit (EITC) in 1975, the Reagan tax cuts in 1981, and the Americans with Disabilities Act of 1990—all enacted under conditions of divided party control. Extravagantly overlooked had been the harvest of domestic regulatory and spending legislation under Nixon and Ford.[31] In the light of today, further examples from divided control might include welfare reform in 1996, telecommunications reform in 1996, the Children's Health Insurance Program (CHIP) of 1997, the USA Patriot Act of 2001, and the No Child Left Behind Education Act of 2002. All along, it was a complex constitutional system that was generating laws, not just an us-against-them party system. Chapter 4 also surveys major congressional investigations of the executive branch during 1947 through 1900, and there too it finds not much of an edge in incidence correlated with conditions of party control, although on this front, it must be admitted, the later Republican hearings of 1998 fostering the impeachment of President Clinton threw a big new weight onto the scales. Chapter 4 in its original essay form had no tables, but I add here a summary one chalking up numbers of major legislative enactments per Congress, sorted by conditions of party control, from 1947 through 2006.[32] In general, as a fast track to lawmaking, unified party control hasn't performed any more remarkably since 1990 than it did before that time.

A more extensive treatment of the party-control question appears in Chapter 5, "Clinton, the 103d Congress, and Unified Party Control: What Are the Lessons?" A test case came down the historical pipeline. In 1992, by sending Bill Clinton to the White House and renewing a Democratic Congress, the American electorate gave over the government to one party for the first time since the Carter administration. What would happen? In terms of legislative production, would we see the New Deal or the Great Society all over again? Well, no, it turned out. There were significant victories — the Family Leave Act of 1993; the Clinton budget package of 1993; the North American Free Trade Agreement (NAFTA), thanks to Republican votes — but the president's health-care reform went down in flames and there were other difficulties. After a discussion of methodology, Chapter 5 takes up the legislative achievements, the nonachievements, the level of party conflict, and the congressional investigations of this soon to be halted all-Democratic phase of the Clinton era, as well as possible explanations of all the foregoing.

If party government, or unified party control, hasn't been anything like a unique, surefire recipe for policy production in the American system, then what has been? Are there deeper causes of legislative surges, like those of the Progressive era and the New Deal era and the lawmaking "bulge," it has been called, of the 1960s and 1970s under Johnson and Nixon (not just Johnson)?[33] In Chapter 6 here, "U.S. Policy Waves in Comparative Context," I cast a century backward into American history as well as cross-nationally into the records of comparable developed nations for clues. This is a sketchy, speculative essay. In principle it draws on a time-space matrix although my evidence is soft and secondary. Do the Progressive era, New Deal era, Johnson-Nixon era, and Reagan era have transnational analogues, and, if so, what are we to make of that?[34] Yes, there seem to be certain comparabilities, and underlying them is no doubt some mix of contagion and simultaneous autonomous causation.

Chapter 7, "Presidential Elections and Policy Change: How Much of a

Connection Is There?," another essay of the mid-1990s, is in a similar vein. It looks back in U.S. history for illumination of legislative surges, this time accommodating the Civil War and Reconstruction era as well as—here they are again, although addressed more amply this time—the Progressive, New Deal, and Johnson-Nixon eras. Four possible sources of policy change are canvassed for their explanatory utility—presidential elections, party government, ups and downs in the economy, and public moods. As in the previous chapter, the evidence I draw on is mostly soft. On balance, public moods seem to perform rather well.[35]

Off the presidential election calendar, the 1990s served up another kind of contender for policy consequentiality—the congressional midterm sweep, as embodied in the striking victory of the Republicans in 1994 under Newt Gingrich bearing the script of the Contract with America. Was a lasting policy impact in the offing? That question hastened me to the history books and resulted in the essay "Innovative Midterm Elections," appearing as Chapter 8 here. Which if any midterm elections in American history seemed to have brought, or at least indexed, major lasting policy change? Against a background of lesser midterms, what were the distinctive properties of any such elections? These probes required certain judgments about, again, soft evidence, yet I came up with four cases that seemed especially promising—the midterms of 1810 (a green light for expansion through war), 1866 (Reconstruction), 1910 (Progressive reform), and 1938 (a shift from the New Deal into the ascendancy of the so-called conservative coalition). Then the clincher question: Did the 1994 midterm exhibit the distinctive properties of those earlier hinge elections? On the whole, I concluded no, and on this basis I ended up chiefly skeptical about the long-run policy consequences of the Gingrich revolution. The same reasoning gives pause about the long-run consequences of the Democratic takeover of Congress in 2006.

Capstoning these essays of the 1990s about elections is Chapter 9, "Electoral Realignments," a rehearsal for a later book bearing that title.[36] Given life by E. E. Schattschneider, V. O. Key Jr., James L. Sundquist, and Walter Dean Burnham in the 1950s and 1960s, and elaborated by other authors since that time, the realignments view of American politics has led an exceptionally ambitious and influential life. It centers on the parties. A time-elongated variant of party-government thinking, it segments U.S. history into "realignment eras" thirty or so years in length said to be ushered in by "critical elections" that have lofted new ruling coalitions to power and generated the major exercises of American policy change over two centuries. For policy innovation, it is claimed, nothing else has been a close second in importance. Agreed-on hinge points are the elections of 1800, 1828, 1860, 1896, and 1932. Cyclical regularity is discerned and accounted for. There is a murky discourse about whether any critical realignment has occurred since 1932, yet the question arose again in the 1990s: Should we be spotting or expecting another one?

Chapter 9 is a negative assessment of this genre. Notwithstanding the genre's obviously sensible highlighting of the Civil War and New Deal eras, I had grown skeptical of its overall explanatory and ordering power. In this essay, published in 2000, I resolved the genre into eleven distinct empirical claims, tested them against available evidence, and judged them all to be largely wanting.[37] I do not believe that this contrary exercise was a gratuitous act. For any discipline, the opportunity costs of investing in dubious explanations can be high. What else might be going on that isn't being looked at?

One answer to this question, harking back to an emphasis of my *Congress: The Electoral Connection,* is a more individuated interpretation than party theories allow. In the shaping of policy, what do individual politicians do that is consequential? Even beyond the presidents, shouldn't there be room in a policy-rich account of American history for actors like Henry Clay, Charles Sumner, Robert F. Wagner, Wilbur Mills, Newt Gingrich, Edward Kennedy, and John McCain? Chapter 10, "Actions in the Public Sphere," associated with a larger book project,[38] pursues this line of thinking in an examination of 2,304 "actions" engaged in by members of the U.S. Congress between 1789 and 1988.[39] The members have engineered laws, taken public stands, joined in ideological crusades, arrayed themselves in opposition to the White House, and done several other kinds of things in participating consequentially in the American public sphere since 1789. They were still doing it all in the middle of the first decade of 2000, as witness the stands and resolutions issued against the Iraq war by many senators.[40] A public encasement of maneuvers, conflict, and dialogue moving through time supplies a continuous setting for U.S. policy making, and members of Congress are a central ingredient of that structure.

How do differences in intensity of preference wend their way into policy processes? How do procedural rules do that? Those questions are taken up in Chapter 11, "Supermajority Rule in the U.S. Senate." In the 1990s and the first decade of 2000, rule by three-fifths rather than simple majorities has become the norm in the Senate as effective filibustering or the threat of it is enabled by that chamber's cloture rule.[41] In this brief essay, I place this current context in relief by examining a past juncture. A party majority of unrivaled size dominated the New Deal's Democratic Congress of 1937–38, and that party's policy aspirations were outsized then, too, although many Democrats were tiring of White House liberalism. What actually happened during that historic

Congress? It is interesting to examine the coalitional strategies of opposing sides as they navigated the Senate's rules and sometimes differed a good deal in intensity — how much did each side really care? — in drives to reform ("pack") the Supreme Court (the White House lost), streamline the executive branch (same result), and criminalize lynching (the civil rights side lost). At least three lessons seem to emerge from this study. First, it's a good bet, not to mention a surprise, that decisions by simple majority are in general *harder* to engineer in today's Senate than they were in earlier times famous in legend for their unending windiness. Second, however, as in the case of civil rights in earlier times, intensity matters. The cloture rule is a wondrously sensitive accommodator of it. Third, don't be sure that the cloture rule is written in stone. Given a sufficiently determined majority and a friendly presiding officer, the Senate's procedures may be altered on the spot, as we came to suspect in the near-entertainment of the "nuclear option" on judicial appointments during George W. Bush's first term.

Then came 9/11. Through reading and reflection, I had already been growing uncomfortable with certain familiar assumptions in the study of American policy making. I had shared them myself. That American history can be examined in isolation. That an interest in domestic policy should crowd out everything else. That the New Freedom, the New Deal, and the Great Society had been the big bangs worth analyzing.[42] That the parties and their programs had been the main drivers of change. That peacetime is normal. That the 1930s had dwarfed the 1940s as a source of policy change — consider our customary obliviousness, for example, to the revolutions in federal revenue policy brought about during World War II and also earlier during World War I.[43] That 1945 is an apt location to start a time series, as is often done — doesn't that take out the bumps, as with histories beginning in 1066 or 1492?

At the least, in the light of 9/11, a change in emphasis seemed to be in order. In Chapter 12, "Wars and American Politics," I examine five of this country's major wars — the War of 1812, the War with Mexico, the Civil War, World War I, and World War II — as sources of lasting change in public policy, the issue content of politics, electoral coalitions, and party ideologies. There is much to be said for this line of thinking. Policies regarding taxation, the tariff, civil rights, the suffrage, and higher education, to cite some major areas, have owed much of their shape to the wars. In the early 2000s, we are seeing the policy and electoral consequences of the 9/11 attack and the Iraq war.

Chapter 13, "Events as Causes: The Case of American Politics," looks beyond wars to events in general — economic depressions and assassinations are added to the mix — as causes of policy and electoral change.[44] In general, contingency itself seems to merit a spot on the causal menu along with interests, movements, moods, parties, and the other usual suspects, in any serious account of American politics and history.[45]

The final chapter, "Incumbency Advantage in U.S. Presidential Elections," blends ideas from several of the previous essays. Incumbency advantage makes another appearance, this time at the level of presidential elections. Wars, events, and contingency reappear. Party strategies reappear. Canonical realignment theory is questioned again. The existence of long-lasting "party systems" or "realignment eras" is cast into doubt once more. Going all the way back to the choice of George Washington in 1788, it seems, American presidential elections can be ordered by a very simple formula. A party running an incumbent candidate keeps the White House roughly two-thirds of the time. A party *not* running an incumbent candidate keeps the White House exactly half the time. In short, in party terms, presidential politics in an open-seat contest reverts on average to a toss-up.

There are policy implications. A party lucky enough to capture the White House needs to seize the day, as did Wilson immediately in 1913, FDR in 1933, Reagan in 1981 (his tax and spending cuts), Clinton in 1993 (his budget package), and Bush in 2001 (his tax cuts). Good politicians intuitively know this. It is unwise to assume that anything like a friendly "party era" or "realignment coalition" will guarantee long-continuing policy successes. They may come, but that will be the luck of the draw as early enthusiasms wear off and unanticipated events help or hinder. Rock-solid long-lasting eras, including "the New Deal era," are largely a mirage. In fact, the policy creativity of the New Deal ended with the 1938 midterm, and we might be coding the 1940s rather differently if Nazi aggression against France and Britain during the 1940 election season hadn't made American voters see a renewal of FDR as the best prospect for foreign-policy leadership given that crisis. There is a lesson for today. In the early twenty-first century, it was often argued that the Republicans under Karl Rove had somehow gained an off-normal ideological and organizational edge that would keep them in power forever, or at least a very long time.[46] Another long-lasting era was at hand. I never believed it.[47] There is too much contingency in political life for that.

All but one of the essays in this book have appeared in print previously. Throughout, I have altered some framing, corrected some mistakes and infelicities, removed some dated material, and, in the case of Chapter 13, eliminated some repetition. But for the most part I have left the essays alone. I have not degendered the pieces from the 1970s, which featured "congressmen." I have not tampered with certain interpretative dissonances across the essays.

Dissonance is, among other things, the flip side of learning. I have not eliminated certain lesser instances of repetition, which I do not believe will cause the reader trouble. Save for Chapter 13, a section of which relies on Chapter 12, the essays can be read as autonomous works.

Notes

1. See, for example, Samuel H. Beer, "Causal Explanation and Imaginative Reenactment," *History and Theory* 3:1 (1963), 6–29, at 7–10.

2. V. O. Key Jr., *Southern Politics in State and Nation* (New York: Knopf, 1949).

3. For a reflection on this coincidence, see Morris P. Fiorina, "*Keystone* Reconsidered," ch. 7 in Lawrence C. Dodd and Bruce I. Oppenheimer (eds.), *Congress Reconsidered* (Washington, D.C.: Congressional Quarterly Press: 2005), at pp. 159–60. The relevant Fiorina works of the 1970s are *Representatives, Roll Calls, and Constituencies* (Lexington, Mass.: Lexington Books, 1974) and *Congress, Keystone of the Washington Establishment* (New Haven, Conn.: Yale University Press, 1977).

4. Morris P. Fiorina, *Divided Government* (New York: Macmillan, 1992); Gary C. Jacobson, *The Electoral Origins of Divided Government* (Boulder, Colo.: Westview Press, 1990).

5. See, for example, John H. Aldrich and Richard G. Niemi, "The Sixth American Party System: Electoral Change, 1952–1992," ch. 5 in Stephen C. Craig (ed.), *Broken Contract? Changing Relationships Between Americans and Their Government* (Boulder, Colo.: Westview Press, 1996); Walter Dean Burnham, "Whole Lotta Shakin' Goin' On: A Political Realignment Is on the Way," *The Nation*, April 17, 2000, pp. 11–15.

6. Keith Krehbiel, *Pivotal Politics: A Theory of U.S. Lawmaking* (Chicago: University of Chicago Press, 1998); Gregory J. Wawro and Eric Schickler, *Filibuster: Obstruction and Lawmaking in the U.S. Senate* (Princeton, N.J.: Princeton University Press, 2006).

7. My iconoclasm on this matter has been noticed: "A third school, best articulated by David Mayhew of Yale University, is that political scientists have attributed too much importance to party dynamics. They matter, but less so than the professional literature has suggested." Richard M. Valelly, "Who Needs Political Parties?" *The American Prospect*, August 14, 2000, pp. 48–50, quotation at 48.

8. Anthony Downs, *An Economic Theory of Democracy* (New York: Harper and Row, 1957).

9. David R. Mayhew, *Congress: The Electoral Connection* (New Haven, Conn.: Yale University Press, 1974), Part I.

10. On position taking, see also Arthur Denzau, William Riker, and Kenneth Shepsle, "Farquharson and Fenno: Sophisticated Voting and Home Style," *American Political Science Review* 79:4 (1985), 1117–34.

11. An inventive advance in this line of thinking appears in R. Douglas Arnold, *The Logic of Congressional Action* (New Haven, Conn.: Yale University Press, 1990). For one thing, members need to worry about whether whatever they do or vote for is "traceable" in the future as consequences occur.

12. See the argument in Mayhew, *Congress: The Electoral Connection*, pp. 132–40.

13. See Diana Evans, *Greasing the Wheels: Using Pork Barrel Projects to Build Majority Coalitions in Congress* (New York: Cambridge University Press, 2004).

14. See Thomas E. Mann and Norman J. Ornstein, *The Broken Branch: How Congress Is Failing America and How to Get It Back on Track* (New York: Oxford University Press, 2006), pp. 175–79.

15. See Gregory L. Bovitz and Jamie L. Carson, "Position-Taking and Electoral Accountability in the U.S. House of Representatives," *Political Research Quarterly* 59:2 (2006), 297–312. The study covers 1973 through 2000.

16. "Rarely has a high-ranking senator provoked more displeasure from his own party colleagues." Helen Dewar, "Baucus Deal on Tax Cut Upsets Senate Democrats," *Washington Post*, May 12, 2001. In July 2001, it was reported that the senator had "managed to score important points in his conservative state by helping Bush broker the biggest tax cut in 20 years." Shailagh Murray, "Uneasy Head: Mr. Baucus's Finance Perch Has Its Perils — Democratic Senator from Conservative Montana Must Tread More Carefully Than Ever," *Wall Street Journal*, July 2, 2001. Bush had carried Montana by 25 points in 2000. Baucus, his role in the tax cut on record, carried the state by 31 points in 2002.

17. In another instance of wave scholarship, also making an appearance around that time was Robert Erikson, "The Advantage of Incumbency in Congressional Elections," *Polity* 3 (1971), 395–405.

18. See also Bruce E. Cain, John Ferejohn, and Morris Fiorina, *The Personal Vote: Constituency Service and Electoral Independence* (Cambridge, Mass.: Harvard University Press, 1987).

19. See Stephen Ansolabehere, David Brady, and Morris Fiorina, "The Vanishing Marginals and Electoral Responsiveness," *British Journal of Political Science* 22:1 (1992), 21–38, at p. 33. See also Stephen Ansolabehere and Alan Gerber, "Incumbency Advantage and the Persistence of Legislative Majorities," *Legislative Studies Quarterly* 22:2 (1997), 161–78.

20. Joseph Sempolinski, "The Effects of Marginality," unpublished manuscript, Yale University, 2007.

21. Stephen Ansolabehere and James M. Snyder Jr., "The Incumbency Advantage in U.S. Elections: An Analysis of State and Federal Offices, 1942–2000," *Election Law Journal* 1 (2002), 315–38.

22. Notwithstanding a good deal of excellent scholarship on incumbency advantage in especially U.S. House elections. The works include Gary C. Jacobson, "The Marginals Never Vanished: Incumbency and Competition in Elections to the U.S. House of Representatives, 1952–82," *American Journal of Political Science* 31 (1987), 126–41; John Zaller, "Politicians as Prize Fighters: Electoral Selection and Incumbency Advantage," ch. 6 in John G. Geer (ed.), *Politicians and Party Politics* (Baltimore: John Hopkins University Press, 1998); Gary W. Cox and Jonathan N. Katz, "Why Did the Incumbency Advantage in U.S. House Elections Grow?" *American Journal of Political Science* 40 (1996), 478–97; Steven D. Levitt and Catherine D. Wolfram, "Decomposing the Sources of Incumbency Advantage in the U.S. House," *Legislative Studies Quarterly* 45 (1997), 45–60.

23. As witnessed in *Toward a More Responsible Two-Party System*, the report issued

by the Committee on Political Parties of the American Political Science Association in 1950 (New York: Rinehart).

24. See David R. Mayhew, *Divided We Govern: Party Control, Lawmaking, and Investigations, 1946–2002* (New Haven, Conn.: Yale University Press, 2005), p. 198.

25. Quoted in James L. Sundquist, "Needed: A Political Theory for the New Era of Coalition Government in the United States," *Political Science Quarterly* 103 (Winter 1988–89), 613–35, at p. 618. At pp. 616–24, Sundquist presents an especially useful review of the theoretical case for unified party control.

26. For an argument that emphasizes choice, see Fiorina, *Divided Government.*

27. Senator James Jeffords, elected by Vermont voters as a Republican, brought about an expansion all by himself in mid-2001 by switching his allegiance to the one-member-shy Democrats, thus levering a new combination of Republican presidency, Republican House, and Democratic Senate that lasted until November 2002.

28. The two exceptions: As of the mid-2000s, the Republicans had not controlled *only* the Senate since 1885–89 or *only* the House since 1859–61. To be technical about it, even these two combinations did come to pass very briefly in recent times. As new presidencies begin, there is a two-week constitutional window between the meeting of a new Congress and the inauguration of a new president and vice president (the latter of whom presides over the Senate as a possible tiebreaker, as did the outgoing Al Gore in the new evenly divided pre–Dick Cheney Senate of January 2001). That window allowed a flickering appearance of each of these two exceptions in, respectively, 1981 and 2001.

29. The relative ordinariness of divided party control in recent times, and the implications of that fact, are discussed in Charles O. Jones, *The Presidency in a Separated System* (Washington, D.C.: Brookings Institution Press, 2005, 2nd edition).

30. See, for example, George C. Edwards III, Andrew Barrett, and Jeffrey Peake, "The Legislative Impact of Divided Government," *American Journal of Political Science* 41 (1997), 545–63; Sarah A. Binder, *Stalemate: Causes and Consequences of Legislative Gridlock* (Washington, D.C.: Brookings Institution Press, 2003). The question figures in Keith Krehbiel, *Pivotal Politics.* For a longer time span regarding major U.S. laws, see John Lapinski and Joshua Clinton, "Measuring Legislative Accomplishment, 1877–1946," *American Journal of Political Science* 50 (2006), 232–49.

31. For a recent discussion of the surprising legislative productivity of the Nixon years, see David Greenberg, *Nixon's Shadow: The History of an Image* (New York: W.W. Norton, 2003), ch. 8.

32. The data plus a discussion for the years 1991–2002 may be found in the 2005 edition of *Divided We Govern* at pp. 200–226. Data on enactments for those years as well as for 2003–6 are available at http://pantheon.yale.edu/~dmayhew/data3.html. There are slight discrepancies between the data on legislative enactments reported in this volume of essays in chapters four and five, and those reported in the 2005 edition of *Divided We Govern.* That is for two reasons. In preparing the 2005 edition, with the advantage of a synoptic view, I made a very few changes in the judgments about which laws to list that I had been making biennially at the ends of the Congresses starting with that of 1991–92. Also, in the epilogue to the 2005 edition I corrected what I now regard as an unfortunate earlier omission. I added major joint resolutions enacted by Congress.

That would have accommodated three additional such measures between 1947 and 1990, and it added three after that date — the Gulf Resolution of 1991, the Use of Force Resolution of 2001, and the Iraq Resolution of 2002. As a legal and practical matter, joint resolutions are virtually indistinguishable from laws. See the discussion in the 2005 edition at pp. 202–5. For some further reflections on this continuing measurement enterprise, see also David R. Mayhew, "Lawmaking and History," ch. 10, in E. Scott Adler and John S. Lapinski, *The Macropolitics of Congress* (Princeton, N.J.: Princeton University Press, 2006).

33. On the "bulge," see William Howell, Scott Adler, Charles Cameron, and Charles Riemann, "Divided Government and the Legislative Productivity of Congress, 1945–94," *Legislative Studies Quarterly* 25 (2000), 285–312, at pp. 297–99. See also Mayhew, *Divided We Govern* (2005), pp. 81–91, 246–51.

34. For the Progressive era, a work I would have relied on had it been available at the time of my writing is Daniel T. Rodgers, *Atlantic Crossings: Social Politics in a Progressive Age* (Cambridge, Mass.: Harvard University Press, 1998).

35. On public moods and policy making, see the important later work by Robert S. Erikson, Michael B. MacKuen, and James A. Stimson, *The Macro Polity* (New York: Cambridge University Press, 2002). See also Mayhew, *Divided We Govern*, pp. 142–74.

36. David R. Mayhew, *Electoral Realignments: A Critique of an American Genre* (New Haven, Conn.: Yale University Press, 2002).

37. In my later book, I expand the number of tested claims to fifteen.

38. David R. Mayhew, *America's Congress: Actions in the Public Sphere, James Madison Through Newt Gingrich* (New Haven, Conn.: Yale University Press, 2000).

39. On the place of such "actions" in a congressional career, see Daniel Diermeier, Michael Keane, and Antonio Merlo, "A Political Economy Model of Congressional Careers," *American Economic Review* 95:1 (2005), 347–73.

40. For one apparent consequence of oppositional moves like this, see Dennis M. Foster, "An 'Invitation to Struggle'? The Use of Force Against 'Legislatively Vulnerable' American Presidents," *International Studies Quarterly* 50 (2006), 421–44.

41. See Krehbiel, *Pivotal Politics.*

42. As in Arthur M. Schlesinger Jr., "The Cycles of American Politics," ch. 2 in Schlesinger (ed.), *The Cycles of American History* (Boston: Houghton Mifflin, 1986), pp. 31–34.

43. For the importance of those wartime junctures in generating longlasting revenue policy, see W. Elliot Brownlee, "Woodrow Wilson and the Financing of the Modern State: The Revenue Act of 1916," *Proceedings of the American Philosophical Society* 129:2 (1985), 173–210; Brownlee, "Tax Regimes, National Crises, and State-building in America," in Brownlee (ed.), *Funding the Modern American State, 1941–1995* (New York: Cambridge University Press, 1996), pp. 37–104; Brownlee, "The Public Sector," in Stanley L. Engerman and Robert E. Gallman, *The Cambridge Economic History of the United States*, vol. 3, *The Twentieth Century* (New York: Cambridge University Press, 2000), pp. 1013–60. The Revenue Act of 1916, although Congress did enact it before the United States entered World War I, was a "preparedness" measure.

44. On assassinations in this regard, see also Bruce Ackerman, "The Living Constitution," *Harvard Law Review* 120:7 (2007), 1738–1812.

45. For an interesting effort to model such an expanded menu, see Robert W. Fogel, "Problems in Modeling Complex Dynamic Interactions: The Political Realignment of the 1850s," *Economics and Politics* 4:3 (1992), 215–54. For a classic argument that events can open up "windows" of policy opportunity, see John Kingdon, *Agendas, Alternatives, and Public Policies* (Boston: Little, Brown, 1984).

46. See Jacob S. Hacker and Paul Pierson, *Off Center: The Republican Revolution and the Erosion of American Democracy* (New Haven, Conn.: Yale University Press, 2005); Thomas B. Edsall, *Building Red America: The New Conservative Coalition and the Drive for Permanent Power* (New York: Basic Books, 2006).

47. "Such claims had always been overblown," argues John J. Pitney Jr., in a reflection on the Democratic victory in 2006: "The Midterm: What Political Science Should Ask Now," *The Forum: The Berkeley Electronic Press,* 4:3 (2006), article 2, p. 3.

I

The Electoral Incentive

What animates members of Congress? The discussion to come will hinge on the assumption that United States congressmen[1] are interested in getting reelected — indeed, in their role here as abstractions, interested in nothing else. Any such assumption necessarily does some violence to the facts, so it is important at the outset to root this one as firmly as possible in reality. A number of questions about that reality immediately arise.

First, is it true that the United States Congress is a place where members wish to stay once they get there? Clearly there are representative assemblies that do not hold their members for very long. Members of the Colombian parliament tend to serve single terms and then move on.[2] Voluntary turnover is quite high in some American state legislatures — for example, in Alabama. In his study of the unreformed Connecticut legislature, Barber labeled some of his subjects "reluctants" — people not very much interested in politics who were briefly pushed into it by others.[3] An ethic of "volunteerism" pervades the politics of California city councils.[4] And in the Congress itself voluntary turnover was high throughout most of the nineteenth century.

Yet in the modern Congress the "congressional career" is unmistakably upon us.[5] Turnover figures show that over the past century increasing proportions of members in any given Congress have been holdovers from previous Congresses — members who have both sought reelection and won it.

Membership turnover noticeably declined among southern senators as early as the 1850s, among senators generally just after the Civil War.[6] The House followed close behind, with turnover dipping in the late nineteenth century and continuing to decline throughout the twentieth.[7] Average number of terms served has gone up and up, with the House in 1971 registering an all-time high of 20 percent of its members who had served at least ten terms.[8] It seems fair to characterize the modern Congress as an assembly of professional politicians spinning out political careers. The jobs offer good pay and high prestige. There is no want of applicants for them. Successful pursuit of a career requires continual reelection.[9]

A second question is this: Even if congressmen seek reelection, does it make sense to attribute that goal to them to the exclusion of all other goals? Of course the answer is that a complete explanation (if one were possible) of a congressman's or any one else's behavior would require attention to more than just one goal. There are even occasional congressmen who intentionally do things that make their own electoral survival difficult or impossible. The late President Kennedy wrote of congressional "profiles in courage."[10] Former Senator Paul Douglas (D., Ill.) tells of how he tried to persuade Senator Frank Graham (D., N.C.) to tailor his issue positions in order to survive a 1950 primary. Graham, a liberal appointee to the office, refused to listen. He was a "saint," says Douglas.[11] He lost his primary. There are not many saints. But surely it is common for congressmen to seek other ends alongside the electoral one and not necessarily incompatible with it. Some try to get rich in office, a quest that may or may not interfere with reelection.[12] Fenno assigns three prime goals to congressmen—getting reelected but also achieving influence within Congress and making "good public policy."[13] These latter two will be given attention further on in this discussion. Anyone can point to contemporary congressmen whose public activities are not obviously reducible to the electoral explanation; Senator J. William Fulbright (D., Ark.) comes to mind. Yet, saints aside, the electoral goal has an attractive universality to it. It has to be the *proximate* goal of everyone, the goal that must be achieved over and over if other ends are to be entertained. One former congressman writes, "All members of Congress have a primary interest in getting re-elected. Some members have no other interest."[14] Reelection underlies everything else, as indeed it should if we are to expect that the relation between politicians and public will be one of accountability.[15] What justifies a focus on the reelection goal is the juxtaposition of these two aspects of it—its putative empirical primacy and its importance as an accountability link. For analytic purposes, therefore, congressmen will be treated in the pages to come as if they were single-minded reelection seekers. Whatever else they may seek will be given passing attention, but the analysis will center on the electoral connection.

Yet another question arises. Even if congressmen are single-mindedly interested in reelection, are they in a position as individuals to do anything about it? If they are not, if they are inexorably shoved to and fro by forces in their political environments, then obviously it makes no sense to pay much attention to their individual activities. This question requires a complex answer, and it will be useful to begin reaching for one by pondering whether individual congressmen are the proper analytic units of an investigation of this sort. An important alternative view is that parties rather than lone politicians are the prime movers in electoral politics. The now classic account of what a competitive political universe will look like with parties as its analytic units is Downs's *Economic Theory of Democracy*.[16] In the familiar Downsian world parties are entirely selfish. They seek the rewards of office, but in order to achieve them they have to win office and keep it. They bid for favor before the public as highly cohesive point-source "teams." A party enjoys complete control over government during its term in office and uses its control solely to try to win the next election. In a two-party system a voter decides how to cast his ballot by examining the record and promises of the party in power and the previous record and current promises of the party out of power; he then calculates an "expected party differential" for the coming term, consults his own policy preferences, and votes accordingly. These are the essential lineaments of the theory.[17] Legislative representatives appear only as modest "intermediaries." If of the governing party, they gather information on grassroots preferences and relay it to the government, and they try to persuade constituents back home that the government is doing a worthy job.[18]

How well a party model of this kind captures the reality of any given regime is an empirical question. One difficulty lies in the need for parties as cohesive teams (members whose "goals can be viewed as a simple, consistent preferences-ordering").[19] In all nonautocratic regimes governments are made up of a plurality of elective officials — not just one man. How can a group of men be bound together so that it looks something like a Downsian team? Probably nowhere (in a nonautocratic regime) does a group achieve the ultimate fusion of preference-orderings needed to satisfy the model; party government in Britain, for example, proceeds substantially by intraparty bargaining.[20] Nonetheless, it is plain that some regimes fit the model better than others. For some purposes it is quite useful to study British politics by using parties as analytic units. Britain, to start with, has a constitution that readily permits majoritarian government. But, beyond that, at the roll call stage British M.P.s act as cohesive party blocs that look something like teams. It is not inevitable that they should do so, and indeed there was a good deal of individualistic voting in the Commons in the mid-nineteenth century.[21] Why do contemporary M.P.s submit to party discipline? There are at least three reasons why they do so, and it will be profitable here to examine them in order to allow later contrasts with the American regime.

First of all, in both British parties the nominating systems are geared to produce candidates who will vote the party line if and when they reach Parliament. This happens not because nominations are centrally controlled, but because the local nominating outfits are small elite groups that serve in effect as nationally oriented cheerleaders for the Commons party leadership.[22]

Second, British M.P.s lack the resources to set up shop as politicians with bases independent of party. Television time in campaigns goes to parties rather than to scattered independent politicians.[23] By custom or rule or both, the two parties sharply limit the funds that parliamentary candidates can spend on their own in campaigns.[24] Once elected, M.P.s are not supplied the kinds of office resources — staff help, free mailing privileges, and the like — that can be used to achieve public salience.[25] These arguments should not be carried too far; M.P.s are not ciphers, and obviously dissident leaders like Aneurin Bevan and Enoch Powell manage to build important independent followings. But the average backbencher is constrained by lack of resources. It comes as no surprise that individual M.P.s add little to (or subtract little from) core partisan electoral strength in their constituencies; the lion's share of the variance in vote change from election to election is chargeable to national swings rather than to local or regional fluctuations.[26]

Third, with the executive entrenched in Parliament the only posts worth holding in a Commons career are the ones doled out by party leaders. Up to a third of majority party M.P.s are now included in the Ministry.[27] "For the ambitious backbencher, the task is to impress ministers and particularly the Prime Minister."[28] Party loyalty is rewarded; heresy is not.

The upshot of all this is that British M.P.s are locked in. The arrangement of incentives and resources elevates parties over politicians. But the United States is very different. In America the underpinnings of "teamsmanship" are weak or absent, making it possible for politicians to triumph over parties. It should be said that Madisonian structure and Downsian teamsmanship are not necessarily incompatible.[29] Connecticut state government, in which party organizations exercise substantial control over nominations and political careers, comes close to the British model; governorship and state legislative parties are bound together by party organization.[30] But Connecticut is exceptional, or, more accurately, it is at one end of a spectrum toward the other end of which there are states in which parties have little binding effect at all.[31] In American politics the place where Downsian logic really applies is in the election of individuals to executive posts — presidents, governors, and big-city mayors. To choose among candidates for the presidency or the New York City mayoralty is to choose among "executive teams" — candidates with their retinues of future high administrators, financial supporters, ghostwriters, pollsters, student ideologues, journalistic flacks, hangers-on, occasionally burglars and spies. In executive elections the candidates are highly visible; they bid for favor in Downsian fashion; they substantially control government (or appear to) and can be charged with its accomplishments and derelictions (President Nixon for inflation, Mayor Lindsay for crime); elections are typically close (now even in most old machine cities); voters can traffic in "expected differentials" (between executive candidates rather than parties). When the late V. O. Key Jr., wrote *The Responsible Electorate*,[32] a book in the Downsian spirit, he had the empirical good sense to focus on competition between incumbent and prospective presidential administrations rather than more broadly on competition between parties. Indeed, it can be argued that American representative assemblies have declined in power in the twentieth century (especially at the city council level) and executives have risen chiefly because it is the executives who offer electorates something like Downsian accountability.[33]

But at the congressional level the teamsmanship model breaks down. To hark back to the discussion of Britain, the specified resource and incentive arrangements conducive to party unity among M.P.s are absent in the congressional environment: First, the way in which congressional candidates win party nominations is not, to say the least, one that fosters party cohesion in Congress. For one thing, 435 House members and 98 senators (all but the Indiana pair) are now nominated by direct primary (or can be, in the few states with challenge primaries) rather than by caucus or convention. There is no reason to expect large primary electorates to honor party loyalty. (An introduction of the direct primary system in Britain might in itself destroy party cohesion in the Commons.) For another, even where party organizations are still strong enough to control congressional primaries,[34] the parties are locally rather than nationally oriented; local party unity is vital to them, national party unity is not. Apparently it never has been.[35]

Second, unlike the M.P. the typical American congressman has to mobilize his own resources initially to win a nomination and then to win election and reelection. He builds his own electoral coalition and sustains it. He raises and spends a great deal of money in doing so. He has at his command an elaborate set of electoral resources that the Congress bestows upon all its members. There will be more on these points later. The important point here is that a congressman can — indeed must — build a power base that is substantially in-dependent of party.[36] In the words of a House member quoted by Clapp, "If we depended on the party organization to get elected, none of us would be here."[37]

Third, Congress does not have to sustain a cabinet and hence does not engage the ambitions of its members in cabinet formation in such a fashion as to induce party cohesion. It would be wrong to posit a general one-to-one relation here between party cohesion and cabinet sustenance. On the one hand, there is nothing preventing congressmen from building disciplined con-gressional parties anyway if they wanted to do so. On the other hand, as the records of the Third and Fourth French republics show, cabinet regimes can be anchored in relatively incohesive parties. Yet, to pose the proposition in statis-tical rather than deterministic form, the need for an assembly to sustain a cabinet probably raises the likelihood that it will spawn disciplined parties.[38]

The fact is that no theoretical treatment of the United States Congress that posits parties as analytic units will go very far. So we are left with individual congressmen, with 535 men and women rather than two parties, as units to be examined in the discussion to come. The style of argument will be somewhat like that of Downs, but the reality more like that of Namier.[39] Whether the choice of units is propitious can be shown only in the facts marshaled and the arguments embellished around them. With the units nailed down, still left unanswered is the question of whether congressmen in search of reelection are in a position to do anything about it.

Here it will be useful to deal first with the minority subset of congressmen who serve marginal districts or states — constituencies fairly evenly balanced between the parties. The reason for taking up the marginals separately is to consider whether their electoral precariousness ought to induce them to en-gage in distinctive electoral activities. Marginals have an obvious problem; to a substantial degree they are at the mercy of national partisan electoral swings. But general voter awareness of congressional legislative activities is low.[40] Hence national swings in the congressional vote are normally judgments on what the president is doing (or is thought to be doing) rather than on what Congress is doing. In the familiar case where parties controlling the presidency lose House seats in the midterm, swings seem to be not judgments on anything at all but rather artifacts of the election cycle.[41] More along a judgmental line, there has been an impressive relation over the years between partisan voting for the House and ups and downs in real income among voters. The national electorate rewards the congressional party of a president who reigns during economic prosperity and punishes the party of one who reigns during adver-sity.[42] Rewards and penalties may be given by the same circuitous route for other states of affairs, including national involvement in wars.[43] With voters behaving the way they do, it is in the electoral interest of a marginal congressman to help insure that a presidential administration of his own party is a popular success or that one of the opposite party is a failure. (Purely from the standpoint of electoral interest there is no reason why a congressman with a safe seat should care one way or another.)

But what can a marginal congressman do to affect the fortunes of a presidency? One shorthand course a marginal serving under a president of his own party can take is to support him diligently in roll call voting; there is ambiguous evidence that relevant marginals do behave disproportionately in this fashion.[44] This strategy may not always be the best one. During the 1958 recession, for example, it may have been wise for marginal Republicans to support Democratic deficit-spending bills over the opposition of President Eisenhower; in the 1958 election Eisenhower's policies seem to have been ruinous for members of his own party. How about marginals of the opposition party? By the same logic it might be advantageous for opposition marginals to try to wreck the economy; if it were done unobtrusively the voters would probably blame the president, not them.

There are a number of intriguing theoretical possibilities here for marginals of parties both in and out of power. Yet marginals seem not to pay much attention to strategies of this sort, whether ingenuous or ingenious. What we are pondering is whether individual marginals can realistically hope to do anything to affect the national component of the variance over time in congressional partisan election percentages.[45] And the answer seems to be no — or at least extraordinarily little. Leaving aside the problem of generating collective congressional action, there is the root problem of knowing what to try to do. It is hard to point to an instance in recent decades in which any group of congressmen (marginals or not) has done something that has clearly changed the national congressional electoral percentage in a direction in which the group intended to change it (or to keep it stationary if that was the intention). There are too many imponderables. Most importantly, presidents follow their own logic. So do events. Not even economists can have a clear idea about what the effects of economic measures will be. The election cycle adds its own kind of perversity; the vigorous enactment of President Johnson's Great Society legislation (by all the survey evidence popular) was followed in 1966 by the largest Republican gain in House popular vote percentage of the last quarter century. Hence there is a lack of usable lore among congressmen on what legislative actions will produce what national electoral effects.[46]

And there is after all the problem of generating collective action — especially action among nonmarginal congressmen who can watch national election percentages oscillate and presidents come and go with relative equanimity. All in all the rational way for marginal congressmen to deal with national trends is to ignore them, to treat them as acts of God over which they can exercise no control. It makes much more sense to devote resources to things over which they think they can have some control. There is evidence that marginals do think and act distinctively. House marginals are more likely than nonmarginals to turn up as "district-oriented" and "delegates" in role studies;[47] they introduce more floor amendments;[48] in general, marginals of both houses display more frenzy in their election-oriented activities. But these activities are not directed toward affecting national election percentages. And although they may differ in intensity, they do not differ in kind from the activities engaged in by everybody else.

Are, then, congressmen in a position to do anything about getting reelected? If an answer is sought in their ability to affect national partisan percentages, the answer is no. But if an answer is sought in their ability to affect the percentages in their own primary and general elections, the answer is yes. Or at least so the case will be presented here. More specifically, it will be argued that they think that they can affect their own percentages, that in fact they can affect their own percentages, and furthermore that there is reason for them to try to do so. This last is obvious for the marginals, but perhaps not so obvious for the nonmarginals. Are they not, after all, occupants of "safe seats"? It is easy to form an image of congressmen who inherit lush party pastures and then graze their way through careers without ever having to worry about elections. But this image is misconceived, and it is important to show why.

First, when looked at from the standpoint of a career, congressional seats are not as safe as they may seem. Of House members serving in the Ninety-third Congress 58 percent had at least one time in their careers won general elections with less than 55 percent of the total vote, 77 percent with less than 60 percent of the vote. For senators the figures were 70 percent and 86 percent (the last figure including fifteen of the twenty-two southerners). And aside from these November results there is competition in the primaries. The fact is that the typical congressman at least occasionally has won a narrow victory.[49]

Second — to look at the election figures from a different angle — in United States House elections only about a third of the variance in partisan percentages over time is attributable to national swings. About half the variance is local (or, more properly, residual, the variance not explained by national and state components).[50] The local component is probably at least as high in Senate elections. Hence vote variation over which congressmen have reason to think they can exercise some control (i.e. the primary vote and the local component of the November vote) is substantial. What this comes down to in general elections is that district vote fluctuations beyond or in opposition to national trends can be quite striking. For example, between 1968 and 1970 the Republican share of the national House vote fell 3.3 percent, but the share of Congressman Chester L. Mize (R., Kans.) fell from 67.6 percent to 45.0 percent, and he lost his seat. In 1972 four incumbent Republican senators lost their seats; in general 1972 was not a bad year for congressional Republicans, and all four senators had won in 1966 with at least 58 percent of the vote. And so it goes. In addition, there are the primaries.[51] It is hard for anyone to feel absolutely secure in an electoral environment of this sort. In Kingdon's interview study of candidates who had just run for office in Wisconsin (about a third of them running for Congress) the proportion who recalled having been "uncertain" about electoral outcome during their campaigns was high, and the incidence of uncertainty was only modestly related to actual electoral outcome.[52] But the local vote component cuts two ways; if losses are possible, so presumably are gains. In particular, it seems to be possible for some incumbents to beef up their November percentages beyond normal party levels in their constituencies. In the House (but apparently not in the Senate) the overall electoral value of incumbency seems to have risen in the last decade — although of course some House incumbents still do lose their seats.[53]

Third, there is a more basic point. The ultimate concern here is not how probable it is that legislators will lose their seats but whether there is a connection between what they do in office and their need to be reelected. It is possible to conceive of an assembly in which no member ever comes close to losing a seat but in which the need to be reelected is what inspires members' behavior. It would be an assembly with no saints or fools in it, an assembly packed with skilled politicians going about their business. When we say "Congressman Smith is unbeatable," we do not mean that there is nothing he could do that would lose him his seat. Rather we mean, "Congressman Smith is unbeatable as long as he continues to do the things he is doing." If he stopped answering his mail, or stopped visiting his district, or began voting randomly on roll calls, or shifted his vote record eighty points on the ADA scale, he would bring on primary or November election troubles in a hurry. It is difficult to offer conclusive proof that this last statement is true, for there is no congressman willing to make the experiment. But normal political activity among politicians with healthy electoral margins should not be confused with inactivity. What characterizes "safe" congressmen is not that they are beyond electoral reach, but that their efforts are very likely to bring them uninterrupted electoral success.

Whether congressmen think their activities have electoral impact, and whether in fact they have impact, are of course two separate questions. Of the former there can be little doubt that the answer is yes. In fact in their own minds successful politicians probably overestimate the impact they are having. Kingdon found in his Wisconsin candidates a "congratulation-rationalization effect," a tendency for winners to take personal credit for their victories and for losers to assign their losses to forces beyond their control.[54] The actual impact of politicians' activities is more difficult to assess. The evidence on the point is soft and scattered. It is hard to find variance in activities undertaken, for there are no politicians who consciously try to lose. There is no doubt that the electorate's general awareness of what is going on in Congress is something less than robust.[55] Yet the argument here will be that congressmen's activities in fact do have electoral impact. Pieces of evidence will be brought in as the discussion proceeds.[56]

The next step here is to offer a brief conceptual treatment of the relation between congressmen and their electorates. In the Downsian analysis what national party leaders must worry about is voters' "expected party differential."[57] But to congressmen this is in practice irrelevant, for reasons specified earlier. A congressman's attention must rather be devoted to what can be called an "expected incumbent differential." Let us define this "expected incumbent differential" as any difference perceived by a relevant political actor between what an incumbent congressman is likely to do if returned to office and what any possible challenger (in primary or general election) would be likely to do. And let us define "relevant political actor" here as anyone who has a resource that might be used in the election in question. At the ballot box the only usable resources are votes, but there are resources that can be translated into votes: money, the ability to make persuasive endorsements, organizational skills, and so on. By this definition a "relevant political actor" need not be a constituent; one of the most important resources, money, flows all over the country in congressional campaign years.[58]

It must be emphazied that the average voter has only the haziest awareness of what an incumbent congressman is actually doing in office.[59] But an incumbent has to be concerned about actors who do form inpressions about him, and especially about actors who can marshal resources other than their own votes. Senator Robert C. Byrd (D., W.Va.) has a "little list" of 2,545 West Virginians he regularly keeps in touch with.[60] A congressman's assistant interviewed for a Nader profile in 1972 refers to the "thought leadership" back in the district.[61] Of campaign resources one of the most vital is money. An incumbent not only has to assure that his own election funds are adequate, but has to try to minimize the probability that actors will bankroll an expensive campaign against him. There is the story that during the first Nixon term Senator James B. Pearson (R., Kans.) was told he would face a well-financed opponent in his 1972 primary if he did not display more party regularity in his voting.[62]

Availability of money can affect strength of opposition candidacy in both primary and general elections.[63]

Another resource of significance is organizational expertise, probably more important than money among labor union offerings. Simple ability to do electioneering footwork is a resource the invoking of which may give campaigns an interesting twist. Leuthold found in studying ten 1962 House elections in the San Francisco area that 50 percent of campaign workers held college degrees (as against 12 percent of the Bay area population), and that the workers were more issue oriented than the general population.[64] The need to attract workers may induce candidates to traffic in issues more than they otherwise would. Former Congressman Allard K. Lowenstein (D., N.Y.) has as his key invokable resource a corps of student volunteers who will follow him from district to district, making him an unusually mobile candidate.

Still another highly important resource is the ability to make persuasive endorsements. Manhattan candidates angle for the imprimatur of the *New York Times*. New Hampshire politics rotates around endorsements of the *Manchester Union Leader*. Labor union committees circulate their approved lists. Chicago Democratic politicians seek the endorsement of the mayor. In the San Francisco area and elsewhere House candidates try to score points by winning endorsements from officials of the opposite party.[65] As Neustadt argues, the influence of the president over congressmen (of both parties) varies with his public prestige and with his perceived ability to punish and reward.[66] One presidential tool is the endorsement, which can be carefully calibrated according to level of fervor, and which can be given to congressmen or to challengers running against congressmen. In the 1970 election Senator Charles Goodell (R., N.Y.), who had achieved public salience by attacking the Nixon administration, was apparently done in by the resources called forth by that attack; the vice president implicitly endorsed his Conservative opponent, and the administration acted to channel normally Republican money away from Goodell.[67]

What a congressman has to try to do is to insure that in primary and general elections the resource balance (with all other deployed resources finally translated into votes) favors himself rather than somebody else. To maneuver successfully he must remain constantly aware of what political actors' incumbent differential readings are, and he must act in a fashion to inspire readings that favor himself. Complicating his task is the problem of slack resources. That is, only a very small proportion of the resources (other than votes) that are conceivably deployable in congressional campaigns are ever in fact deployed. But there is no sure way of telling who will suddenly become aroused and with what consequence. For example, just after the 1948 election the American

Medical Association, unnerved by the medical program of the Attlee Government in Britain and by Democratic campaign promises here to institute national health insurance, decided to venture into politics. By 1950 congressmen on record as supporters of health insurance found themselves confronted by a million-dollar AMA advertising drive, local "healing arts committees" making candidate endorsements, and even doctors sending out campaign literature with their monthly bills. By 1952 it was widely believed that the AMA had decided some elections, and few congressmen were still mentioning health insurance.[68]

In all his calculations the congressman must keep in mind that he is serving two electorates rather than one — a November electorate and a primary electorate nested inside it but not a representative sample of it. From the standpoint of the politician a primary is just another election to be survived.[69] A typical scientific poll of a constituency yields a congressman information on the public standing of possible challengers in the other party but also in his own party. A threat is a threat. For an incumbent with a firm "supporting coalition"[70] of elite groups in his party the primary electorate is normally quiescent. But there can be sudden turbulence. And it sometimes happens that the median views of primary and November electorates are so divergent on salient issues that a congressman finds it difficult to hold both electorates at once. This has been a recurrent problem among California Republicans.[71]

A final conceptual point has to do with whether congressmen's behavior should be characterized as "maximizing" behavior. Does it make sense to visualize the congressman as a maximizer of vote percentage in elections — November or primary or, with some complex trade-off, both? For two reasons the answer is probably no. The first has to do with his goal itself, which is to stay in office rather than to win all the popular vote. More precisely his goal is to stay in office over a number of future elections, which does mean that "winning comfortably" in any one of the them (except the last) is more desirable than winning by a narrow plurality. The logic here is that a narrow victory (in primary or general election) is a sign of weakness that can inspire hostile political actors to deploy resources intensively the next time around. By this reasoning the higher the election percentages the better. No doubt any congressman would engage in an act to raise his November figure from 80 percent to 90 percent if he could be absolutely sure that the act would accomplish the end (without affecting his primary percentage) and if it could be undertaken at low personal cost. But still, trying to "win comfortably" is not the same as trying to win all the popular vote. As the personal cost (e.g. expenditure of personal energy) of a hypothetical "sure gain" rises, the congressman at the 55 percent November level is more likely to be willing to pay it than his colleague at the 80 percent level.

The second and more decisive reason why a pure maximization model is inappropriate is that congressmen act in an environment of high uncertainty. An assumption of minimax behavior therefore gives a better fit. Behavior of an innovative sort can yield vote gains, but it can also bring disaster (as in Senator Goodell's case). For the most part it makes sense for congressmen to follow conservative strategies. Each member, after all, is a recent victor of two elections (primary and general), and it is only reasonable for him to believe that whatever it was that won for him the last time is good enough to win the next time. When a congressman has a contented primary electorate and a comfortable November percentage, it makes sense to sit tight, to try to keep the coalition together. Where November constituencies are polarized in the conventional fashion—labor and liberals on one side, business on the other—there is hardly any alternative. Yet simply repeating the activities of the past is of course impossible, for the world changes. There are always new voters, new events, new issues. Congressmen therefore need conservative strategies for dealing with change. And they have some. For members with conventional supporting coalitions it can be useful to accept party cues in deciding how to cast roll call votes;[72] a Republican House member from Indiana can hardly go wrong in following the party line (though for an Alabama Democrat or a Massachusetts Republican it would be madness to do so). It may be useful to build a voting record that blends in with the records of party colleagues in one's state delegation.[73] It is surely useful to watch other members' primary and general elections to try to gain clues on voter temperament. But conservatism can be carried only so far. It requires a modest degree of venturesomeness just to hold an old coalition together. And for members in great electoral danger (again, Goodell) it may on balance be wise to resort to ostentatious innovation.

Whether they are safe or marginal, cautious or audacious, congressmen must constantly engage in activities related to reelection. There will be differences in emphasis, but all members share the root need to do things—indeed, to do things day in and day out during their terms. The next step here is to present a typology, a short list of the *kinds* of activities congressmen find it electorally useful to engage in. The case will be that there are three basic kinds of activities. It is important to lay them out with some care.

One activity is *advertising*, defined here as any effort to disseminate one's name among constituents in such a fashion as to create a favorable image but in messages having little or no issue content. A successful congressman builds what amounts to a brand name, which may have a generalized electoral value for other politicians in the same family. The personal qualities to emphasize are experience, knowledge, responsiveness, concern, sincerity, independence, and the like. Just getting one's name across is difficult enough; only about half the electorate, if asked, can supply their House members' names. It helps a congressman to be known. "In the main, recognition carries a positive valence; to be perceived at all is to be perceived favorably."[74] A vital advantage enjoyed by House incumbents is that they are much better known among voters than their November challengers.[75] They are better known because they spend a great deal of time, energy, and money trying to make themselves better known.[76] There are standard routines — frequent visits to the constituency, nonpolitical speeches to home audiences,[77] the sending out of infant care booklets and letters of condolence and congratulation. Of 158 House members questioned in the mid-1960s, 121 said that they regularly sent newsletters to their constituents;[78] 48 wrote separate news or opinion columns for newspapers; 82 regularly reported to their constituencies by radio or television;[79] 89 regularly sent out mail questionnaires.[80] Some routines are less standard. Congressman George E. Shipley (D., Ill.) claims to have met personally about half his constituents (i.e. some 200,000 people).[81] For over twenty years Congressman Charles C. Diggs, Jr. (D., Mich.) has run a radio program featuring himself as a "combination disc jockey–commentator and minister."[82] Congressman Daniel J. Flood (D., Pa.) is "famous for appearing unannounced and often uninvited at wedding anniversaries and other events."[83] Anniversaries and other events aside, congressional advertising is done largely at public expense. Use of the franking privilege has mushroomed in recent years; in early 1973 one estimate predicted that House and Senate members would send out about 476 million pieces of mail in the year 1974, at a public cost of $38.1 million — or about 900,000 pieces per member with a subsidy of $70,000 per member.[84] By far the heaviest mailroom traffic comes in Octobers of even-numbered years.[85] There are some differences between House and Senate members in the ways they go about getting their names across. House members are free to blanket their constituencies with mailings for all boxholders; senators are not. But senators find it easier to appear on national television — for example, in short reaction statements on the nightly news shows. Advertising is a staple congressional activity, and there is no end to it. For each member there are always new voters to be apprised of his worthiness and old voters to be reminded of it.[86]

A second activity may be called *credit claiming,* defined here as acting so as to generate a belief in a relevant political actor (or actors) that one is personally responsible for causing the government, or some unit thereof, to do something that the actor (or actors) considers desirable. The political logic of this, from the congressman's point of view, is that an actor who believes that a member can make pleasing things happen will no doubt wish to keep him in office so that he can make pleasing things happen in the future. The emphasis here is on individual accomplishment (rather than, say, party or governmental accomplishment) and on the congressman as doer (rather than as, say, expounder of constituency views). Credit claiming is highly important to congressmen, with the consequence that much of congressional life is a relentless search for opportunities to engage in it.

Where can credit be found? If there were only one congressman rather than 535, the answer would in principle be simple enough.[87] Credit (or blame) would attach in Downsian fashion to the doings of the government as a whole. But there are 535. Hence it becomes necessary for each congressman to try to peel off pieces of governmental accomplishment for which he can believably generate a sense of responsibility. For the average congressman the staple way of doing this is to traffic in what may be called "particularized benefits."[88] Particularized governmental benefits, as the term will be used here, have two properties: (1) Each benefit is given out to a specific individual, group, or geographical constituency, the recipient unit being of a scale that allows a single congressman to be recognized (by relevent political actors and other congressmen) as the claimant for the benefit (other congressmen being perceived as indifferent or hostile). (2) Each benefit is given out in apparently ad hoc fashion (unlike, say, social security checks) with a congressman apparently having a hand in the allocation. A particularized benefit can normally be regarded as a member of a class. That is, a benefit given out to an individual, group, or constituency can normally be looked upon by congressmen as one of a class of similar benefits given out to sizable numbers of individuals, groups, or constituencies. Hence the impression can arise that a congressman is getting "his share" of whatever it is the government is offering. (The classes may be vaguely defined. Some state legislatures deal in what their members call "local legislation.")

In sheer volume the bulk of particularized benefits come under the heading of "casework" — the thousands of favors congressional offices perform for supplicants in ways that normally do not require legislative action. High school students ask for essay materials, soldiers for emergency leaves, pensioners for location of missing checks, local governments for grant information, and on and on. Each office has skilled professionals who can play the bureaucracy like an organ — pushing the right pedals to produce the desired effects.[89] But many benefits require new legislation, or at least they require important allocative decisions on matters covered by existent legislation. Here the congressman fills the traditional role of supplier of goods to the home district. It is a believable role; when a member claims credit for a benefit on the order of a dam, he may well receive it.[90] Shiny construction projects seem especially useful.[91] In the decades before 1934, tariff duties for local industries were a major commodity.[92] In recent years awards given under grant-in-aid programs have become more useful as they have become more numerous. Some quests for credit are ingenious: in 1971 the story broke that congressmen had been earmarking foreign aid money for specific projects in Israel in order to win favor with home constituents.[93] It should be said of constituency benefits that congressmen are quite capable of taking the initiative in drumming them up; that is, there can be no automatic assumption that a congressman's activity is the result of pressures brought to bear by organized interests. Fenno shows the importance of member initiative in his discussion of the House Interior Committee.[94]

A final point here has to do with geography. The examples given so far are all of benefits conferred upon home constituencies or recipients therein (the latter including the home residents who applauded the Israeli projects). But the properties of particularized benefits were carefully specified so as not to exclude the possibility that some benefits may be given to recipients outside the home constituencies. Some probably are. Narrowly drawn tax loopholes qualify as particularized benefits, and some of them are probably conferred upon recipients outside the home districts.[95] (It is difficult to find solid evidence on the point.) Campaign contributions flow into districts from the outside, so it would not be surprising to find that benefits go where the resources are.[96]

How much particularized benefits count for at the polls is extraordinarily difficult to say. But it would be hard to find a congressman who thinks he can afford to wait around until precise information is available. The lore is that they count — furthermore, given home expectations, that they must be supplied in regular quantities for a member to stay electorally even with the board. Awareness of favors may spread beyond their recipients,[97] building for a member a general reputation as a good provider. "Rivers Delivers." "He Can Do More For Massachusetts."[98] A good example of Capitol Hill lore on electoral impact is given in this account of the activities of Congressman Frank Thompson, Jr. (D., N.J., 4th district):

> In 1966, the 4th was altered drastically by redistricting; it lost Burlington County and gained Hunterdon, Warren, and Sussex. Thompson's performance at the polls since 1966 is a case study of how an incumbent congressman, out of line with his district's ideological persuasions, can become unbeatable. In 1966, Thompson carried Mercer by 23,000 votes and lost the three new counties by 4,600, winning reelection with 56% of the votes. He

then survived a district-wide drop in his vote two years later. In 1970, the Congressman carried Mercer County by 20,000 votes and the rest of the district by 6,000, finishing with 58%. The drop in Mercer resulted from the attempt of his hard-line conservative opponent to exploit the racial unrest which had developed in Trenton. But for four years Thompson had been making friends in Hunterdon, Warren, and Sussex, busy doing the kind of chores that congressmen do. In this case, Thompson concerned himself with the interests of dairy farmers at the Department of Agriculture. The results of his efforts were clear when the results came in from the 4th's northern counties.[99]

So much for particularized benefits. But is credit available elsewhere? For governmental accomplishments beyond the scale of those already discussed? The general answer is that the prime mover role is a hard one to play on larger matters — at least before broad electorates. A claim, after all, has to be credible. If a congressman goes before an audience and says, "I am responsible for passing a bill to curb inflation," or "I am responsible for the highway program," hardly anyone will believe him. There are two reasons why people may be skeptical of such claims. First, there is a numbers problem. On an accomplishment of a sort that probably engaged the supportive interest of more than one member it is reasonable to suppose that credit should be apportioned among them. But second, there is an overwhelming problem of information costs.

For typical voters Capitol Hill is a distant and mysterious place; few have anything like a working knowledge of its maneuverings. Hence there is no easy way of knowing whether a congressman is staking a valid claim or not. The odds are that the information problem cuts in different ways on different kinds of issues. On particularized benefits it may work in a congressman's favor; he may get credit for the dam he had nothing to do with building. Sprinkling a district with dams, after all, is something a congressman is supposed to be able to do. But on larger matters it may work against him. For a voter lacking an easy way to sort out valid from invalid claims the sensible recourse is skepticism. Hence it is unlikely that congressmen get much mileage out of credit claiming on larger matters before broad electorates.[100]

Yet there is an obvious and important qualification here. For many congressmen credit claiming on nonparticularized matters is possible in specialized subject areas because of the congressional division of labor. The term "governmental unit" in the original definition of credit claiming is broad enough to include committees, subcommittees, and the two houses of Congress itself. Thus many congressmen can believably claim credit for blocking bills in subcommittee, adding on amendments in committee, and so on. The audience for transactions of this sort is usually small. But it may include important political actors (e.g. an interest group, the president, the *New York Times,* Ralph Nader) who are capable of both paying Capitol Hill information costs and deploying electoral resources. There is a well-documented example of this in Fenno's treatment of post office politics in the 1960s. The postal employee unions used to watch very closely the activities of the House and Senate Post Office Committees and supply valuable electoral resources (money, volunteer work) to members who did their bidding on salary bills.[101] Of course there are many examples of this kind of undertaking.

The third activity congressmen engage in may be called *position taking,* defined here as the public enunciation of a judgmental statement on anything likely to be of interest to political actors. The statement may take the form of a roll call vote. The most important classes of judgmental statements are those prescribing American governmental ends (a vote cast against the war; a statement that "the war should be ended immediately") or governmental means (a statement that "the way to end the war is to take it to the United Nations"). The judgments may be implicit rather than explicit, as in: "I will support the president on this matter." But judgments may range far beyond these classes to take in implicit or explicit statements on what almost anybody should do or how he should do it: "The great Polish scientist Copernicus has been unjustly neglected"; "The way for Israel to achieve peace is to give up the Sinai."[102] The congressman as position taker is a speaker rather than a doer. The electoral requirement is not that he make pleasing things happen but that he make pleasing judgmental statements. The position itself is the political commodity. Especially on matters where governmental responsibility is widely diffused, it is not surprising that political actors should fall back on positions as tests of incumbent virtue. For voters ignorant of congressional processes the recourse is an easy one. The following comment by one of Clapp's House interviewees is highly revealing: "Recently, I went home and began to talk about the _____ act. I was pleased to have sponsored that bill, but it soon dawned on me that the point wasn't getting through at all. What was getting through was that the act might be a help to people. I changed the emphasis: I didn't mention my role particularly, but stressed my support of the legislation."[103]

The ways in which positions can be registered are numerous and often imaginative. There are floor addresses ranging from weighty orations to mass-produced "nationality day statements."[104] There are speeches before home groups, television appearances, letters, newsletters, press releases, ghostwritten books, *Playboy* articles, even interviews with political scientists. On occasion congressmen generate what amount to petitions; whether or not to sign the 1956 Southern Manifesto defying school desegregation rulings was an important decision for southern members.[105]

Outside the roll call process the congressman is usually able to tailor his positions to suit his audiences. A solid consensus in the constituency calls for ringing declarations; for years the late Senator James K. Vardaman (D., Miss.) campaigned on a proposal to repeal the Fifteenth Amendment.[106] Division or uncertainty in the constituency calls for waffling; in the late 1960s a congressman had to be a poor politician indeed not to be able to come up with an inoffensive statement on Vietnam ("We must have peace with honor at the earliest possible moment consistent with the national interest"). On a controversial issue a Capitol Hill office normally prepares two form letters to send out to constituent letter writers — one for the pros and one (not directly contradictory) for the antis.[107] Handling discrete audiences in person requires simple agility, a talent well demonstrated in this selection from a Nader profile:

> "You may find this difficult to understand," said Democrat Edward R. Roybal, the Mexican-American representative from California's thirtieth district, "but sometimes I wind up making a patriotic speech one afternoon and later on that same day an anti-war speech. In the patriotic speech I speak of past wars but I also speak of the need to prevent more wars. My positions are not inconsistent; I just approach different people differently." Roybal went on to depict the diversity of crowds he speaks to: one afternoon he is surrounded by balding men wearing Veterans' caps and holding American flags; a few hours later he speaks to a crowd of Chicano youths, angry over American involvement in Vietnam. Such a diverse constituency, Royal believes, calls for different methods of expressing one's convictions.[108]

Indeed it does. Versatility of this sort is occasionally possible in roll call voting. For example a congressman may vote one way on recommittal and the other on final passage, leaving it unclear just how he stands on a bill.[109] Members who cast identical votes on a measure may give different reasons for having done so. Yet it is on roll calls that the crunch comes; there is no way for a member to avoid making a record on hundreds of issues, some of which are controversial in the home constituencies. Of course, most roll call positions considered in isolation are not likely to cause much of a ripple at home. But broad voting patterns can and do; member "ratings" calculated by the Americans for Democratic Action, Americans for Constitutional Action, and other outfits are used as guidelines in the deploying of electoral resources. And particular issues often have their alert publics. Some national interest groups watch the votes of all congressmen on single issues and ostentatiously try to reward or punish members for their positions; over the years some notable examples of such interest groups have been the Anti-Saloon League,[110] the early Farm Bureau,[111] the American Legion,[112] the American Medical Association,[113] and the National Rifle Association.[114] On rare occasions single roll calls achieve a rather high salience among the public generally. This seems especially true of the Senate, which every now and then winds up for what might be called a "showdown vote," with pressures on all sides, presidential involvement, media attention given to individual senators' positions, and suspense about the outcome. Examples are the votes on the nuclear test-ban treaty in 1963, civil rights cloture in 1964, civil rights cloture again in 1965, the Haynsworth appointment in 1969, the Carswell appointment in 1970, and the ABM in 1970. Controversies on roll calls like these are often relived in subsequent campaigns, the southern Senate elections of 1970 with their Haynsworth and Carswell issues being cases in point.

Probably the best position-taking strategy for most congressmen at most times is to be conservative — to cling to their own positions of the past where possible and to reach for new ones with great caution where necessary. Yet in an earlier discussion of strategy the suggestion was made that it might be rational for members in electoral danger to resort to innovation. The form of innovation available is entrepreneurial position taking, its logic being that for a member facing defeat with his old array of positions it makes good sense to gamble on some new ones. It may be that congressional marginals fulfill an important function here as issue pioneers — experimenters who test out new issues and thereby show other politicians which ones are usable.[115] An example of such a pioneer is Senator Warren Magnuson (D., Wash.), who responded to a surprisingly narrow victory in 1962 by reaching for a reputation in the area of consumer affairs.[116] Another example is Senator Ernest Hollings (D., S.C.), a servant of a shaky and racially heterogeneous southern constituency who launched "hunger" as an issue in 1969 — at once pointing to a problem and giving it a useful nonracial definition.[117] One of the most successful issue entrepreneurs of recent decades was the late Senator Joseph McCarthy (R., Wis.); it was all there — the close primary in 1946, the fear of defeat in 1952, the desperate casting about for an issue, the famous 1950 dinner at the Colony Restaurant where suggestions were tendered, the decision that "Communism" might just do the trick.[118]

The effect of position taking on electoral behavior is about as hard to measure as the effect of credit claiming. Once again there is a variance problem; congressmen do not differ very much among themselves in the methods they use or the skills they display in attuning themselves to their diverse constituencies. All of them, after all, are professional politicians. There is intriguing hard evidence on some matters where variance can be captured. Schoenberger has found that House Republicans who signed an early pro-Goldwater petition plummeted significantly farther in their 1964 percentages than their colleagues who did not sign.[119] (The signers appeared genuinely to believe that identification with Goldwater was an electoral plus.) Erikson has found that roll call records are interestingly related to election percentages: "[A] reasonable estimate is that an unusually liberal Republican Representative gets at least 6 per cent more of the two-party vote . . . than his extreme conservative counterpart would in the same district."[120] In other words, taking some roll call positions that please voters of the opposite party can be electorally helpful. (More specifically, it can help in November; some primary electorates will be more tolerant of it than others.) Sometimes an inspection of deviant cases offers clues. There is the ideological odyssey of former Congressman Walter Baring (D., Nev.), who entered Congress as a more or less regular Democrat in the mid-1950s but who moved over to a point where he was the most conservative House Democrat outside the South by the late 1960s. The Nevada electorate reacted predictably; Baring's November percentages rose astoundingly high (82.5 percent in 1970), but he encountered guerrilla warfare in the primaries which finally cost him his nomination in 1972 — whereupon the seat turned Republican.

There can be no doubt that congressmen believe positions make a difference. An important consequence of this belief is their custom of watching each other's elections to try to figure out what positions are salable. Nothing is more inportant in Capitol Hill politics than the shared conviction that election returns have proven a point. Thus the 1950 returns were read not only as a rejection of health insurance but as a ratification of McCarthyism.[121] When two North Carolina nonsigners of the 1956 Southern Manifesto immediately lost their primaries, the message was clear to southern members that there could be no straying from a hard line on the school desegregation issue. Any breath of life left in the cause of school bussing was squeezed out by House returns from the Detroit area in 1972. Senator Douglas gives an interesting report on the passage of the first minimum wage bill in the Seventy-fifth Congress. In 1937 the bill was tied up in the House Rules Committee, and there was an effort to get it to the floor through use of a discharge petition. Then two primary elections broke the jam. Claude Pepper (D., Fla.) and Lister Hill (D., Ala.) won nominations to fill vacant Senate seats. "Both campaigned on behalf of the Wages and Hours bill, and both won smashing victories . . . Immediately after the results of the Florida and Alabama primaries became known, there was a stampede to sign the petition, and the necessary 218 signatures were quickly obtained."[122] The bill later passed. It may be useful to close this section on position taking with a piece of political lore on electoral impact that can stand beside the piece on the impact of credit claiming offered earlier. The discussion is of the pre-1972 sixth California House district:

> Since 1952 the district's congressman has been Republican William S. Mailliard, a wealthy member of an old California family. For many years Mailliard had a generally liberal voting record. He had no trouble at the polls, winning elections by large majorities in what is, by a small margin at least, a Democratic district. More recently, Mailliard seems caught between the increasing conservatism of the state's Republican party and the increasing liberalism of his constituency.
>
> After [Governor Ronald] Reagan's victory [in 1966], Mailliard's voting record became noticeably more conservative. Because of this, he has been spared the tough conservative primary opposition that Paul McCloskey has confronted in the 11th. But Mailliard's move to the right has not gone unnoticed in the 6th district. In 1968 he received 73% of the vote, but in 1970 he won only 53% — a highly unusual drop for an incumbent of such long standing. Much of the difference must be attributed to the war issue. San Francisco and Marin are both antiwar strongholds; but Mailliard, who is the ranking Republican on the House Foreign Affairs Committee, has supported the Nixon Administration's war policy. In the 6th district, at least, that position is a sure vote-loser.[123]

These, then, are the three kinds of electorally oriented activities congressmen engage in — advertising, credit claiming, and position taking. It remains only to offer some brief comments on the emphases different members give to the different activities. No deterministic statements can be made; within limits each member has freedom to build his own electoral coalition and hence freedom to choose the means of doing it.[124] Yet there are broad patterns. For one thing senators, with their access to the media, seem to put more emphasis on position taking than House members; probably House members rely more heavily on particularized benefits. But there are important differences among House members. Congressmen from the traditional parts of old machine cities rarely advertise and seldom take positions on anything (except on roll calls), but devote a great deal of time and energy to the distribution of benefits. In fact they use their office resources to plug themselves into their local party organizations. Congressman William A. Barrett (D., downtown Philadelphia), chairman of the Housing Subcommittee of the House Banking and Currency Committee, claimed in 1971 to have spent only three nights in Washington in the preceding six years. He meets constituents each night from 9:00 P.M. to 1:00 A.M. in the home district; "Folks line up to tell Bill Barrett their problems."[125] On the other hand congressmen with upper-middle-class bases (suburban, city reform, or academic) tend to deal in positions. In New York City the switch from regular to reform Democrats is a switch from members who emphasize benefits to members who emphasize positions; it reflects a shift in consumer taste.[126] The same difference appears geographically rather than temporally as one goes from the inner wards to the outer suburbs of Chicago.[127]

Another kind of difference appears if the initial assumption of a reelection quest is relaxed to take into account the "progressive" ambitions of some members — the aspirations of some to move up to higher electoral offices rather than keep the ones they have.[128] There are two important subsets of climbers in the Congress — House members who would like to be senators (over the years about a quarter of the senators have come up directly from the House),[129] and senators who would like to be presidents or vice presidents (in the Ninety-third Congress about a quarter of the senators had at one time or another run for these offices or been seriously "mentioned" for them). In both cases higher aspirations seem to produce the same distinctive mix of activities. For one thing credit claiming is all but useless. It does little good to talk about the bacon you have brought back to a district you are trying to abandon. And, as Lyndon Johnson found in 1960, claiming credit on legislative maneuvers is no way to reach a new mass audience; it baffles rather than persuades. Office advancement seems to require a judicious mixture of advertising and position taking. Thus a House member aiming for the Senate heralds his quest with press releases; there must be a new "image," sometimes an ideological overhaul to make ready for the new constituency.[130] Senators aiming for the White House do more or less the same thing — advertising to get the name across, position taking ("We can do better"). In recent years presidential aspirants have sought Foreign Relations Committee membership as a platform for making statements on foreign policy.[131]

There are these distinctions, but it would be a mistake to elevate them over the commonalities. For most congressmen most of the time all three activities are essential. The following vignette of Senator Strom Thurmond (R., S.C.) making his peace with universal suffrage is a good picture of what the electoral side of American legislative politics is all about. The senator was reacting in 1971 to a 1970 Democratic gubernatorial victory in his state in which black turnout was high:

> Since then, the Republican Senator has done the following things:
> — Hired Thomas Moss, a black political organizer who directed Negro voter registration efforts for the South Carolina Voter Education Project, for his staff in South Carolina, and a black secretary for his Washington office.

— Announced Federal grants for projects in black areas, including at least one occasion when he addressed a predominantly black audience to announce a rural water project and remained afterwards to shake hands.

— Issued moderate statements on racial issues.

In a statement to Ebony magazine that aides say Thurmond wrote himself, he said, "In most instances I am confident that we have more in common as Southerners than we have reason to oppose each other because of race. Equality of opportunity for all is a goal upon which blacks and Southern whites can agree."[132]

Notes

For their most useful comments as I was preparing this work, I thank Chris Achen, Albert Cover, Joseph LaPolombara, David Price, Douglas Rae, and David Seidman. This essay originally appeared as Part 1 in David R. Mayhew, *Congress: The Electoral Connection* (New Haven: Yale University Press, 1974). It remained the same in the 2004 edition of the book.

1. Where the context does not suggest otherwise, the term *congressmen* will refer to members of both House and Senate.

2. James L. Payne, *Patterns of Conflict in Colombia* (New Haven: Yale University Press, 1968), pp. 19–20.

3. James D. Barber, *The Lawmakers* (New Haven: Yale University Press, 1965), ch. 4.

4. Kenneth Prewitt, "Political Ambitions, Volunteerism, and Electoral Accountability," 64 *American Political Science Review* 5–17 (1970).

5. H. Douglas Price, "The Congressional Career Then and Now," ch. 2 in Nelson W. Polsby (ed.), *Congressional Behavior* (New York: Random House, 1971).

6. H. Douglas Price, "Computer Simulation and Legislative 'Professionalism': Some Quantitative Approaches to Legislative Evolution," paper presented to the annual convention of the American Political Science Association, 1970, pp. 14–16.

7. Nelson W. Polsby, "The Institutionalization of the U.S. House of Representatives," 62 *American Political Science Review* 146 (1968).

8. Charles S. Bullock III, "House Careerists: Changing Patterns of Longevity and Attrition," 66 *American Political Science Review* 1296 (1972).

9. Indeed, it has been proposed that professional politicians could be gotten rid of by making reelection impossible. For a plan to select one-term legislators by random sampling of the population, see Dennis C. Mueller et al., "Representative Government via Random Selection," 12 *Public Choice* 57–68 (1972).

10. John F. Kennedy, *Profiles in Courage* (New York: Harper and Row, 1956).

11. Paul H. Douglas, *In the Fullness of Time* (New York: Harcourt Brace Jovanovich, 1972), pp. 238–41.

12. In the case of the late Senator Thomas Dodd (D., Conn.) these two goals apparently conflicted. See James Boyd, *Above the Law* (New York: New American Library, 1968).

Using office for financial profit is probably less common in Congress than in some of the state legislatures (e.g. Illinois and New Jersey).

13. Richard F. Fenno Jr., *Congressmen in Committees* (Boston: Little, Brown and Co., 1973), p. 1.

14. Frank E. Smith (D., Miss.), *Congressman from Mississippi* (New York: Random House, 1964), p. 127. It will not be necessary here to reach the question of whether it is possible to detect the goals of congressmen by asking them what they are, or indeed the question of whether there are unconscious motives lurking behind conscious ones. In Lasswell's formulation "political types" are power seekers, with "private motives displaced on public objects rationalized in terms of public interest." Harold D. Lasswell, *Power and Personality* (New York: Viking, 1948), p. 38.

15. Of other kinds of relations we are entitled to be suspicious. "There can be no doubt, that if power is granted to a body of men, called Representatives, they, like any other men, will use their power, not for the advantage of the community, but for their own advantage, if they can. The only question is, therefore, how can they be prevented?" James Mill, "Government," in *Essays on Government, Jurisprudence, Liberty of the Press, and Law of Nations* (New York: Augustus M. Kelley, 1967), p. 18. Madison's view was that the United States House, by design the popular branch, "should have an immediate dependence on, and an intimate sympathy with, the people. Frequent elections are unquestionably the only policy by which this dependency and sympathy can be effectively secured." *The Federalist Papers,* selected and edited by Roy Fairfield (Garden City, N.Y.: Doubleday Anchor, 1961), no. 52, p. 165.

16. Anthony Downs, *An Economic Theory of Democracy* (New York: Harper and Row, 1957). Downs gives a formal touch to a political science literature of both normative and empirical importance, extending from Woodrow Wilson through E. E. Schattschneider and V. O. Key Jr.

17. Ibid., chs. 2, 3.

18. Ibid., pp. 88–90. Because the information and opinions supplied by representatives are important in decision making, Downs says that in effect some decision power devolves to the representatives. But there is this constraint: "Theoretically, the government will continue to decentralize its power until the marginal gain in votes from greater conformity to popular desires is outweighed by the marginal cost in votes of lesser ability to co-ordinate its actions." Pp. 89–90.

19. Ibid., p. 26.

20. See, for example, Richard E. Neustadt, "White House and Whitehall," *The Public Interest,* Winter 1966, pp. 55–69.

21. See William O. Aydelotte, "Voting Patterns in the British House of Commons in the 1840's," 5 *Comparative Studies in Society and History,* 134–63 (1963).

22. Austin Ranney, *Pathways to Parliament: Candidate Selection in Britain* (Madison: University of Wisconsin Press, 1965), p. 281; Leon D. Epstein, "British M.P.'s and Their Local Parties: The Suez Case," 54 *American Political Science Review* 385–86 (1960).

23. Jay G. Blumler and Denis McQuail, *Television in Politics* (Chicago: University of Chicago Press, 1969), pp. xi–xxviii.

24. R. T. McKenzie, *British Political Parties* (New York: St. Martin's, 1955), pp. 252–53, 555.

25. "An American Congressman, it is said, collapsed with shock on being shown the writing-rooms and the Library of the Commons full of men writing letters in longhand: members of Parliament answering the constituency mail." Bernard Crick, *The Reform of Parliament* (Garden City, N.Y.: Doubleday, 1965). p. 58; and, generally, Crick, pp. 58–59. Things have changed somewhat since Crick's account, but the contrast is still valid. See also Anthony Barker and Michael Rush, *The Member of Parliament and His Information* (London: Allen and Unwin, 1970). Loewenberg reports that, in West Germany, "the average member of the Bundestag works under Spartan conditions." Gerhard Loewenberg, *Parliament in the German Political System* (Ithaca: Cornell University Press, 1967), p. 53.

26. Donald E. Stokes, "Parties and the Nationalization of Electoral Forces," ch. 7 in William N. Chambers and Walter D. Burnham, *The American Party Systems* (New York: Oxford University Press, 1967), pp. 188–89.

27. Crick, *The Reform of Parliament,* pp. 30–31. Crick adds: "A modern Prime Minister has a patronage beyond the wildest dreams of political avarice of a Walpole or a Newcastle." P. 31.

28. John P. Mackintosh, "Reform of the House of Commons: The Case for Specialization," in Loewenberg (ed.), *Modern Parliaments,* p. 39.

29. Indeed in city studies there is the standard functional case that cohesive parties may arise to deal with problems caused by constitutional diffusion. See, for example, on Chicago, Edward C. Banfield, *Political Influence* (New York: Free Press, 1961), ch. 8. American parties have traditionally been strongest at the municipal level. But something interesting happens to Downs on the way to the city. Where parties are held together by patronage, and where there are no geographically subsidiary governments that can serve as independent political bases, there is a strong tendency for party politics to become monopolistic rather than competitive. Ambitious politicians have little incentive to sustain an opposition party and every incentive to join the ruling party. The same argument generally holds for national politics in mid-eighteenth-century England.

30. See Duane Lockard, *New England State Politics* (Princeton: Princeton University Press, 1965), chs. 9, 10: Joseph I. Lieberman, *The Power Broker* (Boston: Houghton Mifflin, 1966); James D. Barber, "Leadership Strategies for Legislative Party Cohesion," 28 *Journal of Politics* 347–67 (1966).

31. In the California Senate, for example, at least until recently, committee chairmanships were given out to the most senior members regardless of party. Alvin D. Sokolow and Richard W. Brandsma, "Partisanship and Seniority in Legislative Committee Assignments: California after Reapportionment," 24 *West Political Quarterly* 741–47 (1971).

32. V. O. Key Jr., *The Responsible Electorate* (Cambridge: Harvard University Press, 1966).

33. There is Huntington's point that sweeping turnover of a Jacksonian sort now occurs in national politics only at the top executive level. Samuel P. Huntington, "Congressional Responses to the Twentieth Century," ch. 1 in David B. Truman (ed.), *The Congress and America's Future* (Englewood Cliffs, N.J.: Prentice-Hall, 1965), p. 17.

34. In Chicago, for example. See Leo M. Snowiss, "Congressional Recruitment and Representation," 60 *American Political Science Review* 627–39 (1966).

35. On the fluid behavior of machine congressmen back when there were a good many

more of them, see Moisei Ostrogorski, *Democracy and the Organization of Political Parties,* vol. II, *The United States* (Garden City, N.Y.: Doubleday, 1964), pp. 286–89. Tammany Democrats broke party ranks to save Speaker Joseph G. Cannon from Insurgent and Democratic attack in the Sixtieth Congress, a year before his downfall. See Blair Bolles, *Tyrant from Illinois* (New York: Norton, 1951), p. 181.

36. See Charles L. Clapp, *The Congressman: His Work as He Sees It* (Washington, D.C.: Brookings, 1963), pp. 30–31; Robert J. Huckshorn and Robert C. Spencer, *The Politics of Defeat* (Amherst, Mass.: University of Massachusetts Press, 1971), pp. vii, 71–72; David A. Leuthold, *Electioneering in a Democracy* (New York: Wiley, 1968), passim.

37. Clapp, *The Congressman,* p. 351.

38. See the argument in Leon D. Epstein, "A Comparative Study of Canadian Parties," 58 *American Political Science Review* 46–59 (1964).

39. Lewis Namier, *The Structure of Politics at the Accession of George III* (London: Macmillan, 1960). For a Namier passage on assemblies without disciplined parties see p. 17.

40. Donald E. Stokes and Warren E. Miller, "Party Government and the Saliency of Congress," ch. 11 in Angus Campbell et al., *Elections and the Political Order* (New York: Wiley, 1966), p. 199.

41. Angus Campbell, "Surge and Decline: A Study of Electoral Change," ch. 3 in ibid; Barbara Hinckley, "Interpreting House Midterm Elections: Toward a Measurement of the In-Party's 'Expected' Loss of Seats," 61 *American Political Science Review* 694–700 (1967).

42. Gerald H. Kramer, "Short-Term Fluctuations in U.S. Voting Behavior, 1896–1964," 65 *American Political Science Review* 131–43 (1971). See also the symposium on the Kramer findings in 63 *American Economic Review* 160–80 (May 1973).

43. Kramer, "U.S. Voting Behavior," p. 140. Wars seem to earn penalties.

44. David B. Truman, *The Congressional Party* (New York: Wiley, 1959), pp. 213–18.

45. As in Stokes, "Parties and the Nationalization of Electoral Forces."

46. Nonetheless there are interesting questions here that have never been explored. Do marginal congressmen—or members generally—of the party not in control of the presidency try to sabotage the economy? Of course they must not appear to do so, but there are "respectable" ways of acting. How about Republicans in the Eightieth Congress with their tax cutting in time of inflation? Or Democrats with their spending programs under President Nixon—also in a time of inflation? The answer is probably no. It would have to be shown that the same congressmen's actions differ under presidencies of different parties, and they probably do not. Strategies like this require not only duplicity, but also a vigorous consciousness of distant effects of a sort that is foreign to the congressional mentality.

47. Davidson, *Role of the Congressman,* p. 128.

48. David M. Olson and Cynthia T. Nonidez, "Measures of Legislative Performance in the U.S. House of Representatives," 16 *Midwest Journal of Political Science* 273–74 (1972).

49. Over the long haul the proportion of seats switching from party to party is quite surprising. Of senators serving in the Ninety-third Congress, 56 had succeeded members of the opposite party in initially coming to the Senate, 43 had succeeded members of the

same party, and 1 (Hiram Fong: R., Hawaii) had come into the Senate at the same time his state entered the union. (Predecessors here are taken to be the last elected predecessors; i.e. interim appointees are ignored.) Of House members serving in the same Congress, 157 had originally succeeded members of the opposite party; 223 members of the same party; and 55 had originally taken newly created seats. (District continuity at the time of member transition is assumed here if a new district took in substantially the same territory as an old one.)

50. Stokes, "Parties and the Nationalization of Electoral Forces," p. 186. Thus the American ranking of vote components in order of importance differs from the British ranking. Richard S. Katz has recently introduced a measurement technique that yields higher national components. Katz, "The Attribution of Variance in Electoral Returns: An Alternative Measurement Technique," 67 *American Political Science Review* 817–28 (1973). But the British-American disparity presumably remains. There is a Stokes rejoinder at pp. 829–34.

51. In the 1964–72 period ten House committee chairmen lost their primaries.

52. John W. Kingdon, *Candidates for Office: Beliefs and Strategies* (New York: Random House, 1968), pp. 86–89. Richard F. Fenno Jr., who has recently been traveling with incumbent congressmen in their districts — some of them very "safe" districts indeed — detects a pervasive feeling of electoral insecurity: "One of the dominant impressions of my travels is the terrific sense of *uncertainty* which animates these congressmen. They perceive electoral troubles where the most imaginative outside observer could not possibly perceive, conjure up or hallucinate them." Fenno, "Congressmen in Their Constituencies," unpublished manuscript, pp. 6–7.

53. From about 2 percent in the 1950s to about 5 percent in 1966 and maybe higher in 1970–72. See Robert S. Erikson, "The Advantage of Incumbency in Congressional Elections," 3 *Polity* 395–405 (1971); Erikson, "Malapportionment, Gerrymandering, and Party Fortunes in Congressional Elections," 66 *American Political Science Review* 1240 (1972); David R. Mayhew, "Congressional Elections: The Case of the Vanishing Marginals," forthcoming in *Polity*, Spring 1974. It is not clear what accounts for the rise in incumbency value, not even certain that it is attributable to the election-oriented activities of incumbents. But some of the electoral sagas of recent years are truly startling. There is the case of the Wisconsin seventh district, strongly Republican for years in the hands of Melvin R. Laird. Laird's last percentages were 65.1 percent in 1966 and 64.1 percent in 1968. When Laird went to the cabinet, David R. Obey took the seat for the Democrats with 51.6 percent in a 1969 by-election. Obey won with 67.6 percent in 1970 and then with 63.5 percent in a 1972 election in which he was forced to run against an incumbent Republican in a merged district. On Obey's election-oriented actitivies see Norman C. Miller, "Privileges of Rank: New Congressman Finds Campaigning Is Easier Now That He's in Office," *Wall Street Journal*, August 4, 1969, p. 1.

54. Kingdon, *Candidates for Office*, p. 31. Charles S. Bullock III has recently found the same effect in a study of United States House incumbents and challengers in the 1972 election. Bullock, "Candidate Perceptions of Causes in Election Outcome," paper presented to the annual convention of the American Political Science Association, 1973.

55. Stokes and Miller, "Party Government."

56. The most sophisticated treatment of this subject is in Warren E. Miller and Don-

ald E. Stokes, "Constituency Influence in Congress," ch. 16 in Campbell et. al., *Elections and the Political Order*, pp. 366–70. Note that a weird but important kind of accountability relationship would exist if congressmen thought their activities had impact even if in fact they had none at all.

57. Downs, *Economic Theory of Democracy*, pp. 38–45.

58. To give an extreme example, in the North Dakota Senate campaign of 1970 an estimated 85 to 90 percent of the money spent by candidates of both parties came from out of state. Philip M. Stern, *The Rape of the Taxpayer* (New York: Random House, 1973), p. 384.

59. For thousands of November voters totally unaware of candidate particularities the commonest election criterion is no doubt the party label on the ballet. These voters are normally left undisturbed in their ignorance, although candidates may find it useful to deploy resources to get the right ones to the polls. But it must not be assumed that there are no circumstances under which such voters can be aroused into vigorous candidate awareness.

60. Robert Sherrill, "The Embodiment of Poor White Power," *New York Times Magazine*, February 28, 1971, p. 51.

61. Ellen Szita, Ralph Nader Congress Project profile on Garner E. Shriver (R., Kans.) (Washington, D.C.: Grossman, 1972), p. 14. Shriver's administrative assistant was asked about the district value of the congressman's Appropriations Committee membership. His answer: "Projectwise, it's been valuable. . . . I wouldn't say the majority of his constituents recognize that the Appropriations Committee is one of the most important — just those I would term the 'thought leadership' in the district." The interviewer adds that it must be the "community leadership in Wichita" the assistant was referring to, for, when asked, "with few exceptions . . . the leaders listed more than ten different federally-subsidized projects that Representative Shriver had brought to the fourth district." (Congress Project profiles referred to in future footnotes will be called "Nader profiles" for short. For all of them the more complete citation is the one given here.)

62. Dennis Harvey, "How GOP Sen. Pearson Went from Sure Loser to Sure Winner in 1972," *Wall Street Journal*, September 29, 1972, p. 1.

63. There is the following report of an election problem suffered by Congressman Torbert H. Macdonald (D., Mass.), chairman of the Communications and Power Subcommittee of the House Interstate and Foreign Commerce Committee: "His fear of opposition from some of these industries is so overwhelming that they have succeeded in immobilizing him with regard to regulatory legislation. For example several years ago he received a political scare when the electric companies bankrolled his opponent in the general election. Since then, according to [Congressman Robert O.] Tiernan [D., R.I.], 'Macdonald will not touch them.' That interpretation is confirmed by Macdonald's former aid, Marty Kuhn, who states that 'Even though Torby easily defeated his opponent, the experience made him sort of paranoid. He is now reluctant to do anything that would offend the power people.' " John Paris's chapter on "Communications" in David E. Price (ed.), "The House and Senate Committees on Commerce" (unpublished manuscript), p. 161. The reference is apparently to the election of 1968, when Macdonald's percentage fell to 62.5. It is normally well over 65.

64. Leuthold, *Electioneering in a Democracy*, pp. 92–94.

65. Ibid., p. 44.

66. Richard E. Neustadt, *Presidential Power* (New York: New American Library, 1964), chs. 4, 5.

67. Of course when the president's poll ratings drop, so do his ability to punish and reward and his influence over congressmen. When they drop very low, it becomes politically profitable for congressmen of his own party to attack him — as with Democrats in 1951–52 and Republicans in 1973–74.

68. "The American Medical Association: Power, Purpose, and Politics in Organized Medicine," 63 *Yale Law Journal* 1011–18 (1954). Senator Douglas's recollection: "Legislators accepted the conclusion that the voters were opposed to all forms of health insurance and that they should avoid an open conflict with the AMA." Douglas, *In the Fullness of Time,* p. 390.

69. The convention system of the late nineteenth century offered comparable perils. Bryce comments that House seats were highly prized and that there was an ethic that they should be rotated. "An ambitious Congressman is therefore forced to think day and night of his re-nomination, and to secure it not only by procuring, if he can, grants from the Federal Treasury for local purposes, and places for the relatives and friends of the local wire-pullers who control the nominating conventions, but also by sedulously 'nursing' the constituency during the vacations." James Bryce, *The American Commonwealth* (New York: Putnam's, 1959), I: 40–41.

70. The term is Kingdon's. *Candidates for Office,* p. 45.

71. Although the direct primary system is uniquely American, there are variants that pose similar problems for politicans. In Italian parliamentary elections each voter registers a vote for a favored party's candidate list, but then can also cast preference votes for individual candidates on that list. Whether a given candidate gets elected depends both on how well his party does against other parties and on how well he does against nominees of his own party. Mass organizations (e.g. labor and farm groups) capable of mobilizing preference votes reap benefits in the parliament, "where nothing seems to count so much as the ability to deliver the required number of preference votes." Joseph LaPalombara, *Interest Groups in Italian Politics* (Princeton: Princeton University Press, 1964), pp. 248–49.

72. On cues generally see Donald R. Matthews and James A. Stimson, "Cue-Taking by Congressmen: A Model and a Computer Simulation," paper presented at Conference on the Use of Quantitative Methods in the Study of the History of Legislative Behavior, 1972; and John E. Jackson, "Statistical Models of Senate Roll Call Voting," 65 *American Political Science Review* 451–70 (1971).

73. See Aage Clausen, *How Congressmen Decide: A Policy Focus* (New York: St. Martin's Press, 1973), ch. 7. Fiellin writes on the New York delegation: "Most important of all, perhaps, is that the member in taking cues from the New York group cannot get into electoral difficulties as a result of deviation. There is security in numbers." Alan Fiellin, "The Functions of Informal Groups: A State Delegation," ch. 3 in Robert L. Peabody and Nelson W. Polsby (eds.), *New Perspectives on the House of Representatives* (Chicago: Rand McNally, 1969), p. 113.

74. Stokes and Miller, "Party Government," p. 205. The same may not be true among, say, mayors.

75. Ibid., p. 204. The likelihood is that senators are also better known than their challengers, but that the gap is not so wide as it is on the House side. There is no hard evidence on the point.

76. In Clapp's interview study, "Conversations with more than fifty House members uncovered only one who seemed to place little emphasis on strategies designed to increase communications with the voter." *The Congressman,* p. 88. The exception was an innocent freshman.

77. A statement by one of Clapp's congressmen: "The best speech is a non-political speech. I think a commencement speech is the best of all. X says he has never lost a precinct in a town where he has made a commencement speech." *The Congressman,* p. 96.

78. These and the following figures on member activity are from Donald G. Tacheron and Morris K. Udall, *The Job of the Congressman* (Indianapolis: Bobbs-Merrill, 1966), pp. 281–88.

79. Another Clapp congressman: "I was looking at my TV film today—I have done one every week since I have been here—and who was behind me but Congressman X. I'll swear he had never done a TV show before in his life but he only won by a few hundred votes last time. Now he has a weekly television show. If he had done that before he wouldn't have had any trouble." *The Congressman,* p. 92.

80. On questionnaires generally see Walter Wilcox, "The Congressional Poll—and Non-Poll," in Edward C. Dreyer and Walter A. Rosenbaum (eds.), *Political Opinion and Electoral Behavior* (Belmont, Calif.: Wadsworth, 1966), pp. 390–400.

81. Szita, Nader profile on Shipley, p. 12. The congressman is also a certified diver. "When Shipley is home in his district and a drowning occurs, he is sometimes asked to dive down for the body. 'It gets in the papers and actually, it's pretty good publicity for me,' he admitted." P. 3. Whether this should be classified under "casework" rather than "advertising" is difficult to say.

82. Lenore Cooley, Nader profile on Diggs, p. 2.

83. Anne Zandman and Arthur Magida, Nader profile on Flood, p. 2.

84. Norman C. Miller, "Yes, You Are Getting More Politico Mail; And It Will Get Worse," *Wall Street Journal,* March 6, 1973, p. 1.

85. Monthly data complied by Albert Cover.

86. After serving his two terms, the late President Eisenhower had this conclusion: "There is nothing a Congressman likes better than to get his name in the headlines and for it to be published all over the United States." From a 1961 speech quoted in the *New York Times,* June 20, 1971.

87. In practice the one might call out the army and suspend the Constitution.

88. These have some of the properties of what Lowi calls "distributive" benefits. Theodore J. Lowi, "American Business, Public Policy, Case-Studies, and Political Theory," 16 *World Politics* 690 (1964).

89. On casework generally see Kenneth G. Olson, "The Service Function of the United States Congress," pp. 337–74 in American Enterprise Institute, *Congress: The First Branch of Government* (Washington, D.C.: American Enterprise Institute for Public Policy Research, 1966).

90. Sometimes without justification. Thus this comment by a Republican member of

the House Public Works Committee: "The announcements for projects are an important part of this. . . . And the folks back home are funny about this — if your name is associated with it, you get all the credit whether you got it through or not." James T. Murphy, "Partisanship and the House Public Works Committee," paper presented to the annual convention of the American Political Science Association, 1968, p. 10.

91. "They've got to *see* something; it's the bread and butter issues that count — the dams, the post offices and the other public buildings, the highways. They want to know what you've been doing." A comment by a Democratic member of the House Public Works Committee. Ibid.

92. The classic account is in E. E. Schattschneider, *Politics, Pressures, and the Tariff* (New York: Prentice-Hall, 1935).

93. "Israeli Schools and Hospitals Seek Funds in Foreign-Aid Bill," *New York Times,* October 4, 1971, p. 10.

94. Fenno, *Congressmen in Committees,* p. 40. Cf. this statement on initiative in the French Third Republic: "Most deputies ardently championed the cause of interest groups in their district without waiting to be asked." Bernard E. Brown, "Pressure Politics in France," 18 *Journal of Politics* 718 (1956).

95. For a discussion of the politics of tax loopholes see Stanley S. Surrey, "The Congress and the Tax Lobbyist — How Special Tax Provisions Get Enacted," 70 *Harvard Law Review* 1145–82 (1957).

96. A possible example of a transaction of this sort: During passage of the 1966 "Christmas tree" tax bill, Senator Vance Hartke (D., Ind.) won inclusion of an amendment giving a tax credit to a California aluminum firm with a plant in the Virgin Islands. George Lardner, Jr., "The Day Congress Played Santa," *Washington Post,* December 10, 1966, p. 10. Whether Hartke was getting campaign funds from the firm is not wholly clear, but Lardner's account allows the inference that he was.

97. Thus this comment of a Senate aide, "The world's greatest publicity organ is still the human mouth. . . . When you get somebody $25.00 from the Social Security Administration, he talks to his friends and neighbors about it. After a while the story grows until you've single-handedly obtained $2,500 for a constituent who was on the brink of starvation." Matthews, *U.S. Senators,* p. 226.

98. For some examples of particularistically oriented congressmen see the Nader profiles by Sven Holmes on James A. Haley (D., Fla.), Newton Koltz on Joseph P. Addabbo (D., N.Y.), Alex Berlow on Kenneth J. Gray (D., Ill.), and Sarah Glazer on John Young (D., Tex.). For a fascinating picture of the things House members were expected to do half a century ago see Joe Martin, *My First Fifty Years in Politics* (New York: McGraw-Hill, 1960), pp. 55–59.

99. Michael Barone, Grant Ujifusa, and Douglas Matthews, *The Almanac of American Politics* (Boston: Gambit, 1972), pp. 479–80.

100. Any teacher of American politics has had students ask about senators running for the presidency (Goldwater, McGovern, McCarthy, any of the Kennedys), "But what bills has he passed?" There is no unembarrassing answer.

101. Fenno, *Congressmen in Committees,* pp. 242–55.

102. In the terminology of Stokes, statements may be on either "position issues" or

"valence issues." Donald E. Stokes, "Spatial Models of Party Competition," ch. 9 in Campbell et al., *Elections and the Political Order*, pp. 170–74.

103. Clapp, *The Congressman*, p. 108. A difficult borderline question here is whether introduction of bills in Congress should be counted under position taking or credit claiming. On balance probably under the former. Yet another Clapp congressman addresses the point: "I introduce about sixty bills a year, about 120 a Congress. I try to introduce bills that illustrate, by and large, my ideas — legislative, economic, and social. I do like being able to say when I get cornered, 'yes, boys, I introduced a bill to try to do that in 1954.' To me it is the perfect answer." Ibid., p. 141. But voters probably give claims like this about the value they deserve.

104. On floor speeches generally see Matthews, *U.S. Senators*, p. 247. On statements celebrating holidays cherished by ethnic groups, Hearings on the Organization of Congress before the Joint Committee on the Organization of the Congress, 89th Cong., 1st sess., 1965, p. 1127; and Arlen J. Large, "And Now Let's Toast Nicolaus Copernicus, the Famous German," *Wall Street Journal*, March 12, 1973, p. 1.

105. Sometimes members of the Senate ostentatiously line up as "cosponsors" of measures — an activity that may attract more attention than roll call voting itself. Thus in early 1973, seventy-six senators backed a provision to block trade concessions to the U.S.S.R. until the Soviet government allowed Jews to emigrate without paying high exit fees. "Why did so many people sign the amendment?' a Northern Senator asked rhetorically. 'Because there is no political advantage in not signing. If you do sign, you don't offend anyone. If you don't sign, you might offend some Jews in your state.'" David E. Rosenbaum, "Firm Congress Stand on Jews in Soviet Is Traced to Efforts by Those in U.S.," *New York Times*, April 6, 1973, p. 14.

106. ". . . an utterly hopeless proposal and for that reason an ideal campaign issue." V. O. Key Jr., *Southern Politics* (New York: Knopf, 1949), p. 232.

107. Instructions on how to do this are given in Tacheron and Udall, *Job of the Congressman*, pp. 73–74.

108. William Lazarus, Nader profile on Edward R. Roybal (D., Cal.), p. 1.

109. On obfuscation in congressional position taking see Raymond A. Bauer, Ithiel de Sola Pool, and Lewis A. Dexter, *American Business and Public Policy* (New York: Atherton, 1964), pp. 431–32.

110. "Elaborate indexes of politicians and their records were kept at Washington and in most of the states, and professions of sympathy were matched with deeds. The voters were constantly apprised of the doings of their representatives." Peter H. Odegard, *Pressure Politics: The Story of the Anti-Saloon League* (New York: Columbia University Press, 1928), p. 21.

111. On Farm Bureau dealings with congressmen in the 1920s see Orville M. Kile, *The Farm Bureau through Three Decades* (Baltimore: Waverly Press, 1948), ch. 7.

112. V. O. Key Jr., "The Veterans and the House of Representatives: A Study of a Pressure Group and Electoral Mortality," 5 *Journal of Politics* 27–40 (1943).

113. "The American Medical Association," pp. 1011–18. See also Richard Harris, *A Sacred Trust* (New York: New American Library, 1966).

114. On the NRA generally see Stanford N. Sesser, "The Gun: Kingpin of 'Gun Lobby'

Has a Million Members, Much Clout in Congress," *Wall Street Journal,* May 24, 1972, p. 1. On the defeat of Senator Joseph Tydings (D., Md.) in 1970: "Tydings himself tended to blame the gun lobby, which in turn was quite willing to take the credit. 'Nobody in his right mind is going to take on that issue again [i.e. gun control],' one Tydings strategist admitted." John F. Bibby and Roger H. Davidson, *On Capitol Hill: Studies in the Legislative Process* (Hinsdale, Ill.: Dryden, 1972), p. 50.

115. A cautious politician will not be sure of an issue until it has been tested in a campaign. Polling evidence is suggestive, but it can never be conclusive.

116. David Price, *Who Makes the Laws?* (Cambridge, Mass.: Schenkman, 1972), p. 29. Magnuson was chairman of the Senate Commerce Committee. "Onto the old Magnuson, interested in fishing, shipping, and Boeing Aircraft, and running a rather sleepy committee, was grafted a new one: the champion of the consumer, the national legislative leader, and the patron of an energetic and innovative legislative staff." P. 78.

117. Marjorie Hunter, "Hollings Fight on Hunger Is Stirring the South," *New York Times,* March 8, 1969, p. 14. The local reaction was favorable. "Already Senator Herman E. Talmadge, Democrat of Georgia, has indicated he will begin a hunger crusade in his own state. Other Senators have hinted that they may do the same."

118. Robert Griffith, *The Politics of Fear: Joseph R. McCarthy and the Senate* (New York: Hayden, 1970), p. 29. Rovere's conclusion: "McCarthy took up the Communist menace in 1950 not with any expectation that it would make him a sovereign of the assemblies, but with the single hope that it would help him hold his job in 1952." Richard Rovere, *Senator Joe McCarthy* (Cleveland: World, 1961), p. 120.

119. Robert A. Schoenberger, "Campaign Strategy and Party Loyalty: The Electoral Relevance of Candidate Decision-Making in the 1964 Congressional Elections," 63 *American Political Science Review* 515–20 (1969).

120. Robert S. Erikson, "The Electoral Impact of Congressional Roll Call Voting," 65 *American Political Science Review* 1023 (1971).

121. Griffith, *The Politics of Fear,* pp. 122–31. The defeat of Senator Millard Tydings (D., Md.) was attributed to resources (money, endorsements, volunteer work) conferred or mobilized by McCarthy. "And if Tydings can be defeated, then who was safe? Even the most conservative and entrenched Democrats began to fear for their seats, and in the months that followed, the legend of McCarthy's political power grew." P. 123.

122. Douglas, *In the Fullness of Time,* p. 140.

123. Barone et al., *Almanac of American Politics,* p. 53. Mailliard was given a safer district in the 1972 line drawing.

124. On member freedom see Bauer et al., *American Business and Public Policy,* pp. 406–7.

125. Linda M. Kupferstein, Nader profile on William A. Barrett (D., Pa.), p. 1. This profile gives a very useful account of a machine congressman's activities.

126. One commentator on New York detects "a tendency for the media to promote what may be termed 'press release politicians.'" A result is that "younger members tend to gravitate towards House committees that have high rhetorical and perhaps symbolic importance, like Foreign Affairs and Government Operations, rather than those with bread-and-butter payoffs." Donald Haider, "The New York City Congressional Delega-

tion," *City Almanac* (published bimonthly by the Center for New York City Affairs of the New School for Social Research), vol. 7, no. 6, April 1973, p. 11.

127. Snowiss, "Congressional Recruitment and Representation."

128. The term is from Joseph A. Schlesinger, *Ambition and Politics: Political Careers in the United States* (Chicago: Rand McNally, 1966), p. 10.

129. Ibid., p. 92; Matthews, *U.S. Senators,* p. 55. In the years 1953–72 three House members were appointed to the Senate, and eighty-five gave up their seats to run for the Senate. Thirty-five of the latter made it, giving a success rate of 41 percent.

130. Thus upstate New York Republicans moving to the Senate commonly shift to the left. For a good example of the advertising and position-taking strategies that can go along with turning a House member into a senator see the account on Senator Robert P. Griffin (R., Mich.) in James M. Perry, *The New Politics* (New York: Clarkson N. Potter, 1968), ch. 4.

131. Fenno, *Congressmen in Committees,* pp. 141–42.

132. "Thurmond Image Seen as Changing," *New York Times,* October 17, 1971, p. 46.

2

Congressional Elections
The Case of the Vanishing Marginals

Of the electoral instruments voters have used to influence American national government few have been more important than the biennial "net partisan swing" in United States House membership. Since Jacksonian times ups and downs in party seat holdings in the House have supplied an important form of party linkage.

The seat swing is, in practice, a two-step phenomenon. For a party to register a net gain in House seats there must occur (*a*) a gain (over the last election) in the national proportion of popular votes cast for House candidates of the party in question. That is, the party must be the beneficiary of a national trend in popular voting for the House.[1] But there must also occur (*b*) a translation of popular vote gains into seat gains.[2] Having the former without the latter might be interesting but it would not be very important.

The causes of popular vote swings have only recently been traced with any precision. There is voter behavior that produces the familiar mid-term sag for parties in control of the presidency.[3] There is the long-run close relation between changes in economic indices and changes in the House popular vote.[4] There are doubtless other matters that can give a national cast to House voting, including wars.[5]

The consequences of partisan seat swings (built on popular vote swings) have been more elusive but no less arresting. As in the case of the Great Society

Congress (1965–66), House newcomers can supply the votes to pass bills that could not have been passed without them. Presidents with ambitious domestic programs (Woodrow Wilson, Franklin Roosevelt, Lyndon Johnson) have relied heavily on the votes of temporarily augmented Democratic House majorities. No clear argument can be made, of course, that a bill-passing binge like that of 1965–66 offers a direct conversion of popular wishes into laws. The evidence is more ambiguous. At the least a House election like the one of 1964 produces a rotation of government elites that has policy consequences; at the most there is some detectable relation between what such temporarily empowered elites do and what popular wishes are. Over time the working of the seat swing has sometimes given a dialectical cast to national policy making, with successive elites making successive policy approximations. A case in point is the enactment of the Wagner Act in the Democratic Seventy-fourth Congress followed by its Taft-Hartley revision in the Republican Eightieth. Because of all the translation uncertainties the House seat swing has been a decidedly blunt voter instrument, but it has been a noteworthy instrument nonetheless.

The foregoing is a preface to a discussion of some recent election data. The data, for the years 1956–72, suggest strongly that the House seat swing is a phenomenon of fast declining amplitude and therefore of fast declining significance. The first task here will be to lay out the data — in nearly raw form — in order to give a sense of their shape and flow. The second task will be to speculate about causes of the pattern in the data, the third to ponder the implications of this pattern.

I.

The data are presented in Figure 2.1, a multi-page array of 22 bar graphs. If the pages are turned sideways and read as if they were one long display, the graphs appear in three columns of nine, nine, and four. It will be useful to begin with an examination of the four graphs in the right-hand column.

Each of the four right-hand graphs is a frequency distribution in which congressional districts are sorted according to percentages of the major-party presidential vote cast in them in one of the four presidential elections of the years 1956–68.[6] The districts are cumulated vertically in percentages of the total district set of 435 rather than in absolute numbers. The horizontal axis has column intervals of five percent, ranging from a far-left interval for districts where the Democratic presidential percentage was 0–4.9 to a far-right interval where the percentage was 95–100. Thus the 1956 graph shows that

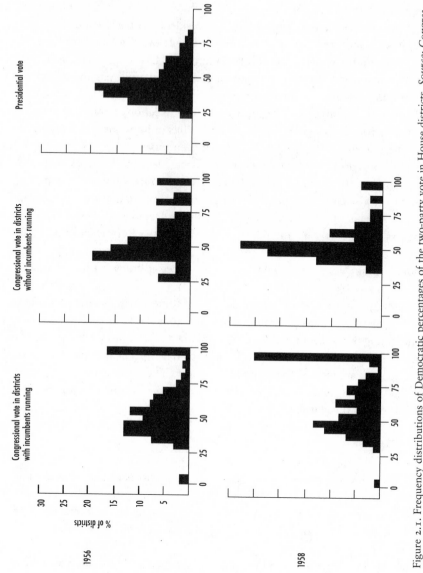

Figure 2.1. Frequency distributions of Democratic percentages of the two-party vote in House districts. *Source: Congressional Quarterly Weekly.*

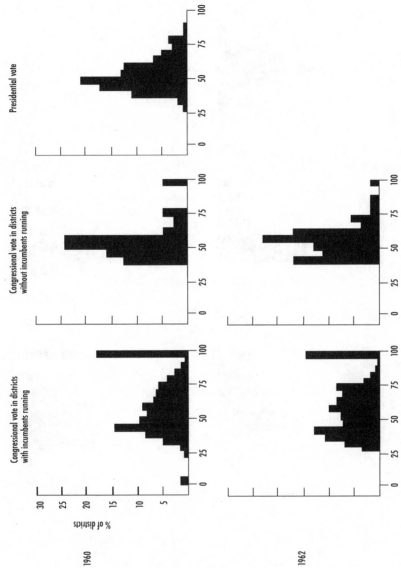

Congressional vote in districts with incumbents running

Congressional vote in districts without incumbents running

Presidential vote

% of districts

1960

1962

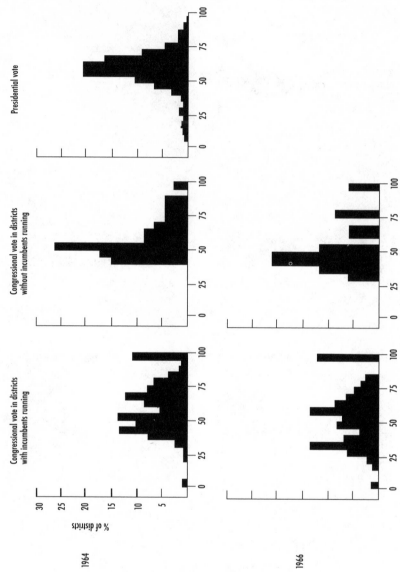

Presidential vote

Congressional vote in districts without incumbents running

Congressional vote in districts with incumbents running

% of districts

30

25

20

15

10

5

0   25   50   75   100

1964

1966

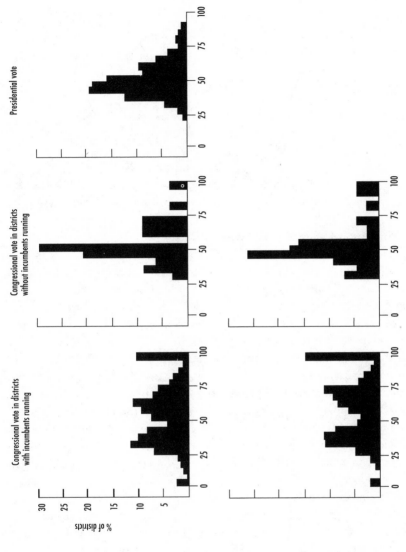

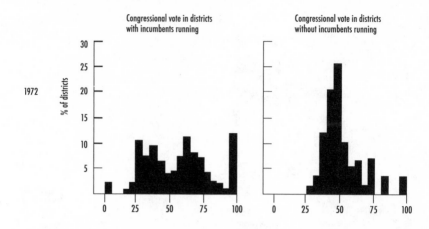

the Stevenson-Kefauver ticket won 50 to 54.9 percent of the major-party vote in about 7 percent of the districts (actual district N = 30) and a modal 40 to 44.9 percent of the vote in about 20 percent of the districts (actual N = 87).

In themselves these presidential graphs hold no surprises; they are presented for the purpose of visual comparison with the other data. The presidential mode travels well to the left of the 50 percent mark in 1956 and well to the right in 1964, but the four distributions are fundamentally alike in shape — highly peaked, unimodal, not far from normal.

The center and left columns give frequency distributions, organized on the same principles as the four presidential graphs, in which House districts are sorted according to percentages of the major-party House vote cast in them in each of the nine congressional elections in the years 1956–72. But for each House election there are two graphs side by side. For each year the graph in the left column gives a distribution of returns for all districts in which an incumbent congressman was running, the center column a set of returns for districts with no incumbents running.[7]

The center graphs, the "open seat" distributions, are erratically shaped because the Ns are small. The number of House districts without incumbents running averages 43 (about a tenth of the membership) and ranges from 31 (in 1956) to 59 (in 1972); there is no discernible upward or downward trend in the series. With allowances made for erratic shape these nine "open seat" distributions are much alike. All are highly peaked and centrally clustered. In 1958 and 1968 nearly 30 percent of the readings appear in the modal interval (in both cases the 50–54.9 percent Democratic interval). Over the set of nine elections the proportion of "open seat" outcomes falling in the 40–59.9 percent area ranges from 54.8 percent to 70.2 percent, the proportion in the 45–

54.9 percent area from 29.0 percent to 50.1 percent. All of which imparts the simple and obvious message that House elections without incumbents running tend to be closely contested.

The nine graphs in the left-hand column give distributions for districts with incumbents running.[8] Thus in 1956 about 9 percent of districts with incumbents running yielded returns in the 45–49.9 percent Democratic interval. In some of these cases the incumbents were Democrats who thereby lost their seats; in any of these nine graphs the election reading for a losing incumbent will appear on what was, from his standpoint, the unfortunate side of the 50 percent line. In an Appendix the nine data sets are disaggregated to show where in fact incumbents lost.

Immediately visible on each of these incumbency graphs is the isolated mode in the 95–100 percent interval, recording the familiar phenomenon of uncontested Democratic victories — mostly in the South. But, if these right-flush modes can be ignored for a moment, what has recently been happening in the contested range is far more interesting. In 1956 and 1960 the distributions in the contested range are skewed a little to the right, but still not far from normal in shape. In the 1958 and 1962 midterm years the distributions are somewhat flatter and more jagged.[9] In 1964 and 1966 they appear only tenuously normal. In 1968, 1970, and 1972 they have become emphatically bimodal in shape. Or, to ring in the uncontested Democratic seats again, the shape of incumbency distributions has now become strikingly trimodal. Thus in the 1972 election there was a range of reasonably safe Republican seats (with the 25–29.9 percent and 35–39.5 percent intervals most heavily populated), a range of reasonably safe Democratic seats (peaked in the 60–64.9 percent interval), and a set of 44 uncontested Democratic seats.

The title of this essay includes the phrase, "The Case of the Vanishing Marginals." The "vanishing marginals" are all those congressmen whose election percentages could, but now do not, earn them places in the central range of these incumbency distributions. In the graphs for the most recent elections the trough between the "reasonably safe" Republican and Democratic modes appears in the percentage range that we are accustomed to calling "marginal." Figure 2.2 captures the point, with time series showing how many incumbent congressmen have recorded percentages in the "marginal" range in each election from 1956 through 1972.[10] The lower series on the two Figure 2.2 graphs show, for comparative purposes, the number of "open seat" outcomes in the marginal range. In one graph marginality is defined narrowly (45–54.9 Democratic percentage of the major-party vote), in the other broadly (40–59.9 percent). By either definition the number of incumbents running in the

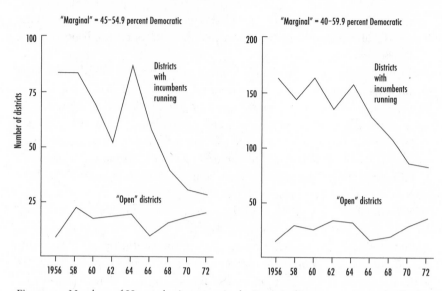

Figure 2.2. Numbers of House elections won in the "marginal" range, 1956–72, in districts with and without incumbents running. *Source: Congressional Quarterly Weekly.*

marginal zone has roughly halved over the sixteen-year period.[11] For some reason, or reasons, it seems to be a lot easier now than it used to be for a sitting congressman to win three-fifths of the November vote.

II.

Why the decline in incumbent marginality? No clear answer is available.[12] Adding complexity to the problem is the fact that the proportion of House seats won in the marginal range has been slowly declining for over a century.[13] Whatever mix of causes underlies the long-run change could account for much of the rapid current change as well. On the assumption that the contemporary decline is not ephemeral, perhaps the most useful thing to do here is to set out some hypotheses which may singly or in combination account for it. Five hypotheses are offered below. Some have a more persuasive ring than others; none is wholly implausible. The first has to do with district line-drawing, the next three with congressmen's actions designed to attract votes, the last with voter behavior not inspired by congressmen's actions.

(1) The line-drawing explanation is easy to reach for. In the last decade of chronic redistricting the possibility of building districts to profit incumbents has not been lost on House members or others acting in their interest. With

county lines less sacred than they once were, ingenious districts can be and have been drawn. And there are good examples of cross-party districting deals among congressmen of large state delegations.[14] But the problem with the line-drawing hypothesis is that it seems not to explain very much. Manipulation of the aggregate national data does not yield an impressive relation between redistricting and electoral benefit.[15] Moreover, if the voters are being partitioned into safe House districts it can be argued that bimodal patterns ought to appear sooner or later in presidential and "open seat" distributions of the sort displayed in Figure 2.1. Of bimodalism the relevant Figure 2.1 graphs give no trace, although it must be said that the evidence is inconclusive. The evidence on redistricting generally is incomplete and inconclusive. But the odds are that it will not explain very much. If all 435 congressmen were suddenly to retire in 1974, and if elections to replace them were conducted in the 1972 district set, the odds are that a distribution of new member percentages would look like a presidential or an evened out "open seat" distribution — unimodal and roughly normal, though perhaps still with a modest isolated mode for uncontested Southerners.

The next four hypotheses hinge on the assumption that House incumbency now carries with it greater electoral advantages than it has in the past. There is evidence that it does.[16] One way to try to find out is to look at what happens to party fortunes in districts where congressmen die, retire, or lose primaries — to compare the last November percentages of veteran incumbents with the percentages of their successor nominees. Table 2.1 does this for the six elections in the years 1962–72. Figures are given for transitions in which the retirees were at least two-term veterans and where the bracketing elections were both contested by both parties. It is hard to tease conclusions out of these data; the universes for the six elections are small, the districts in each inter-election set vary widely in their change percentages, national trends affect Democrats and Republicans differently, and there is the redistricting problem throughout. But these are all of the data there are on the point. Most of the columns in the table include figures on districts with line changes. Including these raises the obvious problem that redistricting itself can affect party percentages. But there is some justification for the inclusion. For one thing, no systematic difference appears here between what happens electorally in redrawn and untouched districts. For another, it is impossible to get any reading at all on the 1972 election without inspecting the redrawn districts; 25 of the 27 "succession nominations" occurred in 1972 in districts with line changes. If handled carefully the altered districts can yield information. Redrawn districts are covered here if they were treated in the press as being more or less "the same" as districts

Table 2.1 Change in Party Percentage in House Districts Where Incumbents Have Retired, Died, or Lost Primaries

	Transitions in Districts without Line Changes						Transitions in Districts with Line Changes	
	Democratic Districts		Republican Districts		All Districts		All Districts	
	N	MEAN	N	MEAN	N	MEAN	N	MEAN
1962	(4)	−5.2	(4)	−0.2	(8)	−2.7	(9)	+1.3
1964	(12)	+5.5	(13)	−8.2	(25)	−1.6	*	
1966	(3)	−6.2	(3)	−2.5	(6)	−4.3	(7)	−7.7
1968	(4)	+1.1	(3)	−14.9	(7)	−5.8	(12)	−8.6
1970	(15)	−4.9	(17)	−7.9	(32)	−6.5	(4)	−5.7
1972	(2)	−26.7	*		(2)	−26.7	(25)	−9.5

Transitions in Districts with and without Line Changes

	Democratic Districts		Republican Districts		All Districts		All Districts		All Districts	
								WGHTD		
	N	MEAN	N	MEAN	N	MEAN	N	MEAN	N	MEDIAN
1962	(5)	−6.0	(12)	+1.8	(17)	−0.5	(17)	−2.1	(17)	−3.1
1964	(12)	+5.5	(13)	−8.2	(25)	−1.6	(25)	−1.3	(25)	−3.1
1966	(8)	−8.9	(5)	−1.8	(13)	−6.2	(13)	−5.4	(13)	−8.2
1968	(10)	−1.4	(9)	−14.5	(19)	−7.6	(19)	−8.0	(19)	−4.7
1970	(19)	−5.1	(17)	−7.9	(36)	−6.4	(36)	−6.0	(36)	−5.6
1972	(12)	−13.1	(15)	−9.0	(27)	−10.8	(27)	−11.1	(27)	−10.2

Source: Congressional Quarterly Weekly.

preceding them; thus, for example, Paul Cronin is commonly regarded as Bradford Morse's successor in the fifth Massachusetts district although Cronin's 1972 boundaries are somewhat different from Morse's old ones.

What to look for in Table 2.1 is whether switches in party nominees bring about drops in party percentages. The bigger the drop the higher the putative value of incumbency. Inter-election changes in party percentage are calculated here by comparing party shares of the total congressional district vote in the bracketing elections.[17] The first three columns in the table give data only on districts without line changes. Thus in 1962 there were four Democratic retirements (or deaths, etc.) in districts with 1960 lines intact; the Democratic share of the total vote fell an average of 5.2 percent in these four districts between 1960 and 1962. In the four Republican retirement districts in 1962 the Republican share of the total vote fell an average of 0.2 percent. In 1964 there was an understandable party gain in the Democratic retirement districts, and an especially heavy mean loss in the Republican set. Fortuitously the numbers of retirement districts for the two parties are almost identical in each of the five elections in 1962 through 1970, so it makes sense to calculate mean change values for all retirement districts regardless of party in each year in order to try to cancel out the effects of election-specific national trends. This is done in the third column, a list of cross-party percentage change means for the six elections. (Thus in 1964 the average change in the 25 retirement seats was a negative 1.6 percent even though the average party values were far apart; Republicans generally lost more in their transitions than Democrats gained in theirs.) Here there emerges some fairly solid evidence. Mean drops in percentage were higher in 1966, 1968, and 1970 than in 1962 and 1964. (1972, with its N of 2, can be ignored.) The best evidence is for 1964 and 1970, with their large Ns. Loss of incumbents cost the parties a mean of 1.6 percent in 1964, a mean of 6.5 percent in 1970.

In the fourth column figures on transitions in redrawn districts are introduced. The values are mean changes for redrawn retirement districts by year regardless of party. It will be seen that these values differ in no systematic way from the values for undisturbed districts in the third column. There is the same general trend toward bigger drops in percentage. Especially striking is the 1972 value of minus 9.5 percent, lower than any other reading in the list of values for redrawn districts. The fifth, sixth, and seventh columns of the table give mean values by year, respectively, for Democratic, Republican, and all retirement districts, with no distinctions being made between altered and unaltered districts. The eighth column gives a weighted mean for each year, a simple average of the party averages. Finally the ninth column gives a median value for the set of all readings in each year.

These readings, tenuous as they are, all point in the same direction. Incumbency does seem to have increased in electoral value, and it is reasonable to suppose that one effect of this increase has been to boost House members of both parties out of the marginal electoral range. If incumbency has risen in value, what accounts for the rise? The second, third, and fourth hypotheses below focus on electorally useful activities that House members may now be engaging in more effectively than their predecessors did ten or twenty years ago.

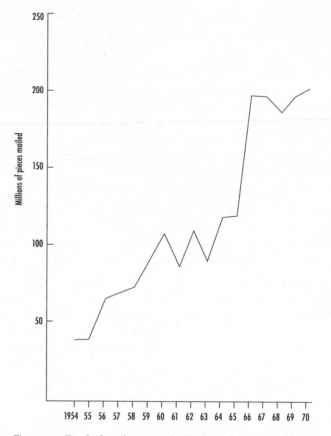

Figure 2.3. Franked mail sent out by House and Senate members, in millions of pieces, 1954–70. *Source:* U.S. Congress, House, Committee on Appropriations, *Hearing Before a Subcommittee of the Committee on Appropriations, Legislative Branch Appropriations for 1970,* 91st Cong., 1st sess., 1969, p. 501 has 1954–1968 data. Subsequent annual hearings update estimated franking use.

(2) House members may now be advertising themselves better. Simple name recognition counts for a lot in House elections, as the Survey Research Center data show.[18] A name perceived with a halo of goodwill around it probably counts for more. If House members have not profited from accelerated advertising in the past decade, it is not from want of trying. The time series in Figure 2.3 shows, in millions of pieces, how much mail was sent out from the Capitol (by both House and Senate members) in each year from 1954 through 1970.[19] The mail includes letters, newsletters, questionnaires, child-care pamphlets, etc., some of them mailed to all district box-holders. Peak mailing months are

the Octobers of even-numbered years. Mail flow more than sextupled over the sixteen-year period, with an especially steep increase between 1965 and 1966. In fact the mail-flow curve matches well any incumbency-advantage curve derivable from the data in Table 2.1. There is no letup in sight; one recent estimate has it that House members will send out about 900,000 pieces of mail per member in 1974, at a total public cost of $38.1 million.[20] So the answer to the incumbency advantage question could be a remarkably simple one: the more hundreds of thousands of messages congressmen rain down on constituents, the more votes they get. Whether all this activity has significantly raised the proportion of citizens who know their congressmen's names is uncertain. There are some Gallup readings showing that the share of adults who could name their congressmen rose from 46 to 53 percent between 1966 and 1970.[21]

(3) Another possibility is that House members may be getting more political mileage out of federal programs. The number of grant-in-aid programs has risen in the past decade at something like the rate of Capitol mail flow. The more programs there are, the more chances House members have to claim credit ostentatiously for the local manifestations of them — housing grants, education grants, anti-pollution grants, etc.

(4) Yet another possibility is that House members have become more skilled at public position taking on "issues." The point is a technological one. If more congressmen are commissioning and using scientific opinion polls to plumb district sentiment, then House members may have become, on balance, more practiced at attuning themselves to district opinion.[22] There is a possibility here, however hard it is to try to measure. There may be a greater general sophistication today about polling and its uses. In 1964, forty-nine Republican House members running for reelection signed a pre-convention statement endorsing Senator Goldwater. It was claimed that Goldwater's nomination would help the party ticket. The forty-nine suffered disproportionately in November.[23] In 1972 there was no comparable rush among House Democrats to identify themselves with Senator McGovern.

(5) The fifth and last hypothesis has to do with changes in voter behavior not inspired by changes in incumbent activities. It is possible that incumbents have been profiting not from any exertions of their own but from changes in voter attitudes. A logic suggests itself. Voters dissatisfied with party cues could be reaching for any other cues that are available in deciding how to vote. The incumbency cue is readily at hand. This hypothesis assumes a current rise in discontent with parties; it assumes nothing about changes in the cues voters have been receiving from congressmen.

There is no point in speculating further here about causes. But it is important that the subject be given further treatment, if for no other reason than that some of the variables can be legally manipulated. The congressional franking privilege comes first to mind.

III.

If fewer House members are winning elections narrowly, and if the proportion of "open seats" per election is not rising, it ought to follow that congressional seat swings are declining in amplitude. The argument requires no assumption that national swings in the House popular vote are changing in amplitude — and indeed there is no evidence in the contemporary data that they are. It does require the assumption that a congressman's percentage showing in one election supplies information on his strength as he goes into the next. That is, a House member running at the 60 percent level is less likely to be unseated by an adverse 5 percent party trend next time around than one running at the 54 percent level. It is easy to predict that a popular voting trend will cut less of a swath through a set of congressmen whose last-election percentages are arrayed like those in the 1968, 1970, and 1972 incumbency graphs of Figure 2.1 than through a set whose percentages are centrally and normally distributed.

There is evidence suggesting that the flight from marginality is having its posited effect. Edward Tufte has found that a "swing ratio" — a rate of translation of votes into seats — built on data from the 1966, 1968, and 1970 elections yields an exceptionally low value when compared with ratios for other election triplets over the past century.[24] The figures in Table 2.2 point in the same direction. Supplied here are data on popular vote swings, net partisan seat swings, and incumbency defeats for each and both parties in the election years from 1956 through 1972.[25] It is worth noting that the large seat swings of 1958, 1964, and 1966 were heavily dependent upon defeats of incumbents. Very few incumbents have lost since 1966. (Almost all the 1972 losers were victims of line changes.) Especially interesting are the figures for 1970, a year in which the popular vote swing was a fairly sizable 3.3 percent. Yet only nine incumbents of the disfavored party lost and the net swing over 1968 was only twelve — of which three changed over in 1969 by-elections. Part of the explanation here is doubtless that the disfavored party had relatively few incumbents in the vulnerable range to protect. Only 47 Republicans running in 1970 had won under the 60 percent mark in 1968, whereas there had been 82 comparably exposed Republicans running in 1958, 76 Republicans in 1964, and 79 Democrats in 1966.

What general conclusions can be drawn? If the trends hold, we are witnesses to the blunting of a blunt instrument. It may be too soon to say that seat

Table 2.2 House Vote Swings and Seat Swings, 1956–72

	Change in National Popular Vote over Last Election	Net Partisan Seat Swing over Last Election	Incumbent Losses to Opposite Party Challengers		
			D	R	Total
1956	1.5% D	2 D	8	7	15
1958	5.1% D	49 D	1	34	35
1960	1.1% R	20 R	22	3	25
1962	2.2% R	2 R	9	5	14
1964	4.7% D	36 D	5	39	44
1966	6.2% R	47 R	39	1	40
1968	0.4% R	5 R	5	0	5
1970	3.3% D	12 D	2	9	11
1972	1.4% R	12 R	6	3	9

Source: Congressional Quarterly Weekly.

swings of the 1958 or 1964 variety can be consigned to the history books, but it is hard to see how they could be equaled in the newer electoral circumstances. There is probably another manifestation here of what Walter Dean Burnham calls "electoral disaggregation" — a weakening of the peculiar links that party has supplied between electorate and government.[26] There is a triumph for Madison's idea of checks and balances: A Congress less affected by electoral tides may be less susceptible to manipulation by the strong twentieth-century presidency. But there is a long-run danger that a Congress that cannot supply quick electoral change is no match for a presidency that can.

Notes

This essay was originally published in *Polity* 6:3 (Spring 1974), pp. 295–317.

1. To put it yet another way, voting for House candidates must have a "national component" to it. See Donald E. Stokes, "Parties and the Nationalization of Electoral Forces," ch. 7 in William N. Chambers and Walter D. Burnham, *The American Party Systems* (New York: Oxford University Press, 1967).

2. The best analysis of translation formulas is in Edward R. Tufte, "The Relation Between Seats and Votes in Two Party Systems," *American Political Science Review*, 67 (June, 1973), 540–54.

3. Angus Campbell, "Surge and Decline: A Study in Electoral Change," ch. 3 in Campbell et al., *Elections and the Political Order* (New York: Wiley, 1966).

4. Gerald H. Kramer, "Short-Term Fluctuations in U.S. Voting Behavior, 1896–1964," *American Political Science Review,* 65 (1971), 131–43.

5. Ibid., p. 140.

6. At the time of writing no comparable figures were yet available for the 1972 election. Dealing with the 1968 returns by calculating percentages of the major-party vote poses obvious problems — especially in the South — but so does any alternative way of dealing with them. Congressional district data used in Figure 2.1 and following tables and figures were taken from *Congressional Quarterly* compilations.

7. An incumbent is defined here as a congressman who held a seat at the time he was running in a November election, even if he had first taken the seat in a recent by-election.

8. The center graphs cover districts with no incumbents, the left-hand graphs districts with one incumbent. This leaves no place in the diagram for districts with two opposite-party incumbents running against each other. There were 16 of these throw-in cases over the period: 7 in 1962, 1 in 1966, 4 in 1968, 1 in 1970, 3 in 1972. Republicans won in 10 of them.

9. On balance it can be expected that distributions will be more centrally clustered in presidential than in midterm years, for the reason that presidential elections enroll expanded electorates in which disproportionate numbers of voters violate district partisan habits in their congressional voting. See Harvey Kabaker, "Estimating the Normal Vote in Congressional Elections," *Midwest Journal of Political Science,* 13 (1969), 58–83.

10. Again, the 16 throw-in cases are not included. It should be recalled here that some of these incumbents in the marginal range moved across the 50 percent mark and lost their seats. (See the Appendix.) Of the 198 incumbents who lost elections to opposite-party challengers in the 1956–72 period, only 4 plummeted far enough to fall outside the broadly defined (40–59.9 percent) marginal range.

11. The decline has come in spite of Republican inroads in Southern House districts. One reason here is that, once they have gotten their seats, Southern Republican incumbents tend to win elections handily; 16 of 22 of them won with over 60 percent of the major-party vote in 1970, 18 of 22 in 1972.

12. For current work on this subject, see Albert D. Cover, "The Advantage of Incumbency in Congressional Elections," Ph.D. dissertation, Yale University, 1976.

13. I owe this point to Walter D. Burnham. On long-run decline in House turnover see Charles O. Jones, "Inter-Party Competition for Congressional Seats," *Western Political Quarterly,* 17 (1964), 461–76.

14. Some strategies and examples are discussed in David R. Mayhew, "Congressional Representation: Theory and Practice in Drawing the Districts," ch. 7 in Nelson W. Polsby, ed., *Reapportionment in the 1970's* (Berkeley: University of California Press, 1971), pp. 274–84.

15. On the 1966 election see Robert J. Erikson, "Malapportionment, Gerrymandering, and Party Fortunes in Congressional Elections," *American Political Science Review,* 66 (1972), 1238.

16. Robert Erikson estimates that incumbency status was worth about 2 percent of the vote in the 1950s and early 1960s, but about 5 percent in 1966 and thereafter. Erikson,

"The Advantage of Incumbency in Congressional Elections," *Polity,* 3 (1971), 395–405. Erikson, "Malapportionment, Gerrymandering, and Party Fortunes in Congressional Elections," 1240.

17. Figures 2.1 and 2.2 are built on candidate percentage of the major-party vote, Table 2.1 on percentages of the total vote.

18. Donald E. Stokes and Warren E. Miller, "Party Government and the Saliency of Congress," ch. 11 in Angus Campbell, et al., *Elections and the Political Order* (New York: Wiley, 1966), pp. 204–9.

19. Data supplied by Albert D. Cover.

20. Norman C. Miller, "Yes, You Are Getting More Politico Mail; And It Will Get Worse," *Wall Street Journal,* March 6, 1973.

21. Gallup survey in *Washington Post,* September 20, 1970.

22. There is a discussion of roll-call position taking and its electoral effects in Robert Erikson, "The Electoral Impact of Congressional Roll Call Voting," *American Political Science Review,* 65 (1971), 1018–32.

23. Robert A. Schoenberger, "Campaign Strategy and Party Loyalty: the Electoral Relevance of Candidate Decision-Making in the 1964 Congressional Elections," *American Political Science Review,* 63 (1969), 515–20.

24. Tufte, "The Relation Between Seats and Votes," pp. 549–50.

25. The incumbency defeat figures cover only losses to opposite-party challengers. Thus once again the 16 throw-in cases are disregarded. Also ignored are the November losses of two highly visible Democrats — Brooks Hays (1958) and Louise Day Hicks (1972) — to independents who thereupon enrolled as Democrats themselves in Washington. It might be added here that some incumbents do after all lose their primaries. The figures for losses to primary challengers are: 6 in 1956, 4 in 1958, 5 in 1960, 8 in 1962, 5 in 1964, 5 in 1966, 3 in 1968, 9 in 1970, 8 in 1972. The figures for losses where redistricting has thrown incumbents into the same primary: 5 in 1962, 3 in 1964, 3 in 1966, 1 in 1968, 1 in 1970, 6 in 1972. Whatever their qualitative effects, primaries have not rivaled the larger November swings in turnover leverage.

26. "The End of American Party Politics," *Trans-Action,* 7 (December, 1969), 18–20.

Appendix

The columns of figures in Table 2.A are frequency distributions of Democratic percentages of the November two-party House vote recorded in districts with incumbents of either (but not both) of the parties running, in biennial elections from 1956 through 1972, with separate columns for each year for districts harboring Democratic and Republican incumbents. Thus in 1956 there were twenty-eight districts with Republican incumbents running in which Democratic percentages were in the 45–49.9 percent range. There were also eight districts with Democratic incumbents running in which Democratic percentages were in the 45–49.9 percent range; these eight Democrats thereby lost their seats. Squares or rectangles are drawn around cells below which contain values for incumbents who lost seats to opposite-party challengers.

Table 2.A Party Electoral Fortunes in Incumbent-held House Districts, 1956–72

	Numbers of Districts, by Year and by Party of Incumbent																	
	1956		1958		1960		1962		1964		1966		1968		1970		1972	
Democratic % of the Two-Party Vote	D	R	D	R	D	R	D	R	D	R	D	R	D	R	D	R	D	R
0– 4.9		3		1		3		1		1		4		9		5		7
5– 9.9																		
10– 14.9														1				
15– 19.9						1								3		2		2
20– 24.9														6		5		7
25– 29.9		13				3		11		1		3		25		15		38
30– 34.9		28		11		16		24		7		8		47		40		27
35– 39.9		54		27		33		39	[2]	25	[1]	24		39		41		36
40– 44.9		54		44		56	[2]	45	[2]	47	[8]	53		31		34	[2]	22
45– 49.9	[8]	28	[1]	50	[3]	19	[7]	19	[1]	38	[30]	26	[5]	10	[2]	15	[4]	10
50– 54.9	40	[6]	4	[27]	28	[3]	23	[4]	14	[35]	28	[1]	26		8	[7]	15	[2]
55– 59.9	28	[1]	11	[7]	36		36	[1]	18	[4]	53	3	38		20	[1]	27	[1]
60– 64.9	28		33		27		32		35		34	[1]	43		28	[1]	40	
65– 69.9	21		19		26		27		45		26		24		35		30	
70– 74.9	10		26		21		31		29		20		22		42		26	
75– 79.9	7		17		16		11		24		13		12		15		16	
80– 84.9	2		10		11		4		13		9		10		12		9	
85– 89.9	4		1		4		2		4				4		4		7	
90– 94.9	1		5		3		1		2				1		1		1	
95–100.0	68		95		72		56		40		51		41		56		44	

Source: Congressional Quarterly Weekly.

3

Why Did V. O. Key Draw Back from His "Have-Nots" Claim?

In *Southern Politics* in 1949, V. O. Key Jr. made one of his most interesting and influential claims: "Over the long run the have-nots lose in a disorganized politics."[1] That is, they do worse in a one-party factional politics like much of the South's than in a setting where organized political parties compete closely in elections. Yet seven years later, in writing *American State Politics*, a work also about states, parties, factions, organized vs. disorganized politics, and the favorable effects of party competition, Key entirely abandoned the "have-nots" claim.[2] Or at least he carefully refrained from restating it. What accounts for his switch? In this essay I speculate about why he may have stepped back from the "have-nots" claim, though I do so without having sought out private documents or information that may bear on the matter. I draw on Key's published work in the 1949 and 1956 books and the 1952 edition of his *Politics, Parties and Pressure Groups* text, as well as on the changing political and intellectual background of the 1950s.[3] Before undertaking the speculation, I try to set out with some care the structures of the main arguments about parties that Key made in the two books about state politics.

The status of the *Southern Politics* "have-nots" claim is not entirely clear. It can be read as a theoretical statement of universalistic form, in which case its universe, within which organized and disorganized politics might be compared, is all democratic regimes, or all relatively autonomous regional subdivisions within such regimes, or both. It might apply in principle to municipalities, though Key does not consider them. Or the claim can be read as an empirical assertion, a hypothesis, or, more loosely, a question about co-variation between patterns of party structure and service to "have-nots" within the universe of existent democratic regimes or their sub-units,[4] or — as most readers have understandably interpreted it — within the universe of the then 48 American states.

Key plainly had in mind the North's two-party states as a comparison group for the South's one-party states as he cast his arguments,[5] though he stopped short, for lack of northern evidence, of making much of the contrast. In his analysis in *Southern Politics,* he resorted to a surrogate strategy which built on a judgment that some southern states — e.g. North Carolina — had party systems that resembled conventional two-party systems much more closely than did those of other southern states — e.g. Arkansas or South Carolina. "Hence," he proposed, "comparisons of the workings of different types of southern factional systems along with casual allusions to commonly understood features of two-party politics ought to yield some sort of estimate of the significance of the southern one- or non-party system" (299). To achieve such an estimate, he presumably meant, would be to suggest or establish something more general about one-party vs. two-party systems.

What warrants the "have-nots" claim? In Key's logic, differences in the characteristics of party systems produce differences in the conduct of politics or government, which in turn produce differences in policies regarding "have-nots." To advance this logic, Key's fertile mind produced, by my count, twenty separate assertions or propositions in *Southern Politics* that linked differences between a disorganized one-party and an organized two-party politics to differences in the conduct of politics or government. In some of these cases — including all the most important ones — Key explicitly made the further connection to differences in "have-nots" policies himself in his theoretical chapter 14; in other cases he implied the connection; and in others, where he developed lines of argument elsewhere than in chapter 14 and did not pick them up there, his points about parties, politics, and government are so similar to, or blend in so well with, the ones he does connect that making the connection for him seems unproblematical.[6]

I present here the twenty statements that link party systems with the conduct of politics or government. Some of these statements are more important than others, some overlap others, and some could be said to contain others; the presentation of them here is designed to bring out the nuances of Key's thinking. All are presented as assertions or propositions that draw contrasts, at least implicitly, between disorganized one-party and organized two-party systems in general. This is the way Key commonly framed his general points in *Southern Politics,* though often his contrasts featured well-organized southern bi-factional systems like North Carolina's as stand-ins for full blown two-party systems. For most of the twenty statements, Key's further implications about "have-nots" policies will be evident. As a general matter, in his view, the "have-nots" are best served by political processes that mobilize the public, raise "real" issues, offer clear issue choices in elections, make governments clearly accountable, provide competent leaders, facilitate the carrying through of complicated government programs, and above all, probably, foster the sort of organized activity that can overcome inertia in the populace, disorder in government, and obstruction by "haves."

Parties and Issues

1) *Two-party systems raise issues better than disorganized systems do.* The emphasis here is on raising issues, on activation or mobilization.[7] South Carolinians, Key wrote, sometimes wished they had two parties. "Few of them, however, realize what a genuine two-party system would mean in the way of raising issues and of activating the masses politically. By the same token, few of them realize the capacities of a one-party system for muffling protest, postponing issues, preserving the status quo" (150). As a general proposition: "When two distinct groups with some identity and continuity exist, they must raise issues and appeal to the masses if for no other reason than the desire for office" (304).

2) *Two-party systems are better at raising "genuine" issues, striking "funda-mental" cleavages, and supporting "rational" politics.* Class-related economic issues or cleavages, in Key's liberal or progressive way of thinking, had a favored ontological status as "genuine," "fundamental" or "rational."[8] He wrote about Texas, for example: "How the state was to protect its citizens from organizations of wealth, what the state was to undertake by way of public services for its citizens, for which citizens these services were intended, and who should pay the tax bill — these were ultimately the great concerns of democratic government...."[9] However, "in the confusions and distractions of one-party politics broad issues of economic philosophy are often obscured or smothered by irrelevant appeals, sectional loyalties, local patriotism, personal candidacies, and, above all, by the specter of the black man" (255). South Carolina's politics provoked these reflections: "An electorate that lacks party guideposts and traditions and that is also susceptible to manipulation by Negro-baiting, can be whipped into groupings quite contrary to what might

be expected on the basis of rational political behavior."[10] And: "Factions in a one-party state are much more fluid than parties, and such cross-currents as localism force alignments out of the pattern indicated by fundamental cleavages of interest" (147).

3) *National issues percolate down less well into one-party systems than into two-party systems.* Key had in mind the stock socioeconomic issues that divided the American national parties during the first half of the twentieth century: "These debates seep down into the battles between their state subsidiaries, and perhaps become blurred in the process, but even the chance for this sort of issue does not exist in one-party jurisdictions."[11] (Obviously statement #3, considered as a general statement, can apply only to subdivisions of polities.)

4) *Two-party systems suppress localism more effectively.* Key paid considerable attention in *Southern Politics* to politicians' non-issue-based home-county followings that emanated in "friends-and-neighbors" voting patterns.[12] Such localism, he suggested, "may be an indicator of the absence of a class politics or at least the disfranchisement of one class" (302). Key's claim about party systems: "In two-party states the force of party tradition and the strength of party cohesion minimize, although they do not entirely erase, localism" (302).

Parties and Policy Choice

5) *Competing parties, because they have stable roots in quite different socioeconomic bases and sustain relatively stable leadership cores, offer policy proposals to voters that are at once significantly different and, by virtue of being familiar as well as different, rather easily understandable. One-party factionalism offers no such package of services.* This complex, very basic set of ideas is hard to disaggregate; it mixes the idea of distinct options with the idea of understandable options.[13] "Normally," Key wrote, "a political party has its foundation in sectional, class, or group interests. One party draws its strength principally from certain sectors of the population; another depends for its support (in the main) on other groups within the population. The differentiation in the interests of these groups produces a differentiation in the policies that the parties seek to effectuate through government."[14] "Discontinuity of faction," however, "both confuses the electorate and reflects a failure to organize the voters into groups of more or less like-minded citizens with somewhat similar attitudes toward public policy. . . . [In such conditions] the voters' task is not simplified by the existence of continuing competing parties with fairly well-recognized, general-policy orientations. That is, this party proposes to

run the government generally in one way; the opposition, another" (303). In another place Key wrote of a "discontinuous and kaleidoscopic quality of faction [that] contrasts markedly with the stability of electoral loyalty and continuity of leadership of true political parties" (301–2).

6) *Two-party systems reduce confusion by narrowing the range of voter options to two.* This point could easily be incorporated into statement #5, but Key, like other theorists of elections, presented it separately. South Carolina's "multiplicity of candidacies" inspired this reflection: "A party system performs a negative function in repressing candidates, as well as the positive role of choosing and putting forward candidates. The loose factional politics in South Carolina blocks few persons with an inclination to run for governor" (135). And on Florida: "Absence of a factional or a party system with a real function in the narrowing of alternatives poses difficult choices for the electorate" (95).

Parties and Turnout

7) *Competitive party systems induce higher voting participation than disorganized one-party systems, especially by groups in lower socioeconomic brackets whose interests are ignored if they do not vote.* The point goes beyond whatever the effects might be of formal or informal suffrage restrictions. Key made a complicated argument about turnout levels in which he considered, among other things, the South's party history and isolation from national politics.[15] Some components of the general case: "Under American conditions high levels of participation occur when the issues run deeply enough or when massive party machines labor assiduously to bring out the electorate" (526). "One-party politics, re-enforced by suffrage limitations, cannot arouse the electoral interest that accompanies two-party politics" (554). Low turnout produces a bias: "A decline in electoral interest generally operates to a much higher degree among the less prosperous than among the more substantial elements of the community" (507). The result: "The blunt truth is that politicians and officials are under no compulsion to pay much heed to classes and groups of citizens that do not vote" (527).

8) *Organized parties can be expected to build turnout by helping voters past formal impediments to voting.* Key suggested, in a conditional statement, that competitive parties that operated in a jurisdiction with poll taxes would take care to get them paid. "The fact that comparatively so few persons in the poll-tax states meet the taxpaying qualification undoubtedly reflects in considerable measure, not the tax deterrent, but the weak and rudimentary nature of political organization in these states. The existence of party organizations in

genuine competition for power would undoubtedly be accompanied by a substantially higher degree of poll-tax payment, both by and for the voters" (596).

Parties and Campaign Finance

9) *Business communities are not divided by party loyalties in disorganized one-party systems, and hence unite more effectively in such systems when their interests are under general attack.* "Scraps of evidence . . . suggest that perhaps the one-party system, in its more fluid form at least, facilitates the coalition of business interests of all types when broad issues seem to be involved. Campaign finance may take on a different form than when individuals have become traditionally known as Democrats or Republicans. Not even such sentimental attachments as the fact that a man's grandfather was a Copperhead obstructs economic calculus in the allocation of campaign donations. Under such circumstances the financing of candidates in opposition to the dominant cluster becomes a matter of chance."[16]

10) *Legislative candidates in disorganized one-party systems, because they are not protected or supported by parties, can more easily be bought up by vested interests.* Key's statement: "The practice in most one-party states by which legislative candidates run independently of any gubernatorial candidate or statewide factional ticket may enhance the financial power of special interests. The lone legislative candidate must win or lose by his own efforts. He cannot call on a state party headquarters for help when he is in trouble. Nor does he benefit from the general Republican or Democratic trend, as does such a candidate in a two-party state. No party organization exists to function as a counterpoise to special financial interest."[17]

11) *Organized parties, through central handling of campaign money, put some distance between contributors and candidates and may thereby help to free government officials from particularistic obligations.* Key argued: "Possibly the highly personal financial nexus between candidate and contributor inevitable in a loose factionalism creates a special sense of obligation and expectation. . . . The financing of the party as an institution may differ in degree in its effects from the financing of individual candidates" (478).

Parties and Accountability

12) *Two competing parties, through the order they confer in campaigns and in government, offer electorates a relatively easy "ins"-vs.-"outs" way of holding governments accountable.* In Key's words: "The great virtue of the two-party system is, not that there are two groups with conflicting policy

tendencies from which the voters can choose [though see statement #5 above], but that there are two groups of politicians. The fluidity of the factional system handicaps the formation of two such groups within the southern Democratic party, and the inevitable result is that there is no continuing group of 'outs' which of necessity must pick up whatever issue is at hand to belabor the 'ins.' "[18]

13) *In disorganized factional systems, governments lack effective opposi-tions.* This differs at least in emphasis from statement #12 above. "Free and easy movement from loose faction to loose faction results in there being in reality no group of 'outs' with any sort of corporate spirit to serve as critics of the 'ins' or as a rallying point around which can be organized all those discon-tented with the current conduct of public affairs."[19]

14) *Incumbent politicians can switch issue colorations more easily in a one-party system; this confuses voters and reduces accountability.* "Uni-partisanism may make it possible for a politician to shift his general orienta-tion with far less risk to personal political survival than under two-party conditions. Lack of party labels and of party lines means that there are no institutional obstacles to collaboration with erstwhile enemies. . . . Sooner or later the mass of voters catch on to what has happened and retire the unfaith-ful servitor; there may be, however, a considerably longer lag in adjustments between constituency and representative than is the rule in two-party situa-tions" (146).

15) *Politicians who operate in disorganized one-party systems can more easily put together "self-contradictory" coalitions.* Key's instance was Geor-gia's Eugene Talmadge, who "played the ends against the middle. His strength was drawn from the upper and lower reaches of the economic scale. Indus-trialists, bankers, and corporation executives provided funds. Poor farmers provided votes. Both are necessary to win campaigns. That he could not be true to one without betraying the other seemed never to be discovered by the wool hat boys. Probably in the absence of a highly competitive system of parties it is easier for politicians to buid a self-contradictory combination."[20]

Parties and Leadership Recruitment

16) *Organized parties, by virtue of their systems of selection, social-ization, incentives, and constraints, do better than a disorganized politics in producing candidates and public officials who are technically competent, personally stable and trustworthy, and capable of working with others to carry through long-term governmental programs.* This more or less captures Key's range of ideas.[21] "A disorganized politics," he wrote, "probably has a

far-reaching influence on the kinds of individual leaders thrown into power and also on the manner in which they utilize their authority once they are in office. Loose factional organizations are poor contrivances for recruiting and sifting out leaders of public affairs. Social structures that develop leadership and bring together like-minded citizens lay the basis for the effectuation of the majority will. Loose factions lack the collective spirit of party organization, which at its best imposes a sense of duty and imparts a spirit of responsibility to the inner core of leaders of the organization. While the extent to which two-party systems accomplish these ends [is] easily exaggerated, politicians working under such systems must . . . have regard not only for the present campaign but also for the next" (304). "Organization both elevates and restrains leaders; disorganization provides no institutional brake on capriciousness when the will in that direction is present" (305). "A cohesive faction has the power to discipline wild-eyed men. A chaotic factionalism provides no block to unscrupulous and spectacular personalities" (306).

Parties and Government

17) *In two-party systems, party ties bind together governors and legislators to achieve programmatic ends; in disorganized one-party systems they do not.* "A party system provides at least a semblance of joint responsibility between governor and legislature. The independence of candidacies in an atomized politics makes it possible to elect a fire-eating governor who promises great accomplishments and simultaneously to elect a legislature a majority of whose members are committed to inaction."[22]

18) *Disorganized one-party systems lean toward particularism in policy processes: two-party systems are better at adhering to general standards.* "The strength of organization reflecting something of a group or class solidarity creates conditions favorable to government according to rule or general principle. . . . In a loose, catch-as-catch-can politics highly unstable coalitions must be held together by whatever means is [*sic*] available. This contract goes to that contractor, this distributor is dealt with by the state liquor board, [etc.]" . . . "Such practices occur in an organized politics, to be sure, but an organized politics is also better able to establish general standards, to resist individual claims for preference, and to consider individual actions in the light of general policy. Organized groups — with a life beyond that of the particular leader — must perforce worry about the future if they are to survive."[23]

19) *Organized parties, unlike transient factions, can impose on government the discipline needed to carry through long-term policies.* In Key's words: "Weak and kaleidoscopic coalitions built around individual leaders produce

in the operations of government itself a high degree of instability. . . . The erratic changes in personnel and policy associated with control by a succession of unrelated and irresponsible factional groups make the consideration, much less the execution, of long-term governmental programs difficult" (305–6). From a discussion of North Carolina's government: "Party discipline is not simply a matter of neat maps of academic interest only: its consequences for the government of the commonwealth are far-reaching. Fundamentally those consequences come down to the fact that a disciplined faction provides the power to govern."[24]

Parties and Overcoming Obstruction

20) *In general, the features of disorganized one-party systems make it especially easy for "haves" to obstruct government action that would be in the interest of "have-nots."* This important point dovetails with arguments in many of the other 19 statements. "Politics generally comes down, over the long run, to a conflict between those who have and those who have less." In state politics the conflict is over taxes, expenditures, and regulation of business; in all cases the cause of serving the "have-nots" requires politicians and governments to engage in strenuous, complex, and concerted activity. Inertia serves the "haves." "It follows that the grand objective of the haves is obstruction, at least of the haves who take only a short-term view. Organization is not necessary to obstruct; it is essential, however, for the promotion of a sustained program in behalf of the have-nots, although not all party or factional organization is dedicated to that purpose. It follows, if these propositions are correct, that over the long run the have-nots lose in a disorganized politics. They have no mechanism through which to act and their wishes find expression in fitful rebellions led by transient demagogues who gain their confidence but often have neither the technical competence nor the necessary stable base of political power to effectuate a program" (307, see 44–45, 655–56).

In Key's surrogate strategy, some of the South's one-party systems provided important analytic leverage because they could be said to display qualities of, or generate activity identified with, the two-party systems exogenous to the South that anchor the comparisons in statements 1 through 20 above. This was particularly true of Virginia, North Carolina, and Tennessee, whose Democratic parties each had a "relatively tightly organized majority faction" that dominated politics and government, endured over decades, and showed "something of a corporate or collective spirit"; and of Louisiana and Georgia, where Huey Long and Eugene Talmadge had each provoked a lasting division in politics between his supporters and opponents.[25] In all these five states at least rudimentary continuing oppositions existed,[26] localism was tamped down,[27] primary elections were waged between more or less continuing sides,[28] and, Georgia perhaps excepted, a sense of "ins" vs. "outs" came through in campaigns (87, 169, 306). Decisively in Louisiana, and appreciably in Virginia and Georgia, the continuing cleavages featured differences over issues.[29] Louisiana's Longs were certainly good at raising issues and their issues were "genuine," according to Key's standard (although this was true also of ones raised by Theodore Bilbo in Mississippi, James Ferguson in Texas, and James Folsom in Alabama).[30] Slates of candidates conducted joint campaigns in Virginia, Tennessee, and Louisiana (170, 308, 404, 414), and ticket loyalties in Louisiana notably carried over into cooperation in office between governors and legislators (173, 308); the Longs could carry programs (162, 165n14, 167–68, 173, 308). The dominant Democratic factions in Virginia and North Carolina stood out for their production of able, noneccentric, team-spirited candidates (no clowns or demagogues),[31] the striking lack of favoritism in their public officials' policy dealings (32, 205–6, 306), and the effectiveness and sense of corporate responsibility they brought to governing (19–20, 87, 228, 306, 306n7). As for voter participation, North Carolina led the South in turnout in general elections (524–25), and Huey Long provoked, in Louisiana's primaries in the 1930s, a turnout among whites that was "unmatched in the recent history of any other southern state."[32]

What kinds of government action, for Key, qualified as service to the "have-nots"? He dwelt on three: regulation of business, ample revenue production (particularly through corporate taxes), and expenditures for public services.[33] The last is the most important: "If there is a single grand issue it is that of public expenditure" (307). The expenditure category that Key gave the most attention to and very likely considered the most significant was education,[34] followed by highways,[35] and then others including health, old-age pensions, and aid to the needy.[36] Decent treatment of blacks probably should qualify as a fourth kind of government service to "have-nots"; Key discussed this, of course, and it fits the logic and spirit of his general argument, though he did not bring it up explicitly in the passage where he laid out his "have-nots" theory.[37] Despite Key's up-front construction of southern politics in Beardian, zero-sum terms, the taxing and spending components in his model of serving "have-nots" do not add up to progressive "redistribution" in any narrow, cash-register sense. Money for education and highways is not channeled just to lower-income brackets, and at any rate one suspects that he would have judged it a net "have-not" benefit even if it came out of regressive taxes — as a forced saving that in time would make poor people better off. They needed the schools and the rural roads.

What southern states did Key regard as especially good servers of "have-nots"? His style of addressing the subject, throughout *Southern Politics,* is such that we are left in no doubt. Patches of good performance occurred in Texas under Ferguson (264–65) and in Mississippi under Bilbo (241). Virginia's race relations were "perhaps the most harmonious in the South," which seems to have been partly the accomplishment of the ruling Byrd organization (32n11, 26). But the stand-out states were unquestionably North Carolina and Louisiana. North Carolina set a regional example in education policy throughout the first half of the century, bettered all other southern states except perhaps Virginia in race relations, built good roads, and in general showed a "spirit that has not feared to face community needs, and to levy taxes to meet them."[38] Louisiana under the neo-populist leadership of the Longs — spectacularly corrupt and autocratic leadership as well in Huey's case — supplied the region's programmatic success story of the 1930s and 1940s. Among the state's public policies were substantial expenditures on schools, schoolbooks, highways, bridges, old-age pensions, and hospitals, and aggressive taxes levied on corporations operating in the state (157–68, 308, 523–26, 603–4).

Key's 1956 book, *American State Politics,* lacks the rich state-by-state sketches of *Southern Politics.* Yet its concern with party factions, inter-party competition, accountability relations, and other such familiar themes; its use of a competitive two-party model as a standard for appraising reality; as well as its focus on competitive party systems of the northern states[39] that naturally complemented the noncompetitive ones of the South give it the character of a companion volume to the earlier work on the South.

American State Politics, however, has a quite different framework of argument. Absent is the tissue of rather well worked-out propositions, hypotheses, and generalizations that linked process with policy in the earlier work. Instead Key falls back on a more traditional way of constructing arguments in political science, a discussion of "functions": what functions can it be said that party systems, in the American states, at least, do in fact perform, might perform, or should perform; why do they do so; and to what ends?[40] He does not present a clear list of such functions,[41] but his discussion can be sorted reasonably well into six. A well-functioning party system — more specifically a two-party system — will feature parties that 1) compete against each other as organized arrays in elections;[42] 2) "recruit, develop, and advance" competent candidates for office;[43] 3) stand available as able, cohesive, and critical oppositions when out of power;[44] 4) allow electorates to make clear "ins" vs. "outs" account-ability judgments;[45] 5) coordinate the policy-making activity of their officials when in power;[46] and 6) "facilitate," at rare times of crisis, novel questions or great issues, "a popular determination of the direction of the course of public action by offering . . . candidates with sufficient difference in policy orientation to make the choice between them something more than illusory" (12, see 59–61, 62, 75, 212–14). The last is a special "critical-elections" version of issue differentiation.

Perform functions to what end? In *Southern Politics* such party-system per-formances as organized competition, good leadership recruitment, and policy coordination figure in statements that tie them causally to a specified range of policy outcomes — i.e., serving variously the "have-nots." No trace of any such specific policy prediction or finding appears in any statement in *American State Politics*. The new ends that an effective party system might promote, none of which receives sustained attention, include such things as "the fulfill-ment of the mission of the states," "more adequate systems of political man-agement and leadership," "effective administration," "stability, firmness, com-petence," "the prosecution of the public business," "promote the public weal," and "provide administrative direction, powerful enough, honest enough, and stable enough to manage competently the very considerable services of the states."[47] "Preventing wrongs" and "liberty" are mentioned.[48] At least ten times "popular government" is set out as the overall end to be served,[49] along with such similar desiderata as "responsiveness of government" and "expres-sion of popular will."[50]

At one point in *American State Politics,* Key harked back to his earlier southern material, and it is interesting to see what he made of it. The South had undergone an "alteration of form," he wrote, as it shifted from an earlier system of parties to a twentieth-century "conflict of personalities or of more or less amorphous factions within the Democratic party. While that alteration in the form was undoubtedly of significance for the substance of politics, the effects on substance remain extremely difficult of estimation and doubtless vary from time to time and from state to state within the South. In some circumstances non-party politics may place a premium on demagogic quali-ties. In others it may deprive [government] of safeguards by its lack of institu-tionalized opposition to criticize, to harass, and to heckle. It may hinder mass movements by the ambiguity of the choices faced by the electorate. Those choices are in terms of candidates rather than of parties with divergent tradi-tions and contrasting leadership cores. Yet in other instances party factions develop that appear to possess a coherence, a continuity, and a habit of competition not sharply at variance with the two-party model" (23). This is all that Key said about the consequences of amorphous factionalism in the South in his later book. Nothing is carried forward about serving or mis-serving "have-nots."

Four ideas come to mind about why Key may have refrained from presenting the "have-nots" claim again in the 1956 work. The first has to do with the tenor and message of *American State Politics,* which after all turned out to be, like *Southern Politics,* largely a jeremiad against a section of the country for failing to live up to the two-party model. Most of the North, to be sure, had two parties that could win a significant vote, but other problems intruded. Most states had developed "a wondrous damper on party government": constitutional separation-of-powers arrangements that, especially when reinforced by legislative malapportionment or gerrymandering, "virtually foreclose full performance by political parties of their role in the democratic process" (52). One party could not easily, if at all, take over full control of a state government from the other.[51] As for party leadership in most of the states, "only a romantic can say much for [it]" (131). In the North as well as the South, the direct primary had undermined party organization and cooperation (see chs. 4–6): "Even in the more competitive states, to speak of a corporate party leadership is often pure fiction" (118–19). "Wide-open primaries tend both to shatter party organization and to leave it without much of anything to do. In the absence of working party organization or its equivalent, the direct primary often produces almost unbelievable sorts of nominations" (288). In general, in Key's view, "The combination of [an underorganized] party system, separated powers, and overrepresentation of the nonmetropolitan estate often makes irrelevant any conception of party collaboration in the operation of government or any theory of party accountability for its conduct" (74).

There were bright spots. "Inner cores of party leadership" continued to get their candidate slates nominated in briskly competitive New York, Indiana, Connecticut, and Delaware, and a "somewhat different, but lively, party rivalry" prevailed in Colorado, Wyoming, Montana, and Idaho (120, 269). Pre-primary nominating conventions were winning trial in Massachusetts, Utah, and New Mexico (122–27), and informal groups had sprung up to confer some order in party primaries in California and Wisconsin (127, 128n33).

But in general the record of particulars, as Key looked back over preceding decades, was bleak; even some of the bright spots dimmed on close inspection. Democratic parties of course amounted to little in Maine, New Hampshire, and Vermont (24–25), and the Republicans were "a feeble enterprise" in

Rhode Island (275). Democrats very seldom elected governors in Kansas, Iowa, and South Dakota, and in these states plus Nebraska the party spread its minority voting strength across almost all counties, which made it difficult to develop a leadership core of local officials (24n4, 242–46). Iowa's dominant Republican party was such that the Farm Bureau could evidently choose its candidate for governor in 1948 (Key 1952, p. 320).

The Republicans had never elected a governor in Oklahoma (Key 1956, 42–43), and they never at any time during the 1931–52 electoral and policy cycle won simultaneous control of the governorship and both legislative houses in Maryland, West Virginia, Kentucky, Missouri, Utah, New Mexico, or Arizona (62). The Democrats never won simultaneous control during those decades in Massachusetts, Connecticut, New York, New Jersey, Delaware, Oregon, Wisconsin, or California (62–63). Massachusetts' nominating politics, especially in the rising Democratic party, was a disorganized, chancy affair in which "candidates of questionable capacity whose names are household words" sometimes won primaries.[52] Connecticut's lower house had been Republican since 1876, a security that is said to have foreclosed enactment of a state income tax.[53] New York's constitution "virtually assigns control of both houses of the legislature to the Republican party" (Key 1956, 66). In New Jersey no Democratic governor since 1913 had carried in with him a party majority in either legislative house (67). In largely organization-free California, "private interests, at times with the most dubious aims" — notably famed lobbyist Arthur Samish acting in behalf of brewing and related interests — could "work behind the scenes to build up candidates" (271–72). In Pennsylvania, which the Democrats fully controlled for only two years in 1931–52 (62–63), most of the important political decisions had been made for several decades by or within a dominant, well-organized Republican party that was, in Key's view, "unbelievably corrupt."[54] Illinois's Republican party was "an evil combination of North Shore plutocracy and downstate, rural backwardness" (Key 1949, 4).

These many shortcomings did nothing to diminish the "have-nots" claim as an abstract proposition, but they may have diminished it, for Key as he worked up his 1956 volume, as an empirical assertion based on American cross-sectional state evidence. How was one to achieve suitable variance on the independent variable if well-functioning two-party systems proved hard to find in the North as well as in the South? An appropriate answer may be that most of the North was obviously still, after all the qualifications, better two-party territory than the South. But the northern material at least introduced complexities. As deviations from the two-party model, how should South

Carolina's not having any coherent parties at all stack up against Pennsylvania's corrupt, seldom interrupted one-party Republican domination or Connecticut's constitutionally generated blockade against Democratic takeover?

A second line of speculation about why Key may have stepped back from the "have-nots" claim has to do with his writing about the policy performances of northern states. Anyone familiar with Key's scholarship will be aware of his great capacity to build interesting and persuasive general points through induction: a mastery of detail produces a wealth of proper nouns and telling instances, often accompanied by quantitative data, that march the reader to a conclusion. An illustration of the kind of instance he often reached for, and one that in this case might have figured in some general argument about northern or North-vs.-South policy patterns on "have-nots" matters, is this statement about New York's Republican Governor Thomas E. Dewey: "In 1950 Dewey could boast of his program of rent control, public housing, fair employment practices, public health services, and other measures that Washington Democrats might claim as their own. Moreover, he interpreted his election as a mandate for state development of St. Lawrence power" (Key 1952, 324).

But this statement about Dewey is the only member of its species. No such anecdotal material about any other northern state's policy performance pertinent to "have-nots" appears anywhere in *Southern Politics,* in *American State Policies,* or in the chapter on state parties in the 1952 edition of Key's parties text. The absence of such statements is striking. Given Key's knowledge, the subjects of the two books on state politics, his customary style of arguing, and in particular the way he built arguments in *Southern Politics,* one continually expects him to introduce comments about such things as the La Follettes' programs in Wisconsin, the "Little New Deal" in Pennsylvania, or the Democrats' labor-backed programmatic drive in the 1950s in Michigan. But he does not, not even in *American State Politics.* Perhaps the lack of such comments and the nonappearance of the "have-nots" claim in the 1956 book stemmed from the same cause — a continuing overall unsureness or uneasiness about state policy patterns outside the South that dictated silence. As of 1956, after all, no one had investigated the individual nothern states the way Key and his associates had investigated the states of the South.

A third line of speculation reintroduces the analysis internal to the South that Key presented in *Southern Politics* — the analysis in which Virginia, North Carolina, Tennessee, Georgia, and Louisiana figured as instances of dual factionalism. The relation between dual factionalism and "have-nots" performance was there, and it was fascinating, but it was precarious. Louisiana's and

North Carolina's policies notwithstanding, dual factionalism hardly qualified as a *sufficient* condition for government attention to "have-nots." Tennessee's and Georgia's policies were unremarkable, and Virginia's were an embarrass-ment: the reigning Byrd organization "dedicates its best efforts to the mainte-nance of low levels of public service."[55] Nor is it clear that dual factionalism was a *necessary* condition for government solicitude toward "have-nots." In both the North Carolina and Louisiana cases, Key, in addressing the question "Why does this state have such distinctive policies?" relied chiefly on a genetic explanation that had an ambiguous role, or none at all, for organized party or factional competition.[56] Louisiana's durable, issue-laden bi-factionalism seems to have been a concomitant rather than a cause of the state's explosion of policies serving the "have-nots." Huey Long caused both the bi-factional cleavage and the policy turnaround.[57] The rise of Long himself, in Key's tell-ing, owed nothing to organized factionalism, though a state tradition of run-ning on "tickets" probably helped along the new dualism once it got started (156–64, 168–70).

The import of the precariousness is that, although Key's richly textured portrayal of the relation between southern bi-factionalism and "have-nots" policies carried and induced conviction in 1949, its pattern could easily go awry if some elements of southern politics got rearranged. Some did between 1949 and 1956. Louisiana's Long vs. anti-Long dualism stayed nicely in place, but developments in North Carolina and Virginia — the two states with exem-plary party organizations and "responsible" leaders — must have deeply disap-pointed Key. Frank Graham's defeat in North Carolina's 1950 Democratic Senate primary, in which racism emerged as an effective appeal against the nationally prestigious liberal incumbent, took the bloom off the state's pro-gressivism and the 1950s did little to restore it.[58] In Virginia the Byrd organiza-tion, which was moving by the end of 1955 toward its stand of "massive resistance" to the Supreme Court's *Brown* decision, proved to be the only fringe-South state whose ruling politicians defied federal authority on school desegregation considerably more than they had to.[59] On racial matters the South's statesman of the mid-1950s was probably James Folsom of Alabama (279–86).

Finally, as a fourth line of speculation, there may have been a drift in the political science community's way of thinking about parties, between the pub-lication dates of *Southern Politics* and *American State Politics,* that Key both contributed to and adapted to. Around 1950 the idea of parties as instruments for permanent programmatic achievement was riding high. The New Deal was fresh in people's minds and the Attlee government was in power. The American Political Science Association's 1950 report on parties is perhaps emblematic in the high place it gave to program. But by 1956 parties had lost much of their luster as world-changing instruments. The programs of the left were in eclipse, the American Republicans and British Tories had been running consolidationist rather than confrontational governments. Keynesian macroeconomic management was more or less in, and Anthony Downs's *Economic Theory of Democracy,* which dwells on the real or perceived effects of short-term officeholding, was only a year away. The drift, if there was one, was from an emphasis on parties as Promethean program builders to parties as short-term government managers, and this distinction captures much of the thematic difference between *Southern Politics* in 1949 and *American State Politics* in 1956.

Notes

This essay was originally published in Milton C. Cummings, Jr., ed., *V. O. Key, Jr. and the Study of American Politics* (Washington, D.C.: American Political Science Association, 1988), pp. 24–38.

1. V. O. Key Jr., *Southern Politics in State and Nation.* (New York: Alfred A. Knopf, 1949), p. 307. The work was published in 1949, but it was the product of a large project that began in 1946 and drew on precedent-setting field research that yielded 538 interviews with politicians and other informants in eleven southern states. Alexander Heard conducted these interviews in nine states and Donald S. Strong in two. Informative discussions of the project appear in Alexander Heard, "Interviewing Southern Politicians," *American Political Science Review,* 44 (1950), pp. 886–96; and Alexander P. Lamis and Nathan C. Goldman, "V. O. Key's *Southern Politics*: The Writing of a Classic," paper delivered at The Citadel Symposium on Southern Politics, Charleston, S.C., March 29–31, 1984. The pagination of the 1949 edition of *Southern Politics* has fortunately been maintained in the 1984 edition issued by the University of Tennessee Press.

2. V. O. Key Jr., *American State Politics: An Introduction* (New York: Knopf, 1956).

3. V. O. Key Jr., *Politics, Parties and Pressure Groups* (New York: Crowell, 3rd ed., 1952).

4. Competitive party systems in "most of the democratic world" set the South in relief at p. 11.

5. Briefly or in passing, he compares southern states with nonsouthern states at ibid., pp. 4, 46, 299, 303 ("Although it is the custom to belittle the contributions of American parties, their performance seems heroic alongside that of a pulverized factionalism"), 306n7 (public administration), 309n13 (southern vs. northern tax rates), 463 ("Money talks in both North and South, but even in the realm of campaign finance the one-party system has its peculiarities"), 463n1, and 661. The only sustained comparison is of voter turnout rates, at pp. 492–504.

6. Key makes his "have-nots" case on pp. 307–310 of chapter 14. In making that case he presents the arguments of statements #1, 2, 5, 10, 12, 13, 16, 17, 19, and 20, and, by reference to particular material that appears later in the book, #7. The arguments of statements #3, 4, and 18 figure elsewhere in chapter 14, and the ones of statements #6, 8, 9, 11, 14, and 15 appear only in other chapters.

7. In this and ensuing general footnotes on the 20 statements, I cite passages in *Southern Politics* that I have found useful in trying to get a full sense of what Key had in mind on a matter. On statement #1 see pp. 183–89 (on issuelessness in Arkansas), 308 ("when someone stirs the masses issues become sharper"), 310, 472 ("A dual factionalism stimulates the raising of issues"), 523–26 (on Huey Long), 656 ("The mass of nonvoting whites will not arouse on their own motion; they must have a leadership drawn in the main from the upper brackets").

8. See pp. 37 ("A tenuous and impermanent factional organization confuses the voters and makes for electoral decisions based on irrelevancies"), 105 ("genuine" issues, and anti-Catholicism in Florida as one that was not), 131 ("In part, the race issue provides in itself a tool for the diversion of attention from issues"), 144 ("so nonrational a politics"), 184 ("social and economic issues of significance to the people have lain ignored," in Arkansas), 189 ("If real issues are raised, voters may be expected to divide along lines of their fundamental interests"), 255 ("In Texas the vague outlines of a politics are emerging in which irrelevancies are pushed into the background and people divide broadly along liberal and conservative lines"), 302 ("confused alignments explicable on no rational grounds," and "meaningful lines" of cleavage), 308 ("appeals irrelevant to any fundamental interest"), 472 ("the grand issue of the scope and nature of governmental activity").

9. Pp. 262–63. He finished the sentence: ". . . second only to the maintenance of the democratic processes themselves in their importance to the citizenry."

10. P. 146. Race issues Key ordinarily put down as distracting or irrational, though he characterized Georgia's conflict over black voting in 1946 as "genuine." See p. 128.

11. P. 311, and more generally pp. 310–11. See also pp. 263 (percolation takes place better during periods of national tension), 507 (the general argument), 655 ("If in no other way the one-party system, by its insulation of the South from national campaigns, deprives the southern electorate of the stimulation of most grand questions of public policy").

12. See pp. 37–41 (on Alabama), 110–112 (the general argument), 147 (the general argument).

13. The argument is presented most effectively at pp. 302–3. See also pp. 11 (on parties as "means for the organization and expression of competing viewpoints"), 44–46 (on the effects of a lack of continuing organizations in Alabama), 100–103 (on the lack in Florida), 129 (on Georgia), 185 (on Arkansas), 249 (on Mississippi, where was to be found "one of the most significant departures of the one-party system from a two-party arrangement. Absence of continuing factional groupings with which individual candidates are routinely identified confuses the voter, makes choice difficult, and aggrandizes irrelevant considerations such as localism"), and 309 (on "the striking feature of the one-party system, the absence of organized and continuing factions with a lower-bracket orientation").

14. P. 15. This is Key's best statement of the idea that differentiation in sectoral base produces differentiation in policies.

15. For the full argument see pp. 307, 489–90, 507–8, 523–26, 527–28, 551–54.

16. P. 476, and more generally, pp. 476–77, 655–56. At first glance, statement #9 may appear to contradict statement #5. But Key's "principally" and "in the main" qualifications to his point about parties being rooted in different parts of the public, presented here in the text under statement #5, save him from contradiction. American Democrats have always enrolled some appreciable part of the business community.

17. P. 477. See also p. 308 ("A loose factional system gives great negative power to those with a few dollars to invest in legislative candidates"), 154n27 ("In a legislative campaign, less conspicuous and far more ambiguous in its issues than gubernatorial campaigns, groups and interests with their eye on the main chance and their hand on the campaign chest enjoy great advantage").

18. Pp. 309–10. See also pp. 15, 303–4 ("All of it may come down to the proposition that if one considers some southern state governments as a whole, there is really no feasible way of throwing the rascals out").

19. P. 304. See pertinent points also at pp. 124 (organization begets counterorganization), 309 (opposition to business interests in an organized politics), 310, 382 (lack of opposition to southern members of the U.S. House), 476–77 (southern oppositions ill-financed), 656–57 (southern oppositions lack leadership).

20. P. 117. See also p. 144 on Cole Blease of South Carolina, and pp. 117n11, 265–71 on W. Lee "Pappy" O'Daniel of Texas.

21. The best discussion is at pp. 304–5. See also pp. 16, 46, 266–67, 271, 306–7. Leadership, the southern upper class, and the one-party system are discussed at pp. 180–82, 656.

22. P. 308. See also pp. 44–45 (in a loose one-party system: "After the election no disciplined factional group exists to carry out a program in the legislature. A great advantage goes to those who seek to obstruct action"); p. 298.

23. P. 305. See also p. 52 ("In a one-party state, such as Alabama, the building of a faction by a state-wide leader must start almost at the bottom, and an especially heavy reliance probably has to be placed on the dispensation of favors, on the promise of favors, and on the appeal of individual personality").

24. P. 228. See also pp. 306n7 (on the relation between party bases and "integrated public administration"), 307 ("the necessary stable base of political power to effectuate a program"), 308 ("A loose factional system lacks the power to carry out sustained programs of action").

25. Key specifies these five states to be exceptional at pp. 299–300.

26. Pp. 27–34, 70–75, 124–29, 164–68, 299–300, 310, 412, 414.

27. Pp. 29–31, 65–67, 107–12, 168–79, 223–27.

28. Pp. 20–22, 27–34, 59–75, 107–17, 124–29, 169–79, 223–28, 229–301, 412, 413–15.

29. Pp. 27–34 (Viriginia); 107, 128–29 (Georgia); 164–68, 523–26 (Louisiana).

30. Pp. 162, 308, 523–26 (the Longs); 238–46 (Bilbo); 263–65 (Ferguson); 42–45 (Folsom). Huey Long "aroused the long-dormant political consciousness of great numbers of people." P. 524.

31. Pp. 25–26, 206, 210, 214, 228, 306–7.

32. Pp. 523–26, 603–5, quotation at p. 523.

33. See especially pp. 307, 471–72. Revealing comments elsewhere on regulation: pp. 42, 158, 165n15, 241n26, 264; and on revenue production; pp. 9, 27n8, 157, 160, 162, 165, 165n14, 210, 211, 235, 662.

34. Pp. 9, 42, 161n5, 162, 165n14, 208–9, 209n8, 211, 241, 264, 308, 471.

35. Pp. 27n8, 42, 162, 165n14, 211, 471.

36. Pp. 42, 162, 165n14, 211, 241, 308, 471.

37. He discusses it at e.g. pp. 26, 32n11, 128, 165n15, 208–9, 209n8, 662–63.

38. Pp. 27n8, 206–11, 228, 306–7, 524–25, quotation at p. 210.

39. At times in *American State Politics*, Key quite clearly gives his attention to relatively competitive states outside the South, rather than to the complete set of nonsouthern states. See e.g. p. 61.

40. For the gist of Key's "functions" framework, see pp. 11–13 ("functions of parties as a pattern against which to check the performance of the parties," at p. 12), 17, 19, 270. ("functions that need to be carried out if the optimum conditions for popular government are to prevail").

41. He presents three lists, more or less, at pp. 11–15, 17, and 19, but no two are the same.

42. For pertinent material, see pp. 11, 12 ("parties with a relatively high degree of cohesion"), 13–14, 154–63, 167–68, 169, 229, 240–41, 273–75.

43. See pp. 10, 11–12, 13, 118–32, 154–63, 166, 254–65, 271–72, 288, quotation at p. 13.

44. See pp. 12, 24–26, 78–80, 195, 276–77, 279.

45. See pp. 14–15, 52, 59–61, 74–75, 200–201, 216, 275, 276, 278–79.

46. See pp. 56–57 ("supposed role as a solvent of separation of powers," at p. 57), 74 ("meshing the independent organs of government"), 198 ("imposing an informal order and coherence upon an unintegrated governmental structure"), 270 ("collaborative control"), and more generally chapters 3 and 7.

47. Respectively pp. 4, 5, 198, 267, 198, 273, 17.

48. Respectively pp. 14, 11.

49. Respectively pp. 10, 15, 61, 62, 119, 120, 121, 213, 267, 268.

50. Respectively pp. 11, 4.

51. For the general case, see chapter 3 and also chapter 7 on the independent election of members of the executive branch.

52. Pp. 123–24, 154–63, quotation at p. 163.

53. Pp. 66–67, 78. See also Key, *Politics, Parties and Pressure Groups*, p. 328.

54. On the Republican hegemony: Key, *Politics, Parties and Pressure Groups*, pp. 318–19. Quotation at Key, *Southern Politics*, p. 4.

55. Key, *Southern Politics*, p. 27. On Georgia: pp. 116–17, 128. "The highly personal nature of Georgia's Talmadge faction probably diverts attention from needs that might find expression and relief through party government." P. 107.

56. On North Carolina, see pp. 206–10.

57. In a passage that introduces Eugene Talmadge: "The colorful demagogue possessed of an intensely loyal personal following can introduce into the disorganized politics of

one-party states elements of stability and form that are of the utmost importance." P. 106. And: "Huey Long in Louisiana likewise was a potent influence in the division of the electorate into two opposing camps." P. 300.

58. On Graham: Jack Bass and Walter DeVries, *The Transformation of Southern Politics* (New York: Basic Books, 1976), pp. 218–22.

59. See Numan V. Bartley, *The Rise of Massive Resistance* (Baton Rouge: Louisiana State University Press, 1969), pp. 108–15, 134, 137, 144, 326.

Divided Party Control
Does It Make a Difference?

Since World War II, party control of the U.S. national government has been formally divided for twenty-six years and unified for eighteen. (That is the span between the elections of 1946 and 1990.) Truman, Eisenhower, Nixon, Ford, Reagan, and Bush have had to coexist—for at least a two-year stretch in each case—with opposite-party majorities in the Senate or House or both. Truman, Eisenhower, Kennedy, Johnson, and Carter have had—again, for at least a two-year stretch—House and Senate majorities of their own party.

In other respects bearing on relations between the president and Congress, this postwar era shows a high degree of continuity or commonality stemming from events or precedents of the 1930s and 1940s. The New Deal and the war ratcheted the government to new levels of activity, and Franklin Roosevelt permanently strengthened the presidency. The La Follette–Monroney Act of 1946 streamlined the congressional committee system. Soon after the war the government took on new commitments in defense, foreign policy, and macro-economic management that are with us still. Truman developed the custom of presenting "the president's program" to Congress each year. Televising of major congressional investigations began in 1948 with HUAC's probe of Alger Hiss.

The postwar era presents, then, a checkered pattern of unified-versus-divided party control set against a background of commonalities. That makes 1946–90 a good span of experience to look into if one wants to track the consequences of unified party control against divided party control, with at least one congressional house organized by the party not holding the White House. How well any generalizations based on 1946–90 would hold for previous eras in American history is not clear, though they might well hold for the near future.

Recently, I have tried to find out how well two pieces of conventional wisdom about party control stand up against the experience of 1946–90 (Mayhew 1991). The first conventional view is: *Congressional committees, acting as oversight bodies, will give more trouble to administrations run by the opposite party than to those of their own party* (Ogul 1976: 18; Scher 1963). The second view, which comes close to being an axiom of political science, is: *Major laws will pass more frequently under unified party control than under divided control* (Sundquist 1988–89: 616–24; Key 1964: 656, 687–88; Ripley 1983: 347–56; Cutler 1988). A party that controls the House, the Senate, and the presidency, the logic goes, can put through a program. Absent such party control, legislative "deadlock" or "stalemate" will set in. In Woodrow Wilson's words, "You cannot compound a successful government out of antagonisms" (quoted in Sundquist 1988–89: 618).

My conclusion is the both assertions are false — or at least largely or probably false. (I hedge because I use evidence that requires many individual judgments that can be disputed.) On balance, neither the "beat up on the other party's administration" effect nor the "divided control causes deadlock" effect makes a significant showing in the political record of 1946–90.

High-Publicity Investigations

The evidence on oversight is for a particular variety of that activity — congressional investigations that deal with alleged executive misbehavior or malperformance and draw media attention. Included are such amply reported enterprises as HUAC's Hiss-Chambers probe of 1948, Senator McCarran's investigation of China policy in 1951–52, Senator McCarthy's Army and State Department hearings of 1953–54, the House probe of corruption in the regulatory agencies in 1958, Senator Fulbright's hearings on the Indochina war during 1966–70, the Senate and House Watergate inquiries of 1973–74, and the Iran-Contra investigations of 1987.

"Misbehavior or malperformance" here means anything from treason or usurpation through corruption to simply making mistakes. The charges could be true, partly true, or fantasy. The target could be any present or past executive official or agency. An investigation made it onto a final list if it inspired front-page stories in the *New York Times* on at least twenty days. For any day, the test for content was whether anyone connected with a congressional committee made a charge against the executive branch, or someone in the executive branch answered such a charge.

Thirty-one investigations between 1946 and 1990 made the list. First prize went to the McCarthy hearings of 1953–54, which generated front-page stories on 203 days. The Senate and House Watergate inquiries ranked second and third. The results do not sort in any remarkable way according to divided versus unified party control. Probes of corruption split about equally between times of unified and divided control; it is a good bet that the ones conducted by Democratic Congresses against the Truman administration caused the most damage politically (Dunar 1984). The Watergate inquiries, which occurred under divided control, may deserve a status all their own. Still, for overall significance it is hard to surpass the loyalty investigations of 1948 through 1954, and notwithstanding the 1948 Hiss probe, those occurred mostly under unified control. That was notably true of every bit of committee loyalty-probing triggered by McCarthy under Truman and Eisenhower; it was under unified party control during those years that McCarthy colonized a Democratic committee and made Owen Lattimore a household name, then ran his own committee and asked, "Who promoted Peress?"

For 1946–90, at least, there is not a convincing case that Congress increases its high-publicity probes of the executive branch during times of divided party loyalty.

Important Laws

The evidence here is a list of 267 major statutes enacted between 1947 and 1990 — ranging from the Taft-Hartley Labor-Management Relations Act and Marshall Plan of 1947–48 through the Clean Air Act and Americans with Disabilities Act of 1990. The 267 items are the product of two sweeps through the 44-year history. Sweep One picked up enactments that observers of the Washington scene judged (according to my coding) to be particularly important at the times the laws passed. Those observers were journalists who wrote "wrapup stories" at the close of each congressional session, or other witnesses whose appraisals have been relayed or embodied in secondary works. Sweep Two picked up enactments that policy specialists, writing recently in 43 policy areas, have indicated to be particularly important in discussing the postwar histories of their areas. "Important" in these contexts means both innovative and consequential—or at least expected at the time of passage to be consequential.

As expected, Johnson's Great Society Congress of 1965–66 emerges in first place (or at least in a tie for it) with 22 major laws—Medicare, the Voting Rights Act (VRA), the Elementary and Secondary Education Act (ESEA), and many others. Eisenhower's last Democratic Congress of 1959–60, which ended in classic deadlock, finishes in last place with five enactments. Taken alone, these reports ratify the triumph-of-party-government story that Sundquist (1968) wrote concerning the mid-1950s through the mid-1960s.

But precious little else during these decades follows that "party government" script. On average, about as many major laws passed per Congress under divided control as under unified control. In several policy areas where specialists' judgments come through clearly—for example, foreign aid, foreign trade, immigration, agriculture, and tax reform—sets of key enactments became law in time patterns unrelated to conditions of party control. For example, the three post-1950 "major expansions" of Social Security occurred with disability insurance in 1956 (divided control), Medicare in 1965 (unified), and a "quantum increase" in cash benefits in 1969–72 (divided) (Derthick 1979: 296). Otherwise, several notable statutes emerged from Congress and won out over presidential vetoes—for example (besides the Taft-Hartley Act), the McCarran Internal Security Act of 1950, the McCarran-Walter Immigration Act of 1952, the Water Pollution Control Act of 1972, the War Powers Act of 1973, and South Africa sanctions in 1986. The "do-nothing"-ness of Truman's Republican Congress in 1947–48 was largely Democratic propaganda; policy specialists point back, for example, to the precedent-setting Federal Insecticide, Fungicide, and Rodenticide Act (FIFRA) of 1947 and the Water Pollution Control Act of 1948. Under Reagan and Bush, the last few years have featured, for example, the Tax Reform Act of 1986, Speaker Jim Wright's considerable program of 1987–88, and Bush's controversial $500 billion budget-reduction package of 1990.

At the level of ambitious presidential programs, Johnson succeeded memorably in 1964 through 1966 with a Congress of his own party, but so did Reagan in 1981 despite having to deal with a House of the opposite party. Truman's Fair Deal and Kennedy's New Frontier largely failed as legislative enterprises, despite the availability of Congresses of the same party. Carter's years proved a washout for his party's lawmaking aspirations, despite sizable Democratic House and Senate majorities of 292–143 and 62–38 during 1977–78. On the only occasion since 1840 when a party took over at House, Senate, and presidency all at once—in 1952 when the Republicans did—that

Table 4.1 Numbers of Major Laws Enacted by Each Congress, 1947–2006ᵃ

Years	President	Under Unified Party Controlᵇ	Under Divided Party Control
1947–48	Truman		10 (2)
1949–50	Truman	12 (2)	
1951–52	Truman	6	
1953–54	Eisenhower	9	
1955–56	Eisenhower		7
1957–58	Eisenhower		12 (1)
1959–60	Eisenhower		5
1961–62	Kennedy	15 (1)	
1963–64	Kennedy/Johnson	14 (4)	
1965–66	Johnson	22 (3)	
1967–68	Johnson	16 (1)	
1969–70	Nixon		22
1971–72	Nixon		16
1973–74	Nixon/Ford		22 (1)
1975–76	Ford		14
1977–78	Carter	12	
1979–80	Carter	10	
1981–82	Reagan		9 (2)
1983–84	Reagan		7
1985–86	Reagan		9 (1)
1987–88	Reagan		12

party turned out not to have much of a program to enact. As a result, virtually no laws of importance passed in the seemingly favorable circumstances of 1953, though Eisenhower won some victories later.

The real story of these decades is the prominent, continuous lawmaking surge that lasted from late 1963 through 1975 or 1976. That was under Johnson, Nixon, and Ford. Whether one looks at legislative workload in general (Davidson 1988) or major laws passed (Mayhew 1991: ch. 4; see Table 4.1 for an update through 2006), it was during that span of years — or roughly that span; assessments of boundaries differ a bit — that the postwar legislative mill operated at full steam. Everyone knows that happened under Johnson, but the Vietnam war, wrangling over "social issues," and Watergate have clouded our picture of legislating under Nixon and Ford. In fact, the state-enhancing thrust of the 1960s toward greater expenditure and regulation continued with great

Table 4.1 Continued

Years	President	Under Unified Party Control[b]	Under Divided Party Control
1989–90	G. H. W. Bush		9 (1)
1991–92	G. H. W. Bush		8 (1)
1993–94	Clinton	12 (2)	
1995–96	Clinton		15 (2)
1997–98	Clinton		9 (1)
1999–2000	Clinton		6
2001–2	G. W. Bush	1 (1)	15 (4)
2003–4	G. W. Bush	10 (1)	
2005–6	G. W. Bush	14	

[a] Major joint resolutions are included here, as contrasted with the lists in the 1991 and 1993 editions of my *Divided We Govern*. This adds on one enactment apiece to the pre-1992 Congresses that enacted the Formosa Resolution of 1955, the Middle East Resolution of 1957, and the Tonkin Gulf Resolution of 1964. See http://pantheon.yale.edu/~dmayhew/data3.html for discussion of data and sources post-1990. Noted in parentheses are enactments considered especially important by newspaper wrapup sources. After 1990, those are the Gulf Resolution of 1991, Clinton's budget package in 1993, NAFTA in 1993, welfare reform in 1996, telecommunications reform in 1996, the budget-balance deal of 1997, the Bush tax cut of 2001, the Use of Force Resolution of 2001, the USA Patriot act of 2001, the Iraq Resolution of 2002, the Homeland Security Department of 2002, and Medicare reform in 2003. No "Sweep Two" sources are used post-1990.

[b] During the Congress of 2001–2, the first four months (roughly) were conducted under unified party control, the rest after the Jeffords switch under divided party control.

force in the 1970s. Budget growth owed to Johnson's Great Society programs, but also to post-1968 legislative initiatives in the areas of, for example, food stamps, Supplementary Security Income (SSI), CETA jobs, unemployment compensation, housing block grants, mass transit, and water pollution, as well as Social Security benefits (Lampman 1984: 8–9; Conlan 1985: 81; Browning 1986: 79–83; Mayhew 1991: ch. 4). The Earned Income Tax Credit (EITC) was enacted in 1975. The "new social regulation," to use Vogel's term (1981), came to pass largely by statute under Nixon (see also Weidenbaum 1977: 5–10; Higgs 1987: 246–54). That featured, to cite some highlights, the National Environmental Policy Act (NEPA) of 1969, the Occupational Safety and Health Act (OSHA) of 1970, the Clean Air Act of 1970, the Equal Employment Opportunity Act of 1972, the Consumer Product Safety Act of 1972, and the Endangered Species Act of 1973. Campaign finance and private pensions came under comprehensive regulation for the first time through laws enacted in 1974. Statutory regulation of state governments reached new heights under Nixon (Conlan 1985: 84–89). The Equal Rights Amendment (ERA) cleared Congress in 1972, though the states would not buy it (Freeman 1975: ch. 6). These and many other items from the Nixon-Ford years are probably familiar to readers, but I do not think we have appreciated their volume or sifted them through our doctrines about party control and legislative action. In terms of volume and also ideological direction of lawmaking, there arguably existed an era of Johnson-Nixon (or Johnson-Nixon-Ford), and it overlapped different circumstances of party control.

Since World War II, to sum up, neither high-publicity investigations nor major laws have accumulated on a schedule that the rules of party control would predict. Why not? That is too complicated a question to tackle here. The material cited above makes it obvious that no simple arithmetic theory involving Democratic presidents and sizes of cross-party "conservative coalitions" on Capitol Hill can work very well. If that were the key factor, why all the lawmaking under Nixon? Why the slump under Carter? Evidently, speculation about causes needs to center on features of the modern U.S. regime that dominate, override, or blot out parties to a greater degree than we may have supposed. Some good candidates for that role seem to be Capitol Hill electoral incentives that foster lawmaking and investigating, presidential leadership qualities that operate more or less independently of party, the practical need for non-narrow roll-call majorities to pass laws regardless of conditions of party control, forcing public events, public opinion cleavages that crosscut parties, and "public moods" like that of 1963–76 that seem capable of overriding everything else (Mayhew 1991: chs. 5, 6).

Note

This essay was originally published in *PS: Political Science and Politics* 24:4 (December 1991), pp. 637–40.

References

Browning, Robert X. 1986. *Politics and Social Welfare Policy in the United States.* Knoxville: University of Tennessee Press.

Conlan, Timothy. 1985. *New Federalism: Intergovernmental Reform from Nixon to Reagan.* Washington, DC: Brookings.

Cutler, Lloyd N. 1988. "Some Reflections About Divided Government." *Presidential Studies Quarterly* 18: 485–92.

Davidson, Roger H. 1988. "The New Centralization on Capitol Hill." *Review of Politics* 50: 345–64.

Derthick, Martha. 1979. *Policymaking for Social Security.* Washington, DC: Brookings.

Dunar, Andrew J. 1984. *The Truman Scandals and the Politics of Mortality.* Columbia: University of Missouri Press.

Freeman, Jo. 1975. *The Politics of Women's Liberation.* New York: David McKay.

Higgs, Robert. 1987. *Crisis and Leviathan: Critical Episodes in the Growth of American Government.* New York: Oxford University Press.

Key, V. O., Jr. 1964. *Politics, Parties and Pressure Groups,* 5th ed. New York: Crowell.

Lampman, Robert J. 1984. *Social Welfare Spending: Accounting for Changes from 1950 to 1978.* New York: Academic Press.

Mayhew, David R. 1991. *Divided We Govern: Party Control, Lawmaking, and Investigations, 1946–1990.* New Haven, CT: Yale University Press.

Ogul, Morris S. 1976. *Congress Oversees the Bureaucracy: Studies in Legislative Supervision.* Pittsburgh: University of Pittsburgh Press.

Ripley, Randall B. 1983. *Congress: Process and Policy.* New York: W. W. Norton.

Scher, Seymour. 1963. "Conditions for Legislative Control." *Journal of Politics* 25: 526–51.

Sundquist, James L. 1968. *Politics and Policy: The Eisenhower, Kennedy and Johnson Years.* Washington, DC: Brookings.

———. 1988–89. "Needed: A Political Theory for the New Era of Coalition Government in the United States." *Political Science Quarterly* 103: 613–35.

Vogel, David. 1981. "The 'New' Social Regulation in Historical and Comparative Perspective." In Thomas K. McCraw, ed., *Regulation in Perspective: Historical Essays.* Cambridge, MA: Harvard University Press.

Weidenbaum, Murray L. 1977. *Business, Government, and the Public.* Englewood Cliffs, NJ: Prentice-Hall.

5

Clinton, the 103d Congress, and Unified Party Control
What Are the Lessons?

"Divided government is not working," David S. Broder wrote in the summer of 1992. "Only the voters can fix this mess." In November of that year, the voters performed on cue by trading in George Bush for Bill Clinton, keeping solid Democratic majorities in the House and Senate, and consequently opting for single-party control of the U.S. government for the first time since 1977–80, under Jimmy Carter. It was a "dramatic shift," notes Richard E. Cohen, "from a divided government stuck in neutral to one in which a single party was operating the vehicle and had well-defined goals" (1994, 2). At hand was a test of whether unified party control could overcome gridlock and make the system work (Brady 1993). At stake was the role of American parties in governing.

Once Clinton took office in 1993, things went quite well on Capitol Hill, as the president pressed his ambitious budget plan and then the North American Free Trade Agreement (NAFTA). Congress, according to one late-1993 assessment, had generated "a spate of new laws, as Democratic policies and programs . . . flowed freely down the legislative sluice for the first time in more than a decade" (Hook 1993, 3355). Using roll-call data, *Congressional Quarterly* reported in September 1993 that Clinton had scored "the highest success rate in Congress of any first-year president since Dwight D. Eisenhower" (Langdon 1993).[1]

But no one was voicing any such claims a year later, after the downfall of Clinton's health care plan and numerous other Democratic aims. "This will go into the record books as perhaps the worst Congress — least effective, most destructive, nastiest — in 50 years," declared the *Washington Post* (1994). "It's back to gridlock, or so it has seemed lately — but of a nasty, internecine kind that makes the Bush administration seem like a checkers game by comparison" (*Washington Post National Weekly Edition* 1994, 24). Also judging thumbs-down was the *New York Times* (1994), which argued that "Bill Clinton and the Democrats have failed to persuade the American people that they can govern as a party" and pointed to "rising public frustration at the majority party's inability to govern even when it has the keys to the Capitol and the White House." In a national opinion poll reported in September 1994, only 19 percent of respondents said that Congress had accomplished more than it does in a typical two-year period; 52 percent thought it had accomplished less (Clymer 1994d; Toner 1994).

How does the 103d Congress of 1993–94 stack up when examined more closely and placed in historical perspective? I pursue that question here in an analysis that dwells on the enactment of laws and on possible differences between unified and divided party control. The analysis feeds off and extends my 1991 work, *Divided We Govern,* which covers Congresses from 1946 through 1990.[2]

Volume and Direction of Lawmaking

This discussion is organized under ten general "claims" that I believe are backed up by the record of the 103d Congress. All ten deal directly or indirectly with unified versus divided party control. Some are framed as historical generalizations about the U.S. regime (at least since World War II); others, implicitly hedged in by understandings about background conditions, are framed as propositions of universalistic form.

Claim 1: The volume of important laws enacted by Congress does not vary significantly between conditions of divided as opposed to unified party control. On average, that is, the number of major laws passed by Congresses under unified party control (where one party holds the presidency, House, and Senate) does not differ significantly from the number passed by Congresses under divided control (where one party holds two of the three institutions but not the third). This is the central claim of *Divided We Govern* and is given prime attention here. The legislative record of 1993–94 is juxtaposed to those of the twenty-three preceding postwar Congresses of 1947–48 through 1991–92.

Is this a direct probe for the existence of gridlock as opposed to its absence? It is not. "Gridlock" implies proposals not passed — failures that could have been successes. Thus, any search for whether gridlock exists or not seems to call for some kind of ratio measure — a numerator comprising laws successfully passed over a denominator comprising all proposals that might have passed (whether they did or not). An obvious supply of such ratio measures appears in presidential "support scores" or "success scores" of various kinds. But for anyone studying the legislative output of the U.S. regime — and particularly anyone examining how that output may vary under conditions of divided as opposed to unified party control — presidential scores have dubious merit.[3] The president is not the only elected official who has legislative powers and an agenda. As an analogy, it would make little sense to investigate the decision outputs of families by looking only at whether mothers get what they want.

This is not just a quibble. Yes, President Clinton did largely set the legislative agenda for the 103d Congress, but right after that, who set the Contract with America agenda for the 104th? Also, proposals for laws often bubble up from the congressional ranks one by one rather than descend as a packaged program from the White House or a Newt Gingrich–like party leadership. Any realistic, committed conservative knows about the subleadership route to success that produced such major measures as the McCarran Internal Security Act of 1950, the McCarran-Walter Immigration Act of 1952, the so-called Hyde amendments to curb government support of abortion, and the Gramm-Rudman-Hollings antideficit act of 1985. On the liberal side, in the decades after the White House became Republican in 1968, various blocs and entrepreneurs crafted a legislative art form in maneuvering to enactment such initiatives as Senator Edmund Muskie's Water Pollution Control Act of 1972, the War Powers Act of 1973, the Federal Election Campaign Act of 1974, South Africa sanctions in 1986, and the Family Support Act of 1988. In fact, Capitol Hill is a swirl of legislative options that emerge endlessly from all corners and sides — not just from the White House (Lindblom 1965). That makes it hard to isolate a useful "legislative agenda" for a Congress.

My substitute solution in *Divided We Govern* was, in effect, to count the full-grown oaks but ignore the acorns — to try to compile two-year lists of important laws that actually did pass but to ignore any underlying agendas or denominators. This way, we could at least try to see whether levels of successful legislative volume or motion differ under conditions of unified as opposed to divided party control. What are the levels of legislative production? That might be the best answerable question. Accommodated by this course is one plausible theoretical viewpoint about denominators indexing legislative proposals — namely, that they always should be set at infinity, regardless of conditions of party control. In principle, acorns exist without end (Krehbiel 1996). What politicians could propose under specified circumstances is limitless; what they do propose is secondary and, at any rate, likely to be affected by the circumstances.

To canvass for important enactments in *Divided We Govern,* I conducted two independent sweeps through the history of all post–World War II Congresses (Mayhew 1991, ch. 3). By "important" items, I meant in principle ones that were both innovative and consequential — or at least believed likely, at the time of passage, to be consequential. My first sweep relied on contemporary accounts, chiefly a series of stylized end-of-session "wrap-up" stories written by *New York Times* and *Washington Post* journalists, that cited enactments evidently thought by the Washington community to be major initiatives. The test was this: Did the writers seem to think a new law was particularly important or not? The second sweep relied on judgments by specialists in forty-three policy areas, writing mainly in the 1980s, regarding which laws enacted in their areas during the preceding decades had proved to be major measures. This two-pronged methodology has many difficulties, including ones associated with coding elusive materials (Mayhew 1991, 6–7, 34–50, 74–80, 90–91; Mayhew 1993b), but it has the strength of offering cross-time appraisals by two sets of arguably relevant witnesses. The wrap-up journalists, like the policy experts, really do try to place lawmaking in absolute or historical perspective. A quick reality test of this, for example, is that the wrap-up sweep for Lyndon B. Johnson's historic Great Society Congress of 1965–66 yielded nineteen major laws, whereas the one for Eisenhower's last Congress of 1959–60 — a model of meager performance for many historians and political scientists — yielded just four major laws.

All statutes netted by either sweep added up to 274 items for the Congresses of 1947–48 through 1991–92 — and now another 11 for 1993–94. The second column of Table 5.1 presents the number of laws passed by each Congress. In parentheses just to the right are figures for a small number of laws (already included in the larger counts) that seemed to stand out to contemporary witnesses in the first sweep as historically important. Included are the Marshall Plan in 1948, Medicare in 1965, the Voting Rights Act of 1965, Reagan's two budgetary instruments in 1981, and Bush's and Clinton's deficit reduction acts of 1990 and 1993.[4]

Evident in the second column of Table 5.1 is a bulge of lawmaking from the early 1960s through the mid-1970s. I believe the bulge is real — not some methodological fluke (see also Howell et al. 2000, 297–99; Davidson 1988, 351–54). It indexes the immense expansion of the U.S. domestic state through

Table 5.1 Analysis of Laws Passed by Congress, 1947–94

Congress	Total Number of Laws[a]	Part of Presidential Term		Party Control	
		1st Half	2d Half	Unified	Divided
1947–48	10 (2)	—	10	—	10
1949–50	12 (2)	12	—	12	—
1951–52	6	—	6	6	—
1953–54	9	9	—	9	—
1955–56	6	—	6	—	6
1957–58	11 (1)	11	—	—	11
1959–60	5	—	5	—	5
1961–62	15 (1)	15	—	15	—
1963–64	13 (4)	—	13	13	—
1965–66	22 (3)	22	—	22	—
1967–68	16 (1)	—	16	16	—
1969–70	22	22	—	—	22
1971–72	16	—	16	—	16
1973–74	22 (1)	22	—	—	22
1975–76	14	—	14	—	14
1977–78	12	12	—	12	—
1979–80	10	—	10	10	—
1981–82	9 (2)	9	—	—	9
1983–84	7	—	7	—	7
1985–86	9 (1)	9	—	—	9
1987–88	12	—	12	—	12
1989–90	9 (1)	9	—	—	9
1991–92	7	—	7	—	7
1993–94	11 (2)	11	—	11	—
Mean	11.9	13.6	10.2	12.6	11.4

[a] Figures in parentheses represent the number of laws that were considered to be of particular historical importance at the time of their passage. *Source:* For 1947–92: Mayhew 1993a, chap. 3 and p. 200. For 1993–94: Calmes and Harwood 1993; Church 1993; Clymer 1993c, 1994d; Dewar and Cooper 1994; Zuckerman and Farrell 1994.

increased expenditure and regulation that took place under John Kennedy, Lyndon Johnson, Richard Nixon, and Gerald Ford (Mayhew 1991, ch. 4; Sundquist 1968; Vogel 1981; Skocpol 1987, 364–65). Lawmaking really did surge, perform at a high rate, and decline. Since that time, however, the fall-off in law counts does owe partly to two artifactual considerations. First,

Congress switched, around 1980, to large comprehensive or omnibus bills — notably, budgetary instruments — as vehicles of choice for many legislative items that once would have passed as freestanding laws. No doubt this cut down a bit on the number of documentable "major laws" for more recent times. The most embarrassing consequence for this study is the confinement of the 1981 "Reagan revolution" to just two statutes — the president's tax cut (the largest in U.S. history) and the so-called Gramm-Latta II (or OBRA — the Omnibus Budget Reconciliation Act) package of expenditure cuts (Mayhew 1991, 43, 69, 76). Second, my second sweep through the works of "policy experts" — an independent source of listable laws — faltered in the early 1980s and came to a complete halt in 1986. Those writers' works could not be consulted for events occurring after their publication dates. A result is that my methodology, now reduced to the wrap-up stories of the first sweep, has probably grown both stingier and less sound when applied to very recent Congresses. Almost certainly it skips a few additional laws that a continued second sweep would have netted, and it loses the sensibility of policy experts as a useful complement to that of journalists.

This having been said, the middle columns of Table 5.1 document one solid generalization: More major laws pass during the first half of a presidential term than during the second half. The only exception is Reagan's second term, when Democratic House Speaker Jim Wright ushered through a considerable program in 1987–88 (Mayhew 1991, 118–19). (After the 1994 midterm, of course, congressional Republicans aimed for a second exception during 1995–96). But the right-hand columns of Table 5.1, which test for any difference in legislative productivity between conditions of unified (UNI) and divided party control (DIV), show close to a wash. On average, unified control scores a bit higher in volume, but even that slight edge may owe to the fact that the recent use of omnibus measures has cut down on law counts chiefly during the Republican divided-control presidencies of 1981–92. Overall, for legislative productivity, divided as opposed to unified party control seems to be a minor factor at best (Mayhew 1991, 76, 175–78; Howell et al. 2000, 297–99).

Now for the Clinton era's opening contributions. The list that follows presents eleven enactments of Clinton's first Congress of 1993–94.[5] Two of them, the 1993 budget package and NAFTA, were billed by the media as extraordinarily important.[6] In addition, the wrap-up discussions at the close of the 1993 legislative year contributed another four items — the family leave act, the "motor voter" act, Clinton's national service plan, and the Brady bill, which orders a waiting period in the purchase of handguns. These were relatively easy choices.[7] The late-1994 wrap-ups added on three more items unproblematically — that year's onmibus crime bill, the soon-to-be-ratified

GATT (General Agreement on Tariffs and Trade) accord, and a California desert protection plan that surprisingly stayed alive in October 1994 when just about every other initiative was dying. Beyond that, the 1994 sources become harder to read, as they discuss education reforms without always identifying particular bills. I ended up listing the Goals 2000 education measure of 1994 as well as a belatedly dwelt-on reform of college-loan financing that had passed back in 1993. This last is the shakiest of the eleven listed choices. My overall result for 1993–94 corresponds particularly well to the 1994 *Washington Post* and *Boston Globe* wrap-ups.[8]

- *OMNIBUS DEFICIT REDUCTION ACT.* Clinton's centerpiece. A claimed $496 billion in savings over five years including $220 billion in tax hikes; top income-tax bracket rate to go from 31 percent to 36 percent, plus a 10 percent surcharge on the exceptionally wealthy. Expansion of the Earned Income Tax Credit (EITC).
- *NORTH AMERICAN FREE TRADE AGREEMENT (NAFTA) APPROVED.* Bush-Clinton plan for free-trade zone encompassing the United States, Canada, and Mexico.
- *Family and Medical Leave Act of 1993.* Employers required to allow twelve weeks of unpaid leave for family medical emergencies.
- *Motor Voter Act of 1993.* States required to provide voter registration forms in motor vehicle offices, military recruiting stations, and welfare offices.
- *National Service Act of 1993.* Clinton's "AmeriCorps" plan to offer college educational grants in exchange for community service work.
- *Reform of college-student loan financing.* Deprivatization; government to provide money directly rather than through banks. (A provision of the omnibus budget act.)
- *Brady bill.* Requires a five-day waiting period for purchase of handguns.
- *Goals 2000.* Establishes national education goals for all students and schools.
- *Onmibus crime act.* Ban on assault weapons; expansion of the death penalty; $30 billion to finance prison construction, hiring of 100,000 new police officers, and prevention programs.
- *California desert protection.* Creates largest wilderness area outside Alaska. Dianne Feinstein's bill.
- *General Agreement on Tariffs and Trade (GATT) accord approved.* Lowers tariffs among 124 nations and creates World Trade Organization.

The closest also-rans were a revision of the Hatch Act in 1993, which drew marginal interest in the 1993 wrap-ups but faded in 1994; a new injection of aid to the ex-Soviet republics; the killing of the supercollider in 1993; and a measure outlawing blockades of abortion clinics. One or more of these items could surface in any future "policy experts" search in the style of my second sweep. An excellent prospect for such status is a 1994 banking reform unlisted here that authorized interstate branch networks (Bradsher 1994). This key bipartisan measure evidently was not controversial enough to intrude into session-closing wrap-up accounts dominated by Clinton's agenda. So there exist misses that look as if they might have been hits. It is a hazard of the methodology for all Congresses, particularly all recent ones, not just the 103d.

Recently, at least three other political scientists have independently compiled their own list of major laws for a Bush or Clinton Congress (see also Gettinger 1994). The results are shown in Table 5.2.[9] For the 101st Congress, Timothy J. Conlan (1993) uses the same methodology as mine. Charles O. Jones makes his own overall assessments for the 102d and 103d Congresses (1994, 145; 1995), though he may have aimed for an importance cutoff point something like mine, since he refers to my lists for pre-1990 Congresses. For the 103d Congress, Bruce I. Oppenheimer (1996) uses end-of-session appraisals by *Congressional Quarterly Weekly Report*. In general, Conlan's and Jones's lists match mine pretty well in both length and content.[10] Oppenheimer's list for the 103d Congress is longer, but evidently that is because he uses *Congressional Quarterly*, which, unlike the mass-audience newspapers, seems to aim for completeness rather than summary judgments. That is its unique virtue. When I tried to use *Congressional Quarterly Weekly Report* for 1947–90 I ended up with lists that were quite long, and I couldn't tell when to stop counting.[11]

Referring back to Table 5.1 for long-term comparisons, we see that the record of 1993–94 looks like those of most other pre-Kennedy or post-Nixon Congresses held during the opening half of a presidential term — regardless of conditions of party control. It is nothing special. The 103d arguably belongs in a range with, for example, Truman's Congress of 1949–50 (UNI), which likewise featured one big domestic and one big foreign item — the landmark Housing Act of 1949 and the NATO treaty; or Carter's Congress of 1977–78 (UNI), which addressed surface mining, food stamps, clean air, clean water, the minimum wage, Social Security financing, the tax code, civil service reform, energy, the Panama Canal treaties, and airline deregulation.

I invite readers to examine Table 5.2, consult their memories, and see if they think that Clinton's first Congress of 1993–94 (UNI) really proved to be more productive than Bush's first one of 1989–90 (DIV).[12] For "party government" enthusiasts this may be a cruel comparison, but note the 1989–90 items — a deficit reduction package just as prodigious as Clinton's (more about that below), immigration reform, child care, a minimum wage hike, the $50 billion savings-and-loan bailout of 1989, the Americans with Disabilities Act of

Table 5.2 Major Laws for Recent Congresses, According to Four Political Scientists

Congress	D. R. Mayhew	T. J. Conlan	C. O. Jones	B. I. Oppenheime
101st (1989–90)	$N = 9$ minimum wage S & L bailout DEFICIT REDUCTION disabilities clean air child care immigration housing agriculture	$N = 9$ minimum wage S & L bailout DEFICIT REDUCTION disabilities clean air child care immigration housing kill catastrophic		
102d (1991–92)	$N = 7$ transportation civil rights energy arms treaty Russian aid cable TV California water		$N = 9$ transportation civil rights energy Russian aid cable TV Gulf resolution banking unemployment benefits JTPA amendments	

Table 5.2 Continued

Congress	D. R. Mayhew	T. J. Conlan	C. O. Jones	B. I. Oppenheimer
103d (1993–94)	$N = 11$ DEFICIT REDUCTION NAFTA family leave motor voter national service college loans Brady bill Goals 2000 omnibus crime California desert GATT accord		$N = 12$ DEFICIT REDUCTION NAFTA family leave motor voter national service Brady bill Goals 2000 omnibus crime GATT accord amend Hatch Act supercollider banking	$N = 18$ DEFICIT REDUCTION NAFTA family leave motor voter national service Brady bill Goals 2000 omnibus crime GATT accord banking economic stimulus S & L fund foreign aid NIH reauthorization DOD authorization abortion clinics independent counsel DOA reorganization

Source: Data from Conlan 1993; Jones 1994, 145; 1995; Mayhew 1991, chap. 3; 1993a, 200; and Oppenheimer 1996.

1990, and the crowning achievement of Senator George Mitchell's career — the telephone-book-sized Clean Air Act of 1990.[13]

Certain other Congresses are in a higher league. The 103d came nowhere near the Great Society Congress of 1965–66 (UNI), and in my view it fell well short of the "Reagan revolution" Congress of 1981–82 (DIV), whose significance is uniquely underindexed in Table 5.1. (We might ask ourselves whether, even now, Reagan's budget of 1981 leaves more of a trace in U.S. finances, programmatic options, and political discourse than does Clinton's budget of 1993.)

Again, this is an analysis innocent of agendas or denominators. To bring those up is to confront the outsized ambitions adopted by Democrats after the 1992 election. For lawmaking, it was expected to be 1933 or 1965 all over again. But it did not turn out that way. Legislative drives ensued and failed on Clinton's BTU energy tax, his economic stimulus plan (Clymer 1993b), a "freedom of choice" charter for women (Clymer 1993a), statehood for the District of Columbia (Ayres 1993), welfare reform, labor's goal to bar replacement of strikers (Manegold 1994), campaign finance reform (Rosenbaum 1994), lobbying reform (Clymer 1994a), a range of environmental bills addressing clean water, safe drinking water, pesticides, hazardous wastes, Superfund overhaul, mining law, endangered species, and cabinet status for the Environmental Protection Agency (Kenworthy and Lee 1994; *USA Today,* Oct. 6, 1994, 4A; Cushman 1994), and, of course, health care (Clymer 1994c; Priest and Weisskopf 1994; Clymer, Pear, and Toner 1994; Rovner 1995; Johnson and Broder 1996, chs. 14–20). Most or all of these items might have been expected to succeed, given the new Democratic hegemony. There were other agendas in 1993–94. Drives not so clearly partisan failed in the areas of product liability, telecommunications (Andrews 1994), and congressional accountability (that is, a move to make regulatory laws that apply to everyone else apply to Congress, too). Conservatives auditioned for 1995 with unsuccessful drives for term limits, a balanced budget amendment, a line-item veto, a curb on unfunded federal mandates, and the so-called "A to Z" and Penny-Kasich expenditure cuts. In the 103d, there was plenty of failure to go around.

Claim 2: The ideological direction of lawmaking does not vary with patterns of party control as much as we ordinarily think.   A simple, paint-palette model of U.S. policy making would have it that we receive one bright shade of ideological result when the Democrats control the government, another bright shade when the Republicans do, and a blend (if any policies are made at all) when party control is divided. Call it blue, red, and purple.

Obviously, there is a good deal of truth to this model. To contrast certain

Congresses with their immediate predecessors, for example, Truman's Congress of 1949–50 (D-UNI) and Kennedy's of 1961–62 (D-UNI) moved lawmaking policy in a blue direction, and the Taft-led Congress of 1947–48 (DIV), the Reagan-led Congress of 1981–82 (DIV), and the Gingrich-led Republican Congress of 1995 (DIV) moved it in a red direction. The results flashed bright blue during the first two years of Lyndon Johnson's presidency (D-UNI). Both the general point and the details are as well known as any lore about American politics.

But that model is far from the whole story. Try the following experiment: (1) Disregard all actual election returns, party labels and holdings, roll-call scores, and other such paraphernalia we ordinarily rely on. (2) With an eye for ideological direction, look at just the results of lawmaking for each Congress since World War II (as in, for example, Mayhew 1991, table 4.1). (3) Assume that Democrats are liberals (blue) and Republicans are conservatives (red). (4) Guess which party ran the government during each postwar Congress (assume for the moment no divided party control). No peeking at the actual party holdings. Here is a good bet for a guess: The Republicans governed until 1960, the Democrats from 1961 through roughly 1977, and the Republicans have been in control since then. In a census of statutes, you will notice, for example, the anti-Communist laws enacted under Truman (D-UNI) and Eisenhower (R-UNI) from 1950 through 1954 (Mayhew 1991, 43–44, 173–74); the sequence of welfare state expansions from roughly 1964 through 1975 — not just food stamps, Medicare, and Medicaid under Johnson (D-UNI) but also Social Security indexing and Supplementary Security Income (SSI) under Nixon (DIV) and the Earned Income Tax Credit (EITC) under Ford (DIV). You would notice the regulatory explosion under Nixon[14] and the deregulation of securities, railroads, airlines, natural gas, trucking, and banking from 1975 through 1982, chiefly under Carter (D-UNI).[15] Clearly, there exist prominent lawmaking tendencies not explainable by the usual party-based lore; the bents of eras can override those of parties.[16]

Clinton's Congress of 1993–94 bears out the conventional party logic but also, strikingly, its override. On the one hand, yes, as in 1949 and 1961 the new Democratic ascendancy brought successes for the left. The family leave, motor voter, and national service acts of 1993 would almost certainly never have passed in a renewed Bush presidency. Nor would top-bracket income taxes have been raised to the degree they were in the deficit reduction act of 1993 — from 31 percent up to 36 percent, with an extra 10 percent surcharge on income over $250,000. These were prize achievements for the liberal side.

But on the other hand, if placed more generally in a context with preceding Congresses, the 1993–94 record looks a lot like more of the same. Future historians will probably make that judgment. Even family leave, from one perspective, was just one more of a miniseries of strenuous moves to regulate industry that passed starting in 1990. It joined the Americans with Disabilities Act of 1990, the Clean Air Act of 1990, and the Civil Rights Act of 1991 (Weidenbaum 1991). In the trade area, NAFTA and GATT had been Bush projects. Also, the nonactions during 1993–94 came to look surprisingly like those under Bush: the thwarted aims of one side or another on health care, freedom of choice, striker replacement, the environment, campaign finance, term limits, the line-item veto, and the balanced budget amendment. Clinton lost an economic stimulus proposal in 1993, but so had Bush lost one in 1992 (Stein 1993).

And the 1993 Clinton budget package, once Congress had stripped away much of its "investment" and other new ideas, comfortably joined a class of high-aim deficit reduction measures extending back over a decade—those of 1982, 1984, 1987, 1990, and now 1993 (Birnbaum 1993). Republicans charged that the Clinton measure set a record for new tax revenue. That was false: in constant dollars, the 1982 plan had raised more. Clinton himself claimed authorship of "the largest deficit reduction package in history" (Pear 1995). That was false too: the bipartisan act of 1990 had taken a five-year $482 billion bite; given inflation, the 1993 act would have needed a $532 billion bite to match that mark, but in fact it ended up somewhere between $432 and $477 billion.[17] In general, the 1993 package strikingly resembled the now-orphaned one of 1990 (no one was claiming credit for the earlier deal any more). The 1990 act had already raised the top-bracket income tax rate from 28 percent to 31 percent. (In retrospect, it seems clear that the historically low 28 percent rate proudly achieved by the Tax Reform Act of 1986 was just sitting there as a target; it survived only four years of real political life.) The 1993 act, like the 1990 one, relied heavily on post–Cold War defense cuts, placed caps on congressional discretionary spending, slashed Medicare payments to providers (though not beneficiaries), raised the gas tax (up 4.3 cents, as opposed to a 5.0 cent increase in 1990), and went out of its way to include social welfare sweeteners—notably, a new five-year $20.8 billion hike in the Earned Income Tax Credit that topped the $12.4 billion hike in the credit in 1990 (Hager 1993c; Wessel 1993; Yang 1993; *New York Times* 1993).[18] "It tells you a lot about the politics of deficit reduction," remarked former Congressional Budgetary Office director Rudolph G. Penner in mid-1993. "Regardless of who controls the government, you are pushed in the same direction" (quoted in Hager 1993c).

As the Democratic 103d Congress adjourned, several commentators marveled at its surprising friendliness to business and hostility to unions—what with, among other things, the wins on NAFTA and GATT and the losses on health care and striker replacement (Broder and Weisskopf 1994; Birnbaum 1994; Gigot 1994). To the political director of the Sierra Club, the 103d had turned out to be "the worst environmental Congress since the first Earth Day in 1970" (Kenworthy and Lee 1994, 14). In the mix of laws actually passed, the chief themes were arguably deficit reduction, free trade, and crime control. Clearly, much was going on in these two years beyond the reach of the conventional party paint-palette.

Why the Results Even Out

The gist of the two claims given above is that, in both volume and ideological direction, U.S. lawmaking seems to "even out" across conditions of party control. Why this evening out might occur is taken up briefly in the following four claims.[19]

Claim 3: "National moods" help to override conditions of party control (that is, as the U.S. system varies among conditions of party control, "moods" can cut down on the kinds of differences in legislative volume or ideological direction, or both, that conventional "party government" wisdom would lead us to predict). This elusive though arguably basic explanation can only be touched on here (see Mayhew 1991, 142–74). It addresses both volume and ideology. During the Civil War and the Reconstruction era, the Progressive era, the New Deal era, and the 1960s through the early 1970s, the argument goes, an intense public activism drove up the volume of ambitious lawmaking and tilted its product to the left. At other times, less has been undertaken, and on average its tenor has been more conservative. In recent decades, at least, the up-and-down pattern has not corresponded all that well to conditions of party control.

It would be hard to find a better exhibit for this case than Clinton's first Congress. Notwithstanding Democratic Party control in 1993–94, the lions in the background environment were Ross Perot and Rush Limbaugh, not, as with a generation earlier, liberal mobilizers like Ralph Nader and Martin Luther King Jr. No liberal cause of the 1990s — including health care — seemed to draw anywhere near the intense public support given to term limits and other antigovernment causes. For Democrats, it was a jungle out there. First-term congressman Don Johnson (D-Ga.), fresh from voting for the president's allegedly big-government budget, returned home in 1993 to face picketing, demands for his recall, and "a raucous town-hall meeting with 350 people in the small community of Grovetown, during which he was repeatedly booed and shouted down with catcalls" (Cohen 1994, 211).[20] This climate evidently made it very rough for Democrats on Capitol Hill — especially in 1994. "Despite their minority status," observed a reporter late that year, "the Republicans have virtually controlled the legislative agenda since they stalled the crime bill in July" (Seelye 1994). The tactics associated with that stall included a remarkably effective GOP case — it seemed to echo through a receptive public — that the crime measure was loaded with "social pork" (Boyer 1994; Johnson and Broder 1996, 482–86). (A revised crime package later passed.) In this and other areas, intense or whipped-up conservative opinion seemed to override party labels. Grassroots communications to Congress surged on the conservative side during 1993–94 (Goldstein 1995).[21]

A good analogy to the 103d is Truman's Congress of 1949–50. Democrats at that time, excited by their 1948 election triumph, also aimed for a replay of the New Deal and scored a few victories (notably in housing) but soon bogged down in a nasty, stalemate politics in which most of their program — including national health insurance — died and a surge of intense conservatism (then of an anti-Communist variety) prevailed. The McCarran Internal Security Act of 1950 was one landmark result. For liberal Democratic legislators, it was a deadly environment.

Claim 4: Crosscutting opinion cleavages help to override conditions of party control.   In certain areas, the electorate divides intensely and lastingly along lines that do not match party identification. As a result, whether laws pass or not can bear little relation to congressional party holdings (Mayhew 1991, 139–42). Thus, since abortion divides the public the way it complicatedly does, the strong "freedom of choice" initiative could founder in a 1993 House populated by 258 Democrats. As another example, issues of basic labor-management relations tend to unite Republicans but divide Democrats — and also, possibly because business outspends and outlobbies labor, to stiffen Republicans and de-energize Democrats — with the result that Republican Senate filibusters can succeed. It is a complex combination, but the 103d Congress, with the failure of striker replacement, took its place as one more high-tide Democratic one in which labor unions tried hard but could not get their way. (The others since the New Deal have been Truman's Congress of 1949–50, Johnson's of 1965–66, and Carter's of 1977–78. See Mayhew 1991, 78, 140n.)

During 1993–94, however, Exhibit A for the crosscut theory in NAFTA. A new, intense opinion cleavage over free trade versus protectionism seems to have emerged in the 1990s that crosses party lines. One result is the eye-catching 1993 roll-call pattern on NAFTA, a Clinton priority: majorities of

Republicans in both houses voted for it, but majorities of Democrats in both houses voted against it (Black 1994). (Of the 285 major post–World War II laws discussed earlier, only 2 others bore a Republicans-over-Democrats enactment profile like that — the Twenty-second Amendment curbing presidential terms in 1947 and the Gramm-Rudman-Hollings antideficit act of 1985). Could a reelected Bush have maneuvered NAFTA through a Democratic Congress? My guess is yes. Since he largely lacked other priorities, he could have pressed it during his honeymoon period of early 1993 when White House influence would have been high.

Claim 5: Lack of easy majority processes helps to override conditions of party control.   Even under unified party control, that is, Capitol Hill processes can be tortuous and sometimes nonmajoritarian (Mayhew 1991, 119–35). Laws do not "flow freely down the legislative sluice." In 1993–94, for example, disagreements between Senate and House figured in the demise of reforms of mining law and for provision of safe drinking water (Cushman 1994; Clymer 1994d). Also, telecommunications reform, a consensus winner in the House, "collapsed . . . in the Senate amid feuding between rival industry groups" (Andrews 1994). On show here was a kind of politics in which one segment of an industry — in this case, the regional Bells — could pull a log out of a tall pile and bring it down.

As Keith Krehbiel (1996) argues, a notably effective equalizer across conditions of party control is the Senate cloture rule, which erects a 60 percent hurdle for enactments under unified control that can rival the 67 percent hurdle allowed by presidential vetoes under divided control. In effect, President Bush the law blocker in 1991–92 could give way to Minority Leader Dole the law blocker in 1993–94.[22] In at least five instances — Clinton's economic stimulus bill, product liability, striker replacement, lobbying reform, and campaign-finance reform — Senate filibustering was at least the proximate cause of a major bill's defeat in 1993–94, and other bills sagged before such threats (Clymer 1994b; Wirls 1995).

Still, the filibuster weapon needs to be kept in perspective. Many defeats in 1993–94 owed little or nothing to real or anticipated Senate filibusters. Certain of the Democrats' environmental initiatives were dogged by appealing, hard-to-beat amendments that raised questions of unfunded mandates, property rights, or risk assessment — all perspectives that came of age in the succeeding 104th Congress. Welfare reform sank in committee. District of Columbia statehood and "freedom of choice" foundered for lack of House votes. On health care, so far as we know, never at any time was there a House floor majority for any plan the Democrats wished to advance.[23] "There wasn't anything out there they wanted to vote for. We weren't close to a majority on any specific health care plan," Speaker Tom Foley later recalled (Johnson and Broder 1996, 509). Also, a proximate cause of defeat is often just part of the story, as is suggested later in a discussion of campaign finance.

Claim 6: Something like "reason of state" can help to override conditions of party control.   Political scientists delight in models that posit individuals or societal groups whose fixed, distinctive preferences vector toward and explain policy outcomes. Nothing is more basic to the discipline.

But policy making does not always work that way. There seems to exist a class of policy areas in which, over time, outcomes are constant but the coalitions that support them vary. More specifically, an elite "reason of state" view seems to override customary party or district preferences on certain subjects where whoever holds power dutifully takes unpopular actions thought to be necessary. It is a root-canal style of politics. Thus, for example, foreign aid bills enjoyed support only from Democrats under Truman, but once Eisenhower took office in 1953 the roll-call backing for them shifted to bipartisan (Kesselman 1961). Another example is the raising of the national debt limit, which needs to be done occasionally even though it is unpopular back home. To cite one span of congressional history, majorities of both Democrats and Republicans tended to back debt-ceiling hikes under Eisenhower, only Democrats would do so under Kennedy and Johnson, but both Democrats and Republicans did so again under Nixon (*Congress and the Nation, 1945–1964,* 393–95, *1965–1968,* 127–40, *1969–1972,* 64–75; *Congressional Quarterly Almanac, 1966,* 714, 886, 953, *1967,* 316–22, 38H, 48H, 7S, 8S, 28S, *1970,* 293–95, 30H, 32S). Particularly for Republicans, much depended on which party held which office.

A good analogue to these instances is deficit reduction from 1982 through 1993. Senate Republicans took the policy lead through 1986, during which time they controlled that chamber (Hager 1993b). In 1990, under Bush, deficit reduction had a bipartisan coalitional base: the White House and Senate Minority Leader Dole finally struck a deal with House and Senate Democrats. But in 1993, as they had with foreign aid and the debt ceiling at earlier times of unified party control, the ruling Democrats had to act all by themselves. Republican support vanished. This is not to say that exactly the same result occurred in 1993 as earlier or that what happened was inevitable, but in fact a very similar result accrued even though it owed to a very different coalition. The idea of constant outcomes based on varying coalitions could use more study; it might open a window onto "state autonomy."

First-Year versus Second-Year of Congresses

A finer-grained analysis can be obtained from examining the 1993–94 Congress. When Clinton pursued deficit reduction and NAFTA in 1993 but put off health care, many of us asked certain questions. Can this work? How long can a president keep pressing successfully? What is the likely legislative rhythm of a president's first Congress? Below are some suggestive patterns.

Claim 7: In Congresses just after presidential elections, major laws tend to pass during the first year if party control is unified, but during the second year if it is divided. Here, finally, is a straightforward difference between unified and divided control. Table 5.3 divides post–World War II Congresses into four categories — the result of crosscutting a distinction of unified- versus divided-control Congresses against a distinction of the first half versus the second half of a presidential term. Within each of the four categories, the number of major laws passed by each Congress is broken down according to whether it was passed in the first or the second year.[24] Thus, in Clinton's case, NAFTA is a first-year enactment, and GATT is a second-year one.

The top tier in Table 5.3 presents data on initial Congresses under unified party control. This is the milieu of freshly elected Democratic presidents (Eisenhower is the outlier) who claim mandates for their domestic programs, unfold "hundred days" scenarios, and prod Congress to act fast (Kelley 1983; Dahl 1990; Hershey 1992). In fact, lawmaking under these conditions has tilted toward the first year — by an average of 7.3 as opposed to 6.2 major enactments. Clinton's first-year tilt looks like those under Kennedy in 1961–62, Johnson in 1965–66, and Carter in 1977–78. The general relation here is arguably better than it looks. Under Truman, three of the 1950 measures involved the just-begun Korean War. And 1953–54 is a stark, genuine exception. For lawmaking, Eisenhower's first year in office, 1953, stands out as the leanest of all the fifty or so years since World War II, because the new president did not have a legislative program at all in 1953. (Once he swung into gear in 1954, Eisenhower successfully promoted a sizable program: tax code revision, Social Security expansion, flexible farm prices, Food for Peace, urban renewal, authorization of an atomic energy industry, the St. Lawrence Seaway.)[25]

The second tier in Table 5.3 lists the data for initial Congresses under divided party control. Once again, the Congress of 1981–82 requires a warning label: the count of laws for 1981 greatly understates their significance. Notably, this first Reagan Congress is the only one in the category where a president vigorously pursued an early-days mandate strategy. That having been said, the

Table 5.3 Comparison of Number of Laws Passed in First and Second Year of Congress

Presidency	Years	First Year	Second Year
Unified party control: 1st Congress of presidential term			
Truman	1949–50	5 (2)	7
Eisenhower	1953–54	1	8
Kennedy	1961–62	9	6 (1)
Johnson	1965–66	15 (3)	7
Carter	1977–78	7	5
Clinton	1993–94	7 (2)	4
Mean		7.3	6.2
Divided party control: 1st Congress of presidential term			
Eisenhower	1957–58	2 (1)	9
Nixon	1969–70	6	16
Nixon/Ford	1973–74	11 (1)	11
Reagan	1981–82	2 (2)	7
Reagan	1985–86	2	7 (1)
Bush	1989–90	2	7 (1)
Mean		4.2	9.5
Unified party control: 2d Congress of presidential term			
Truman	1951–52	3	3
Kennedy/Johnson	1963–64	6 (1)	7 (3)
Johnson	1967–68	6	10 (1)
Carter	1979–80	3	7
Mean		4.5	6.8
Divided party control: 2d Congress of presidential term			
Truman	1947–48	6 (1)	4 (1)
Eisenhower	1955–56	2	4
Eisenhower	1959–60	3	2
Nixon	1971–72	5	11
Ford	1975–76	6	8
Reagan	1983–84	3	4
Reagan	1987–88	5	7
Bush	1991–92	2	5
Mean		4.0	5.6

Source: Data from Mayhew 1991, 52–73; 1993a, 200.

story for this set of Congresses is that lawmaking tends to be backloaded rather than front-loaded — there is an average of 9.5 measures in the second year versus 4.2 in the first. As for the post-midterm Congresses (see the right half of Table 5.3), lawmaking tilts slightly toward the second year under both conditions of party control.

Some inferences can be drawn from all the data: (1) For whatever reasons, an up-front mandate appeal does seem to work for newly elected presidents operating under unified party control. Only in this circumstance (with due respect to Reagan) does the lawmaking volume of the first year tend to dominate that of the second. (2) With a newly elected president operating under divided party control, lawmaking takes an especially long time. Ordinarily, there exists no mandate claim to help things along; yet the president, who was, after all, just elected, may insist on getting his way; the needed cross-party deals may be especially hard to make. Consider this contrast: it took eight months — until August 1993 — to enact Clinton's deficit reduction plan, yet it took twenty-two months — until October 1990 — to arrange one under Bush. (3) Nevertheless, although pre-midterm Congresses tend to vary according to party control in their timing profiles, they do not vary according to party control in their overall lawmaking volume. Different balance, same mass. Of course, under divided party control the final product does not so clearly reflect presidential tastes.

Bruce I. Oppenheimer (1996, 129–32, tables 6 and 7) confirms the idea that lawmaking takes longer under divided party control — at least in Congresses convening just after presidential elections. He examines the initial Congresses under Carter (1977–78), Reagan (1981–82 and 1985–86), Bush (1989–90), and Clinton (1993–94) and reports this result: budget resolutions and appropriations bills are much more likely to meet their deadlines (or at least come close) under unified control than under divided control. The pattern is nearly perfect. One way to look at it is that, on these budgetary matters, expeditiousness trades off against inclusiveness; under divided control, the coalitions need to be larger, and that takes longer.

Claim 8: Among presidents who have pressed ambitious domestic legislative programs (successfully or not) during their first year after winning election, none has ever had much luck pressing one also during his second year. This is another wrinkle on first year versus second year. (It introduces exactly the kind of ratio thinking I sidestepped earlier, but here the emphasis is on presidential success, not on the system's legislative output.) With health care in 1994, on the heels of deficit reduction in 1993, was Clinton trying to do something that none of his predecessors had ever pulled off? Surprisingly, perhaps, the answer seems to be yes. I arrived at this answer by reading secondary sources to try to get a general sense of past Congresses.

Here is an arguably complete list of twentieth-century presidents who have undertaken ambitious domestic legislative drives during their first postelection year: Wilson in 1913 (the New Freedom), Franklin Roosevelt in 1933 (his "hundred days"), Roosevelt in 1937 (court packing, executive reorganization, etc.), Truman in 1949 (the Fair Deal), Kennedy in 1961 (the New Frontier), Johnson in 1965 (the Great Society), Carter in 1977 (his energy plan), Reagan in 1981 (his budget package), and Clinton in 1993 (his budget package).

These drives enjoyed varying degrees of success. But never has a drive by the same president in a follow-up second year enjoyed notable success.[26] Reagan in 1982 and, it is probably fair to say, FDR in 1934 did not conduct ambitious second-year drives. Although Wilson won some victories in 1914, nonetheless, "the weakening of the administration's antitrust program was only the first sign of a general reaction that began to set in around the beginning of 1914 and increasingly affected the administration and the president" (Link 1954, 75). Johnson in 1966, then receding into conducting the Vietnam War, scored some successes on Capitol Hill but lost out on D.C. home rule, unemployment compensation, open housing, and a Taft-Hartley rollback (Evans and Novak 1966, 499–500, 558–61; *Congressional Quarterly Almanac,* 1966, 69–88). Kennedy won some middle-sized items in 1962 but suffered a drawn-out, dramatic defeat on Medicare (Koenig 1962; Bernstein 1991, ch. 8; *Congressional Quarterly Almanac,* 1962, 62–74). FDR in 1938, though victorious in advancing economic pump priming and the country's first nationwide minimum wage law, suffered a decisive loss on executive reorganization and had to live with a business-oriented congressional tax package he would not sign (Davis 1993, ch. 6; Patterson 1967, ch. 7). Carter in 1978 saw his energy program unravel in the Senate and, like FDR, was confronted with an unwanted probusiness tax package; he signed it (Kaufman 1993, chs. 5, 6, 8). Truman had a disastrous year in 1950, what with the onset of McCarthyism and the loss of virtually all his legislative priorities (Truman 1959, ch. 2; Gosnell 1980, ch. 34; Hamby 1973, ch. 15; McCoy 1984, ch. 8.)

Clinton, in short, joined good company with his health care loss in 1994. Second-year success on a project of that scale would have broken all precedent. If this historical analysis is correct, here is a guess about what drives the trend: a president, on becoming the beneficiary of an act of public authorization (ordinarily a presidential election), gets a shot at one season of legislative leeway; that is it. It seems to be a matter of leadership license and public attention span.

This account is compatible with a few odd cases of legislative drives conducted at times other than first years of presidential terms. Eisenhower saved his shot until his second year, but it was still available. FDR conducted a textbook legislative campaign during his third year in office—the "Second New Deal" of 1935. But that benefited from a unique authorizing event—the 1934 midterm that gave his ruling party an unprecedented gain in congressional seats. And Lyndon Johnson did in fact conduct successful legislative drives during back-to-back years—in 1965 following his election landslide but also before that, between November 1963 and November 1964. From the standpoint of lawmaking, that earlier twelve-month span was arguably the most eventful season since 1935: it yielded food stamps, aid to higher education, the countercyclical Kennedy tax cut, Johnson's antipoverty program, the Wilderness Act of 1964, the landmark Civil Rights Act of 1964, and, to boot, the Tonkin Gulf resolution that paved the way for the Vietnam War. Behind these results, though, seems to have been another kind of authorizing act—the assassination of President Kennedy, which by way of a complex public psychology seems to have awarded his successor great temporary leeway (Mayhew 1991, 90, 182).[27] The implication of all this for 1994 is that Clinton pushed up against the envelope and the envelope held. His ambition was out of line.

Of Partisanship and Indicators

All else aside, wasn't the 103d Congress at least a triumph for political scientists? Didn't "party voting" and related pleasing indicators find their day? Here, the answer is yes.

Claim 9: "Party voting" reached a new high in final passage of major laws by the 103d Congress. There is no doubt about it. Table 5.4 presents roll-call data on final passage for the eleven major enactments of 1993–94 listed earlier. The figures are broken down by party and chamber. In nine of the eleven instances, "party votes" carried the measures in both House and Senate—that is, a majority of Democrats voted one way and a majority of Republicans the other. A near miss is the California desert protection bill, which in fact Republican senators tried to block but finally gave in on. Only GATT drew support from most members of both parties. To look at the results another way, only two of the eleven measures—Goals 2000 and the California desert protection act—drew backing from at least two-thirds of the members of both houses (though GATT and family leave earned that distinction in one house).

No previous postwar Congress had performed anything like this. No previous Congress had enacted more than a quarter of its major laws by "party

Table 5.4 Final Passage Votes on Major Enactments, 1993–94

	House			Senate		
Bill	Dem	GOP	Total[a]	Dem	GOP	Total[b]
1993						
DEFICIT-REDUCTION	217–41	0–175	218–216	50–6	0–44	51–50
NAFTA	102–156	132–43	234–200	27–28	34–10	61–38
Family leave	210–29	36–123	247–152	55–2	16–25	71–27
Motor voter	237–14	21–146	259–160	57–0	5–37	62–37
National service	248–5	26–147	275–152	51–4	6–36	57–40
College loans[c]	217–41	0–175	218–216	50–6	0–44	51–50
Brady bill	184–69	54–119	238–189	47–8	16–28	63–36
1994						
Goals 2000	246–6	59–115	306–121	53–1	10–21	63–22
Crime	188–64	46–131	235–195	54–2	7–36	61–38
California desert	244–6	53–122	298–128		voice vote	
GATT accord	167–89	121–56	288–146	41–13	35–11	76–24

[a] House totals include votes cast by Bernard Sanders (Socialist-Vt.). [b] Vice President Gore broke a 50–50 Senate tie on deficit reduction. [c] College loan reform passed as part of the deficit reduction act. *Source: Congressional Quarterly Almanac.*

votes" in both houses or by narrow (less than two-thirds) majorities in both houses.[28] In these regards the 103d stands out as an extreme exception. This is not to say it came as a complete surprise, however; according to other evidence, it was more like a culmination. David W. Rohde (1991, chs. 1, 3, 5) and others have documented rises dating to the 1980s in party cohesion indexes, party loyalty scores, overall party voting, and other such congressional indicators.

Much might be said about the accentuated partisanship of the 103d Congress, but I make just one brief argument here. On current evidence, the kind of partisanship indexed by "party voting" does not seem to contribute to legislative productivity.[29] It might do so under some specifiable conditions, and it might do so in the future — certainly that is one vision of "party government" doctrine. But it does not seem to have done so to date. Indeed, particularly in light of the programmatic meltdown of the summer of 1994, at least as good a case seems to exist that, in the U.S. constitutional setting today, high partisanship contributes instead to inaction — even under unified party control. The opposition digs in, ugly wrangling ensues, the atmosphere sours, the public loses confidence and turns off, and measures die.

Claim 10: Certain indicators of government performance can be misleading. If partisanship bears an uncertain relation to legislative productivity, so too does an especially well known statistic currently relied on to index government performance.[30] That is *Congressional Quarterly*'s "presidential support score," which presents for each year the proportion of House and Senate roll calls on which the president's side won, from among those on which the White House took a position. It is by this standard that Clinton, as of September 1993, was said to be doing better than any first-year president since Eisenhower in 1953 (Langdon 1993). For 1994, the index reading is a very high 86.4 percent, which ranks that year among the reputed Everests of presidential success — 1953 under Eisenhower, 1963 through 1965 under Kennedy and Johnson, and, yes, 1993 under Clinton (Langdon 1994).[31]

I argued earlier that it is dubious in principle to accept "presidential support scores" as a guide to overall system performance, since the White House's agenda is not the only one.[32] But here the problem goes deeper. The score is not measuring presidential success very well. We were invited to compare 1993 with 1953, when, as it happens, Eisenhower did not have a legislative program. Should that not have counted somehow? That was bad enough, but the 1994 result seems to me to be worse. In fact, given Clinton's health care and lesser defeats, the interesting question arises: How could such a poor year earn such a high score? Here is a guess: congressional Democrats, by the early 1990s, had grown organizationally strong enough to make themselves look good on the floor. Their leaders, by manipulating agendas and rules, could largely detour the party's internal antagonisms away from roll-call processes. But the party was not necessarily strong enough to carry its bills. The disparity became plain in 1994. A tip-off is that health care, which dominated that year's news, politics, and policy processes, eventually figured in no roll calls at all in the House — it never came up — and in only four minor ones in the Senate. For 1994, we are looking at a "presidential support score" that leaves out health care. Little more needs to be said.

But how about presidential vetoes? (This is a standard student question.) Bush cast many vetoes and made them stick; Clinton cast none during the 103d Congress. Surely that disparity somehow indexes legislative productivity? Well, no. An absence of vetoes does not necessarily mean full-throttle lawmaking. Let me proceed by anecdote, using the subject of campaign-finance reform. In the 102d Congress (DIV), the Democrats served up a bill, and Bush vetoed it. In the 103d Congress (UNI), the two houses passed differing bills in 1993, but House Democrats stalled off a compromise until September 29, 1994 — apparently because deep down many of them were not eager for any action at all (they had been no more eager under Bush, but they knew he would veto) — and Senate Republicans finished things off with an end-of-session filibuster the next day, on September 30, 1994. These are the bare facts with a spice of motivation (Donovan 1994; "Legislative Summary" 1994). Note the pattern: identical results in the two Congresses — nothing at all passed — but the smoking gun of a veto only under Bush. There is more than one way to kill a bill.

Not the least of lessons available from the 103d Congress is a caveat about indicators. Only with an awareness of context should they be consulted at all.

Bonus claim: High-publicity congressional investigations of the executive branch occur just as often under unified party control as under divided control. And yes, investigations. "Democrats in Congress won't investigate a Democratic administration," Senator Dole asserted in January 1994, voicing the conventional wisdom of that time as the Whitewater controversy unfolded ("Dole Calls for Whitewater Answers" 1994). But it kept unfolding; nervousness set in among Capitol Hill Democrats who started switching to an "it's best to get the facts out" posture, hearings came to look inevitable, the Democratic leadership signed on to them, and once again a Congress did investigate an administration of its own party.

In fact, at least since World War II, investigations of the executive branch that have drawn high media attention have occurred as often against one background of party control as the other (Mayhew 1991, ch. 2). Table 5.5 lists all probes conducted under Carter, Reagan, Bush, and Clinton that figured in front-page stories of the *New York Times* for at least twenty days. These last four presidents offers a recent illuminating comparison.

In the Whitewater hearings of the summer of 1994, party loyalist Henry B. Gonzalez, chair of the House Banking Committee, caused the Clinton administration little trouble. But the Senate Banking Committee, chaired by Donald W. Riegle Jr., caused a great deal. Roger C. Altman, deputy secretary of the treasury, had to resign after testifying, and the spectacle came at a bad time for a White House still trying to keep stride in its health care march. A year later, in 1995, Republican-run committees took up Whitewater too, but they found it hard to exact as much political damage as Riegle and his committee had done in 1994.

The 103d Congress is receding into history, and it competes in memory with at least the Republican Congress of 1995–96 (DIV), also conducted under

Table 5.5 High-Publicity Congressional Investigations of the Executive Branch under the Past Four Presidents

Congress	President	Party Control	Subject	Number of Days on Front Page of *New York Times*
1977–78	Carter	UNI	Bert Lance bank deals	26
1979–80	Carter	UNI	Billy Carter/Libya	21
1981–82	Reagan	DIV	none	—
1983–84	Reagan	DIV	EPA favoritism	28
1985–86	Reagan	DIV	none	—
1987–88	Reagan	DIV	Iran/Contra	95
1989–90	Bush	DIV	Dept. of Housing and Urban Development	23
1991–92	Bush	DIV	none	—
1993–94	Clinton	UNI	Whitewater	22

Source: Mayhew 1991, ch. 2; 1993a, p. 200.

Clinton. Suffice it to say that those Gingrich-driven years brought a lawmaking disaster rivaling Clinton's health care debacle — the Republicans' shut-down-the-government budget drive that derailed in the winter of 1995–96 — but they also yielded, if actual enactments are considered, a surprisingly large harvest of legislation. Included were significant new laws addressing unfunded mandates, congressional responsibility, lobbying reform, securities stockholder suits, telecommunications, agriculture deregulation, the line-item veto, antiterrorism, pesticides, safe drinking water, welfare reform, health insurance portability, the minimum wage, and immigration. Adam Clymer, fresh from covering both the 103d and 104th Congresses for the *New York Times,* reflected in late 1996: "As for the Congress of 1993–94, in which Democrats ran both the House and the Senate, it did less than its successor" (Clymer 1996).

Notes

For their critiques of earlier versions of this work, I would like to thank R. Douglas Arnold, Fred Greenstein, Rogan Kersh, Keith Krehbiel, Eric Schickler, and Ian Shapiro. This essay was originally published as chap. 10 in John G. Geer (ed.), *Politicians and Party Politics* (Baltimore: Johns Hopkins University Press, 1998), pp. 259–93. © 1998 The Johns Hopkins University Press. Reprinted with permission of The Johns Hopkins University Press.

1. To that date, Clinton's side had prevailed on 88.6 percent of House and Senate roll calls on which the White House had taken a position. Like a successful rumor, this *Congressional Quarterly* report of presidential success traveled through the politics of ensuing months and improved as it traveled. Thus, "It's *the most productive first year* of any president since President Eisenhower's first term," said Senate Majority Leader George Mitchell on "Meet the Press" (as reported in Calmes and Harwood 1993; italics added). And, "Democrats *steered more legislation through Congress* in Clinton's first year as president than at any other similar time since Dwight D. Eisenhower was president" (Zuckman and Farrell 1994; italics added).

2. The Congress of 1991–92 is addressed in Mayhew 1993a, 200.

3. This is not to deny that whether presidents get what they want is an interesting question in its own right. On this subject, see notably Edwards 1980.

4. The other acts appearing in parentheses in Table 5.1 are the Taft-Hartley Act of 1947, the Housing Act of 1949, the NATO Treaty (1949), the Civil Rights Acts of 1957, 1964, and 1968, the Trade Expansion Act of 1962, the Test Ban Treaty (1963), the Anti-Poverty Act of 1964, the Kennedy tax cut of 1964, the Elementary and Secondary Education Act of 1965, the War Powers Act of 1973, the Tax Reform Act of 1986, and NAFTA (1993). These highlighted acts appear in capital letters in Mayhew (1991, 51–74, 91n). This list is reported here with misgivings. More than any other data set used here, its contents can owe to media hype, and such hype is routinely given to presidents deploying a mandate script for their major aims under conditions of unified party control. In fact, in terms of real long-term impact, it is questionable whether Kennedy's trade act or Soviet treaty outranked similar measures under later Republican presidents. (These latter appear in the longer list of 285 laws.) Not on the short list of twenty-one laws are the highly consequential Highway Act of 1956 and the Clean Air Act of 1970, which were enacted without great fanfare during Eisenhower's and Nixon's presidencies under conditions of divided party control. On the general problem, see Mayhew 1991, 90–91.

5. Full books have been written about three of the 1993 items: Cohen 1994 on Clinton's budget, Elving 1995 on family leave, and Waldman 1995 on national service.

6. If an official or customary title of an act proved to be available, brief, and to the point, it was used in this list. The form for these is "Family and Medical Leave Act of 1993." Otherwise, items take a form such as "Omnibus crime act." Laws judged by sources to be of exceptional importance are presented at the beginning of the list and are capitalized.

7. For recent Congresses, I have not been able to resist reaching beyond the *Washington Post* and the *New York Times* to incorporate other journalistic wrap-ups that seem to follow similar standards in discussing achievements, weighing evidence, presenting material hierarchically according to importance, as journalists will, and implicitly or explicitly imposing cutoff points. I give primary attention to the prose discussions in such pieces and much less to the boxes with enactment checklists of varying length that sometimes appear alongside. For 1993, a model wrap-up piece is Church 1993, which gives attention to all six laws discussed above in the text for 1993 and to no others, though it does question the significance of national service ("applies to so few people that it is really only tokenism") and the Brady bill ("has some loose ends") (33). The other sources from late 1993 are Dewar and Cooper 1993; Clymer 1993c; Calmes and Harwood 1993.

8. The *Washington Post*'s writers discuss nine enactments from 1993–94 and also refer summarily to "several education bills" from 1994. Nine of my listings are the same as theirs, if Goals 2000 can serve for the education bills. I have two items they lack (college loans, motor voter), and they have one that I lack (the killing of the supercollider in 1993). The *Boston Globe* writers discuss eleven enactments for 1993–94 plus "significant reforms in primary and secondary education." If Goals 2000 can serve for those reforms, I have one item they lack (California desert protection), and they have two that I lack (aid to the ex-Soviet republics in 1993, which I thought offered little new over 1992; and a 1994 measure outlawing blockades of abortion clinics, which is referred to just briefly in the *Globe* discussion and not taken up in anyone else's wrap-up account). The 1994 *New York Times* wrap-up does not do a good job of incorporating enactments from 1993; NAFTA and deficit reduction are discussed but not family leave, motor voter, national service, or the Brady bill. Otherwise, the *Times* discusses five items (1993 college loans, crime, Goals 2000, California desert protection, and GATT) that are on my list, plus another education measure that is not. The 1994 sources are Dewar and Cooper 1994; Clymer 1994d; Zuckman and Farrell 1994.

9. For space reasons, some of the entries in Table 5.2 for particular laws are cryptic. In the 101st Congress, "disabilities" means the Americans with Disabilities Act. "Kill catastrophic" means repeal of the Medicare Catastrophic Coverage Act of 1988. In the 102d Congress, "Gulf resolution" means the resolution authorizing the Persian Gulf war in early 1991. In Oppenheimer's (1995) list for the 103d Congress, "S&L fund" means a new deposit insurance fund for the savings and loan bailout; "foreign aid" means an authorization that included aid for Russia; "NIH reauthorization" included money for family planning and counseling; "DOD authorization" covered "Star Wars" cuts and gays in the military.

The alert reader of Table 5.2 may wonder about two particular sources of bias inherent in my reliance on journalistic wrap-up sources or in the way I interpret those sources. First, note that my lists, compared with the others, "miss" the repeal of catastrophic insurance in 1989–90 and the killing of the supercollider in 1993–94. My guess is that the wrap-up methodology, as I employ it, underplays somewhat the deaths of laws and programs (as opposed to their births) throughout the post–World War II era. One reason is that terminations tend to slip out of focus by occurring as parts of larger bills. On the methodology's missing of "appropriations erosion," see Mayhew 1991, 41. On the politicians' logic of hiding, so to speak, stiff programmatic budgeting cuts in larger bills, see Arnold 1990, 105. Second, note that my lists, unlike the others, include an overhaul of California water policy in 1991–92 and the California desert protection plan of 1993–94. In both cases, these bills caused a stir just before congressional adjournments. No doubt, they were fresh in journalists' minds as the wrap-up stories took shape. Throughout the post–World War II era, the wrap-up methodology probably overplays a bit such end-of-session success stories.

10. Jones's list for the 102d Congress is closer to mine than it looks, if we take into account his inclusion of the 1991 Persian Gulf resolution; I have not counted such resolutions, even if they are important (as that one surely was). See Mayhew 1991, 40–42.

11. Of the last nine entries in the Oppenheimer list, three are referred to only cursorily in the 1993 and 1994 newspaper wrap-up discussions, and six are not referred to at all.

12. An October 1994 assessment: "Bush's legacy is having a dramatic impact on how Washington operates in the Clinton era because many of the programs implemented by the Republican president, from defense cuts to budget rules to environmental regulations, are only now taking effect. . . . The greatest irony is that the interparty gridlock of the Bush era does not look so intractable in comparison with the sometimes-stalemate of the Clinton era. Bush's accommodation with Democrats resulted in legislation that appears in many ways more activist than Clinton has been able to achieve" (Kranish 1994).

13. The Clean Air Act of 1990 "produced the comprehensive revision (after nearly a decade of deadlock) of one of the most important statutes ever enacted by Congress [that is, the Clean Air Act of 1970 — also enacted under divided party control]. It also serves as proof that divided government can work" (Bryner 1993, xi). See also Cohen 1995.

14. "ATF, CPSC, DEA, the Endangered Species Act, EPA, LSC, NHTSA, NOAA, OSHA — all had their origin during the Nixon administration. In addition, affirmative action and wage and price controls were introduced" (Friedman 1995). See also Vogel 1981.

15. On the conservative shift under Carter, see Mayhew 1991, 93–94, 166–69, 172–73.

16. The most familiar epicycle to a party-based model of U.S. lawmaking involves the "conservative coalition" of Republicans and southern Democrats. That is, Democrats, even if formally in power, cannot flash bright blue because of their Dixie wing (and Republican congressional ranks are augmented by that wing). But this line of argument does not help to explain the liberal lawmaking results under Nixon or the shift to relatively conservative results under Carter.

17. Data are from the Congressional Budgetary Office (CBO) (Hager 1993a). At its time of passage, the 1993 measure was advertised as offering a $496 billion bite, but that figure declined after later CBO calculations. A range, rather than a single value, is offered for 1993 because of alternative assumptions about whether certain savings specified earlier in 1990 were now being double counted. See also Rosenbaum 1993.

18. In loose talk, Clinton supporters sometimes claimed credit for EITC, period. That idea turned up in, for example, a Molly Ivins (1994) column: "Another contender for Most Significant [Legacy] is the earned-income tax credit — the most important part of the first budget package."

19. Discussions of the first three of these explanations appear in Mayhew 1991, chs. 5, 6. (Of the six arguments presented in those chapters, the three taken up here seem to be the most illuminating with regard to 1993–94.)

20. For an account of the abuse heaped on the White House's cross-country bus caravan staged to rally support for health care reform in the summer of 1994, see Johnson and Broder 1996, ch. 18.

21. That public opinion in general shifted in a conservative direction during 1993–94 is reported in Ferejohn, Gaines, and Rivers 1996, 11–18. See also Johnson and Broder 1996, 447–49.

22. Dole usually served as aggregator of the opposition in 1993–94, but he needed forty allies to block a measure. Technically, in any instance, the least "anti" of forty-one naysayers was the pivotal Senate voter.

23. "No postmortems, what-ifs, or finger-pointing can change the fact that the overhaul of the nation's health care system lacked majority support with the American public and in Congress" (Schick 1995, 227). "A whip count in the House showed that the *Democratic* votes weren't there. The Senate was in much the same situation" (Moynihan 1995, 39).

24. The source for the breakdowns through 1990 is Mayhew 1991, 52–73; for the breakdowns from 1991 and 1992, see Mayhew 1993a. Strictly speaking, the year cited for each enactment is the one in which it formally became law (usually through a president's signature). A measure signed, for example, in January of an even year might have received most or all of its congressional treatment during the preceding odd year — though, in fact, the typical pattern for laws listed here as passing in even years was to pass Congress during a late-season crush of the even year. In Table 5.3, the figures in parentheses refer to the twenty-one earlier-mentioned measures that were thought by the media to be historically important; these are already included here as ordinary single items in the larger counts, and they do not play any extra role in the calculations of the averages.

25. For 1953, only the tidelands oil act, a conservative congressional favorite held over from 1952, made the list of 285 postwar enactments. On Eisenhower's presenting a program in 1954 but not in 1953, see Reichard 1975, chs. 5–7; Neustadt 1955.

26. Paul C. Light writes of a "cycle of decreasing influence" that induces newly elected presidents to introduce and fight for their proposals just after taking office (1982, ch. 2).

27. I have avoided discussing the instance of Theodore Roosevelt in 1905–7. Roosevelt certainly advanced an ambitious program then, but the old legislative calendar before the ratification of the Twentieth Amendment makes it difficult to talk about a first versus a second legislative year. Wilson solved this problem, so to speak, in 1913, as did FDR in 1933, by calling a special first session of the incoming Congress for March just after his election. Also unaddressed here is Wilson's successful legislative drive of 1916.

28. See Mayhew 1991, 121–22, for data on 1947 through 1990. In the second Bush Congress of 1991–92, six of the seven allegedly major enactments (all but cable-TV reform) passed with bipartisan support in both houses; six (all but aid to Russia) passed with better than two-thirds majorities in both houses.

29. To make a broader statement, the ups and downs in the standard annual "party voting" index based on all congressional roll calls since World War II do not seem to match the ups and downs in any dimension of government performance worth attending to — including the volume of major lawmaking and the level of White House success in passing programs. See the argument in Mayhew 1991, 126.

30. For another discussion of this subject, see Jones 1994, ch. 6.

31. Langdon is quite aware of the difficulty the index runs into in 1994.

32. Among the troughs in the "presidential support score" series are 1973 and 1987–88, when Nixon and Reagan respectively were on the ropes politically and lacked influence on Capitol Hill. Nevertheless, the overall system's legislative production was quite heavy both times. The year 1973 brought CETA jobs (through the Comprehensive Employment and Training Act), D.C. home rule, a Social Security hike, the Trans-Alaska pipeline, Conrail, HMOs, the War Powers Act, and a landmark foreign aid measure. In 1987–88, Speaker Jim Wright presided over the enactment of a Democratic program.

References

Andrews, Edmund L. 1994. "Bill to Revamp Communications Dies in Congress." *New York Times,* Sept. 24.

Arnold, R. Douglas. 1990. *The Logic of Congressional Action.* New Haven: Yale University Press.

Ayres, B. Drummond, Jr. 1993. "House Soundly Defeats a Proposal on District of Columbia Statehood." *New York Times,* Nov. 22.

Bernstein, Irving. 1991. *Promises Kept: John F. Kennedy's New Frontier.* New York: Oxford University Press.

Birnbaum, Jeffrey H. 1993. "Clinton Follows Predecessors' Path in Wrestling with the Demon Deficit." *Wall Street Journal,* May 21.

———. 1994. "As Clinton Is Derided as Flaming Liberal by GOP, His Achievements Look Centrist and Pro-Business." *Wall Street Journal,* Oct. 7.

Black, Gordon L. 1994. "NAFTA — Clinton's Victory, Organized Labor's Loss." *Political Geography* 13:377–84.

Boyer, Peter J. 1994. "Whip Cracker." *New Yorker,* Sept. 5, 38–54.

Bradsher, Keith. 1994. "Interstate-Banking Bill Gets Final Approval in Congress." *New York Times,* Sept. 14.

Brady, David W. 1993. "The Causes and Consequences of Divided Government: Toward a New Theory of American Politics?" *American Political Science Review* 87:189–94.

Broder, David S. 1992. "Wreckage of Divided Government." *Washington Post,* Aug. 30.

Broder, David S., and Michael Weisskopf. 1994. "Business Prospered in 103d Congress: Despite Democratic Leadership, Labor Had a Sparse Two Years on Hill." *Washington Post,* Sept. 25.

Bryner, Gary. 1993. *Blue Skies, Green Politics: The Clean Air Act of 1990.* Washington, D.C.: Congressional Quarterly Press.

Calmes, Jackie, and John Harwood. 1993. "Congress Rushes to Close Book on One Busy Year, But Clinton Promises to Apply the Spurs in Next." *Wall Street Journal,* Nov. 22.

Church, George J. 1993. "The Gridlock Breakers: Passage of the Brady Bill Caps a Solid Season for the 103d Congress." *Time,* Dec. 6, 32–33.

Clymer, Adam. 1993a. "Bill to Prohibit State Restrictions on Abortion Appears to Be Dead." *New York Times,* Sept. 16.

———. 1993b. "GOP Senators Prevail, Sinking Clinton's Economic Stimulus Bill." *New York Times,* Apr. 22.

———. 1993c. "Sour End to Strong Year." *New York Times,* Nov. 24.

———. 1994a. "GOP Filibuster Deals a Setback to Lobbying Bill." *New York Times,* Oct. 7.

———. 1994b. "Having 'Done Enough Harm,' Senate Inches to Adjournment." *New York Times,* Oct. 5.

———. 1994c. "National Health Program, President's Greatest Goal, Declared Dead in Congress." *New York Times,* Sept. 27.

——— 1994d. "Rancor Leaves Its Mark on 103d Congress." *New York Times,* Oct. 9.

———. 1996. "Clinton and Congress: Partnership of Self-Interest." *New York Times,* Oct. 2.

Clymer, Adam, Robert Pear, and Robin Toner. 1994. "For Health Care, Time Was a Killer." *New York Times,* Aug. 29.

Cohen, Richard E. 1994. *Changing Course in Washington: Clinton and the New Congress.* New York: Macmillan.

———. 1995. *Washington at Work: Back Rooms and Clean Air.* Boston: Allyn and Bacon.

Congress and the Nation, 1945–1964, 1965–1968, 1969–1972. Washington, D.C.: Congressional Quarterly Service, 1965, 1969, 1973.

Congressional Quarterly Almanac, 1962, 1966, 1967, 1970. Washington, D.C.: Congressional Quarterly Service, 1963, 1967, 1968, 1971.

Conlan, Timothy J. 1993. "Intergovernmental Regulatory Enactments in the 1980s." In U.S. Advisory Commission on Intergovernmental Relations, *Federal Regulation of State and Local Governments: The Mixed Record of the 1980s,* A-126. Washington, D.C.: U.S. Government Printing Office.

Cushman, John H., Jr. 1994. "Congress Drops Effort to Curb Public-Land Mining." *New York Times,* Sept. 30.

Dahl, Robert A. 1990. "Myth of the Presidential Mandate." *Political Science Quarterly* 105:355–72.

Davidson, Roger H. 1988. "The New Centralization on Capitol Hill." *Review of Politics* 50:345–64.

Davis, Kenneth S. 1993. *FDR: Into the Storm, 1937–1940: A History.* New York: Random House.

Dewar, Helen, and Kenneth J. Cooper. 1993. "Dust Clears on a Fruitful Legislative Year." *Washington Post,* Nov. 28.

———. 1994. "103d Congress Started Fast but Collapsed at Finish Line." *Washington Post,* Oct. 9.

"Dole Calls for Whitewater Answers." 1994. *Washington Post,* Jan. 17.

Donovan, Beth. 1994. "Democrats' Overhaul Bill Dies on Senate Procedural Votes." *Congressional Quarterly Weekly Report* 42 (Oct. 1): 2757–58.

Edwards, George C., III. 1980. *Presidential Influence in Congress.* San Francisco: W. H. Freeman.

Elving, Donald D. 1995. *Conflict and Compromise: How Congress Makes the Laws.* New York: Simon and Schuster.

Evans, Rowland, and Robert Novak. 1966. *Lyndon B. Johnson and the Exercise of Power.* New York: New American Library.

Ferejohn, John A., Brian J. Gaines, and Douglas Rivers. 1996. "The Failure of Incumbency: Why the Democrats Lost the House in 1994." Unpublished manuscript, Department of Political Science, Stanford University.

Friedman, Milton. 1995. "Getting Back to Real Growth." *Wall Street Journal,* Aug. 1.

Gettinger, Stephen. 1994. "View from the Ivory Tower More Rosy than Media's." 1994. *Congressional Quarterly Weekly Report* 52 (Oct. 8): 2850–51.

Gigot, Paul A. 1994. "103d Congress: Pass the Balloons and Party Hats." *Wall Street Journal,* Oct. 7.

Goldstein, Kenneth M. 1995. "Tremors before the Earthquake: Grass Roots Communications to Congress before the 1994 Election." Paper presented at the annual conference of the American Political Science Association, Chicago, Aug. 31–Sept. 3.

Gosnell, Harold F. 1980. *Truman's Crises: A Political Biography of Harry S. Truman.* Westport, Conn.: Greenwood Press.

Hager, George. 1993a. "Latest CBO Figures Support Clinton Deficit Projection: But Forecasters Deflate Reduction Package Total, Warn That Sustained Economic Health Is a Must." *Congressional Quarterly Weekly Report* 51 (Sept. 11): 2376–77.

———. 1993b. "1985 All Over Again?" *Congressional Quarterly Weekly Report* 51 (July 24): 1936.

———. 1993c. "1993 Deal: Remembrance of Things Past: With Democratic Congresses and Limited Options, New Package Is Similar to 1990 Version." *Congressional Quarterly Weekly Report* 51 (Aug. 7): 2130–31.

Hamby, Alonzo L. 1973. *Beyond the New Deal: Harry S. Truman and American Liberalism.* New York: Columbia University Press.

Hershey, Marjorie Randon. 1992. "The Constructed Explanation: Interpreting Election Results in the 1984 Presidential Race." *Journal of Politics* 54:943–76.

Hook, Janet, and the *Congressional Quarterly* staff. 1993. "Democrats Hail 'Productivity,' But Image Problems Remain." *Congressional Quarterly Weekly Report* 51 (Dec. 11): 3355–57.

Howell, William, Scott Adler, Charles Cameron, and Charles Riemann. 2000. "Divided Government and the Legislative Productivity of Congress, 1945–94." *Legislative Studies Quarterly* 25:285–312.

Ivins, Molly. 1994. "Even Though No One's Looking at the Scoreboard." *Boston Globe,* Nov. 20.

Johnson, Haynes, and David S. Broder. 1996. *The System: The American Way of Politics at the Breaking Point.* Boston: Little, Brown.

Jones, Charles O. 1994. *The Presidency in a Separated System.* Washington, D.C.: Brookings Institution Press.

———. 1995. Personal communication with author, via E-mail.

Kaufman, Burton I. 1993. *The Presidency of James Earl Carter Jr.* Lawrence: University Press of Kansas.

Kelley, Stanley, Jr. 1983. *Interpreting Elections.* Princeton: Princeton University Press.

Kenworthy, Tom, and Gary Lee. 1994. "The Green Gridlock: Hopes for a Flowering of Environmental Laws Are Falling Flat." *Washington Post National Weekly Edition,* Sept. 26–Oct. 2, 14.

Kesselman, Mark. 1961. "Presidential Leadership in Congress on Foreign Policy." *Midwest Journal of Political Science* 5:284–89.

Koenig, Louis W. 1962. "Kennedy and the 87th Congress." In *American Government Annual, 1962–1963,* ed. Ivan Hinderaker. New York: Holt, Rinehart and Winston.

Kranish, Michael. 1994. "Legacy of the Bush Years Blooming in the Clinton Era." *Boston Globe,* Oct. 23.

Krehbiel, Keith. 1996. "Institutional and Partisan Sources of Gridlock: A Theory of Divided and Unified Government." *Journal of Theoretical Politics* 8:7–40.

Langdon, Steve. 1993. "Clinton Prevails on Capitol Hill despite Poor Showing in Polls." *Congressional Quarterly Weekly Report* 51 (Sept. 25): 2527.

———. 1994. "Clinton's High Victory Rate Conceals Disappointments." *Congressional Quarterly Weekly Report* 52 (Dec. 31): 3619–20.

"Legislative Summary." 1994. *Congressional Quarterly Weekly Report* 52 (Nov. 5): 3148–49.

Light, Paul C. 1982. *The President's Agenda: Domestic Policy Choice from Kennedy to Carter (with Notes on Ronald Reagan)*. Baltimore: Johns Hopkins University Press.

Lindblom, Charles E. 1965. *The Intelligence of Democracy: Decision Making through Mutual Adjustment*. New York: Free Press.

Link, Arthur S. 1954. *Woodrow Wilson and the Progressive Era, 1910–1917*. New York: Harper and Brothers.

Manegold, Catherine S. 1994. "Senate Republicans Deal a Major Defeat to Labor." *New York Times,* July 13.

Mayhew, David R. 1991. *Divided We Govern: Lawmaking, Investigations, and Party Control, 1946–1990*. New Haven: Yale University Press.

———. 1993a. *Divided We Govern: Lawmaking, Investigations, and Party Control, 1946–1990*. Rev. ed. New Haven: Yale University Press.

———. 1993b. "Let's Stick with the Longer List." *Polity* 25:485–88.

McCoy, Donald R. 1984. *The Presidency of Harry S. Truman*. Lawrence: University Press of Kansas.

Moynihan, Daniel Patrick. 1995. "The Professionalization of Reform II." *The Public Interest,* no. 121:39.

Neustadt, Richard E. 1955. "Presidency and Legislation: Planning the President's Program." *American Political Science Review* 49:980–1021.

New York Times. 1993. Editorial, July 26.

———. 1994. Editorial, Oct. 9.

Oppenheimer, Bruce I. 1996. "The Importance of Elections in a Strong Congressional Party Era: The Effect of Unified versus Divided Government." In *Do Elections Matter?* ed. Benjamin Ginsberg and Alan Stone, 3d ed. Armonk, N.Y.: M. E. Sharpe.

Patterson, James T. 1967. *Congressional Conservatism and the New Deal*. Lexington: University Press of Kentucky.

Pear, Robert. 1995. "Clinton Decides to Control, but Not Cut, the Deficit." *New York Times,* Feb. 5.

Priest, Dana, and Michael Weisskopf. 1994. "Death from a Thousand Cuts: White House Mistakes and Rabid Washington Partisanship Killed Health Care Reform." *Washington Post National Weekly Edition,* Oct. 17–23, 9–10.

Reichard, Gary W. 1975. *The Reaffirmation of Republicanism: Eisenhower and the Eighty-third Congress*. Knoxville: University of Tennessee Press.

Rohde, David W. 1991. *Parties and Leaders in the Postreform House*. Chicago: University of Chicago Press.

Rosenbaum, David E. 1993. "Beyond the Superlatives: Budget Bill Is Neither Biggest Deficit Cutter Nor the Biggest Tax Rise in Recent Years." *New York Times,* Aug. 5.

———. 1994. "Bill to Revamp Financing of Campaigns Fails Again." *New York Times,* Oct. 1.

Rovner, Julie. 1995. "Congress and Health Care Reform 1993–1994." In *Intensive Care: How Congress Shapes Health Policy,* ed. Thomas E. Mann and Norman J. Ornstein. Washington, D.C.: American Enterprise Institute and Brookings Institution Press.

Schick, Allen. 1995. "How a Bill Did Not Become a Law." In *Intensive Care: How Congress Shapes Health Policy,* ed. Thomas E. Mann and Norma J. Ornstein. Washington, D.C.: American Enterprise Institute and Brookings Institution Press.

Seelye, Katharine Q. 1994. "Clinton and Allies Rediscover Their Voice in Writing Epitaph for Congress." *New York Times,* Oct. 9.

Skocpol, Theda. 1987. "A Society without a 'State'? Political Organization, Social Conflict, and Welfare Provision in the United States." *Journal of Public Policy* 7:349–71.

Stein, Herbert. 1993. "Don't Fault D.C. for the Slow Recovery." *New York Times,* Sept. 19.

Sundquist, James S. 1968. *Politics and Policy: The Eisenhower, Kennedy, and Johnson Years.* Washington, D.C.: Brookings Institution Press.

Toner, Robin. 1994. "Health Impasse Souring Voters, New Poll Finds." *New York Times,* Sept. 13.

Truman, David B. 1959. *The Congressional Party.* New York: Wiley.

USA Today. 1994. "Many Laws Were Left in Limbo This Session." October 6, 4A.

Vogel, David. 1981. "The 'New' Social Regulation in Historical and Comparative Perspective." In *Regulation in Perspective: Historical Essays,* ed. Thomas K. McCraw. Cambridge: Harvard University Press.

Waldman, Steven. 1995. *The Bill.* New York: Viking.

Washington Post. 1994. Editorial, Oct. 7, A24.

Washington Post National Weekly Edition. 1994. Editorial, Sept. 5–11, 27.

Weidenbaum, Murray. 1991. "Return of the 'R' Word: The Regulatory Assault on the Economy." *Policy Review,* no. 58:40–43.

Wessel, David. 1993. "Deficit-Cutting Bill Bears a Resemblance to 1990 Predecessor; But Differences May Be Crucial; Realistic Economic View, Increase in Taxes Are Cited." *Wall Street Journal,* Aug. 3.

Wirls, Daniel. 1995. "United Government, Divided Congress? The Senate and the Democratic Agenda in the 103d Congress." Paper presented at the annual conference of the American Political Science Association, Chicago, Aug. 31–Sept. 3.

Yang, John E. 1993. "Why Does the Budget Argument Sound So Familiar? Because We've Heard It All Before — Three Years Ago." *Washington Post National Weekly Edition,* July 26 – Aug. 1, 20.

Zuckman, Jill, and John Aloysius Farrell. 1994. "Partisanship Derailed Congress's Fast Start." *Boston Globe,* Oct. 9.

6

U.S. Policy Waves in Comparative Context

During the twentieth century, the United States has seen three waves of particularly ambitious lawmaking — the Progressive era, the New Deal era, and the 1960s–70s.[1] (This ignores legislative activity during the two world wars.) The country has also seen a major retrenchment of state activity highlighted by Ronald Reagan's program of 1981.

Patterns of "public politics" have accompanied and largely caused, at least in a proximate sense, these lawmaking waves. By "public politics" I mean a wide range of activities through which people try to affect what governments do, that reach large audiences through media coverage, and that sometimes achieve their aims. Included are elections, strikes, riots, demonstrations, media muckraking, official investigations, and relevant actions by political movements, reformers, think-tank builders, parties, government commissions, and elected officeholders. This is a broad net.

During the same four twentieth-century periods, many other developed countries have experienced quite similar policy waves backgrounded by quite similar patterns of "public politics." The other countries' waves and patterns have not been identical to ours, but they have been intriguingly similar. This holds even for the U.S. Progressive era, which, of all the periods in question, has been studied least often in comparative perspective.

If the above is true, it is food for thought — not least about explanations of policy making that go beyond the proximate ones supplied by the "public politics" of the United States or any other country. Why do policy-making thrusts and attendant styles of "public politics" appear in many places nearly simultaneously? Explanations based on "co-occurring conditions" and "contagion" come to mind.

Before considering these explanations, my argument will proceed through stylized accounts, for each of the four twentieth-century periods, of lawmaking and its associated "public politics" in the United States and elsewhere. Except for the United States in the 1960s–70s, these accounts rely on standard secondary sources. I hope I do not do great injustice to them or the history they cover.

The United States in the Progressive Era

Because much of the pioneering lawmaking of the Progressive era occurred in individual states, it makes sense to examine the states as well as the nation as a whole. Legislative activity was at a high pitch in the states from roughly 1905 through 1914; on Capitol Hill the peak period was 1906 through 1916.[2] Major themes included government efficiency, regulation of industry, progressive taxation, social reform, and democratization of public processes and institutions. In the states, reformers enacted process innovations such as corrupt practices acts and the direct primary, recall, referendum, and initiative throughout the era. Substantively, the state-level agenda shifted from railroad regulation around 1905 to items such as workmen's compensation, child labor codes, mothers' pensions, and maximum-hour laws for women after about 1910. Massachusetts passed the country's first minimum wage law. At the national level, two enactments in 1906 — Theodore Roosevelt's Hepburn Act regulating railroads and his Pure Food and Drug Act — keynoted the era. Congresses under Taft in 1909–13 voted more railroad regulation, created the Department of Labor and the Children's Bureau, approved the Sixteenth Amendment authorizing a federal income tax and the Seventeenth to elect senators directly, and dismantled the conservative House leadership hierarchy developed by Speakers Reed and Cannon. Congresses under Wilson in 1913–16 produced, among other things, the Federal Reserve Act, the Clayton Antitrust Act, the Federal Trade Commission, a progressive income tax code, and a variety of labor enactments — though not welfare-state transfer programs; mothers' pensions at the state level were the chief such U.S. initiative during the Progressive era.[3]

What was the era's "public politics" background? The presidential election of 1904, waged mainly over the tariff, seems to have had little to do with the onset of reform. Rather, analysts write of a "turning-point [in] the weight of opinion" or a "new political mood" of reform activism that set in rather abruptly in 1905–6.[4] With journalistic muckraking serving as a prod, movement activity erupted. The American Federation of Labor, to name one organization, inserted itself into electoral politics with unprecedented energy in 1906–9.[5] Much of the educated public came to enlist in Progressive causes that engendered laws throughout the era — for example, a women's movement that maneuvered the establishment of the Children's Bureau in 1912.[6] In controversy and intensity of public involvement in politics, Taft's years seem to have exceeded Roosevelt's: "The simmering discontents of the previous decade boiled over [in 1909] into full-blown political turmoil. At the same time the insurgencies and reform movements of the time spewed forth a welter of exciting, unsettling ideas and doctrines."[7] The International Workers of the World triggered some of the notable strikes of U.S. history — Los Angeles (printers) in 1911, Lawrence (textile workers) in 1912, and Paterson (textile workers) in 1913. The American Socialist party grew to its peak strength in 1912, electing many mayors after 1910.

In the early Progressive era particularly, elected executives pressed legislatures in the cause of reform. Chiefly, as with Robert La Follette in Wisconsin, Charles Evans Hughes in New York, and Theodore Roosevelt in Washington, D.C., that meant Republican executives confronting Republican legislatures. In general, the executive reformers came away dissatisfied — Congress in 1907–9 stonewalled Theodore Roosevelt and his program, for example. Small surprise that the chief targets of the era's democratizing reforms, aside from party organizations, were the U.S. House and Senate and the state legislatures (which could be circumvented, it was hoped, through initiatives and referenda). After about 1910, cross-party coalitions of insurgent Republicans and Democrats came into their own as enacters of reform legislation — in Massachusetts, North Dakota, and New Jersey, for example, as well as under President Taft in 1911–13. The Republican party self-destructed into Progressive and orthodox fragments in 1912. Wilson as president won his chance at "party government" starting in 1913 (though he had just governed New Jersey no less effectively in harness with a Republican state senate), as did new Democratic majorities in, for example, New York and Ohio and other states. Many of the last Progressive governments were Democratic party affairs.

Elsewhere, 1905 to 1913

In Europe as in the United States, 1905–6 was a political watershed in governments' policy stances and actions. Outside Britain (and unlike the United States), one reason for this was strikes and demonstrations in the revolutionary year of 1905. Verdicts by the then small European electorates do not seem to have played a role. To judge by its issue content, for example, the British Liberals' sweeping election victory of 1906 did not provide any more of the mandate for reform than did Theodore Roosevelt's landslide of 1904.[8]

What were the new stances and actions? According to one account that also brings to mind Theodore Roosevelt, Europe's post-1905 governments "were very consciously 'technocratic,' for they intended to use the power of the State to eliminate social evils." "In most European countries, the years from 1906 to 1909 were self-consciously progressive; technocrats well to the fore."[9] During 1906 through 1909 or so, leaders of many governments announced eye-catching programs that featured some mix of increased central taxation, government efficiency, labor laws, social welfare instruments, and various democratizing moves. That was true, for example, of Clemenceau's 17-point program in 1906 in France, Giolitti's program in Italy, the Campbell-Bannerman then Asquith program in Britain, and also Deakin's 1906 program of welfare-state nationalism in Australia.

But also like Theodore Roosevelt's, most such programs failed or only partly succeeded. Government leaders could not put them through their legislative bodies. Clemenceau won only one of his 17 points. Giolitti encountered resistance. In Britain, Lloyd George's controversial 1909 budget foundered in the House of Lords. Bülow in Germany, in search of more revenue, ran up against the restrictive Prussian voter franchise that colored his parliament. In Britain, Germany, and to some extent Italy, as in the United States, prominent democratizing moves that followed during 1908–11 took aim at obstructive legislative bodies. (Lloyd George won out over the House of Lords through the Parliament Act of 1911, and Giolitti expanded the Italian suffrage, but Germany took no action.)[10]

But that was not all. As in the United States, strikes, demonstrations, and movement activity like that by women's suffragists increased in 1909–10. Labor unrest produced a general strike in Sweden in 1909 and one major strike after another in France during 1909–13 and Britain during 1910–14.[11] "After 1909, almost all European countries went into a period of relative chaos."[12] It was against this background that governments enacted labor reforms and some of their major social-welfare instruments of the century — for example, Britain's National Insurance Act of 1911, a comprehensive German measure that same year (updating Bismarck's), and Sweden's Pension Act of 1913.[13] France also experienced a high tide of welfare-state action during these years, but as in the United States, that high tide was not very high.[14] In general, in Europe as well as the United States in 1906–14, reforms percolated through governments in ways more complicated than theories of party government would suggest. It was not a great party age.

The New Deal Era in the United States

As a surge of lawmaking aimed at recovery or reform, the New Deal era arguably extended from 1932 through 1938. Under Hoover in 1932, a resuscitated coalition of Democrats and insurgent Republicans passed significant labor, relief, and progressive-tax initiatives. Franklin Roosevelt's "hundred days" in the spring of 1933 set a new standard for legislative productivity; that season's National Industrial Recovery Act (NRA) and Agricultural Adjustment Act (AAA) headed an enactment list that included relief, securities regulation, banking deposit insurance, and the Tennessee Valley Authority. Just as remarkable were the second hundred days of the summer of 1935; that season yielded arguably the New Deal's two most important measures — the Wagner Labor Relations Act and the Social Security Act — as well as a controversial tax-the-rich measure and a breakup of public utility holding companies. More disappointing to New Dealers, but still notable, was a series of 1937–38 measures that addressed public housing and farm tenancy, established a national minimum wage, and primed the economy.[15]

The background to the 1932 and 1933 lawmaking was an overriding sense of depression emergency that produced the 1932 Democratic election landslide and licensed Roosevelt's quasi-corporatist experiments with the economy through the AAA and NRA. In general, the enactments of the "First New Deal" had a reformist Democratic or Progressive edge; nonetheless a problem-solving, "coalition of the whole" atmosphere persisted through most of Roosevelt's first two years. Much different was the environment of 1935–37, which brought, in Schlesinger's phrase, a "politics of upheaval." Great nationwide strikes occurred in 1934, evidently with consequence on Capitol Hill: "It is unlikely that the NLRA [the Wagner Act] would have been passed without the labor upsurge of 1934–1935."[16] Talented competitors in a 1935–36 contest to mobilize the public included Huey Long (to whom the Wealth Tax Act of 1935 was said to owe, indirectly), the Townsend movement (whose pressure for old age pensions was felt in Congress in 1935), the radio priest Father Charles E. Coughlin, and the Communist party (working through, for example, the incipient CIO). There was a uniquely powerful upwelling of the Left, and Roosevelt shifted his coalitional base to encompass it — by words and actions and through alliances with, for example, the CIO, the Farm-Labor party in Minnesota, the Progressive party in Wisconsin, and the American Labor party in New York. One result was a bitter ideological polarization of

American politics that, starting in 1938, cast the House Un-American Activities Committees against the New Deal Left. That polarization stayed prominent until the late 1940s.

Elsewhere, 1932 to 1938

For policy making in the 1930s, the first thing one notices across a wide range of countries is *dis*similarity.[17] That does not help my case. To be sure, the United States, in being open to deficits and demand stimulation, resembled Sweden under the Social Democrats and Germany under the Nazis, but that scarcely exhausts the three-way comparison. The decade's politics seem to merit this generalization: Parties really did have distinctive programs — or assembled them on the spot, as in the case of the New Dealers — and it made a considerable difference which parties or coalitions ruled. Britain and Australia, run by Conservative-dominated "national governments" after 1931, stayed close to economic orthodoxy. New Zealand experienced a burst of welfare-state reform when Labour took power in 1935. Sweden had its well-known Social Democratic innovations. France achieved a historic labor-relations pact under Léon Blum's 1936 Popular Front. Belgium, run by a fresh Social Democratic government starting in 1935, enacted "a 'New Deal' type of emergency program" that year and then a comprehensive labor program (emulating France's next door) in 1936. Even Canada fits in a perverse way: A 1935 Tory government, beset by demagoguery and discontent matching those in the United States, enacted all at once a vast program replicating most of the New Deal. But a new Liberal government killed nearly all of it a few months later.[18] One pattern, then, for the decade is: distinctive party programs and action, but not cross-national policy commonality.

Still, one commonality involving the United States does appear. That is the widespread incidence of movement activity, strikes, and other direct action from 1934 onward accompanied by the upwelling of the Left. The second New Deal of 1935, though not the first of 1933, arguably belongs in a category with the 1936 Popular Front governments of France and Spain. Ideological commitment, strikes, and roiling movements supplied an atmosphere for those governments too.[19] Also, directly contemporaneous with the 1935–36 New Deal were the ambitious Canadian Tory program (though not under Left-coalition auspices) and the New Zealand Labour and Belgian Social Democratic programs (though I have not come across evidence of underpinning strikes, mass action, or Popular Front enthusiasm in the latter two cases). In the West in general, as in the United States, the energizing of the Left in the mid-1930s produced a bitter ideological polarization that did much to frame domestic political discourse until the coming of the Cold War in 1947–48.

The United States in the 1960s and 1970s

Elsewhere I have argued that a long surge of national lawmaking took place in the United States from 1963 through 1975 or 1976. Important statutes kept winning passage in unusually high volume, constituting a major, continuous thrust toward greater federal spending and regulation.[20] Robert J. Lampman identifies 1965 through 1976 as the years between which the country's postwar surge in social welfare spending took place — rising from 11.2 to a peak 19.3 percent of GNP.[21] Seventy-seven new social programs were established under Johnson in 1963–68; forty-four under Nixon and Ford in 1969–76.[22] Major items included Medicare, Medicaid, and housing, education, and antipoverty initiatives under Johnson, but also an ambitious expansion of entitlements under Nixon — for example, Supplemental Security Income (SSI) for the aged, disabled, and blind; greatly multiplied food-stamps assistance; publicly financed "CETA jobs" for the unemployed; and a 23 percent hike in social security benefits (controlling for inflation) in 1969–72. Major civil rights acts passed in 1964, 1965, and 1968 under Johnson. Drives to regulate industry gained momentum under Johnson but peaked under Nixon. Fourteen statutes and two new agencies to that end accrued under Johnson; eighteen statutes and six new agencies under Nixon.[23] Instances in the consumer field were the Traffic Safety Act of 1966, the Fair Packaging and Labeling Act of 1966, and the Consumer Product Safety Act of 1972. Landmark environmental acts — all passed under Nixon — included the National Environmental Policy Act (NEPA) of 1969, the Clean Air Act of 1970, and the Water Pollution Control Act of 1972. Other regulatory instruments included the Occupational Safety and Health Act (OSHA) of 1970 and the Federal Election Campaign Act of 1974. This account could go on; the general point is that a great deal kept happening.

Under the heading of public politics, Johnson's leadership in the wake of John Kennedy's assassination counted heavily. That time, until November 1964, was probably the most productive legislative season since 1935; it yielded the Higher Education Act of 1963, the Wilderness Act of 1964, the Food Stamp Act of 1964, the (delayed) Kennedy tax cut, the Civil Rights Act of 1964, and the Economic Opportunity (antipoverty) Act of 1964. The landslide election of 1964, producing a rare two-to-one Democratic edge in the House, empowered that party to enact a program it had been preparing for a decade — including Medicare and the Elementary and Secondary Education Act (ESEA) of 1965. Beyond that, much lawmaking seems to have owed to movement activity, other direct political action, and events. Civil-rights demonstrations, the violence in Birmingham and Selma, and the assassination of the Rev. Martin Luther King Jr. seem to have supplied necessary conditions for enacting the civil rights instruments of 1964 (public accommodations), 1965 (voting rights), and 1968 (open housing). All three acts were passed by large cross-party minorities. Anyone who lived through 1968–74 will remember the extraordinarily political turmoil of that time. Its ingredients were an antiwar movement that pursued legislative and other courses of action; a consumer movement that provoked several statutes; an environmental movement that mushroomed around 1970 and contributed to several more statutes; and a new women's movement that lobbied Congress with great success in 1971–72 (the Equal Rights Amendment won approval then, although the states would not ratify it).[24] In general, congressional liberals responding to various causes had good luck passing laws under Nixon. Often they had administration support, as on entitlements expansion and some of the major environmental moves.

Elsewhere, 1963 through 1976

I will not try to track the equivalent of "regulation" in other countries. But government spending is easier, and the story is familiar and more or less the same everywhere. Figures marshaled by standard sources echo the surge in U.S. social spending between 1965 and 1976: Japan's social spending rose especially sharply (from 14 to 19 percent of the budget) between 1965 and 1975; total British government spending rose from 33.6 to 45.1 percent of GNP between 1964 and 1975. In one study of eighteen countries, the mean social share of GDP rose from 13.7 to 26.5 percent between 1960 and 1981. In another study of eighteen countries, mean government revenue rose from 28.5 to 38.5 percent of GDP between 1960 and 1975.[25] In direction of change, at least, the United States during this era was just one of the pack.

What kinds of public politics accompanied these public sector surges? This subject can only be touched on here, but certain interesting patterns appear. In some countries, ambitious party programs of the early or mid-1960s, presented and carried through in the style of the Democrats' Great Society program, seem to have made the difference. That was true of the Canadian Liberals' pension, assistance, and medical insurance plans of 1965–66; the Dutch confessional parties' "mid-sixties social policy surge"; and the Italian center-left coalition's move into education spending in 1963–68.[26] But in later years, events and pressure seem to have figured more prominently in forcing government policy initiatives. Youth turmoil spread across Europe in 1967–68; leftist assertiveness grew in the Socialist parties; Italy in particular entered "a most extraordinary period of social ferment" featuring labor unrest; strikes rocked British politics in the early 1970s.[27] In this atmosphere, the Italian public sector swelled haphazardly in the early 1970s as a response to pressure.[28] The Japanese government shifted to welfare expansion in the early 1970s in reaction to local election losses to the Left.[29] Edward Heath's Conservative government in Britain took measures between 1970 and 1974 that were not in the Tory tradition — wage controls, nationalization of a major company, a surrender to unions — at the same time the Nixon administration was making un-Republican moves.[30] But note that even in the mid-1960s there had not existed a clear relation of the classical kind between the left- or right-leaningness of parties or coalitions and their records in office. Recall that, for example, a confessional coalition spurred in Dutch welfare expansion of the mid-1960s (Labour was in opposition).[31]

The United States in the Age of Carter and Reagan

Among recent U.S. measures aimed at cutting taxes, trimming expenditures, fostering monetarism, or deregulating industry — today's family of conservative economic thrusts — Ronald Reagan's $750 billion tax cut and omnibus expenditure cut (OBRA, or Gramm-Latta II) unquestionably stand out. But those two major 1981 measures are not all. The legislative history of deregulation is instructive. Starting in 1975, federal acts to deregulate business affected securities (1975), state fair-trade laws (1975), railroads (1976 and 1980), natural gas (1978), airlines (1978), banking (1980 and 1982), and trucking (1980). A Democratic Congress passed a surprisingly business-oriented tax revision in 1978. California adopted its Proposition 13 tax cut in 1978. Helping along conservative causes in the late 1970s were the Sagebrush Rebellion, the newly prominent religious Right, the Business Roundtable, a new cluster of well-funded think tanks, and some aggressive right-wing political action committees. By the end of the Carter administration in 1980, the political environment had been well softened up for Reagan. Much of the policy turnaround associated with his presidency had already come to pass under a Democratic party fast losing faith in its welfarism and Keynesianism.[32]

Elsewhere around 1980

Two commonalities stand out. Especially in the English-speaking world, government policy shifts toward free markets took place at about the same time as the one in the United States. And they were carried out, though with nuances, by parties of both the Left and Right.[33] A British Labour government unraveled in 1976–79 rather as did Carter's: Keynesianism and public spending were abandoned in a muddled and demoralized lead-in to Thatcher's victory in 1979.[34] Mulroney's Tory government in Canada tried out some of the new ideas. In Australia and New Zealand, Labour governments elected in 1983 and 1984 radically deregulated their economies. The New Zealand government (although not Australia's, where unions remained stronger) let unemployment rise and moved abruptly away from progressive taxation.[35] Elsewhere the trends are cloudier, though in general the case for cross-national policy commonality, regardless of party, seems strong enough. France, for example, after "deplanifying" in the late 1970s, experimented with socialist planning following Mitterrand's 1981 election, but then blended back, still under Mitterrand, into what seems to have been a European thrust toward freer markets in the 1980s.[36] One contribution to the policy commonality is that virtually everywhere during these years, parties of the left moved to the right.[37]

Explaining the Commonalities: Coincidence, Contagion, and Public Politics

In each of the four eras, at least in some respects, a wave of policy making and certain patterns of popular politics in America corresponded to a similar wave and patterns in other countries. Here are some reflections about these accounts.

First, they address what and when, not why. If they are halfway plausible, the question of why arises. Why the commonalities across borders? I will not pursue this question here except to suggest that both "co-occurring conditions" and "contagion" explanations seem to figure in varying mixes as answers. In some cases, it is easy to point to conditions co-occurring across national boundaries that no doubt helped to spur governments into similar policy moves nearly simultaneously. The growth of industrial labor forces and union movements in the early twentieth century probably underpinned, somehow, the labor and welfare initiatives undertaken by many governments around 1910. Likewise the coming of age of baby boomers triggered higher-education spending in many countries in the 1960s. Those are slow-acting causes. At a faster level, simultaneous experience of phases of the international business cycle spurred similar actions—as with the depression rate of the 1930s and the oil shocks of the 1970s.

All this is commonplace, but note that social and economic problems do not announce themselves or their remedies unproblematically. Ideas need to intrude. The "contagion" of ideas across national boundaries can shape common responses in a context where conditions co-occur, as in the case of the distinctive and fairly unified response of members of the Organization for Economic Cooperation and Development to economic troubles around 1980. Belgium copied Blum's program in 1936; Canada evidently copied Franklin Roosevelt's in 1935.

More interesting, though, is the wide range of cross-national policy-making commonality where no very clear case for co-occurring conditions exists — at least nothing on the order of a depression or an oil shock. There, contagion explanations look like a particularly good bet. Take, for example, policy making in the United States and elsewhere around 1910. Notwithstanding the parallel growth of industrial labor forces, it would be a tough assignment to anchor the policy-making commonality of that era in co-occurring conditions. A better idea might be shared impulses or aspirations commonly expressed. One critic of American exceptionalism has recently written of the United States during the Progressive era as the "scene of a cosmopolitan interchange" and "a prime site for the study of transnational ideologies."[38] Policy ideas evidently crossed the Atlantic fast both ways. Much U.S. policy making in the twentieth century probably follows this model, although scholarship on the point is sparse.[39]

Contagion, moreover, can apply not just to policy initiatives but to the styles of public politics underpinning them. That is the most intriguing idea suggested by the four foregoing accounts: national leaders aggressively mobilizing publics behind ambitious programs after 1905; movement activity in 1905–14; political strikes in 1909–13; strikes and movements again in 1934–37; the energizing of the Left in the mid-1930s; state-enhancing party programs in the mid-1960s; student protest in 1968; movements and strikes again in 1968–73 — all these were transnational phenomena. All of them shaped policy making in the United States and elsewhere. The cross-national simultaneity of political styles, formations, and tactics strongly suggests idea contagion as an explanation, but, again, evidence needs to be assembled.

A second reflection is that political scientists tend to overrate parties and elections as engines of U.S. policy making. Transfixed by election returns, realignment theories, and models of party government, we tend to ignore other features of public politics and to present an impoverished picture of relations between the public and the government. Much in the foregoing accounts backs up this view. Consider, for example, the policy-rich junctures of 1909–13, 1935–37, and 1969–74 in the United States and elsewhere. To do justice to these times, one needs to give attention to direct action, political movements, ideological impulses, and general turmoil. To be sure, parties won elections during these years and sometimes passed programs. But beyond that, governments got caught up in the currents of ideologies and movements and assumed what looks like a propitiating role. Both the Nixon administration and the Italian government of around 1970, for example, beleaguered by angry elements of their publics, presided over surprising policy initiatives, possibly as a consequence. The expansion of entitlements, after all, can be a remedy for disorder. The same explanation may be applied to the years between 1909 and 1913.

Third, it seems to me that U.S. political parties have played rather different policy roles in different eras of the twentieth century, and political science's theoretical tradition has evolved accordingly. Herbert Croly, who gave short shrift to parties as public instruments — instead emphasizing executive leadership and direct democracy — was as suitable a spokesman as one could imagine for the Progressive era. He gave written form to the politics he witnessed. A generation later, E. E. Schattschneider captured the unique, Promethean promise of parties in the 1930s. Then, here and in Europe, parties exhibited great mobilizing potential and made programmatic commitments that seemed to be distinct and reliable. "Party government" seemed to be a way to reconstruct societies. Another generation later in the 1950s, 1960s, and 1970s, with Keynesian macroeconomics accepted by all sides and incremental state expansion permitted by economic growth, Anthony Downs's model worked well. Party "bidding" at the center for voter support, to use the British term, came to characterize politics. So far, there does not seem to exist a successor model for the 1980s and beyond.

As a last reflection, why have U.S. political scientists addressed this country's policy making in a fashion largely innocent of international comparisons? The comparisons are there to be drawn, and not just during the twentieth century. To go back farther in time, the U.S. switch to conservatism and imperialism in the mid-1890s had European correlates — for example, the new Salisbury-Balfour regime in Britain: "Everywhere in Europe, there were governments of the right."[40] Wouldn't a good look at those turn-of-the-century settings elsewhere promise more payoff — for illuminating *this* country's politics — than yet another study of the McKinley-Bryan realignment of 1896? A bit earlier, American Populism had a striking counterpart in New Zealand — where works by Americans Edward Bellamy and Henry George served as ideological texts — during exactly that movement's high tide here in the early 1890s.[41] It was evidently an earlier transnational reform wave. Even the Civil War and Reconstruction era, which seem about as homegrown as anything can be, had similarities in Europe, where liberal reform enjoyed a continental surge: "This was a decade of reform, of political liberalization, even of some concession to what was called 'the forces of democracy.' "[42] The comparative question is a good one to ask, as, to go back yet farther, R. R. Palmer memorably did for the late eighteeth century in his *Age of the Democratic Revolution.* "Why did X happen in many places?" can sometimes give better traction than "Why did X happen in the United States?"

Notes

For their thoughtful comments on an early draft of this work, I would like to thank John Aldrich, Robert Dahl, Eileen McDonagh, Herbert Kaufman, Joseph LaPalombara, Karen Orren, and David Stebenne. This essay was originally published as chap. 17 in Lawrence C. Dodd and Calvin Jillson (eds.), *New Perspectives on American Politics* (Washington, D.C.: CQ Press, 1994). Copyright © 1994 CQ Press, a division of Congressional Quarterly Inc.

1. See for example Theda Skocpol, "A Society without a 'State'? Political Organization, Social Conflict, and Welfare Provision in the United States," *Journal of Public Policy* 7 (October–December 1987): 364–65; Richard A. Harris, "A Decade of Reform," in *Remaking American Politics*, ed. Richard A. Harris and Sidney A. Milkis (Boulder, Colo.: Westview, 1989), 5, 9; David R. Mayhew, *Divided We Govern: Party Control, Lawmaking, and Investigations, 1946–1990* (New Haven: Yale University Press, 1991), chap. 6.

2. General sources on the states are Richard L. McCormick, "The Discovery That Business Corrupts Politics: A Reappraisal of the Origins of Progressivism," *American Historical Review* 86 (April 1981): 266–68; George E. Mowry, *The Era of Theodore Roosevelt, 1900–1912* (New York: Harper, 1958), 71–84; and David Sarasohn, *The Party of Reform: Democrats in the Progressive Era* (Jackson: University Press of Mississippi, 1989), 112–18. General sources on the national government include Mowry, *Era of Theodore Roosevelt*, chaps. 7, 11–14; Sarasohn, *Party of Reform*, chaps. 1, 3, 4, 6; John Milton Cooper, Jr., *Pivotal Decades: The United States, 1900–1920* (New York: Norton, 1990), 46–48, 90–102, 109–21, 145–57, 162, 195–202, 212–19, 291, 298, 307–8; Lewis L. Gould, *Reform and Regulation: American Politics, 1900–1916* (New York: Wiley, 1978), 32–33, 51–73, 90–96, 105–6, 149–58, 168–75; Paolo E. Coletta, *The Presidency of William Howard Taft* (Lawrence: University Press of Kansas, 1973), chaps. 3, 5–7, 13; Arthur S. Link, *Woodrow Wilson and the Progressive Era, 1900–1917* (New York: Harper, 1954), chaps. 2, 3, 9; Howard W. Allen, "Geography and Politics: Voting on Reform Issues in the United States Senate, 1911–1916," *Journal of Southern History* 27 (1961): 218.

3. See Theda Skocpol, *Protecting Soldiers and Mothers: The Political Origins of Social Policy in the United States* (Cambridge: Harvard University Press, 1992). For sketches of lawmaking at state and national levels during the Progressive era, see Mayhew, *Divided We Govern*, 146–52.

4. McCormick, "The Discovery," 268; Gould, *Reform and Regulation,* 59. See also Mowry, *Era of Theodore Roosevelt,* chap. 4 and pp. 206–11; Cooper, *Pivotal Decades,* 80–89.

5. Julia Greene, " 'The Strike at the Ballot Box': The American Federation of Labor's Entrance into Election Politics, 1906–1909," *Labor History* 32 (Spring 1991): 165–92.

6. Skocpol, "Protecting Soldiers and Mothers," chap. 8.

7. Cooper, *Pivotal Decades,* 123.

8. See for example Derek Fraser, *The Evolution of the Modern British Welfare State* (London: Macmillan, 1973), 136.

9. Norman Stone, *Europe Transformed, 1878–1919* (Glasgow: Fontana, 1983), 129, 141.

10. This reference covers the preceding two paragraphs. On France: David Thomson, *Democracy in France since 1870* (New York: Oxford University Press, 1969), 173–76. On Italy: Denis Mack Smith, *Italy: A Modern History* (Ann Arbor: University of Michigan Press, 1959), section 7. On Britain: R. C. K. Ensor, *England, 1870–1914* (Oxford: Clarendon Press, 1960), chaps. 12, 13. On Australia: Russel Ward, *Australia* (Englewood Cliffs, N.J.: Prentice-Hall, 1965), 85–97. On Germany: A. J. Ryder, *Twentieth-Century Germany: From Bismarck to Brandt* (New York: Columbia Press, 1973), 78–80. In general: Stone, *Europe Transformed,* 141.

11. Franklin D. Scott, *Sweden: The Nation's History* (Minneapolis: University of Minnesota Press, 1977), 416–17; Thomson, *Democracy in France,* 174; Ensor, *England,* 438–41.

12. Stone, *Europe Transformed,* 144.

13. Ryder, *Twentieth-Century Germany,* 80; Hugh Heclo, *Modern Social Politics in Britain and Sweden* (New Haven: Yale University Press, 1974), chaps. 3, 4; David Thomson, *Europe since Napoleon* (New York: Knopf, 1962), 330; Ensor, *England,* 444–55.

14. Thomson, *Europe since Napoleon,* 329; Thomson, *Democracy in France,* 173–76.

15. See Jordan A. Schwarz, *The Interregnum of Despair: Hoover, Congress, and the Depression* (Urbana: University of Illinois Press, 1970), 78–90 and chaps. 5, 6, 8; William E. Leuchtenburg, *Franklin D. Roosevelt and the New Deal, 1932–1940* (New York: Harper and Row, 1963); Arthur M. Schlesinger, Jr., *The Coming of the New Deal* (Boston: Houghton Mifflin, 1958; Arthur M. Schlesinger, Jr., *The Politics of Upheaval* (Boston: Houghton Mifflin, 1960), 261, chaps. 16–18, and 381–84; James T. Patterson, *Congressional Conservatism and the New Deal: The Growth of the Conservative Coalition in Congress, 1933–1939* (Lexington: University Press of Kentucky, 1967), chap. 2 and 77–80. For a sketch, see Mayhew, *Divided We Govern,* 34, 152–56.

16. David Plotke, "The Wagner Act, Again: Politics and Labor, 1935–37," in *Studies in American Political Development,* vol. 3 (New Haven: Yale University Press, 1989), 117.

17. See Peter A. Gourevitch, "Breaking with Orthodoxy: The Politics of Economic Policy Responses to the Depression of the 1930s," *International Organization* 38 (1984): 95–129; Kim Quayle Hill, *Democracies in Crisis: Public Policy Responses to the Great Depression* (Boulder, Colo.: Westview, 1988), chap. 4; Ekkart Zimmermann and Thomas Saalfeld, "Economic and Political Reactions to the World Economic Crisis of the 1930s in Six European Countries," *International Studies Quarterly* 32 (September 1988): 305–34. This is not a well-trodden subject: "There has been surprisingly little comparative

study of the political forces that shaped the policy choices of different nations in the 1930s, and there are no general theories about these matters indicating a parsimonious way to explore this terrain." Hill, *Democracies in Crisis,* 103.

18. Adolf Sturmthal, *The Tragedy of European Labor, 1918–1939* (New York: Columbia University Press, 1943), chaps. 10, 11; David Thomson, *England in the Twentieth Century* (New York: Penguin, 1979), 147–62; Clive Turnbull, *A Concise History of Australia* (South Yarra, Victoria: Currey-O'Neil, 1983), 143–48; Keith Sinclair, *A History of New Zealand* (London: Allen Lane, 1980), 264–70; J. Bartlett Brebner, *Canada: A Modern History* (Ann Arbor: University of Michigan Press, 1970), chap. 28. On Belgium: Zimmermann and Saalfeld, "Economic and Political Reactions," quotations at 314.

19. Sturmthal, *Tragedy of European Labor,* chaps. 10, 11; H. Stuart Hughes, *Contemporary Europe: A History* (Englewood Cliffs, N.J.: Prentice-Hall, 1961), 238–43, 285–88; Raymond J. Sontag, *A Broken World: 1919–1939* (New York: Harper and Row, 1971), chaps. 10, 11.

20. Mayhew, *Divided We Govern,* chaps. 3, 4. Of the eight stylized presentations, this is the one not based on standard secondary sources. To compile, for *Divided We Govern,* a list of major U.S. federal statutes enacted from 1946 through 1990, I made two "sweeps" through materials for those decades. In the first sweep, I used accounts by contemporary witnesses, chiefly journalists, who sized up the importance of laws just passed as they reported on each of the twenty-two postwar Congresses. In the second sweep, I used recent works of policy history by specialists in forty-three areas, probing them for the authors' judgments about the importance of postwar statutes enacted in their areas. The final overall list includes 267 statutes. This is, strictly speaking, a study of motion — does the government do much at all? — rather than ideological direction, but there can be no doubt about the record of 1963 through 1975–76: The period is characterized by a very high volume of legislation as well as a continuous regulatory and spending thrust.

21. Robert J. Lampman, *Social Welfare Spending: Accounting for Changes from 1950 to 1978* (New York: Academic Press, 1984), 8–9. The figures are for federal, state, and local governments combined, but the federal government took the lead during these years.

22. Robert X. Browning, *Politics and Social Welfare Policy in the United States* (Knoxville: University of Tennessee Press, 1986), 79–83.

23. David Vogel, "The 'New' Social Regulation in Historical and Comparative Perspective," in *Regulation in Perspective: Historical Essays,* ed. Thomas K. McCraw (Cambridge: Harvard University Press, 1981), 161; Murray L. Weidenbaum, *Business, Government, and the Public* (Englewood Cliffs, N.J.: Prentice-Hall, 1977), 5–10.

24. On the women's movement, see Jo Freeman, *The Politics of Women's Liberation: A Case Study of an Emerging Social Movement and Its Relation to the Policy Process* (New York: David McKay, 1975), 202.

25. Bradley M. Richardson and Scott C. Flanagan, *Politics in Japan* (Boston: Little, Brown, 1984), 412; Richard Rose, *Do Parties Make a Difference?* (London: Macmillan, 1984), 121–22; Manfred G. Schmidt, "Learning from Catastrophes: West Germany's Public Policy," in *The Comparative History of Public Policy,* ed. Francis G. Castles (Oxford: Polity Press, 1989), 63; David R. Cameron, "The Expansion of the Public Economy: A Comparative Analysis," *American Political Science Review* 72 (1978): 1244.

26. Brebner, *Canada,* 547; Goren Therborn, "'Pillarization' and 'Popular Movements': Two Variants of Welfare State Capitalism: The Netherlands and Sweden," in *Comparative History of Public Policy,* ed. Castles, 211; Roger Morgan, *West European Politics since 1945: The Shaping of the European Community* (London: B. T. Batsford, 1972), 188; Norman Kogan, *A Political History of Italy: The Postwar Years* (New York: Praeger, 1983), 216.

27. Morgan, *West European Politics,* 177–78, 193; Walter Laqueur, *Europe since Hitler: The Rebirth of Europe* (Baltimore: Penguin, 1970), 440–46; Peter Lane, *Europe since 1945: An Introduction* (London: Batsford Academic and Educational, 1985), 159–60; Derek W. Urwin, *Western Europe since 1945: A Short Political History* (New York: Longman, 1981), chap. 15; Paul Ginsborg, *A History of Contemporary Italy: Society and Politics 1943–1988* (New York: Longman, 1990), chap. 9, quotation at 298.

28. Kogan, *Political History of Italy,* chaps. 16–20; Ginsborg, *History of Contemporary Italy,* chaps. 9, 10.

29. Kent E. Calder, *Crisis and Compensation: Public Policy and Political Stability in Japan, 1949–1986* (Princeton, N.J.: Princeton University Press, 1988), 103–5, 215–18, 357–59, 372–74.

30. Geoffrey Alderman, *Modern Britain: A Domestic History* (London: Croon Helm, 1986), 277; Peter Jenkins, *Mrs. Thatcher's Revolution: The Ending of the Socialist Era* (Cambridge: Harvard University Press, 1988), 13–15.

31. On this general point, see Rose, *Do Parties Make a Difference?* 119–26; Cameron, "Expansion of the Public Economy," 1253–54. In Cameron's study, having a leftist government explains a third of the variance in revenue expansion, but many specified countries work against that relation.

32. See Mayhew, *Divided We Govern,* 93–94, 166–69.

33. Frances G. Castles, "The Dynamics of Policy Change: What Happened to the English-Speaking Nations in the 1980s," *European Journal of Political Research* 18 (September 1990): 491–97.

34. Jenkins, *Mrs. Thatcher's Revolution,* 18–28.

35. Castles, "Dynamics of Policy Change," 494–96.

36. Peter Hall, *Governing the Economy: The Politics of State Intervention in Britain and France* (New York: Oxford University Press, 1986), 185–91 and chap. 8.

37. Seymour Martin Lipset, "The Death of the Third Way: Everywhere but Here, That Is," *The National Interest* (Summer 1990): 25–37.

38. Ian Tyrrell, "American Exceptionalism in an Age of International History," *American Historical Review* 96 (October 1991): 1052.

39. For a good concrete account of how a policy idea traveled from the United States to Britain recently, see Michael M. Atkinson and William D. Coleman, "Policy Networks, Policy Communities and the Problems of Governance," *Governance* 5 (April 1992): 154–80.

40. Stone, *Europe Transformed,* 96.

41. Sinclair, *A History of New Zealand,* chap. 2-II.

42. E. J. Hobsbawm, *The Age of Capital, 1848–1875* (New York: Charles Scribner's Sons, 1975), 71–72, 102–6, quotation at 71.

Presidential Elections and Policy Change
How Much of a Connection Is There?

In analyses of American politics, it would be hard to find a more basic claim or assumption than that major policy changes are owing to the outcomes of presidential elections. Old government policies are abandoned and new ones adopted because of election results. The idea is central to theories of "party government" and "electoral realignments," as well as to more conventional accounts of political processes by historians, political scientists, and journalists.

How true is the claim? Probably less than is commonly believed. Partly because most of us get excited by presidential elections, and partly because we see them as great democratic instruments, we tend to overestimate their causal power. Also, we tend to assume that causal power without actually showing it. In our studies, we zero in on the presumed independent variable — elections — without giving anywhere near the same systematic attention to the presumed dependent variable — policy change. The extreme case is the research design where we look only under the streetlight for lost coins and, sure enough, find them — a recurrent failing of "realignments" scholarship that takes cognizance of policy change only if it occurs just after an alleged "critical" election.

By these customary standards, this essay is a backwards enterprise. I dwell on the dependent variable — policy change, of a sort, during American history

—and only later speculate about what may be causing it. Moreover, presidential elections are made to compete here, at least in a thought experiment, against other potential causes. The causal discussion is organized under four rubrics—elections in general, the actions of political parties, the condition of the economy, and public moods—of which the first and second, though not the third and fourth, assign a prominent role to presidential elections. In general, the first two rubrics do not seem to outperform the second two as producers of policy change.

Lawmaking Surges

The policy change to be investigated here is of a particular kind—legislative "surges" that have produced a large share of the significant statutes enacted during American history. Four times since the 1790s, the national government has legislated in a striking surge pattern. In each case, exceptionally large numbers of major laws kept winning enactment year after year, Congress after Congress, under two or three presidents for a half decade or more. These surges of activity had beginnings and endings (although the boundaries are not always entirely clear). It is as if the system's volume could somehow be turned up to a pitch of accelerated change, stay there awhile, then be lowered again to a pitch of normal slow change.

There were also similarities in statutory content. In the laws of each of the four eras, there was a pronounced thrust toward enhancing the powers, activities, or reach of the national state. Among the means to those ends were increased public expenditure and taxation, new federal programs, direct coercion to the extreme of military occupation, government planning, regulation of the economy, and restructuring of the polity or society through such means as guaranteed individual rights. To be sure, not all the enactments of these eras worked. Many had unanticipated consequences or just failed. But there was substantial policy impact, even if it did not live up to the extraordinary levels of legislative ambition exhibited during these four strenuous times.

The first task here is to make the case for the existence of these four legislative "surges." This will be done chronologically, era by era, in what I hope is sufficient, though not overwhelming, detail. Actual statutes will be emphasized, not catchphrases such as "the New Deal" or various statistics that are often taken to be indicators of legislative action. For the first three eras, the sources are standard secondary writings. For the fourth, the proximate source is David R. Mayhew, *Divided We Govern: Party Control, Lawmaking, and Investigations, 1946–1990.*[1]

1. THE CIVIL WAR AND RECONSTRUCTION ERA: 1861 THROUGH 1875

Moves against slavery and in favor of civil rights provide the obvious theme of this first of the four "surge" eras, but, according to many interpretations, there also existed powerful companion themes of constructing a centralized American state and nourishing a nationwide capitalist economy. The laws of the time reflect these various aims. A sequence of unprecedentedly ambitious lawmaking extended through eight Congresses.

In the early years came moves to enact what amounted to an updated version of Henry Clay's Whig blueprint for an "American system." In early 1861, after the South had seceded from the Union, the lame-duck session of the Congress elected in 1858 enacted the Morrill Tariff Act. That measure initiated a Republican high-tariff regime that endured, despite temporary reductions in duties during the Democratic Cleveland and Wilson administrations, until the 1930s.[2] In 1862 came the Homestead Act, offering federal land to homesteaders for a nominal fee, the Morrill Land-Grant College Act, awarding federal land to the states to construct agricultural and engineering colleges, and the Pacific Railroad Act, providing land subsidies to build a transcontinental railroad. Funding the Civil War required banking measures that had an "American system" theme of centralized control: the Legal Tender Act of 1862 (fostering a national currency) and the National Banking Act of 1863 (creating a national, though not tightly centralized, banking system).[3]

Once the war had begun, Congress enacted central antislavery measures that had had no chance of passage until that time — for example, bans on slavery in the western territories and in the District of Columbia. But in 1863, Lincoln bypassed Congress and the regular lawmaking process by abolishing southern slavery through executive order in his Emancipation Proclamation. Conventional legislative processes regained the initiative in this policy area in early 1865, when Congress approved the Thirteenth Amendment, which outlawed slavery and created the Freedmen's Bureau. After Lincoln's assassination, under President Andrew Johnson, the 39th Congress enacted the Civil Rights Act of 1866, the content of which prefigured the Fourteenth Amendment, approved that amendment later in the same year, and passed the First Reconstruction Act over Johnson's veto in March 1867. That measure imposed military rule on the South and revolutionized southern politics by enfranchising blacks and disfranchising many previously rebellious whites. Three additional Reconstruction Acts followed in 1867 and 1868, as well as the Fifteenth Amendment, which guaranteed suffrage for blacks, in February 1869.[4]

The Fifteenth Amendment is sometimes regarded as the concluding legislative measure of the Reconstruction era. In fact, during the two ensuing Congresses, substantial energy, commitment, and public attention were devoted to enacting five "Enforcement Acts" during 1870, 1871, and 1872, which mandated that the attorney general take steps to make the earlier measures, particularly the Fifteenth Amendment, actually work in the South. The third of these acts is sometimes called the Ku Klux Klan Act because, in effect, it outlawed that organization. By 1875, these measures had largely failed, though some of them were to be drawn upon by the federal government much later during the civil rights revolution of the 1950s and 1960s. The Reconstruction era's last notable measure was the Civil Rights Act of 1875, a project promoted by Massachusetts Senator Charles Sumner as his long career ended, which won enactment during the closing lame-duck session of the Republican Congress that had been elected in 1872.[5]

2. THE PROGRESSIVE ERA: 1906 THROUGH 1916

Moves to bring about government regulation of the economy, the polity, and the society keynoted lawmaking drives during the Progressive era. That much is generally agreed upon, notwithstanding scholarly dissensus otherwise about the aims and achievements of the era. Railroad regulation figured prominently during the early years, labor measures during the later ones, and regulation of parties and elections throughout. New instruments of government were created and funded. For purposes of periodizing, it may help to review events at the state level, where much of the significant reform action occurred. The period of roughly 1905 through 1914 is often cited as the time of high-volume lawmaking in the states, where ambitious reform programs were continually being enacted somewhere or other during those years. The principal instances include Wisconsin in 1903, a pacesetting session dominated by Governor Robert La Follette, as well as 1905, Minnesota in 1905 and 1907, New York in 1907, Georgia in 1907 to 1909, California, New Jersey, and North Dakota in 1911, Massachusetts in 1911 to 1914, New York once again in 1913, and Ohio in 1913 to 1914.[6]

At the national level, President Theodore Roosevelt dramatically opened the Progressive era by winning congressional approval of the Hepburn Act of 1906, a plan to regulate railroad rates that, in the words of Jeffrey K. Tulis, "gave birth to the modern administrative state."[7] To pass it, Roosevelt needed to conduct an eighteen-month campaign to mobilize public opinion and assemble congressional support. Also enacted in 1906 were the Pure Food and Drug Act and the Meat Inspection Act. Roosevelt's last Congress of 1907–9, which did little legislating, aside from the Tillman Act that banned corporate contributions in election campaigns, provides a gap in the sequence. This may be because the White House provided the national legislative agenda during these early Progressive years and, as a general rule, presidents almost never have much luck winning congressional approval of their domestic programs after six years in office (these were Roosevelt's seventh and eighth years).[8]

National lawmaking came to life again in 1909 under President William Howard Taft. Spurred by Democrats and insurgent Republicans, the Republican Congress of 1909–11 passed the Mann-Elkins Act (another stab at railroad regulation), a measure establishing a postal savings system (an idea that had been around for about four decades), and the Sixteenth Amendment (authorizing a federal income tax). The Congress of 1911–13, divided between a Republican Senate and a Democratic House, approved the Seventeenth Amendment that required popular election of U.S. Senators, mandated an eight-hour day for private-sector workers on federal contracts, established a federal Children's Bureau and the Department of Labor, and enacted the third and most ambitious of a 1907, 1910, and 1911 sequence of campaign-finance reforms. These measures, which among other things required disclosure of financial transactions by congressional candidates and placed a ceiling on candidate spending, had largely the same goals and enjoyed the same kind of reform backing as the more familiar series of campaign-finance laws enacted in the 1970s, although the instruments of the Progressive era, by comparison, lacked enforcement teeth.[9]

Woodrow Wilson's first Congress of 1913–15 passed the Underwood Tariff Act, which lowered duties and used the new Sixteenth Amendment to inaugurate an income tax; the Federal Reserve Act; the Clayton Antitrust Act; a measure creating the Federal Trade Commission (FTC); and the La Follette Seamen's Act, which regulated maritime working conditions. A second major legislative drive under Wilson in 1916 generated the Federal Farm Loan Act; workmen's compensation for federal employees; a ban on interstate sale of goods produced by child labor (later struck down by the Supreme Court as unconstitutional); the Adamson Act, which mandated an eight-hour day for railroad workers; and the Revenue Act of 1916, which elevated the income tax to the status of chief revenue instrument of the federal government. That year's energetic program was the last of the era. A few congressional initiatives came later — for example, the Eighteenth Amendment (prohibition of alcoholic beverages) in 1917 and the Nineteenth Amendment (women's suffrage) in 1919. But, as a general matter, the Progressive lawmaking impulse faded away at the national level during World War I, in 1917–18.[10]

3. THE NEW DEAL ERA: 1932 THROUGH 1938

The Roosevelt Years. If seen as a sequence of lawmaking aimed at either recovery or reform, as those objectives were regarded at the time, the New Deal era arguably spanned four consecutive Congresses. The two Congresses during Franklin Roosevelt's first term in the White House (1933–36) unquestionably stand out. The famous "hundred days" session of 1933 produced the National Industry Recovery Act, the Agricultural Adjustment Act (inaugurating the modern system of crop subsidies), the Emergency Banking Act, the Federal Emergency Relief Act, the Home Owners' Loan Act, the Securities Act, and measures creating the Civilian Conservation Corps (CCC), the Federal Deposit Insurance Corporation (FDIC), and the Tennessee Valley Authority (TVA). The 1934 session brought the Reciprocal Trade Agreements Act, which lowered tariff rates — not a state-expanding move — but arguably improved the government's planning capacity; the Taylor Grazing Act; the Indian Reorganization Act; and measures creating the Securities and Exchange Commission (SEC); the Federal Communications Commission (FCC); and the Federal Housing Administration (FHA).[11]

The strenuous "second hundred days" of 1935 generated the Social Security Act (setting up the modern U.S. pensions system), the National Labor Relations Act (establishing federal regulation of collective bargaining), the Public Utilities Holding Company Act, the Wealth Tax Act, the Banking Act of 1935 (centralizing monetary authority), and the Guffey-Snyder Coal Act (regulating the coal industry). The Emergency Relief Appropriation Act of 1935 enabled Roosevelt to create the Works Progress Administration (WPA), the New Deal relief agency run by Harry Hopkins. Measures enacted during the 1936 session included the Soil Conservation and Domestic Allotment Act and an act establishing the Rural Electrification Administration (REA) as an independent executive agency.[12]

The Congress of 1937–38 greatly disappointed New Dealers, considering its immense Democratic majorities as Republicans fell to record lows of seventeen Senators and eighty-nine House members. Many initiatives foundered, including TVA-like designs for other river systems and Roosevelt's plans to pack the Supreme Court and reorganize the executive branch. But at least six significant measures passed. These were the Wagner-Steagall Housing Act (a commitment to low-income public housing), the Farm Tenancy Act (a commitment, ultimately not implemented, to sharecroppers and tenant farmers), the Fair Labor Standards Act (the federal government's original minimum-wage law), the Agricultural Adjustment Act of 1938 (an important consolidating move for the commodity programs), the Robinson-Patman Act of 1938 (to curb alleged unfair price discrimination by chain stores), and an expensive antirecession pump-priming measure in 1938, based on Keynesian doctrine.[13] These enactments brought the era to a close. New Deal reform ideas kept percolating during Roosevelt's remaining years, but few had much success on Capitol Hill.[14]

The Hoover Years.   The start of this era still needs discussion. Although the choice of boundary date is unconventional, it arguably occurred in 1932, at a time when President Herbert Hoover faced a Republican Senate and a Democratic House. This extension of the New Deal "surge" era backwards derives from focusing on which laws of which types actually passed rather than, as is customary, on what Franklin Roosevelt, once elected to the presidency, asked for and received. At least five measures enacted in 1932 deserve mention. Hoover's proposed Reconstruction Finance Corporation (RFC), authorized by Congress that year, became the first alphabet agency of the Depression era. The Glass-Steagall Act permitted a more expansionary monetary policy. The Emergency Relief and Construction Act, engineered by Democrats and progressive Republicans, committed the federal government for the first time to countercyclical public works and relief spending. The prounion Norris–La Guardia Act, one of the century's key measures in the area of labor-management relations, outlawed yellow-dog contracts and curbed the use of antiunion injunctions by courts. Finally, the Revenue Act of 1932, which substantially raised taxes and shifted their incidence in a progressive direction through use of corporate, estate, and high-bracket income levies, came to serve as the federal government's basic revenue instrument of the 1930s. It required an uprising on Capitol Hill during the spring of 1932 for that "most progressive tax law of the decade" to pass: backbench Democrats and progressive Republicans rebelled against the leaderships of both parties to defeat a proposed national sales tax and substitute their own plan. As a producer of recovery and reform measures, as those causes were then understood, the Congress of 1931–33 arguably ranks with that of 1937–38.[15]

4. THE JOHNSON-NIXON-FORD ERA: 1963 THROUGH 1975–76

Whether one examines gross indicators of congressional workload or lists of major statutes enacted, the early or mid-1960s through the mid-1970s stands out as the era of exceptional legislative productivity since World War II.[16] Best known is the burst of lawmaking during the mid-1960s, bearing the label of Johnson's Great Society. Hardly less striking in retrospect — although the Vietnam war, Nixon's use of "social issues," and the Watergate scandal overshadowed it at the time — is the record of enactments under Nixon and

Ford during the period 1969–76. The ideological direction was largely the same as under Johnson. In general, in the realm of domestic lawmaking, the entire era amounted to one long successful drive to enact a liberal agenda of increased spending, new federal programs, and increased regulation of the society, polity, and economy.[17]

The New Frontier and the Great Society.   The era's boundary dates are not clear-cut. The Kennedy administration had won a few legislative victories earlier during the period 1961–63, but, in general, the New Frontier domestic program stalled, hence the choice of 1963 as the era's opening date. Soon after Kennedy's assassination late that year, and partly because of the new sympathetic political environment created by that event, legislative output ratcheted upward. Within a year, the results included Kennedy's Keynes-inspired tax cut; the Economic Opportunity Act (Johnson's ambitious anti-poverty program); and the Civil Rights Act of 1964, which addressed public accommodations (the most far-reaching civil rights measure since the 1870s); as well as, for example, the Higher Education Facilities Act of 1963; the Wilderness Act of 1964; the Urban Mass Transportation Act of 1964; and the Food Stamp Act of 1964. November 1963 through November 1964 — between the assassination and the presidential election — was arguably the most productive peacetime legislative year since 1935. Following Johnson's landslide victory in 1964, the hyperactive congressional session of 1965 went on to produce the Elementary and Secondary Education Act (the first broad-based federal funding of local schools), Medicare and Medicaid, and the Voting Rights Act, as well as many other measures addressing, for example, highway beautification, the arts and humanities, Appalachian development, pollution control, higher education, and subsidized housing.[18]

Late Johnson, Nixon, and Ford.   After the Great Society, the story often tails off or becomes cloudy. But in fact, these initiatives under Johnson were just the beginning. In social welfare spending, for example, the country's remarkable post–World War II surge in actual outlays began in 1965 and lasted through 1976, peaking under Ford.[19] Contributing to that surge were many statutes enacted during Johnson's presidency (including major housing acts in 1966 and 1968), but also many passed after 1968 under Nixon and Ford during the period 1969–76. These included the Food Stamp Act of 1970 (increasing that program's funding by an order of magnitude), Supplementary Security Income in 1972 (federalizing an income floor for the aged, blind, and disabled), the Comprehensive Employment and Training Act of 1973 (creating public sector "CETA jobs" for the unemployed), expansions of unemployment insurance in

1970 and 1976, the Housing and Community Development Act of 1974 (inaugurating federal "block grants"), the Higher Education Act of 1972 (creating "Pell grants" for lower income college students), and a series of Social Security hikes in 1969, 1971, and 1972, which raised benefits 23 percent, controlling for inflation. The Earned Income Tax Credit (EITC) for lower income workers—strictly speaking, a "tax expenditure"—came into existence in 1975 under Ford.[20] According to Robert X. Browning's count, a total of seventy-seven new social programs were initiated under Johnson and forty-four under Nixon and Ford.[21] Other spending initiatives during Nixon's time included federal "revenue sharing" with state and local governments and greatly increased funding authorizations for mass transit and water pollution control.[22]

In the regulatory realm, most of the era's initiatives occurred after Johnson's presidency. The "new social regulation" of American industry, according to David Vogel, took place during roughly 1964 through 1977; the peak reform years were 1969 through 1974, under Nixon and Ford. Two new federal regulatory agencies were established under Johnson and seven under Nixon and Ford.[23] In the area of consumer protection, enactments began with the Traffic Safety Act of 1966 (engendered by Ralph Nader) and the Fair Packaging and Labeling Act of 1966, continuing with, for example, the Truth-in-Lending Act of 1968, the Consumer Product Safety Act of 1972, and the Magnuson-Moss Act of 1974 (which empowered the FTC to set industry-wide rules barring unfair practices).[24] Key environmental measures included the National Environmental Policy Act (NEPA) of 1969, which called for "environmental impact statements"; the Clean Air Act of 1970; the Water Pollution Control Act of 1972; and the Endangered Species Act of 1973.[25] Workplace conditions were addressed in the Coal Mine Health and Safety Act of 1969 and the Occupational Safety and Health Act (OSHA) of 1970. Private pensions received detailed federal regulation for the first time in the Employee Retirement Income Security Act (ERISA) of 1974.[26]

Also, federal regulation of state and local governments set new records under Nixon and Ford—as in, for example, statutory requirements for clean air and water; the Equal Employment Opportunity Act of 1972, which banned discrimination in public employment; and the National Health Planning and Resources Development Act of 1974, which induced lower-level governments into new planning assignments.[27] When confronted by economic difficulties in the early 1970s, Congress reached for planning, not market, remedies—as in the Economic Stabilization Act of 1970, which authorized wage and price controls that Nixon later utilized, and the Emergency Petroleum Allocation Act of 1973, which called for the distribution of petroleum products by government formula. The Federal Election Campaign Act of 1974 brought campaign finance under strict, comprehensive regulation for the first time. Westerners who staged the "sagebrush rebellion" in the late 1970s were reacting to, among other things, two ambitious land-planning measures enacted under Ford — the National Forest Management Act (NFMA) of 1976 and the Federal Land Policy Management Act (FLPMA) of 1976. In the area of rights, the civil rights statutes of 1964 and 1965 were followed by the important Open Housing Act of 1968 and, among other initiatives, an unprecedented variety of women's rights measures enacted during the period 1971–72, which included the Equal Rights Amendment to the Constitution (ERA), though not enough states finally ratified that initiative.[28]

The preceding highlights the lawmaking thrust of the 1960s–70s era, which, to be sure, did not end abruptly. A 1977 measure to regulate strip mining, for example, continued the impulse. But, in general, further plans for expenditure and regulation fared poorly under President Carter during the period 1977–80. Proposals for national health insurance and a consumer protection agency, for example, went nowhere despite sizable Democratic majorities in the House and Senate. Legislative production in general, and of major statutes in particular, fell off. The content shifted; under Carter, *de*-regulation of industry arguably became the leading theme in statutes actually passed as trucking, airlines, railroads, banking, and natural gas shed government controls. The program-building dynamism of the 1960s and early 1970s was no longer evident. The stage was set for Reagan.[29]

ASSESSMENT

These, then, are the four striking legislative surges of U.S. history. Obviously, they do not account for all important laws passed. Virtually any Congress enacts at least some significant legislation. Briefer bursts of lawmaking have occurred that one can categorize as expanding the reach of the national state — starting with basic statutory designs of government institutions and Alexander Hamilton's program to construct a national economy during the period 1789–91. There was the so-called billion-dollar Congress of 1889–91, under President Benjamin Harrison, run by Republicans, which passed the Sherman Antitrust Act, the Sherman Silver Purchase Act, the McKinley Tariff Act (raising duties), the Naval Act of 1890 (paving the way for the modern Navy), and the Dependent Pension Act of 1890 (greatly expanding the Civil War veterans' pension system).[30] Government size and scope mushroomed as a result of war-mobilization enactments under Wilson during the period 1916–18 and Roosevelt during the period 1940–45.[31]

Furthermore, not all major legislation sets out to expand the reach of the national state. Sometimes *dis*engagement of the state from the society or the economy requires major legislative action. That was true of, for example, Reagan's tax and domestic expenditure cuts in 1981, the deregulation moves under Carter, the Twenty-first Amendment repealing Prohibition in 1933, Secretary of the Treasury Andrew Mellon's steep tax cuts in the 1920s, Jefferson's measures to cut taxes, defense, and the national debt after he assumed the presidency in 1801, and Jackson's veto of the bill to recharter the Bank of the United States in 1832. (The latter may be the chief instance of a major American policy change — not just a preservation of the status quo — that derived from using the legislative process to block a bill rather than to pass one.)

Still, the four surges of 1861 through 1875, 1906 through 1916, 1932 through 1938, and 1963 through 1975–76 seem to stand out for their programmatic ambition, length of time, and volume of major enactments. And it is probably no accident that all four of them exhibited drives to expand the reach of the national state, which is, after all, a kind of undertaking that is likely to require a great deal of strenuous legislative action.

Causes of Legislative Surges

What can be said about the causes — or at least correlates — of the four major legislative surges outlined above? Chiefly at issue here is the causal force of presidential elections, but that factor can perhaps be explored most illuminatingly by placing it in a more general context. The causal discussion here will proceed under four rubrics, of which the first two afford a role for presidential elections.

1. ELECTIONS

Are legislative surges traceable in a more or less direct way to election outcomes? That is, have elections proximately preceded, or at least occurred at prominent junctures within, the legislative surges and arguably brought them about or spurred them on?

Realignment Elections. This is to raise, for one thing, the subject of "electoral realignments" — the major reconfigurations in American popular voting patterns that are said to have taken place in or around 1800, 1828, 1860, 1896, and 1932. In the well-known literature on this subject, these elections are seen as boundary points between successive "party systems."[32] Such "realignments" evidently helped to spur the lawmaking surges during the periods 1861–75 and 1932–38. It is difficult to imagine the former surge without the Republicans' rise to power from 1854 to 1860 or the latter without the

Democrats' sizable congressional gains in 1930 and 1932 and Franklin Roosevelt's landslide victory in 1932. The analogy between the Civil War and Reconstruction era Republicans and the New Deal era Democrats is perhaps the most attractive feature of realignment theory.

But aside from those two junctures, "electoral realignments" do not explain or illuminate legislative surges.[33] Consider American history since the 1870s. The surges of the Progressive era and the 1960s through the 1970s are not traceable to any electoral revolutions that "realignment" theorists include in their canon. And the realignment of 1896, historic though that may have been by virtue of its changes in popular voting patterns, its defeat of William Jennings Bryan's bid for the presidency, and its production of a new dominant Republican coalition, did not provoke any legislative surge. The new McKinley Republicans, possessing solid congressional majorities, might have been expected to repeat their party's lawmaking dynamism of a decade earlier under Benjamin Harrison, but they did not. Their legislative record during the period 1897–1901 was at best ordinary.[34] The leading enactments of that time seem to have been the Gold Standard Act of 1900, which upheld the gold standard that Grover Cleveland's Democratic administration had protected so tenaciously during the period 1893–97, and the Dingley Tariff Act of 1897, which, following reductions under Cleveland, returned rates to high Republican levels (higher ones for dutiable imports, though lower ones for all imports, than in the party's McKinley Tariff Act of 1890).[35] The legislative doldrums experienced under McKinley decisively disconfirm any theory that posits a one-to-one relationship between electoral realignments and activist lawmaking.

Authorizing and Deauthorizing Elections.   But a more commonsensical question can be asked about elections. Are there particular ones — besides the "realigning" ones already noted — that seemed to have helped authorize or deauthorize Congress to undertake legislative surges? There are obvious candidates for those roles, although, to be fair to the evidence, the search for them needs to be broad enough to accommodate congressional midterm elections as well as presidential contests. On the authorizing side, the post–Civil War midterm of 1866 was viewed by many contemporaries as a showdown referendum between President Andrew Johnson and Congress's radical Republicans, over how to deal with the conquered South; the latter won and Reconstruction ensued. The 1910 midterm election brought not only a generally Democratic tide but also a decisive defeat for the Republicans' conservative wing in state and district primaries; these results probably helped along the Progressive agenda in the next Congress. Woodrow Wilson and the Democratic party claimed a mandate for their brand of Progressivism after the 1912 election; lawmaking under the New Freedom banner ensued. The 1964 election contributed to the Great Society cause by producing Johnson's landslide mandate as well as a rare new two-to-one Democratic edge in the House; the energetic legislative session of 1965 followed. To be very contemporary, the 1994 midterm seemed to many at the time to authorize fulfillment of Newt Gingrich and the House Republicans' "Contract with America."

On the deauthorizing side, the Republicans' disastrous defeat in the 1874 midterm election is almost certainly part of the reason why the lawmaking of the Reconstruction era came to an end. And the 1918 and 1938 midterms, occasioning decisive Democratic losses under Woodrow Wilson and Franklin Roosevelt in their second terms, are often associated with the flagging reform impulses of Progressivism and the New Deal, although that argument should not be carried too far. World War I is more often cited as having put an end to Progressivism at the national level, and the New Deal was already suffering from conflict between Roosevelt supporters and increasingly powerful conservative forces on Capitol Hill in the two years leading to the 1938 election.

Particular elections help — midterm as well as presidential ones — but they leave a good deal unaccounted for. Notably left unexplained is the spurring of Progressivism at the national level by Theodore Roosevelt during the period of 1905–6; this is not ordinarily attributed to any electoral mandate (although it is possible that Roosevelt's record-setting landslide victory of 1904 has not been properly interpreted). Also, the move away from government activism under Carter during the period 1977–80 does not seem to have stemmed from any deauthorizing election, presidential or congressional (although Reagan's victory in 1980 may be said to have ratified it).

Leadership Conversion.   Of course, the subject of electoral connections is not exhausted by pointing to particular elections and their alleged sweeping verdicts. Incumbent parties or politicians can accommodate major changes in public opinion by switching along with it, if they are alert. Major changes in government policy can thus occur without the stimulus of any party's election gains or losses, though these often contribute. In the 1870s, for example, Republican politicians dialed downward their support for Reconstruction on a schedule that evidently matched northern public opinion. During the period 1977–78, Senate and House members seem to have gone along with what they saw as a swell of opinion against government spending and regulation. Some just changed their positions. In 1975, Republican Congressman John B. Anderson of Illinois had supported the controversial Naderite proposal to create a consumer protection agency; in 1977, apparently in response to new constituency sentiment, he came out against it. During those same years, liberal

Democratic Senator Edward Kennedy surprisingly took on deregulation of industry as a new personal cause. Broad policy change can come about through conversion of incumbent members as well as membership change through election upheavals.[36]

2. POLITICAL PARTIES

Party Government.   To what degree can the laws of any surge be credited to one political party that controls government and monopolizes the legislative initiative and thus shapes an era? That is perhaps the leading question to ask about parties. By extension, it is also a question about elections, both presidential and congressional, since whether a party gets a chance to exercise such monopoly power owes to configurations of election results. If "party government" always functioned unambiguously in the United States, the answer to the question as posed would be obvious: legislative surges would always be entirely traceable to one party. But the reality is more complicated and it varies over time.

Without much doubt, the leading instance of a surge driven by one party was that of the Civil War and Reconstruction era. To be sure, serious disagreement occurred between "radicals" and moderates of the ruling Republican party and between President Andrew Johnson and Congress. In addition, because the southern states seceded from Congress in 1861, the lawmaking afterward has the flavor of a northern, not just a Republican party, surge. The absence of the Southerners permitted not only the antislavery measures, but also such Whiggish initiatives as the tariff and transcontinental railroad acts. Still, the Republican party won every presidential and congressional election between 1860 and 1874, and its leaders advanced all the important laws during that time.

Much more complicated was the record of the Progressive era. Parties or their leaders had lawmaking roles, but those varied over time and often departed from the "party government" model. Through 1908, at both state and national levels, reform-oriented executive leaders of the Republican party provided most of the era's programmatic impulse. The most prominent instances are Theodore Roosevelt as president and Governors Robert La Follette of Wisconsin and Charles Evans Hughes of New York. But Republicans supplied the chief opposition also—the Aldrich-Cannon regime on Capitol Hill and comparable conservative factions in the state legislatures. From 1909 through 1912, the progenitors of notable reform programs were typically cross-party coalitions of Democrats and progressive Republicans. That happened in the national government under President Taft as well as in, for example, Massachusetts, New Jersey (under Democratic Governor Woodrow Wilson), and

North Dakota. After the 1912 election, the Democratic party took over as the successful proposer and carrier of legislative programs — in the national capital under President Wilson, but also in states such as New York and Ohio (under Governor James M. Cox).[37]

The New Deal was obviously engineered by the Democratic party or its leaders. It consisted largely of enactments initiated by Franklin Roosevelt or other liberal Democrats — Senator Robert F. Wagner of New York, for example, in the cases of the National Labor Relations Act of 1935 and the Wagner-Steagall Housing Act of 1937 — and enacted by Congresses containing immense Democratic majorities. As a matter of electoral accountability, the Democrats certainly won credit for the achievements of the era. Still, the record was somewhat more muddled at the level of actual lawmaking. In fact, the 1930 election and the Great Depression revived the cross-party coalition of Democrats and insurgent Republicans who had won congressional victories — notably in initiating the progressive income tax — during the Taft and Wilson presidencies. That coalition put across, for example, the Revenue Act of 1932 and the Emergency Relief and Construction Act of 1932. Progressive Republicans (or former Republicans) took the lead on some key measures that year and also afterward. An example is Senator George Norris's role in enacting the Norris–La Guardia Act of 1932 (New York's Fiorello La Guardia was also then an insurgent Republican) and establishing the Tennessee Valley Authority in 1933. Progressive Republicans receded in significance as the decade wore on, but after 1934, another development swerved the New Deal away from any single textbook model of "party government." President Roosevelt's policy initiatives increasingly divided his own party. By 1937, with the Republican party devastated and silent, congressional Democrats provided the president's chief opposition as well as his chief ranks of Capitol Hill support. The anti-Roosevelt Democratic faction included more than just conservative Southerners: one leader in the winning struggles against Roosevelt's court-packing and executive reorganization plans during the period of 1937–38 was, for example, Senator Burton Wheeler of Montana, who had accrued excellent progressive as well as Democratic party credentials. This was an odd brand of "party government."

No one would contest a general claim that the Democratic party was responsible for enacting Johnson's Great Society program in the mid-1960s. The major civil rights acts of 1964, 1965, and 1968 were something of an exception: on these measures the House and Senate roll calls pitted Northerners against Southerners, regardless of party, rather than Democrats against Republicans. Nevertheless, the Great Society's housing, health insurance, education, and antipoverty initiatives unquestionably offer a leading instance of party-based lawmaking. Yet, as the era's lawmaking impulse continued beyond 1968, the simplicity of rule by one party gave way. In general, the legislative initiative stayed with the Democrats—but now it was lodged in that party's congressional branch. Thus, for example, the National Environmental Policy Act of 1969 was advanced by Senator Henry Jackson of Washington, the Clean Air Act of 1970 by Senator Edmund Muskie of Maine, the 23 percent Social Security hike of 1972 by Congressman Wilbur Mills of Arkansas, the Equal Rights Amendment in 1972 by Senator Birch Bayh of Indiana, and the Earned Income Tax Credit of 1975 by Senator Russell Long of Louisiana. One Democratic legislative campaign after another succeeded. But the Nixon administration played a role also. Many spending and regulatory measures were championed by the White House—for instance, the major expansion of the food stamp program in 1970—or at least enjoyed Nixon's collaboration or acquiescence. At odds on many matters, Nixon and congressional Democrats shared a surprising joint responsibility for the era's domestic spending and regulatory record.

In summary, the clearest case for a "party government" model of lawmaking, notwithstanding the adversarial role played by President Andrew Johnson, is probably that of the 1861–75 period. The New Deal is a good case. In the 1960s and 1970s, there was an approximation of "party government" under Johnson but bipartisan cooperation and conflict under Nixon. In the Progressive era, even though one party or the other promoted many legislative victories at various times at state and national levels, the overall pattern is exceptionally diverse.

Unified versus Divided Control.   To ask a slightly different question about parties, to what extent have legislative surges occurred during times of unified party control of the national government—that is, times when one party, by virtue of election results, possessed formal majorities in the Senate and House and also held the presidency? This is worth asking, since it is a common view in political science, and more generally, that such unified control is a necessary condition for major lawmaking. Otherwise, it has been argued by James L. Sundquist and others, "deadlock" or "stalemate" between the parties will occur.[38]

The surge of the 1861–75 period offers a nearly pure case. Republicans controlled the presidency, the House, and Senate during those years, and they used that control to enact laws. The "nearly" qualification derives from taking account of President Andrew Johnson, in power during the period 1865–69, whose connection to the Republican party was ambiguous and whose vetoes had to be overridden during those years for the program of the party's congressional majority to prevail. In general, they were and it did, at least at the level of passing laws; implementation proved more difficult.

The New Deal era presents another nearly pure case. Unified Democratic control of the government underlay all the legislative action beginning with the "hundred days" in 1933. The qualification owes to the era's initial burst of lawmaking in 1932 under Hoover, who, to be sure, blocked certain important initiatives but promoted or at least signed others.

The 1960s and 1970s are a mixed case. Unified Democratic control provided the setting for Johnson's Great Society and lasted until the 1968 election. But major legislative initiatives continued to pass under Nixon and even Ford, despite the shift in 1968 to divided control as Democrats kept their majorities in the House and Senate.

Various patterns prevailed during the Progressive era. Some major legislative programs were enacted under conditions of unified-control "party government." That was particularly true about Woodrow Wilson's presidential program during the period 1913–16, as national party leader Wilson worked through Democratic party caucuses on Capitol Hill. At the state level, Democrats in control of governorships and legislatures enacted ambitious programs during those same years, for example, in New York and Ohio. Theodore Roosevelt won his program from a Republican Congress during the period 1905–6 (though in fact his fellow partisans balked at times and he needed Democratic help), as did Governor Hughes from a Republican legislature in New York in 1907. Wisconsin's government was formally all-Republican when La Follette enacted his program in 1903 and 1905, as was California's when Hiram Johnson's program passed in 1911. But in fact that is misleading since the chief opposition to reform in these latter states, out of power because of losses in nominating processes, was also Republican. And many notable legislative programs at the state level — including those referred to above in North Dakota, Minnesota, Massachusetts, and New Jersey (under Woodrow Wilson as governor) — were enacted under circumstances of formally divided party control. Nationally, that was also the story under Taft during the period 1911–13, when much lawmaking occurred despite a switch to divided control. During the Progressive era, major legislative programs were enacted in an impressive variety of formal party circumstances.[39]

"Party Voting" in Congress.   One more question might be asked about parties. Does congressional "party voting," as political scientists define the concept, rise during times of legislative surges? The idea might be that that kind of party-versus-party confrontation is required to enact major laws. A "party voting" score, which can be calculated for the House or Senate for any Congress,

reports the proportion of all roll calls on which a majority of Democrats opposed a majority of Republicans. The overall answer to the question is close to an unqualified no.[40] For the House, for example, between 1861 and 1984, the mean "party voting" score for Congresses during the four legislative surges was sixty; for other Congresses it was fifty-seven. There is a long-term decline in the statistic, it should be said, that makes simple averaging problematic. The best bits of evidence for a positive connection are that the 1861–75 Congresses scored about four points higher, on average, than those of 1875–91 (perhaps a fair comparison); and that the Congresses of 1931–38 scored some nine points higher than those of the preceding Republican decade (1921–30). Those results, which juxtapose the Civil War–Reconstruction and New Deal eras to neighboring periods of relatively low legislative productivity, show at least a modest relation between high "party voting" and legislative surges. But "party voting" did not stand out during the Progressive era, and it reached its nadir during Nixon's presidency, hitting an all-time low of 29 percent during the period of 1969–70. A fair inference is that "party voting" rises slightly during legislative surges where one party in fact produces the laws, but that it will not rise — it may even fall — during surges otherwise. That would be understandable. The overall relation between the two variables, therefore, is weak or nonexistent. Confronted by just a time series on congressional "party voting," from 1861 to the present, one would have no way of knowing when the legislative surges took place. That holds for the Senate as well as the House. In very recent years — the late 1980s and early 1990s — congressional "party voting" has risen to heights not seen for many decades, without being accompanied by remarkable records of lawmaking.

Assessment of Parties. Are parties, then, the producers of legislative surges? The historical trend is mixed and complicated. For the Civil War–Reconstruction and New Deal eras, yes is a plausible answer. The Progressive era presents the opposite extreme, for it is a good bet that ambitious lawmaking would somehow have occurred anyway — that the parties were secondary, even though they sometimes played prominent roles. Furthermore, in regard to party, the dominant impulse of the era was largely *against* parties. In the 1960s and 1970s, the Democratic party, or at least entrepreneurs within it, supplied most of the legislative dynamism, though the Nixon administration figured importantly too, and divided party control reigned after 1968. There is no clear trend in party role between the 1860s and the 1990s: the New Deal, for example, ranks higher in legislative achievement by one dominant party than does the Progressive era. Still, the pre-1900 data on party control, party voting, and legislative surges are compatible, at least, with the idea that parties were more central to governmental functioning in the nineteenth century than they have become in the twentieth. Possibly, they were.

Beyond that, there exists a plausible argument that conditions allowing a greater detachment of energetic lawmaking from single-party control of the government have arisen since World War II. It is during these recent decades that elections have taken a turn toward candidate-specific (as opposed to party) appeals, and that both Congress and the presidency have adopted legislative practices that transcend, in a sense, parties. These include the annual presentation of "the president's program," and Congress's immensely improved staffing that permits countless legislative initiatives regardless of which parties control which branches. We may see more of the kind of ambitious cross-party lawmaking that took place under Nixon.

3. THE ECONOMY

There are at least two routes by which the state of the economy might be hypothesized to underpin legislative surges. The first does not involve elections in any clear way. The second may or may not involve elections, but when it does, they recede into the secondary role of transmitting economic signals to the government. Causal power, from this perspective, resides in the economy.

Underlying Economic Conditions.   The first route is a relatively static model in which basic underlying conditions in the economy might distinctively affect legislative action. Thus, it is sometimes argued that the lawmaking surge under Johnson and Nixon during the 1960s and 1970s required a high-growth economy as a base—that is, to provide the necessary slack for spending commitments and regulatory experiments. But lower the growth rate, bring on budgetary pressure, and the lawmaking would tail off as it indeed did in the mid-1970s. Possibly a similar prosperity-based argument could be made about the Progressive era. Unfortunately, the New Deal era presents an exactly opposite scenario: the uniquely dismal economy of the 1930s accommodated pathbreaking spending and regulatory drives by an activist government. The New Deal is a devastating disconfirmation of any theory that associates economic prosperity with lawmaking.

Economic Downturns.   Precipitous economic downturns offer the second possibility—as either provokers or dampeners of legislative surges. They might cause election upheavals that in turn cause legislative moves on Capitol Hill or, without that, they might cause alarm in the public that impinges in turn on elected officials. The leading instance is the Great Depression of 1929, which triggered huge electoral gains for the Democratic party that unquestionably set the stage for the legislative surge of the 1930s.

However, economic slumps seem to have helped close, rather than open, at least two of the surge eras — those of the Civil War–Reconstruction and the New Deal. The depression of 1873 was evidently one major cause of the Republicans' decisive loss of the House in 1874. The precipitous recession of late 1937 through early 1938 seems to have helped turn public opinion against further New Deal experiments; that in turn hobbled Roosevelt's legislative drive well before the 1938 election.

Some economic downturns, moreover, may not lead to legislative surges. The major depression of 1893, for example, instrumental as it probably was in elevating the Republican party to power for a generation, did not open, close, or figure in any of the prominent legislative surges of American history. Thus, economic slumps may encourage or discourage legislative surges, or they may have negligible impact. In general, sharp economic downturns delegitimize any governing party along with its economic policies; the opposition, whatever it stands for, comes to look like a good bet for power.[41]

4. MOODS AND MOVEMENTS

Public Moods.   Another view of the causes of lawmaking surges would emphasize "public moods." Arthur M. Schlesinger Jr. has argued that Americans periodically become caught up in moods of "public purpose" — a kind of secular revivalism. Large numbers of citizens throw themselves into public affairs for periods as long as a decade with the aim of reforming politics and society — and then tire of such efforts and recede into private pursuits like those associated with the quiet generations of the 1920s and 1950s. Schlesinger points to the Progressive era, the New Deal era, and the 1960s–70s period as twentieth-century instances of activist eras. Obviously, the activist "moods" said to be exhibited during these eras map very well onto the century's three legislative surges.[42]

"Public moods" are more difficult to get an empirical handle on than are economic downturns or election results, but in fact, historians and other witnesses have often pointed precisely to "mood changes" as the reasons why legislative surges began or ended. All four endings have been given that interpretation: in each case, after years of unending energetic reform, there occurred a quite abrupt onset of activism fatigue that brought lawmaking and other reform endeavors to a halt. In the mid-1870s, the North is said to have lost its faith that Reconstruction might work and, hence, its activist drive.[43] Under Woodrow Wilson, World War I is said to have drained away all remaining public purpose for domestic as well as international causes: a "mood change" thus took place that in turn affected Capitol Hill.[44] A pronounced anti–New Deal "mood shift" is detected during the period 1937–38; the economy's new downturn at that time combined with other events to sow pessimism about the New Deal enterprise in general.[45] Finally, the activism of the 1960s and 1970s is said to have lost out to a "mood shift" under Carter: the idea that society could be improved through government action gave way to pessimism, apathy, successful drives to deregulate industry, the "Sagebrush Rebellion," and the low tax ideology of California's Proposition 13.[46]

As for the beginnings of legislative surges, analysts assign prominence to a "mood change" in only one case, though there it is the leading interpretation. It involves the Progressive era, whose onset of lawmaking surges at both state and federal levels is conventionally traced to a "mood shift" toward reform activism occurring roughly in 1905. Muckraking by journalists such as Ida Tarbell and Lincoln Steffens had set the stage for it since 1902. Neither an election result nor a downturn in the economy seems to have played a role.[47] In all of American history, the beginning of the Progressive era stands out as the juncture where a "mood" account decisively outperforms competing theories.

Political Movements.   Much of the dynamism of "public purpose" moods seems to be provided by political movements. The Progressive era was animated either by one long-lasting, all-embracing movement or by a variety of narrower allied ones, depending on one's interpretation. Some of that era's lawmaking can be directly traced to movement action, as Theda Skocpol has claimed for the women's movement and Congress's establishment of the Children's Bureau in 1912.[48] In the 1960s and 1970s, a sizable number of loosely allied movements—civil rights, consumer, antiwar, labor, student, women's liberation, environmental, and "public interest" groups—pursued reform campaigns. Again, particular laws enacted largely as a result can be cited: the civil rights movement, through demonstrations led by Martin Luther King Jr. in Birmingham and Selma, was instrumental in bringing about the Civil Rights Acts of 1964 and 1965; the consumer movement, the Fair Packaging and Labeling Act of 1966, and the Consumer Product Safety Act of 1972; the environmental movement, the major clean air and water measures of 1970 and 1972; the women's movement, congressional approval of the ERA in 1972; and the public interest group Common Cause, the Federal Election Campaign Act of 1974.[49] In the case of the 1860s and 1870s, Eric Foner interprets Reconstruction as having had a movement activist base that took form as early as 1863 and lasted into the 1870s.[50] The New Deal is least satisfactorily explicable by reference to movements. Roosevelt's "hundred days" of lawmaking in 1933 seems to have drawn on the country's obvious sense of economic emergency at that time, not movement effervescence. Still, it is becoming increasingly evident that lively movement activity by Townsendite pension advocates, share-the-wealth followers of Huey Long, labor union organizers, and even the Communist party provided an important part of the underpinning of Roosevelt's "second hundred days" in 1935.[51] Some analysts credit that session's Social Security Act, National Labor Relations Act, and Wealth Tax Act substantially to background movement pressure; members of Congress felt it and responded.[52] It was not just huge Democratic congressional majorities in Washington; there was an upwelling of the left outside.

Conclusion

These four accounts of legislative surges — addressing parties, elections, the economy, and public moods and movements — obviously overlap. An economic downturn, for example, may bring about an electoral upheaval or a mood shift. A mood shift may contribute to an electoral shift. An election turnover may be read by contemporaries as evidence of a mood shift. Movement activism may colonize a party and provide it dynamism, as evidently happened with the Republican party during Reconstruction (though no longer after the mid-1870s). But no one neat set of causal or correlative relations applies to all four of the prominent legislative surges of American history. Lawmaking via "party government" has occurred in some eras but not others. Economic downturns have started or stopped legislative activity at some times but not at others. Public moods and movements seem to be the most reliable factor; they somehow have figured in the dynamics of every legislative surge, though they are so elusive empirically that it is hard to get a fix on exactly when they exist or what they may be causing.

As for presidential elections — the chief concern of this essay — they play a role but not as consequentially or frequently as we imagine. In particular, "realigning elections," which are often advanced as the paramount political events of U.S. history, have not mapped all that well onto legislative surges. They have proven to be neither a necessary cause of such surges — consider the Progressive era and the 1960s–70s period — nor a sufficient one — consider the 1890s. Beyond that, individual presidential elections can of course contribute to surges — consider 1912 and 1964 — as can congressional midterms — consider 1866 and 1910. But such contributions are normally wrapped up in a multicausal package whose ingredients include events in the economy and the gyrations of public moods and movements.

At least, one might think, elections would leave a deposit of distinctive policy-making capacity whenever they elevate one party to simultaneous control of the presidency, the Senate, and the House. But there also the historical record is muddled: legislative surges have not corresponded all that neatly to times of unified party control. Consider, for example, the strenuous lawmaking during Nixon's years of divided party control, as compared with the relatively fallow legislative records under Truman, Kennedy, and Carter—all of whom enjoyed periods of one-party rule.

There is a lesson here for the 1990s. What happened at the time of Clinton's election in 1992, the argument goes here, is that analysts who predicted a new legislative surge were buying too heavily into the causal power of elections. In fact, a presidential election victory, even if clothed in a claimed mandate, is not enough. Solid one-party control of the government is not enough. Just about entirely lacking in the United States during the period 1993–94 was the mix of activist public mood and movement effervescence that, in the past, has probably done more than anything else to foster legislative surges. A president or party unfortified by such public enthusiasm faces an uphill struggle.

Notes

This essay was published as chap. 5 in Harvey L. Schantz, *American Presidential Elections: Process, Policy, and Political Change* (Albany: State University of New York Press, 1996). © 1996 State University of New York. All rights reserved. Reprinted by permission. That essay was an adapted and expanded version of "Parties, Elections, Moods, and Lawmaking Surges" by David R. Mayhew. Used by permission of Charles Scribner's Sons, a Division of Simon & Schuster, New York, from *Encyclopedia of the American Legislative System*, Joel H. Silbey, Editor in Chief. Vol. II, pp. 885–95. Charles Scribner's Sons, 1994.

1. David Mayhew, *Divided We Govern: Party Control, Lawmaking, and Investigations, 1946–1990* (New Haven: Yale University Press, 1991).

2. John Mark Hansen, "Taxation and the Political Economy of the Tariff," *International Organization* 44 (Autumn 1990): 527–51.

3. Leonard P. Curry, *Blueprint for Modern America: Nonmilitary Legislation of the First Civil War Congress* (Nashville: Vanderbilt University Press, 1968), chaps. 2–8, 11; J. G. Randall and David Donald, *The Civil War and Reconstruction* (Boston: Little, Brown, 1969), pp. 283–92, 344–53.

4. Randall and Donald, *Civil War and Reconstruction*, pp. 284–85, 372–73, 576–86, chap. 34, pp. 641–43; Curry, *Blueprint for Modern America*, chaps. 2, 3; William Gillette, *Retreat from Reconstruction, 1869–1879* (Baton Rouge: Louisiana State University Press, 1979), pp. 17–20.

5. Ibid., chaps. 2, 8, 11; S. G. F. Spackman, "American Federalism and the Civil Rights Act of 1875," *Journal of American Studies* 10 (1976): 313–28.

6. Richard L. McCormick, "The Discovery That Business Corrupts Politics: A Reappraisal of the Origins of Progressivism," *American Historical Review* 86 (April 1981): 266–68; George E. Mowry, *The Era of Theodore Roosevelt, 1900–1912* (New York: Harper and Brothers, 1958), pp. 71–84; David Sarasohn, *The Party of Reform: Democrats in the Progressive Era* (Jackson: University Press of Mississippi, 1989), pp. 112–18; Mayhew, *Divided We Govern,* pp. 146–48.

7. *The Rhetorical Presidency* (Princeton, N.J.: Princeton University Press, 1987), p. 101.

8. On lawmaking during Theodore Roosevelt's second administration: Mowry, *Era of Theodore Roosevelt,* chap. 11; John Morton Blum, *The Republican Roosevelt* (Cambridge, Mass.: Harvard University Press, 1977), pp. 87–105; John Milton Cooper Jr., *Pivotal Decades: The United States, 1900–1920* (New York: Norton, 1990), chap. 4; Lewis L. Gould, *Reform and Regulation: American Politics, 1900–1916* (New York: Wiley, 1978), chap. 3; Stephen Skowronek, *Building a New American State: The Expansion of National Administrative Capacities, 1877–1920* (New York: Cambridge University Press, 1982), pp. 255–59; Robert M. Crumden, *Ministers of Reform: The Progressives' Achievement in American Civilization* (New York: Basic Books, 1982), chap. 6; Elmer E. Cornwell Jr., *Presidential Leadership of Public Opinion* (Bloomington: Indiana University Press, 1965), pp. 24–26; Mayhew, *Divided We Govern,* pp. 118–19, 148–149, 157.

9. On lawmaking under Taft: Mowry, *Era of Theodore Roosevelt,* chap. 12; Cooper, *Pivotal Decades,* chap. 5; Gould, *Reform and Regulation,* chap. 4; Paolo E. Coletta, *The Presidency of William Howard Taft* (Lawrence: University Press of Kansas, 1973), chaps. 3, 5–7, 13; Kenneth W. Hechler, *Insurgency: Personalities and Politics of the Taft Era* (New York: Columbia University Press, 1940), chap. 8; Sarasohn, *Party of Reform,* chap. 4; Mayhew, *Divided We Govern,* pp. 149–51; Skowronek, *Building a New American State,* pp. 261–67; Robert E. Mutch, *Campaigns, Congress, and Courts: The Making of Federal Campaign Finance Law* (New York: Praeger, 1988), pp. 1–16.

10. On lawmaking under Wilson: Arthur S. Link, *Woodrow Wilson and the Progressive Era, 1910–1917* (New York: Harper and Brothers, 1954), chaps. 2, 3, 9; Gould, *Reform and Regulation,* chap. 6; Sarasohn, *Party of Reform,* pp. 183–89; Cooper, *Pivotal Decades,* chap. 7; W. Elliot Brownlee, "Wilson and Financing the Modern State: The Revenue Act of 1916," *Proceedings of the American Philosophical Society* 129 (1985): 173–210; Mayhew, *Divided We Govern,* pp. 151–52.

11. William E. Leuchtenburg, *Franklin D. Roosevelt and the New Deal, 1932–1940* (New York: Harper and Row, 1963), chap. 3 and pp. 85–86, 90–91, 135, 203–5; Arthur M. Schlesinger Jr., *The Coming of the New Deal* (Boston: Houghton Mifflin, 1958), chaps. 2, 3, 6, 15–17, 19, 20, 26, 28; Albert U. Romasco, *The Politics of Recovery: Roosevelt's New Deal* (New York: Oxford University Press, 1983), chap. 3.

12. Leuchtenburg, *Franklin D. Roosevelt and the New Deal,* pp. 124–33, chap. 7, pp. 171–73; Schlesinger, *Coming of the New Deal,* chaps. 18, 24; Arthur M. Schlesinger Jr., *The Politics of Upheaval* (Boston: Houghton Mifflin, 1960), pp. 261–70, chaps. 16–18, pp. 381–84; James T. Patterson, *Congressional Conservatism and the New Deal: The*

Growth of the Conservative Coalition in Congress, 1933–1939 (Lexington: University Press of Kentucky, 1967), chap. 2 and pp. 77–80.

13. Leuchtenburg, *Franklin D. Roosevelt and the New Deal,* pp. 135–42 and chaps. 10, 11; Patterson, *Congressional Conservatism,* pp. 11, 159, 233–46; James MacGregor Burns, *Roosevelt: The Lion and the Fox* (New York: Harcourt, Brace, 1956), chaps. 15–17; Barry D. Karl, *The Uneasy State: The United States from 1915 to 1945* (Chicago: University of Chicago Press, 1983), pp. 167–69.

14. John W. Jeffries, "The 'New' New Deal: FDR and American Liberalism, 1937–1945," *Political Science Quarterly* 105 (Fall 1990): 397–418; Edwin Amenta and Theda Skocpol, "Redefining the New Deal: World War II and the Development of Social Provision in the United States," chap. 2 in Margaret Weir, Ann Shola Orloff, and Theda Skocpol, eds., *The Politics of Social Policy in the United States* (Princeton, N.J.: Princeton University Press, 1988).

15. David Burner, *Herbert Hoover: A Public Life* (New York: Knopf, 1979), pp. 270–82, quotation at 282; Harris G. Warren, *Herbert Hoover and the Great Depression* (New York: Oxford University Press, 1959), chaps. 9–13; Jordan A. Schwarz, *The Interregnum of Despair: Hoover, Congress, and the Depression* (Urbana: University of Illinois Press, 1970), pp. 78–98 and chaps. 5, 6, 8; Mayhew, *Divided We Govern,* pp. 154–56. (Note that Congress traditionally held lame-duck postelection sessions — such as in early 1933 — until the Twentieth Amendment abolished them, starting in 1935.)

16. Post–World War II legislative workload is discussed in Roger H. Davidson, "The New Centralization on Capitol Hill," *Review of Politics* 50 (Summer 1988): 349–50. Major statutes enacted by Congress between 1946 and 1990 are listed and discussed in Mayhew, *Divided We Govern,* chaps. 3, 4. This study is based on two sweeps through the history of those years, one using judgments rendered at the time by contemporaries (chiefly journalists) about the importance of statutes just enacted by each Congress, the other using retrospective judgments by policy specialists (writing chiefly in the 1980s) about the importance of statutes enacted in their fields during the preceding decades.

17. For analyses that explicitly compare the lawmaking record of the 1960s and 1970s (not just that of the Great Society) with those of the Progressive and New Deal eras, see Theda Skocpol, "A Society without a 'State'? Political Organization, Social Conflict, and Welfare Provision in the United States," *Journal of Public Policy* 7 (1987): 364–65; and Richard A. Harris, "A Decade of Reform," chap. 1 in Harris and Sidney M. Milkis, eds., *Remaking American Politics* (Boulder, Colo.: Westview, 1989), pp. 5, 9.

18. James L. Sundquist, *Politics and Policy: The Eisenhower, Kennedy, and Johnson Years* (Washington, D.C.: Brookings, 1968); Mayhew, *Divided We Govern,* chaps. 3, 4.

19. Robert J. Lampman, *Social Welfare Spending: Accounting for Changes from 1950 to 1978* (New York: Academic Press, 1984), pp. 8–9.

20. Christopher Howard, "The Hidden Side of the American Welfare State," *Political Science Quarterly* 108 (Fall 1993): 403–36.

21. Robert X. Browning, *Politics and Social Welfare Policy in the United States* (Knoxville: University of Tennessee Press, 1986), pp. 79–83.

22. On spending initiatives under Nixon and Ford: Timothy Conlan, *New Federalism: Intergovernmental Reform from Nixon to Reagan* (Washington, D.C.: Brookings, 1988), pp. 81–82; Jodie T. Allen, "Last of the Big Spenders: Richard Nixon and the Greater

Society," *Washington Post,* February 24, 1983, p. A15; Browning, *Politics and Social Welfare Policy,* pp. 79–83, 95, 110–11, 142–48, 161; James T. Patterson, *America's Struggle Against Poverty, 1900–1985* (Cambridge, Mass.: Harvard University Press, 1986), pp. 158, 165, 197–98; R. Allen Hays, *The Federal Government and Urban Housing: Ideology and Change in Public Policy* (Albany: State University of New York Press, 1985), pp. 150–53; Martha Derthick, *Policymaking for Social Security* (Washington, D.C.: Brookings, 1979), chap. 17; Mayhew, *Divided We Govern,* pp. 81–85.

23. David Vogel, "The 'New' Social Regulation in Historical and Comparative Perspective," in Thomas K. McCraw, ed., *Regulation in Perspective: Historical Essays* (Cambridge, Mass.: Harvard University Press, 1981), p. 161.

24. Kenneth J. Meier, *Regulation: Politics, Bureaucracy, and Economics* (New York: St. Martin's Press, 1985), chap. 4.

25. Ibid., chap. 6.

26. Sar A. Levitan, Peter E. Carlson, and Isaac Shapiro, *Protecting American Workers: An Asssessment of Government Programs* (Washington, D.C.: Bureau of National Affairs, 1986), chaps. 6, 10; Meier, *Regulation,* chap. 8.

27. Conlan, *New Federalism,* pp. 84–89.

28. General sources on regulatory expansion in the 1960s and 1970s: Richard A. Harris, "A Decade of Reform"; David Vogel, "The Power of Business in America: A Reappraisal," *British Journal of Political Science* 13 (1983): 24; Robert Higgs, *Crisis and Leviathan: Critical Episodes in the Growth of American Government* (New York: Oxford University Press, 1987), pp. 246–54; Murray L. Weidenbaum, *Business, Government, and the Public* (Englewood Cliffs, N.J.: Prentice-Hall, 1977), pp. 5–10; Mayhew, *Divided We Govern,* pp. 83, 85–87. On women's rights: Jo Freeman, *The Politics of Women's Liberation: A Case Study of an Emerging Social Movement and Its Relation to the Policy Process* (New York: David McKay, 1975), chap. 6.

29. On Carter's years: Mayhew, *Divided We Govern,* pp. 75, 76, 93–94, 98, 166–69.

30. Ibid., p. 144.

31. On state expansion during the two world wars, see Higgs, *Crisis and Leviathan,* chaps. 7, 9.

32. See, for example, Walter Dean Burnham, "Party Systems and the Political Process," chap. 10 in William Nisbet Chambers and Burnham, eds., *The American Party Systems: Stages of Political Development* (New York: Oxford University Press, 1967), pp. 287–304. The most unqualified claim that a one-to-one correspondence has existed between "electoral realignments" and (consequent) bursts of innovative national lawmaking appears in David W. Brady, *Critical Elections and Congressional Policy Making* (Stanford, Calif.: Stanford University Press, 1988).

33. See Mayhew, *Divided We Govern,* pp.143–44.

34. See, for example, Richard L. McCormick, "Walter Dean Burnham and 'The System of 1896,'" *Social Science History* 10 (1986): 245.

35. Brady, *Critical Elections,* chap. 3. On the tariff: Hansen, "Taxation and the Political Economy of the Tariff," p. 540.

36. On 1977–78: Mayhew, *Divided We Govern,* pp. 107, 168–69.

37. Ibid., pp. 146–48.

38. See, for example, James L. Sundquist, "Needed: A Political Theory for the New Era

of Coalition Government in the United States," *Political Science Quarterly* 103 (Winter 1988–89): 616–24.

39. Mayhew, *Divided We Govern,* pp. 146–48, 159.

40. For data on "party voting," see Jerome M. Clubb and Santa A. Traugott, "Partisan Cleavage and Cohesion in the House of Representatives, 1861–1974," *Journal of Interdisciplinary History* 7 (Winter 1977): 375–401; Patricia A. Hurley and Rick K. Wilson, "Partisan Voting Patterns in the U.S. Senate, 1877–1986," chap. 3 in John R. Hibbing and John G. Peters, eds., *The Changing World of the U.S. Senate* (Berkeley, Calif.: IGS Press, 1990); and Samuel C. Patterson and Gregory A. Caldeira, "Party Voting in the United States Congress," *British Journal of Political Science* 18 (January 1988): 111–31.

41. This conclusion may be inferred from many works on elections and the economy—for example, Gerald H. Kramer, "Short-Term Fluctuations in U.S. Voting Behavior, 1896–1964," *American Political Science Review* 65 (March 1971): 131–43.

42. Arthur M. Schlesinger Jr., "The Cycles of American Politics," chap. 2 in Schlesinger, *The Cycles of American History* (Boston: Houghton Mifflin, 1986).

43. Gillette, *Retreat from Reconstruction,* chaps. 7–12, 15; Eric Foner, *Reconstruction: America's Unfinished Revolution, 1863–1877* (New York: Harper and Row, 1988), pp. 524–34.

44. Richard Hofstadter, *The Age of Reform: From Bryan to F.D.R.* (New York: Vintage Books, 1955), p. 282.

45. Mayhew, *Divided We Govern,* p. 165.

46. Ibid., pp. 166–69.

47. Ibid., pp. 163–64.

48. Theda Skocpol, *Protecting Soldiers and Mothers: The Political Origins of Social Policy in the United States* (Cambridge, Mass.: Harvard University Press, 1992), chap. 9.

49. Mayhew, *Divided We Govern,* pp. 162–63.

50. Eric Foner, *Reconstruction: America's Unfinished Revolution.*

51. Arthur M. Schlesinger Jr., *The Politics of Upheaval* (Boston: Houghton Mifflin, 1960), part I.

52. Mayhew, *Divided We Govern,* pp. 161–62.

8

Innovative Midterm Elections

For a party out of the White House, there is an age-old way to conduct midterm elections: Talk retrospective and make vague promises. The Republicans' "Had Enough?" campaign against the Truman administration in 1946 is a classic instance. In midterms, a retrospective focus makes sense because it is so inviting to blame everything on an incumbent president's two-year record. Vagueness helps along a "coalition-of-disaffected-minorities" strategy at a time when not having presidential candidates on the ballot lets House and Senate candidates run on local issues; what works in Alabama may not work in Rhode Island.

All the more surprising, then, that the Republicans of 1994 should present a campaign appeal—the Contract with America—that was both prospective and specific. For a congressional party, it broke new ground to commit hundreds of candidates to an action program and then use that program as respectively a campaign theme, a lens for interpreting the election outcome, and a centerpiece for a "hundred-days" legislative drive. Many presidential candidates have acted out this familiar mandate scenario—consider Ronald Reagan's use of the Kemp-Roth tax cut plan in the 1980 campaign and subsequently in his 1981 budget—as have U.S. national parties more generally by writing platforms every four years and then sometimes paying attention to

them after winning. But it was a first for a congressional party — more specifically, for just a House-of-Representatives party.

Of course, election mandates are largely a matter of social construction
(Hershey 1992): Who can be sure what voters intend when they vote or if their
individual intentions can be successfully added up? But being socially constructed does not make a mandate any the less consequential. Believable electoral connections can be immensely consequential, as is evident in the records
of William Gladstone, Woodrow Wilson, and others who pioneered in the
genre of election programs and their governmental use. Perceived mandates
can legitimize. Partly because presidents discovered this fact, the twentieth-
century presidency shot ahead of Congress in power. An intriguing question is
whether congressional "contracts" like Newt Gingrich's, played out into the
future, could serve as something of an institutional equalizer. Congress to
president: "My mandate and hundred days are better than yours." Is this a
possible future? We should stay tuned.

Placing 1994 in U.S. History

But if the apparatus of the contract is new, midterm elections that make
a difference are not. My chief aim here is to develop this historical generalization, not to dwell on 1994's uniqueness. If the 1994 midterms turn out to have
spurred a decisive long-term policy shift — we can't be sure yet that it has — this
will not be the first time midterms have done that, contract or no contract. In
fact, presidential elections, transfixing as they are for most of us, have had to
compete with midterms as boundary events in U.S. policy history. This is an
important, largely untold story.

More specifically, I will try in this chapter to isolate and discuss a class of
past midterms that meet the following four criteria: Each of them (1) elevated
to power a new dominant congressional coalition that (2) anchored in place a
new national policy agenda and (3) enjoyed considerable (though never complete) success in enacting that agenda, and (4) the coalition, the agenda, and
the enacting capacity lasted for not just two years but eight or ten years or even
longer. In short, these are midterms that triggered new policy eras. It is hard to
imagine a more ambitious role for midterm elections, and the Gingrich Republicans will be delighted if theirs can eventually be said to have met this stiff
standard. We cannot know if it will, but if it does, it will join an already-
populated historical class.

The evidence to document midterms of the stipulated type will center on
relevant innovativeness shown by post-midterm Congresses rather than on

events inherent in the midterm elections themselves. What happens afterward is what counts. Just how the midterms may have engendered such innovativeness is another matter, and I will do the best I can with that question in a follow-up discussion, though without confidence that I have gotten anywhere near closure. The sources for this electoral and policy analysis are standard secondary works on U.S. political history.

I will close the chapter on a different note. It is entirely possible, after all, that the 1994 midterms have engendered not a new policy era but a flash in the pan. The "Age of Gingrich" may come and go in a hurry, leaving little trace. I will take a look at a past flash-in-the-pan midterm victory that arguably approximates best some relevant properties of 1994 — the Republican midterm victory of 1946.

Innovative Midterms of the Past

The ambitious criteria outlined above seem to be met by four past midterms, two from the nineteenth century and two from the twentieth.

1810

Here is a case we all learned about in elementary school but that later professional training in election analysis seems to have taught us to ignore. The election of 1810, at the midpoint of James Madison's first term in the White House, "swept in a new generation of Republicans" to power in the House of Representatives. This breath of fresh air came from within the dominant Jeffersonian Republican party rather than from the declining Federalist opposition. "War Hawks" was the familiar label given to the new faction of some 30 members who took the lead in organizing the new House in November 1811, electing freshman Henry Clay to the Speakership.

The War Hawks' new agenda featured nationalism, aggressive expansionism, economic development, and, in the short term, war against England. They got much of what they wanted. The new Congress led off with military legislation and nudged Madison toward requesting a declaration of war, which he did in mid-1812. Beyond that, House Republican pressure for such initiatives as a new national bank, internal improvements, higher tariffs, and admission of new states continued through the 1810s and into the 1820s, often winning success though often losing out to White House opposition (as with Madison's veto of an internal improvements bill on his last day in office). The House had become the center of initiative in the government. If today's media had operated back then, it is a good bet that more TV bytes per year would have gone to Clay, who served as Speaker most of the time between 1811 and 1825, than to Presidents James Madison (1809–17) or James Monroe (1817–25) (White

1951: 57–62; Peters 1990: 33–34; Smelser 1968: 208–13; Davidson et al. 1994: 325–26; Jordan 1994: 98–99; Boyer et al. 1993: 267–68).

1866

This was the election that ushered in congressional Reconstruction. Consolidated in veto-proof two-thirds majorities in both House and Senate, the dominant radical faction of the Republican party proceeded to seize the initiative from President Andrew Johnson and enact its own blueprint for the conquered South. Representative Thaddeus Stevens, though not Speaker, assumed a leadership role something like Henry Clay's earlier.

Following the election, in January 1867, the outgoing 39th Congress arranged a special session of the incoming 40th Congress for March 1867. (Without that, the new Congress wouldn't have met until November 1867, as was the norm before the 20th "Lame-Duck" Amendment was added to the Constitution in the 1930s.) In ambition and decisiveness, the legislative record of March 1867 resembles that of early 1933 under Franklin Roosevelt. Actually, the victorious Republicans initiated their blueprint in the closing days of the lame-duck session just *before* the new Congress convened. On March 2, 1867, three major acts were approved: the Tenure of Office Act restricting the president's control over executive personnel; the Command of the Army Act requiring the president to issue all military orders through the general of the army; and above all, the First Reconstruction Act dividing the South into five military districts to the end of writing new state constitutions and forming new governments based on enfranchisement of African-Americans but restricted suffrage for rebel whites (Cashman 1993: 211–12; Randall and Donald 1969: ch. 34). The programmatic drive went on from there in a smooth transition as the new Congress convened on March 4.

In general, though with flagging commitment after the late 1860s, the Republicans' Reconstruction majority held in place on Capitol Hill until the midterm election of 1874. In the realm of lawmaking, three more Reconstruction Acts ensued during 1867 and 1868 (though the coalition fell one Senate vote short of evicting the impeached Johnson from office in 1868), the 15th Amendment enfranchising blacks cleared Congress in February 1869, and subsequent Congresses followed with the five Enforcement Acts of 1870 through 1872 and the era-closing Civil Rights Act of early 1875.

1910

No opening big bang this time, and no new leader as prominent as Clay or Stevens. At this midpoint of the William Howard Taft administration, the Republicans kept formal control of the Senate while losing the House. But in coalitional terms, the election gave decisive control of Capitol Hill to a cross-party coalition of Democrats and progressive Republicans who pursued a reform agenda until U.S. entry into World War I in 1917 (or perhaps until the 1918 midterm). Congressional conservatives had lost their ascendancy and largely their blocking power; as of 1910, the House's Cannon regime and the Senate's Allison-Aldrich regime came to an end.

Many notable laws were to win enactment during Woodrow Wilson's legislative drives of 1913–14 and 1916, but the Congress of 1911–13 compiled a busy record before that. It included the 17th Amendment requiring direct election of U.S. Senators, first voted by the House in 1892 and now finally endorsed by the Senate; an eight-hour day for workers on federal contracts, favored by the House against Senate opposition since 1896; a ban on phosphorus matches whose manufacture was said to cause a hideous disease; establishment of the federal Children's Bureau, championed by that era's women's movement; creation of the Department of Labor; and a campaign-finance measure placing a ceiling on candidate expenditures (Mowry 1958: 262–65; Kobach 1994: 1776–79; Moss 1994; Mutch 1988: 1–16). In 1912, the House broke new ground with its so-called Money Trust Investigation — "the first Congressional investigation conducted in the 'grand manner' of modern times, and geared to the avowed purpose of proving and publicizing the need for major legislative enactments in new fields." Wall Street received a major roasting (Taylor 1961: 81–84).

1938

"It was not the 1936 Roosevelt landslide, but the more ambiguous [in party terms] result of 1938, that set the pattern that was followed, with relatively minor variations until after World War II was over and Roosevelt was dead" (Barone 1990: 122). The 1938 midterm brought to dominance the so-called conservative coalition of Republicans and southern Democrats who now had the resolve, numbers, and institutional bases to block liberal initiatives, conduct investigations serving conservative ends, and sometimes enact their own laws. Special attention was to go to cutting back New Deal programs, hunting for alleged subversives, and curbing the then muscle-flexing labor movement. The coalition's major actors included Edward Cox (D.–Ga.), Howard Smith (D.–Va.), and Charles Halleck (R.–Ind.), a formidable trio on the House Rules Committee which served as a kind of cross-party headquarters; Martin Dies (D.–Tex.) as chairman of a special committee to investigate un-American activities; House Republican Minority Leader Joseph Martin of Massachusetts; and, as the years went on, Senator Robert Taft of Ohio (Patterson 1967: ch. 9).

No new major New Deal initiative won enactment after the 1938 election (Jeffries 1990; Amenta and Skocpol 1988). In 1939–40, Congress slashed relief spending, ended Roosevelt's prized undistributed-profits tax, and killed two key White House proposals in the areas of public works and housing. Congressman Clifton A. Woodrum (D.–Va.) ran a damaging investigation of the Works Progress Administration (WPA), Congressman Smith conducted a yearlong probe of the National Labor Relations Board (NLRB), and the Dies committee targeted the left in general. Notable laws actually passed during those years included the Hatch Act of 1939 curbing executive use of patronage jobs and the Smith Act of 1940 requiring aliens to register and penalizing subversion of the Armed Forces (Patterson 1967: ch. 9). By the end of 1943, Congress had directly or indirectly killed such New Deal instruments as the Federal Theatre Project, the Civilian Conservation Corps, the WPA, the National Youth Administration, the Home Owners' Loan Corporation, and the National Resources Planning Board (Leuchtenburg 1963: 273; Brinkley 1995: 141, 255). Labor unions suffered constraints through the Smith-Connally Act of 1943 and later the Taft-Hartley Act of 1947.

Just how long the "conservative coalition" can be said to have prevailed on Capitol Hill is a slippery subject, partly because there were ups and downs. One account, using roll-call data, points to 1939 through 1955 as the era of particular coalition success in the House: On occasions during those years when most Republicans and most southern Democrats lined up against most northern Democrats, the conservative side won 92.8 percent of the time. A comparable Senate era, exhibiting a lag as the Senate, for staggered-election reasons, often does, was 1942 through 1958 (Shelley 1983: 29–41). Liberal Democrats reaching for power under Kennedy still found it necessary to "pack" the House Rules Committee with their own loyalists in a celebrated showdown in 1961.

ALSO-RANS

Those are the four midterms that seem to stand out. In the nineteenth century, according to standard sources, no other midterm comes close to 1810 or 1866 in the stipulated kind of policy impact. As for more recent times, I gave serious consideration to the 1958 election during Eisenhower's second term, which elected immense Democratic majorities that contributed to party projects later in the 1960s. But 1958 doesn't work well. Eisenhower kept surprisingly good control of the national policy agenda in 1959 through 1960 by attacking government spending and promoting reform of labor unions — the latter coming to fruition in the Landrum-Griffin Act of 1959 (Evans and Novak 1966: ch. 10). The liberals had to wait. I considered the 1974 midterm, which elected the 75 famed "Watergate babies" who forced an overhaul of the

House seniority system in the winter of 1974–75. But what did they do after that? What policy regime did they inaugurate? Not much on the socio-economic front, and the era's chief Watergate-related procedural reforms — the War Powers Act, the Budget and Impoundment Act, and the Campaign Finance Reform Act — were enacted by the preceding Congress of 1973–74.

Possibly the closest call was the midterm of 1930 under Hoover, which has much in common with that of 1910 under Taft. In March through June of 1932, a cross-party congressional coalition of Democrats and progressive Republicans erupted to enact important new statutes in the areas of taxation and relief. A New Deal reform impulse that would last into 1937–38 was investing Capitol Hill before Roosevelt reached Washington. But it is not easy to credit this eruption in any direct way to the 1930 midterm, notwithstanding the large seat shifts that year to the Democrats. The Congress of 1931–33 started out in a spirit of bipartisan cooperation. Perhaps this is surprising, given the background of the Depression, but the antiestablishment reform eruption came later and seems to have had later causes. It was one of those things — no doubt induced by the Depression getting worse. Unlike 1910, the 1930 midterm did not itself empower a new coalition bearing a new policy agenda (Schwarz 1970: chs. 4–6; Mayhew 1991: 154–56).

Explaining Innovative Midterms

What might account for midterm aftermaths as striking as those associated with 1810, 1866, 1910, and 1938? Four models come to mind. Each model will be discussed briefly here, with an eye for all past U.S. experience with midterms, innovative and noninnovative, insofar as that is possible. The recent 1994 midterms will be brought in where relevant. We know that 1994 elevated to power a new congressional coalition bearing a new policy agenda; as of this writing in May 1995, notwithstanding the House's remarkable early-year "one hundred days" campaign, we cannot tell how much luck this coalition will finally have enacting its agenda into law during 1995–96, and we certainly can't tell whether the new regime will exhibit decadelong staying power. But it will be interesting to see whether midterm features associated with past exceptional innovativeness, insofar as those can be teased out of history, obtained in 1994.

LARGE PARTY SEAT SWINGS

A simple and obvious idea is that new, aggressive, long-lasting policy regimes on Capitol Hill might have origins in midterm seat gains for the out-party that are abnormally large — whatever might cause those gains. It is a proximate explanation. This is unquestionably part of the story for 1910, when the Democrats gained 56 House seats and 10 Senate seats and took over the House (though not the Senate); for 1938 when the Republicans gained 80 House seats and 6 Senate seats (though still fell well short of capturing either body); and, to compare with the present, for 1994 with its Republican gains of 52 and 8 seats.

Unfortunately, as a general proposition, this seat-gain diagnostic is not much better than most of those offered by pre-modern medicine. The 1810 midterms don't help the discussion much, since they occurred before competition between mass-based parties kicked into place in the 1830s (though still: Those War Hawks weren't a Federalist party opposition). But note that the 1866 midterms brought scarcely any partisan seat change at all—3 House seats and 1 Senate seat to the Democrats, compared with the results for 1864. For the radical Republicans in the 1866 midterm, holding even was a victory. Moreover, a great many midterms have brought large partisan seat swings without generating aggressive, long-lasting new policy orders—for example, Democratic gains of 93 House seats in 1874, 70 in 1882, 75 in 1890, 75 in 1922, and (as previously discussed) 49 in both 1958 and 1974 and Republican gains of 120 in 1894, 66 in 1914, and 47 in 1966. Spot quiz: What was undertaken or achieved by that Congress of 1895–97 fortified by a record 120 new House Republicans? The history books are a blank. Large partisan seat swings may help, but on the evidence they have been neither a necessary nor a sufficient condition for an innovative post-midterm policy order.

PUBLIC OPINION CHANGE

At a much more basic level, Capitol Hill policy change may be motored by ups and downs in public opinion. Politics may finally be that simple. Assume a universe in which U.S. public opinion is ordinarily stable but sometimes shows breaking points—"public moods," for example, may come and go—that the breaking points occur randomly across electoral cycles, and that both the stabilities and the breaking points are reflected on Capitol Hill. One result is that off-election-season "policy eruptions" will occasionally take place in Congress, as in, say, the Progressive-Democratic uprising of the spring of 1932 or the onset of McCarthyism in early 1950. But another result, given the stickiness inherent in electing politicians for terms, is that opinion breaking points will need to wait for the next even-year November to find full expression in Washington.

Nothing is particularly strange about this universe, though note one thing that it predicts: Elections that elevate new Capitol Hill policy coalitions will occur as often in midterms as in presidential years. And that may be a basic fact of U.S. politics (though, yes, a freshly elected coalition may run into more enactment trouble after midterms than after a presidential election since it faces holdover politicians in both the White House and two-thirds of the Senate rather than just in two-thirds of the Senate). In this scenario, Clay or Stevens (or Gingrich), as leader of a new policy coalition, should be no more surprising than Franklin Roosevelt in that role.

I have a hunch that this model accounts for a good deal in general and helps to explain innovative midterms. Survey evidence for 1937–38, and moves by elite actors around 1810, in 1865–66, and in 1909–10 that admit inference of substantial underlying opinion shifts also at those junctures, help the model along—and for comparison, 1993–94 showed evidence of an opinion shift too. But this analysis has to stay in the realm of hunch. Most of U.S. history lacks opinion data, and at any rate, for recent times, assuming agreement on which kinds of data to look for, we would very likely find instances of sizable pre-midterm shifts of opinion that did not trigger new post-midterm policy regimes. Consider Truman's first two years or Reagan's. A hypothesized relation between large opinion shifts and new policy regimes would likely pan out across U.S. history, as a statistical matter, but there would be a lot of error.

RESOLUTION OF HIGH-STAKES CONFLICT

To switch to an elite setting more easily documented and more proximate to the phenomenon being explained, consider the following scenario for the opening two years of a president's term. For a year or more, dramatic battles take place on Capitol Hill as Congress lines up for and against White House positions. The stakes are enormous as the future seems to be presenting itself for basic shaping; by historical standards, one of the opposing sides is pressing an exceptionally prodigious agenda. There are wins, losses, and standoffs. The overall outcome remains uncertain going into a midterm season where a self-conscious opposition confronts the White House in elections seen by many as showdowns. The opposition wins and stands ready with its own agenda.

Let me concede that this scenario misdescribes the lead-up to the midterm of 1810. Spectacular as the War Hawks may be as an instance of a post-midterm policy coalition, the early-nineteenth-century politics surrounding their rise sometimes fits into the discussion here aptly, sometimes not so aptly. Part of the story of 1810 is that the House, for various reasons, was succeeding at that time in surging temporarily past the presidency as a national representative institution (it still far surpassed the Senate). U.S. institutions, parties, and voters were all getting their sea legs back then.

But of 1865–66, 1909–10, and 1937–38, this resolution-of-conflict model provides a quite good description. From late 1865 through 1866, radical Republicans in Congress squared off against Andrew Johnson, winning some victories over his vetoes but not able to dominate yet. In 1909–10, aggressive Capitol Hill reformers went to the mat with Taft-backed conservatives over the tariff, taxation, conservation, and railroad regulation. It remained unclear who would prevail. In these Johnson and Taft instances the transformative agendas came from the Capitol Hill side, but in 1937–38 FDR bore that distinction with his post-landslide program to pack the Supreme Court, tighten presidential control of the executive branch, help along labor union organization, and press legislative initiatives in such areas as housing, minimum wage, public-works spending, and more river-valley developments like the Tennessee Valley Authority (TVA). Intense reaction to these aims brought a "conservative manifesto" by Senate dissidents in late 1937, landmark White House defeats on court packing and executive reorganization, a customizing of the House Rules Committee to serve as a base for congressional conservatism, and a first round of Dies committee hearings damaging to New Deal interests in 1938. It was a warm-up for 1939, though until the 1938 midterms it wasn't certain which side would come out ahead (Randall and Donald 1969: ch. 33; Cooper 1990: 145–57; Patterson 1967: chs. 6–8).

These three Congresses were unquestionably among the most contentious in U.S. history. In the cases of 1865–66 and 1909–10, though not as clearly 1937–38 when congressional support for the White House plummeted during the recession of late 1937 through early 1938 but then rose again in mid-1938, elite-level events during the two-year intervals are consistent with a model of gradual underlying public-opinion drift away from the White House side. House insurgents, for example, failed in an attempt to cripple the conservative Cannon Speakership in March 1909 but succeeded a year later in March 1910.

All three Congresses discussed here may remind the reader of 1993–94. The Democrats are back! it was proclaimed at the start of 1993, and the Clinton administration's drive to rival the New Deal and Great Society ensued. Health care reform in 1994 raised the stakes about as high as they get in U.S. domestic politics, and the resulting coalitional combat up through the 1994 midterms does not need to be reviewed.

Leaving aside the circumstances of 1810, very-high-stakes, unresolved conflict before midterms looks like a necessary condition for a new policy regime after the midterms. The logic is good, as are the facts; not least, it is important for an opposition to discover and steel itself through conflict before midterms so as to be ready with an agenda afterward. But a sufficient condition, it is probably not. Other relevant historical junctures seem to register fairly high on the "high-stakes-and-unresolved-conflict-before-midterms" scale, for example, the first two years of Theodore Roosevelt's second term (which brought wins and losses for the Square Deal), of Truman's second term (the Fair Deal's ups and downs, McCarthyism), of Kennedy's presidency (the stalemate over civil rights, the losing White House drives for education aid and Medicare), of Nixon's first term (lots of conflict on many fronts), and of Carter's presidency (the close-fought stalemate over energy policy). Still, to be fair to the idea being pressed here, most beginnings of presidential terms do *not* seem to exhibit such unresolved high-stakes conflict—some examples (when the presidents all got what they wanted, more or less) are Woodrow Wilson's first two years in 1913–14, Franklin Roosevelt's in 1933–34, Lyndon Johnson's in 1965–66, and Reagan's in 1981–82; Eisenhower's in 1953–54 (low-temperature politics); and (when the presidents didn't want much) Reagan's in 1985–86 and Bush's in 1989–90.

MAJORITY-PARTY FACTIONALISM

The fourth model is compatible with the public-opinion and conflict-resolution accounts presented previously but makes a distinctive claim. It is this: The decisive lead-up to a new post-midterm policy regime is a fundamental, take-no-prisoners conflict over an era's central policy issues *within* the ruling majority party during the preceding midterm-election season, from which an anti–White House faction emerges victorious and then constitutes or joins a dominant new policy regime on Capitol Hill.

I have not found evidence of such intraparty conflict during the 1810 election season, which hasn't been written up all that much. Perhaps the War Hawks of 1811–12—who were certainly a prime instance of a party faction—emerged from such election-related conflict within the dominant Jeffersonian Republican party of that era, perhaps not. But for U.S. history after, say, 1860—this gets past the confusing reconfiguration of parties during the 1850s—the factionalism model works very well. There seems to be a one-to-one relation between exceptional factionalism within the majority party and the advent of new long-lasting policy regimes.

Here is the evidence. In the post–Civil War election year of 1866, beyond the usual contesting between Republicans and Democrats, much hinged on which kinds of Republicans managed to get nominated and elected. Nominating showdowns took place at the district level between radicals and conservatives. President Andrew Johnson, a deposit of the Lincoln-led Union ticket of 1864 but now well distanced from the Republican median on Reconstruction policy, undertook an extraordinary speaking tour across the North during the late summer of 1866 aimed at electing a cross-party coalition of "Douglas

Democrats" and conservative Republicans to Congress. No president before that time had intruded so boldly into electoral politics, and none would do so again during the nineteeth century; Johnson's campaign was "the stark exception." The radicals won; the opposing cross-party coalition lost. On balance, radicals triumphed over conservatives in the Republican party's nominating processes that year; later, the party kept virtually all its congressional seats in a general election lacking conventional "in-party" versus "out-party" dynamics; and Johnson ended the election season discredited (Tulis 1987: 87–93; Powell 1973; Stampp 1970: 114–18; Randall and Donald 1969: 589–91).

In 1910 President Taft and his allies undertook the first great midterm party purge of the twentieth century — an effort to aid Republican party regulars and defeat progressive insurgents in Republican primaries in the Midwest and West. Disloyal incumbents were targeted. Statewide networks of "Taft Republican clubs" appeared and were answered by "progressive Republican clubs." The result was a disaster for the White House — "an almost unbroken string of reverses" as some 40 incumbent Republican regulars lost their House nominations (mostly to progressives), anti-Taft incumbents held their seats, and aggressive reform factions led by Robert La Follette and Hiram Johnson won eye-catching complete victories in Wisconsin and California (Mowry 1958: 266–68, 272–73; Cooper 1990: 157; Patterson 1967: 270–87).

And in 1938 Franklin Roosevelt, exasperated by a growing faction of anti–New Deal Democrats on Capitol Hill, undertook the second and last great midterm party purge of the twentieth century. The result was another White House disaster, or at least it was seen as such: In three of the best-known confrontations, conservative Senators Walter George of Georgia, "Cotton Ed" Smith of South Carolina, and Millard Tydings of Maryland easily won their primaries against FDR-backed challengers (Patterson 1967: 270–87). In fact, more seems to have gone on in the 1938 Democratic primaries than we see in the conventional Roosevelt-centered accounts. (Both the 1910 and 1938 primary seasons could use more scholarly attention.) Through random reading, for example, I have come across instances of incumbent liberal Democrats losing House nominations in 1938 in San Antonio, where the defeat of Maury Maverick was a major blow to the left, and in Norfolk, Virginia. A nationwide grinding of party teeth seems to have occurred, not always involving the White House (Koeniger 1982: 878, 884; Weiss 1971).

In short, the majority-party factional showdowns of 1866, 1910, and 1938 stand out as distinctive; no other midterm season since 1860 has exhibited such dynamics. Certainly the three presidential intrusions at those times are distinctive. And in all three cases an anti–White House faction that won out overall (the radical Republicans in 1866) or in a substantial section of the country (the progressive Republicans in 1910, the conservative Democrats in 1938) went on to constitute or join a new Capitol Hill policy coalition that prevailed for a long time.

What might explain this apparent cause-and-effect relationship? One answer is that such factional showdowns do not do anything more than efficiently index emerging conflicts in U.S. society that are particularly severe and lasting. New societal cleavages are the real causal factor; that loud noise you hear is just a new issue cutting the political sector at a new joint. But another plausible answer is that such showdowns between party factions, whatever their origins, have causal power of their own: They may generate a psychology that something basic has been "settled" in a whole party or a large geographic region within one party (those Walter George types just can't be beaten); they may stir lasting animosities among elite actors, convert historical opponents into friends and old comrades-in-arms into enemies, and result in blocs of voters being cued by factional leaders once old party images and signals become muddled. Whichever way, the effect on the system as a whole is to permanently weaken one actual or potential governing coalition (the anti-Reconstructionists, the Taft-Cannon-Aldrich Republicans, the New Dealers) and strengthen another (the radical Republicans, the progressives/Democrats, the "conservative coalition").

There is no easy way to choose between these two accounts, but it may be illuminating to note that intraparty conflict can play a large and analogous role in other settings. Consider the factional showdowns that occasionally occur in U.S. nominating conventions with the result of ushering in a new durable policy coalition within a presidential party and affecting the national balance between the parties—the 1896 Democratic convention that elevated the Silverite faction led by William Jennings Bryan and alienated the more conservative Gold Democrats; the 1964 Republican convention that nominated Barry Goldwater, jarred that party toward conservatism of a southwestern variety, and ostracized the Rockefeller moderates; and the 1972 Democratic convention that nominated George McGovern and shifted that party's base toward candidate organizations catering to race, gender, and age categories at the expense of the old establishment of labor unions, regular state organizations, and city machines. In British politics, to cite another analogy, nothing has been more productive of dominant, long-lasting coalitions in the House of Commons than having one major party hive off a faction through serious internal policy conflict and thus improve the competitive position of the other major party—as did the Tories over repeal of the Corn Laws in 1846, the Liberals over Irish Home rule in 1886 and again over conduct of World

War I in 1916, and the Labor Party over policy toward the Depression in 1931 and again through defection of its centrist Social Democratic faction in 1981.

But obviously, nothing even faintly resembling the midterm factional show-downs of 1868, 1910, and 1938 took place within the Democratic party during the 1994 election season. Imagine a counterfactual scenario in which the Clinton White House, fed up with less than 100 percent Democratic sup-port for the president's budget and health care programs, stage-manages a party purge in mid-1994. "Clinton Clubs" sprout up around the country. Disloyalists are listed and denounced. Liberal money cascades out from New York and California. In a whirlwind speaking tour through the relevant states and districts, the president appeals in person to Democratic primary voters to nominate unabashed liberals to replace Senators Richard Bryan of Nevada and Bob Kerrey of Nebraska; Congressmen Gary Condit of California, Bill Brewster of Oklahoma, Charles Stenholm of Texas; and others. House members Sam Gejdenson and David Obey are tapped by the White House to enter primaries against two other senators of uncertain reliability—Joseph Lieberman of Connecticut and Herb Kohl of Wisconsin. In the event, virtually all the White House–backed candidates lose out to a now-angry collection of party veterans who have taken to calling themselves "The True Democratic Center." Nothing like this happened in 1994.

BACK TO 1994

In general, then, where does this analysis of past "innovative midterms" leave us as regards 1994? For one thing, it throws a comparative light on Gingrich. Followers as we are of the twentieth-century presidency, we tend to forget that House leaders elevated by elections—such as Clay and Stevens—can sometimes seize the policy initiative too. It may be just historical accident that no congressional leader has assumed this role in recent times. (Senator Robert Taft may be the closest twentieth-century approximation until now—see the following discussion.)

For another thing, in *some* background respects 1994 bears resemblance to some or all of the past innovative midterm years: Witness the yearlong drift of public opinion against the Clinton White House, the exceptionally high-stakes conflict over health care, the impressive November seat gains for the opposition. This is food for thought. Yet, in the final analysis, the trademark characteristic of relevant past midterms—the no-holds-barred conflict between factions of the majority party—was entirely missing in 1994. The new Republican policy coalition of 1995 is not propelled by any such explosion. Yes, the Democrats suffered a major election loss in 1994, but they did not tear themselves apart in that year's election processes and thus they remain a formidable instrument. The normal gyrations of politics can bring them back. The implication: We may be witnessing not the start of a long-lasting new policy regime but rather the start of conventional toss-up politics in which Congress goes back and forth between the parties and key policy options stay up for grabs.

The Analogy of 1946

If 1810, 1866, 1910, and 1938 are high rungs to reach for, 1946 is a very low rung — at least in terms of the durability of the new policy coalition produced by that midterm. The analogy is haunting to today's Republicans since 1946 looks so much like 1994. Then, Harry Truman, a first-term Democratic president floundering in his job and low in the polls, saw his party lose control of both houses of Congress as Republicans gained 58 House members and 13 senators and surged to 54.7 percent of the national major-party House vote. The comparable statistics for 1994 are 52 House members, 9 senators, and some 53.8 percent of the House popular vote. Between the two dates, the Republicans never captured control of the House or Senate at midterms (they did *keep* the Senate in 1982) or won a decisive edge in the House popular vote at any time.

Yet, of course, the party majorities of 1946 hemorrhaged away two years later. Besides reelecting Truman in 1948, the Democrats gained 75 House members, 9 senators, and formal control of both houses that lasted with one brief interlude (1953–54) for three decades. In hindsight, the Republican 80th Congress of 1947–48 proved to be a classic instance of up the hill and down again. It didn't begin a long-lasting new policy regime; instead it just offered a sort of local peak experience for the cross-party "conservative coalition" that reigned during those times anyway. From the Republican long-term perspective, 1946 is an awful precedent for 1994.

But how about a more modest perspective in which short-term slogging is the norm in politics and can make a difference? With that standard in mind, it is worth closing with a brief look at the Republicans' last exercise in post-midterm rule. They didn't employ a "contract" or a hundred-days script in 1947, but they did have a program of sorts and a talented leader in Robert Taft.

What was the result? (Hartmann 1971; Witte 1985: ch. 7; Meier 1985: 142, 159). The phrase "do-nothing 80th Congress" has echoed down through the years, but that was largely Democratic campaign propaganda. It meant that, no surprise, a Republican Congress refused to enact Truman's Fair Deal program. (As it happens, the ensuing 81st Congress, run by Democrats, enacted a major housing bill but balked as the 80th did at Truman's education, health insurance, river-valley, and civil rights proposals and wouldn't support the president on agriculture or labor-management relations; the conservative coalition lived on.)

Otherwise, there was considerable legislative motion in 1947–48. In the area of foreign and defense policy, teamwork across party lines generated the Truman Doctrine authorizing aid to Greece and Turkey, the Marshall Plan, and the National Security Act unifying the armed services under one cabinet secretary. The 80th's domestic initiatives that remained influential long afterward included the Federal Insecticide, Fungicide, and Rodenticide Act (FIFRA) of 1947, inaugurating federal control of pesticides, and the Water Pollution Control Act of 1948, the federal entry into that policy realm; it was still a program-building era, even if many initiatives failed.

As for the Taft Republicans' distinctive policy agenda, three enactments deserve mention. The 22nd Amendment limiting presidents to two terms — the "term-limits" formula of those times — cleared Congress easily in early 1947. A sizable tax cut lost out twice to Truman vetoes in 1947, but a third version attracted the needed votes for an override in the spring of 1948. Most important by far, the pro-management Taft-Hartley Act, which rolled back the Wagner Act and has regulated labor relations for the past half century despite energetic union efforts to repeal it under Truman (in 1949), Johnson, and Carter, won passage over Truman's veto in mid-1947.

By conservative standards, that was quite a successful two years. It is not entirely clear that the current 104th Congress will surpass it, though probably it will.

At any rate, long-term electoral prospects for the Republicans are scarcely as grim today as they must have looked back in 1947–48. Republican winners in 1946 included no senators and only 2 House members from the still solidly Democratic South, which meant that the GOP needed to win immense — and, after the New Deal realignment, unlikely — victories outside the South to organize Congress. House delegations from the North in 1947–48 had Republican edges as extreme as 8–1 in Minnesota, 10–0 in Wisconsin, 14–3 in Michigan, 20–6 in Illinois, 9–2 in Indiana, 19–4 in Ohio, 12–2 in New Jersey, and 28–5 in Pennsylvania. All 6 Philadelphians were Republicans. Numbers like these were not likely to last very long. Today, given the Republican surge in the South, they are no longer needed.

And beyond this, we now have Gingrich and the Contract with America. The 80th Congress's Robert Taft, for all his pugnacity and energy, his analytic capacity, his encyclopedic knowledge of policy areas, his ability to bore in day after day with telling critiques, amendments, and counterproposals, never made much of a mark as a dramatizer, stage manager, or salesman—as witness his failed presidential drives. Gingrich, like some presidents, possesses exactly those merchandising capabilities—as witness the contract and the programmatic House drama built on it in early 1995. At the least, this should guarantee that we won't hear a great deal about a "do-nothing 104th Congress."

Note

I would like to thank Joseph LaPalombara and Eric Schickler for their helpful comments on an early draft. This essay was originally published as chap. 10 in Philip A. Klinkner (ed.), *Midterm: The Elections of 1994 in Context* (Boulder, Colo.: Westview Press, 1996). © 1996 Westview Press. Reprinted by permission of Westview Press, a member of Perseus Books Group.

References

Amenta, Edwin, and Theda Skocpol. 1988. "Redefining the New Deal: World War II and the Development of Social Provision in the United States." Ch. 2 in Margaret Weir, Ann Shola Orloff, and Theda Skocpol, eds. *The Politics of Social Policy in the United States.* Princeton: N.J.: Princeton University Press.

Barone, Michael. 1990. *Our Country: The Shaping of America from Roosevelt to Reagan.* New York: Free Press.

Boyer, Paul S., et al. 1993. *The Enduring Vision.* Lexington, Mass.: D.C. Heath.

Brinkley, Alan. 1995. *The End of Reform: New Deal Liberalism in Recession and War.* New York: Alfred A. Knopf.

Cashman, Sean Dennis. 1993. *America in the Gilded Age: From the Death of Lincoln to the Rise of Theodore Roosevelt.* New York: New York University Press.

Cooper, John Milton, Jr. 1990. *Pivotal Decades: The United States, 1900–1920.* New York: W.W. Norton.

Davidson, James West, et al. 1994. *Nation of Nations.* Vol. 1. New York: McGraw-Hill.

Evans, Rowland, and Robert Novak. 1966. *Lyndon B. Johnson: The Exercise of Power.* New York: New American Library.

Hartmann, Susan. 1971. *Truman and the 80th Congress.* Columbia, Mo.: University of Missouri Press.

Hershey, Majorie Randon. 1992. "The Constructed Explanation: Interpreting Election Results in the 1984 Presidential Race," *Journal of Politics* 54:943–76.

Jeffries, John W. 1990. "The 'New' New Deal: FDR and American Liberalism, 1937–1945." *Political Science Quarterly* 105:397–418.

Jordan, Winthrop D. 1994. *The United States.* Englewood Cliffs, N.J.: Prentice Hall.

Kobach, Kris W. 1994. "Rethinking Article V: Term Limits and the Seventeenth and Nineteenth Amendments." *Yale Law Journal* 103:1971–2007.

Koeniger, A. Cash. 1982. "The New Deal and the States: Roosevelt versus the Byrd Organization in Virginia." *Journal of American History* 68:876–96.

Leuchtenburg, William E. 1963. *Franklin D. Roosevelt and the New Deal, 1932–1940.* New York: Harper Torchbook.

Mayhew, David R. 1991. *Divided We Govern: Party Control, Lawmaking, and Investigations, 1946–1990.* New Haven: Yale University Press.

Meier, Kenneth J. 1985. *Regulation: Politics, Bureaucracy, and Economics.* New York: St. Martin's Press.

Moss, David A. 1994. "Kindling a Flame under Federalism: Progressive Reformers, Corporate Elites, and the Phosphorus Match Campaign of 1909–1912," *Business History Review* 68: 244–75.

Mowry, George E. 1958. *The Era of Theodore Roosevelt, 1900–1912.* New York: Harper and Brothers.

Mutch, Robert E. 1988. *Campaigns, Congress, and Courts: The Making of Federal Campaign Finance Law.* New York: Praeger.

Patterson, James T. 1967. *Congressional Conservatism and the New Deal: The Growth of the Conservative Coalition in Congress, 1933–1939.* Lexington, Ky.: University Press of Kentucky.

Peters, Ronald M., Jr. 1990. *The American Speakership.* Baltimore, Md.: Johns Hopkins Press.

Powell, Lawrence N. 1973. "Rejected Republican Incumbents in the 1866 Congressional Nominating Conventions: A Study in Reconstruction Politics." *Civil War History* 5: 219–37.

Randall, J. G., and David Donald. 1969. *The Civil War and Reconstruction.* Lexington, Mass.: D.C. Heath.

Schwarz, Jordan A. 1970. *The Interregnum of Despair: Hoover, Congress, and the Depression.* Urbana, Ill.: University of Illinois Press.

Shelley, Mack C., II. 1983. *The Permanent Majority: The Conservative Coalition in the United States Congress.* University, Ala.: University of Alabama Press.

Smelser, Marshall. 1968. *The Democratic Republic, 1801–1815.* New York: Harper & Row.

Stampp, Kenneth M. 1970. *The Era of Reconstruction, 1865–1877.* New York: Alfred A. Knopf.

Taylor, Telford. 1961. *Grand Inquest: The Story of Congressional Investigations.* New York: Ballantine.

Tulis, Jeffrey K. 1987. *The Rhetorical Presidency.* Princeton, N.J.: Princeton University Press.

Weiss, Stuart L. 1971. "Maury Maverick and the Liberal Bloc." *Journal of American History* 57:880–95.

White, Leonard. 1951. *The Jeffersonians: A Study in Administrative History, 1801–1829.* New York: Macmillan.

Witte, John F. 1985. *The Politics and Development of the Federal Income Tax.* Madison, Wisc.: University of Wisconsin Press.

9

Electoral Realignments

Introduction

The study of U.S. electoral realignments, which enjoyed its heyday in the 1960s and 1970s, was one of the most creative, engaging, and influential intellectual enterprises undertaken by American political scientists during the past half century. It rivaled the Michigan election studies. It offered certifiable science, in the sense of a conceptual scheme, a theory, and quantitative analysis; breadth, in tackling large political questions associated with all of American national history; and even an eschatology, in the sense that it has induced generations of students and others, armed with a key to historical development, to keep asking, "Is an electoral realignment about to happen?" or "Have we been witnessing an electoral realignment this year?"

Fundamental to the appeal and influence of the realignments enterprise was the talent of four major entrepreneurs during its creative early days. First came V. O. Key Jr. and E. E. Schattschneider, who contributed important groundwork, and then James L. Sundquist and Walter Dean Burnham, who provided the principal statements in the genre. All four of these writers exhibited a prodigious, sure-footed command of the factual particulars of American political history as well as a rare capacity to generalize by detecting patterns. Small wonder that the genre made such a mark.

Here I address what might be called the classic phase of the realignments genre, which means chiefly works by these four writers. I touch on subsequent claims by David W. Brady; I take up critical commentaries by the trio of Jerome M. Clubb, William H. Flanigan, and Nancy H. Zingale, and by Larry M. Bartels; and I refer to a few works outside the genre, but I do not address the rest of the now vast follow-up literature amending, extending, or critiquing the classical realignments genre as it emerged in political science, or the parallel literature contributed by academics in the history profession. The sideline topic of party identification is not touched.

I start by explicating the classic realignments genre and end by critiquing it. I briefly take up certain works by the four principal authors but then shift gears and consider what might be thought of as a fully fleshed-out, maximally ambitious version of the realignments perspective — an ideal type of a scholarship already featuring ideal types. This ideal version relies heavily on the work of Burnham, whose theoretical and empirical claims have been particularly ambitious, and on Schattschneider, whose claims were just as ambitious if less completely worked out. It relies somewhat less on Sundquist, who has been more cautious, and least of all on Key, whose claims were the most conservative. I risk misconstruing all four authors by adopting this course, but along the way I try to signal how the four have differed from each other. What I call the fully fleshed-out version of the realignments perspective has proven to be particularly engaging and influential.

The Classic Realignments Perspective
THE FOUR PRINCIPALS: KEY, SCHATTSCHNEIDER, SUNDQUIST, AND BURNHAM

The idea of realignments had been broached by earlier authors (see Schantz 1998), but it was Key who crystallized and popularized the concept. His 1955 article, "A Theory of Critical Elections," demonstrates the basic, trademark dichotomizing move of the realignments school — the idea of sorting American elections into two categories: a few that are critical elections, in Key's terminology, and a great residual many that are not. Critical elections are those "in which voters are, at least from impressionistic evidence, unusually deeply concerned, in which the extent of electoral involvement is relatively quite high, and in which the decisive results of the voting reveal a sharp alteration of the preexisting cleavage within the electorate" (Key 1955:4). As "perhaps . . . the truly differentiating characteristic of this sort of election," Key emphasized that "the realignment made manifest in the voting in such elections seems to persist for several succeeding elections" (Key 1955:4). Using data from townships in selected New England states, Key tagged the elections of 1896 and 1928 as critical elections that brought sharp and long-lasting changes in voting patterns. That was all. Not a word appears in Key's article about any critical elections prior to 1896, any possible periodicity in the occurrence of such elections, or any distinctive kinds of issue innovations or government policy results that might be associated with such elections. Also, Key seemed to back off critical elections somewhat four years later (Key 1959) by pointing up patterns of "secular realignment" — that is, gradual change — in voter coalitions. Still, in 1955, courtesy of Key, the idea of critical elections came out of the bottle.

Schattschneider weighed in with a different kind of contribution in 1956, which he reissued largely intact as a chapter in his *Semisovereign People* in 1960. This evocative framing of realignments was chatty rather than data-driven. Unlike Key's circumspect articles, it was laden with far-reaching if often elusive empirical and theoretical claims. Schattschneider zeroed in on the election of 1896, "one of the decisive elections in American history," which brought on a party coalitional alignment "powerful enough to determine the nature of American politics for more than thirty years." The realignment of 1896 was "perhaps the best example in American history of the successful substitution of one conflict [that is, one cleavage between opposing clusters of interests] for another" — a signature Schattschneider concern (1960:78, 81–82). Later, the "revolution of 1932" produced "the greatest reversal of public policy in American history" (Schattschneider 1960:86).

Key and Schattschneider provided materials to build with. A half generation later, Sundquist presented a large, well-worked-out construction entitled *Dynamics of the Party System* (1973, revised and reissued 1983). Probably most undergraduate students have learned about electoral realignments through this zestful, accessible volume that organizes so much of American political history so interestingly. Sundquist addresses realigning periods or eras rather than just single elections — a realignment "reaches its climax in one or more critical elections" (Sundquist 1973:294) — and he dwells on three such eras that by about 1970 had become canonical: the 1850s, the 1890s, and the 1930s. In Sundquist's account of voter realignments, as in Schattschneider's, the content of new voter cleavages (not just their statistical existence, as in Key's account) is the signal feature. However, in an updating touch, Sundquist indexes the cleavages according to opposing issue positions, not (like Schattschneider) according to opposing interests from which issue propensities could in principle be easily predicted. Sundquist is cautious. He is quick with a proposition or a generalization about behavior by voters or parties, but I find no claims in his work about the likely periodicity of voter realignments, or about the governmental policy consequences of realignments.

Of Burnham's many works on electoral realignments, the following three are perhaps the best guides to his thinking: his indirectly relevant, much-cited article "The Changing Shape of the American Political Universe" (1965), his chapter in the classic volume *The American Party Systems* (1967), and his *Critical Elections and the Mainsprings of American Politics* (1970). Burnham adopted the essentials set forth by Key and Schattschneider and pointed the realignments scholarship toward additional instances of realigning elections, toward periodicity throughout American history, and toward policy effects said to be systematically associated with realignments. With these extensions, the realignments genre at the level of graduate instruction became largely Burnham's.

THE MOST AMBITIOUS VERSION: ELEVEN CLAIMS ABOUT REALIGNMENTS

A fully fleshed-out, maximally claim-laden version of the realignments perspective can be sorted into a series of distinct claims about reality. I present eleven such claims from the relevant literature. There is nothing magic about these particular eleven; anyone else who happened to scrutinize the same literature would probably code it differently, though not radically differently. Any analyst approaching this literature can get tied up in knots over whether the features allegedly associated with realignments are causes, defining properties, concomitants, or consequences of them. I have devised my series of claims so as to try to bypass those knots, which probably cannot be untied. The eleven claims are all in principle empirically testable. The first ten are universalistic in form — at least across the domain of American national history. The eleventh is historical. The first three claims, taken together, sum to the appropriate kind of content of a cyclical theory of history — such as business-cycles theory.

1. National elections in American history can be sorted into two kinds: a few realigning ones and a great many nonrealigning ones. This is the genre's foundational claim. The terminology can be blurry; not all authors agree on the definitions of "critical" and "realigning." There is the messy matter of eras as opposed to single elections: 1860 often sprawls back to encompass most of the 1850s; 1896 is often joined to the sweeping congressional midterm result of 1894; 1928 and 1932 are variously treated as distinct and unrelated events, related events, or part of the same continuing event. For the most part, the literature addresses presidential elections only, but some authors take up congressional ones. Still, Key's 1955 claim has remained central: Voter alignment changes that are "both sharp and durable" are brought by some elections but not by others (Key 1955:11). There is consensus on the requirement of durability (Sundquist 1983:4;

Burnham 1967:288–89, 1970:4–5). As for the elections in question, "There has long been agreement among historians that the elections of those of [sic] 1800, 1828, 1860, 1896, and 1932, for example, were fundamental turning points in the course of American electoral politics" (Burnham 1970:1) — a judgment that has not drawn much dissent within the genre.

2. Electoral realignments have appeared in patterns of regular periodicity. Key and Sundquist make no such claim, as noted above, but Burnham gives it prominence, titling a chapter "The Periodicity of American Critical Realignments" (1970:ch. 2). Burnham asserts that a realignment cycle emerges "approximately once every thirty years" (1967:288). "Historically speaking, at least, national critical realignments have not occurred at random. Instead, there has been a remarkably uniform periodicity in their appearance." "[T]his periodicity has had an objective existence" (Burnham 1970:8). There has been a "periodic rhythm," a "cycle of oscillation" (Burnham 1970:181).

3. A dynamic exists that motors history through this pattern of cyclical oscillations into and out of realignments. This is Burnham's claim, with an assist from Sundquist. This line of thinking has relied on tantalizing suggestions and metaphors rather than sustained argument, but it has probably been no less influential for that, and the case for a dynamic is worth teasing out. In brief, political "stress" (Burnham 1970:4, 135) or "tension" (1970: 10, 181) builds up over a period of roughly thirty years until it reaches a "flash point" (1970:10, 136) or a "boiling point" (1970:27), at which time a "triggering event" (1970:181) brings on an electoral realignment. The terms *flash point* and *boiling point* bear an Engels-like connotation of a change in quantity being overtaken by a change in quality.

To put it more elaborately, there exists a "dynamic, even dialectic polarization between long-term inertia and concentrated bursts of change" (Burnham 1970:27). Ordinarily, American institutions tend toward "underproduction of other than currently 'normal' policy outputs. They may tend persistently to ignore, and hence not to aggregate, emergent political demand of a mass character until a boiling point of some kind is reached" (1970:27). In another of Burnham's passages, "[T]he socioeconomic system develops but the institutions of electoral politics and policy formation remain essentially unchanged" (1970:181). Thus stacked up are "dislocations," "dysfunctions," and "increasingly visible social maladjustments" (1970:181, 135), which are not sufficiently attended to until the political system catches up with a lurch as "incremental bargaining politics" gives way to "nonincremental change" (1970:137).

Sundquist, reflecting the standard interpretation imparted by Progressive historians, gives a corresponding cast to the politics of the latter part of the nineteenth century leading up to the mid-1890s (Sundquist 1973:92–94,

144). "Patronage, rather than program, became the object of politics" (1973:93). For twenty years, the party system was based on "dead issues of the past," offering voters "no means of expressing a choice on the crucial issues of domestic economic policy around which the country had been polarizing" (1973:144). Then, with the nomination of Bryan in 1896, "the party system took on meaning once again. . . . The day of political unresponsiveness, of evasion and straddling on fundamental, burning questions, was over" (1973:144).

These first three claims offer a dichotomizing concept, periodicity, and a dynamic — the necessary components of a cyclical theory.

4. Voter concern and turnout are unusually high in realigning elections. This property could be tucked into claim #1 as an additional defining property, but on balance it is a recessive property in the literature, and there is probably no harm in considering it here as a distinct empirical claim. The idea goes back to Key, as noted above, and it is embraced by at least Burnham (1970:7–8): "The rise in intensity is also normally to be found in abnormally heavy voter participation for the time."

5. In an electoral realignment, a new dominant voter cleavage over interests or issues replaces an old one. This claim is central to Schattschneider's and Sundquist's work, though not to Key's. I do not see it as a clear, up-front assertion in Burnham's.

6. Politics at realigning junctures is exceptionally ideological. This is Burnham's idea. "The rise in intensity [during realignments] is associated with a considerable increase in ideological polarizations" (Burnham 1970:7). "In the campaign or campaigns [during a realignment] . . . , the insurgents' political style is exceptionally ideological by American standards; this in turn produces a sense of grave threat among defenders of the established order, who in turn develop opposing ideological positions" (Burnham 1967:288).

7. At least as regards the U.S. House of Representatives, realigning elections hinge on national issues, nonrealigning elections on local ones. This claim is a recent contribution by Brady (1988) that I have not come across in any previous scholarship. "Certain elections, however, are dominated by national rather than local issues" (Brady 1988:14). "[D]uring realignments," Brady undertakes to demonstrate, "the House is elected on national, not local issues, thus giving a sense of mandate to the new majority party" (Brady 1988:18).

8. Electoral realignments are associated with major changes in government policy. This claim is absent from Key's work and recessive at best in Sundquist's, but it figures in both Schattschneider's and Burnham's, albeit complicatedly. Schattschneider finds it obvious that the 1932 realignment ushered in important changes in policy, and the voter alignment caused by

the 1896 election no less obviously underpinned major policy results for a generation (1956:208, 205), but he stops short of asserting that the 1896 election brought about changes in policy — not least, evidently, owing to his judgment that the newly dominant post-1896 Republican party "*had no important positive program of legislation*" (italics in original). Catering to business interests that wanted the government off their backs, the party gauged its policy success "in terms of *what was prevented*" (italics in original) — not in terms of what was initiated or enacted (Schattschneider 1956:197–98). Burnham, in his more recent writings, has acknowledged this lack of post-1896 innovation: "Unlike the turnovers of 1828, 1860, or 1932, the realignment of 1894–1896 *did not* result in a major reversal of dominant public policy" (Burnham 1986:269, italics in original; see also Burnham 1981:175).

However, in the realignment genre's classic days, Burnham did not shrink from rendering bold, unasterisked assertions. A critical realignment constitutes "a turning point in the mainstream of national policy formation" (Burnham 1967:289). Critical realignments "are intimately associated with and followed by transformations in large clusters of policy" (1970:9). These assertions have had a life. Brady (1988) takes it as a given that the aftermaths of alleged realignments are times to canvass for successful major policy innovations. He examines the three chief canonical aftermaths (although no other times) and claims to detect such major innovations during those aftermaths. Through overcoming "policy incrementalism," his reasoning goes, "realigning or critical elections create conditions under which majorities are capable of legislating clusters of policy changes" (Brady 1988:4). "The Congresses of the Civil War, 1890's, and New Deal eras were responsible, in part, for outpourings of new comprehensive public policies" (Brady 1988:vii). Thus has the genre evolved.

9. Electoral realignments are distinctively associated with "redistributive" policies. This is a recent Burnham idea, building on Theodore J. Lowi's (1964) well-known three-category typology. There is no reason to expect distributive or regulatory policy making to map onto realignment cycles in any predictable way, Burnham states or implies, but "[m]atters become quite different when we turn to *redistributive policies*. . . . Such policies are the heart of critical-realignment periods and are among the most important of their 'symptoms' " (Burnham 1986:270, italics in original).

10. The American voting public expresses itself effectively and consequentially during electoral realignments, but not otherwise. This is an exceptionally large claim that capstones, and to some degree duplicates or incorporates, the rest (for example, claim #3), but it is worth stating independently. Note the language used in assertions such as the following: "[T]he voting public has made vitally important contributions to American political development approximately once in a generation" (Burnham

1967:287). That is, the public has done that on those occasions but not otherwise. Sundquist states that the public had "no means of expressing a choice on the crucial issues of domestic economic policy" for twenty years, but then in 1896 "the party system took on meaning once again" (Sundquist 1973:144). In Schattschneider's view, the voter alignment brought on by the 1896 election "determined" — an unusually strong verb — "the nature of American politics for more than thirty years" (1960:78). That is, voters could not or did not do anything effective or consequential thereafter for a third of a century.

11. There existed a "system of 1896." This historical claim figures so prominently in the work of both Schattschneider and Burnham — it is something like a large container packed with its own content yet snugly insertable into the general realignments vehicle — that it merits special mention. The "function" of the voter alignment struck by the 1896 election, Schattschneider wrote, using an explanatory style in vogue in the 1950s, was to award political and economic supremacy to the American business class — a result that stuck for a "determined" thirty-six years. The Republican party, "the political instrument of business," ordinarily ruled during that time (Schattschneider 1956:197). The sectional shape of the post-1896 alignment — that is, the newly accentuated one-party rule by Democrats in the South and Republicans in much of the North — was a key aspect of that hegemony. "Both sections became extremely conservative because one-party politics tends strongly to vest political power in the hands of people who already have economic power" (Schattschneider 1956:202). In addition, "the sectional party alignment was unfavorable to the development and exploitation of new alternatives in public affairs" (Schattschneider 1956:205).

Insulation of the business sector from mass pressures has been a leading theme in Burnham's interpretation of post-1896 politics. By now the reader may be tired of quotations, but because they convey both content and flavor, here are a few more. Burnham claims that the 1896 alignment "almost certainly" depressed voter turnout for a generation or more, notably through depositing noncompetitive one-partyism across both North and South; accordingly, "the functional result of the 'system of 1896' was the conversion of a fairly democratic regime into a rather broadly based oligarchy" (Burnham 1965:23). In general terms, according to Burnham (1965:25), the realignment of 1896 "brought victory beyond expectation to those who had sought to find some way of insulating American elites from mass pressures." The "chief function" of the post-1896 party system was "the substantially complete insulation of elites from attacks by the victims of the industrializing process" (Burnham 1967:301). Burnham has "no doubts that *in general* the system established in the 1890s was in fact a political matrix which insulated

industrial and finance capital from adverse mass pressures for a generation afterward" (1986:269, italics in original).

Let no one underestimate the intellectual aspiration of these Schattschneider and Burnham claims about the system of 1896. There is a line
out to Barrington Moore Jr.: "The takeoff phase of industrialization has
been a brutal and exploitative process everywhere, whether managed by
capitalists or commissars. A vital functional political need during this
phase [that is, during the early twentieth century in the American case] is
to provide adequate insulation of the industrializing elites from mass
pressure" (Burnham 1965:24). There is an answer to the question: Why is
there no socialism in the United States? "One is indeed inclined to suspect
that the large hole in voter participation which developed after 1900
roughly corresponds to the area in the electorate where a viable socialist
movement 'ought' to have developed" (Burnham 1967:301). And there is
an answer to the question: Why is there no European-style welfare state in
the United States? "The accomplishments of the [post-1896] Republican
party might be measured more accurately, therefore, by the gap produced
between the social legislation of western European countries and that of
the United States before 1932" (Schattschneider 1956:198).

Those are the eleven claims. I hope that I have stayed true to the texts and
that I have expressed fairly the ambitions of the various authors.

A Critique of the Genre

How does the realignments genre stand up at the close of the twentieth
century, well past its historical evidence base and a generation or two beyond
the main assertions by its chief exponents?

All the claims I have presented here can, in principle, be assessed for their
empirical validity, and that assessment is my principal task in the remainder of
the essay. In some instances, reasonably hard empirical information is available in published works and can be mobilized. In most instances, that course is
not possible, and I resort to my understanding of the conventional wisdom
piled up by generations of historians writing standard works about American
political history. For recent times, I rely also on my own experience of living under and witnessing the American regime. These are fallible reliances,
yet what are the options? It is bankrupt and irresponsible, as the realignment writers would likely agree, to throw up one's hands when confronted by
provocative assertions on large, important, not easily tractable matters.

A second concern, beyond validity, is the illuminative power of the realignments genre. What has it added to the discipline? What would we be thinking

about American electoral history otherwise? What did we think before the realignments genre came along? It has always been obvious that some American elections have surpassed others in engaging voters, generating a sense of high stakes among voters, shaking up received voter alignments, or causing important policy or other effects down the line. Elections are not all equal. Also, the Civil War and New Deal eras have always stood out for both their electoral turbulence and their policy innovations. It is reasonable to ask, what has the realignments genre fruitfully added beyond these baselines?

Probably the chief contemporary charge against the realignments genre is that it has ceased to be relevant. No certifiable realignment has occurred since 1932. A sixty-eight-year gap is a heavy cross to bear for a theory of thirty-year electoral cycles, and it has been variously borne. The concepts of party "decomposition" and "dealignment" have been introduced. Burnham has argued that "there in fact *was* a critical realignment in the 1968–72 period. One of its essential features lay in the very dissolution of the traditional partisan channels that had been implicitly incorporated as a nonproblematic part of the classic realignment model. People therefore looked for it with the wrong tools and in the wrong places" (Burnham 1991:107). Translation: For evidence of electoral realignments, don't bother to rely on patterns of election returns anymore. To support this point, Burnham draws on "the very perceptive political commentator Sidney Blumenthal" (Blumenthal 1982), with his idea of "the permanent campaign," who "was perhaps the first to get the basic story right" (Burnham 1991:107).

I do not wish to deal with the problem of a post-1932 absence of realignments here. The decomposition and dealignment ideas are not implausible, and, at any rate, a perspective that managed to illuminate the first century and a half of American political history, even if for whatever reasons it ceased to work in recent times, would be an impressive achievement.

But how does the realignment perspective stand up when applied to its apparently most favorable century and a half? Not very well, I argue here in assessing the empirical validity (and occasionally the illuminative power) of the eleven claims presented above. The genre's performance across the claims, which I take up one by one, ranges from mediocre to poor.

DICHOTOMIZATION OF ELECTION TYPES

Of efforts to detect presidential elections in American history that have generated especially large and durable changes in voter alignments, I am aware of two sophisticated ones that were undertaken without regard for the conventional wisdom of the realignments genre about what results to expect. (Peter F. Nardulli's 1995 work, with its inventive time series on subregions, does not seem to be "blind" in this sense.) No such work is unimpeachable. Countless decisions about data use need to be made; third parties are always a nightmare. Moreover, no one to my knowledge has used statistical methods to tackle the slippery and probably intractable task of detecting realigning eras as opposed to single elections. Still, impressive work has been done using data sets based on individual elections.

Clubb and colleagues (1980; for a somewhat different version see Flanigan and Zingale 1974) were appropriately sensitive to two distinct connotations of the realignments genre. Using aggregate presidential election data by state, they probed for two kinds of electoral change: "surge," as when, in a limiting case, every state becomes 10 percent more Democratic in election year B than in previous election year A (a fitting accommodation of, for example, the election of 1932); and "interaction," as when, in a limiting case, half the states become 10 percent more Democratic and the other half 10 percent more Republican, yet despite the considerable disruption in cleavage there is no (necessary) net national party percentage change between election years A and B. Either kind of change is "realigning" if its end-state persists during a span of succeeding elections—again, a necessary requirement for the realignments genre. Otherwise, any A-to-B change is merely "deviating." Clubb and colleagues proceed by analyzing successive election quadruplets (A through D, B through E, etc.)—the logic being to situate each election in a context of both its predecessors and its successors. Their technology requires them to calculate results separately for each party (at least because of third parties, one major party's record is not simply the mirror of the other's). Calculations are provided for the Democrats from 1836 through 1976, the Republicans from 1868 through 1976.

Clubb and colleagues' table 3.1a (1980:92–93) warrants close inspection. For the Democrats, the notable realigning surge elections, in order of magnitude of change, are the following: 1932, +16.3% (a bull's-eye for the realignments perspective); 1948, −8.2%; 1868, +6.1%; 1848, −5.6%; 1840, −3.6%; 1920, −1.8%; 1876, +1.5%; 1960, +1.3%. The notable Democratic realigning interactive elections are as follows: 1836, 5.7%; 1860, 2.8%; 1964, 2.1%; 1928, 1.9%; 1864, 1.7%; 1948, 1.2%; 1904, 1.1%. (In these latter cases the values are absolute—that is, no directional plus or minus signs.) On the Republican side, the realigning surge elections are the following: 1932, −11.3% (another, or the same, bull's-eye); 1920, +7.7%; 1896, +5.2%; 1876, −4.7%; 1952, +2.5%; 1964, −2.5%. The Republican realigning interactive elections are as follows: 1952, 1.3%; 1936, 1.2%; 1964, 1.2%.

The election of 1932 performs spectacularly in these calculations. The election of 1860 is something of a washout, but that is understandable. No such comparative statistical analysis could adequately accommodate the breaking in half of the Democratic party that year (although note that the same thing happened to the Republican Party in 1912, and the 1912 election is not ordinarily regarded as realigning). But what about the unremarkable statistical performance of the election of 1896?

Bartels (1998), employing a more complex methodology, also relies on aggregate state-level election data and is sensitive to both surge and interactive types of change (though those are Clubb and colleagues' terms) if they turn out to be durable. Tracked in the Bartels case, from 1868 through 1996 — which rules out of bounds the election of 1860 — is the Republican minus the Democratic percentage of the popular vote for president. The calculations allow a summary realignment score for each election. In Bartels's key figure 8 (1998:315), the election of 1932 emerges a runaway winner in "average effect, 25-year horizon," but what then? An easy second-place finisher is the election of 1880, followed by, in order, those of 1920, 1972, 1936, 1876, 1912, 1896, and 1924.

From the viewpoint of the realignments genre, setting aside the anomaly of 1860, the problem posed here is that, confronted by the Clubb and colleagues (1980) and Bartels (1998) analyses alone, probably not one reader in a hundred would seize on the election of 1896 as a realigning event. In Bartels's assessment (1998:316): "[T]he electoral pattern established in 1896 was much less durable than previous scholarship has suggested. . . . [T]he electoral impetus of 1896 was diminished by half within four years; the state-by-state voting pattern in 1900 reflected the divisions of 1888 . . . as much or more than those of 1896." The 1896 result comes to look suspiciously like a deviating one.

At a more general level, Bartels casts doubt on the very idea of sorting elections into two types. "Rather than consisting of a few great peaks separated by broad plateaus reflecting long periods of political stasis, the distribution of long-term effects in Fig. 8 reflects a complex intermixture of large, medium, and small effects" (Bartels 1998:315).

In the face of such numbers, one way to try to keep 1896 on its pedestal is to argue that all such quantitative analysis is impeachable, and, at any rate, quantitative analysis is not enough. Relevant contextual information is needed, and certainly the decade of the 1890s offers a rich supply of it — the Populist revolt in 1892, the country's second worst depression in 1893, the astounding (still unmatched) 120-seat shift to the Republicans in the House elections of 1894, the fracturing of both major parties over silver and other questions in 1896, the capture of the Democratic party by anti–Wall Street insurgents, William Jennings Bryan's unprecedented nationwide campaign of speechmaking, Mark Hanna's mobilizing of the business community behind McKinley, and the Republican domination that resulted. It is a familiar and riveting story.

But there exist other riveting stories, even if, partly courtesy of the realignments genre, they may not be quite as familiar. In light of the impressive showings of the 1876 and 1880 elections in, respectively, Clubb and colleagues' and Bartels's results, and in line with the realignment genre's practice of weaving narratives about short sequences of allegedly related elections (not just one election), consider the following three-paragraph sketch. It is a stylized account of the politics of the 1870s that I have composed for this occasion.

In the 1874 congressional midterm election, spurred by Reconstruction fatigue and a poor economy, the American electorate rendered one of its most decisive results ever—a sweeping Democratic takeover of the House that rendered federal Reconstruction policy unsustainable. The state Republican regime in Mississippi soon crumbled, paving the way for the extraordinary election campaign waged by white "Redeemers" to take back South Carolina in 1876—a successful politicomilitary drive conducted largely by army veterans that featured guerrilla organization, intimidation, and murder (Zuczek 1996). It was an innovative mix that would be seen again in Germany and Italy after World War I. At the national level, the high-stakes presidential contest of 1876—which party would control the army?—ended in a hung result and, for the only time in American history, an extra-constitutional settlement. This cross-party, cross-regional deal involving an ad hoc commission has been brought to life in possibly the most distinguished work ever written about the events surrounding an American election—C. Vann Woodward's *Reunion and Reaction* (1951). In effect, although the Republicans kept control of the presidency, southern Democratic whites gained control of their home affairs with a program of keeping whites on top, blacks down, and Yankees out. Full African-American disfranchisement came a generation later, but that was an afterthought. Redeemer governments came to enjoy solid control of the South by the late 1870s—notably of South Carolina (historically the Deep South's style-setter), Mississippi, and Louisiana, which were the chief spots of contention because they had African-American population majorities or near majorities.

In its southern aspect, the 1876–77 settlement was so unusual that it has seldom figured in cross-national analysis. It featured constitutional politics for one race, but a caste system and suppression for another. The nearest analogy may be the South African Nationalist election victory of 1948. In terms of voting statistics, the full effect of the 1876–77 settlement was not felt until 1880, when notably Louisiana and South Carolina, which had narrowly voted Republican at the presidential level in 1876 — the beleaguered, biracial Republicans were still in control of counting ballots then at that office level — swung dramatically to the Democratic column, where they remained for generations. In major respects, the southern electoral victories of the mid-1870s determined (to use Schattschneider's verb, which works better here than in most contexts owing to the not easily reversible suppression of southern African-Americans) the course of American politics and society for most of a century, until the civil rights revolution of the 1960s unraveled them.

One of the aftermaths of the 1876–77 settlement was an abrupt shift in the national policy agenda. Reconstruction questions receded. The issue of civil rights was abandoned — not least by a Supreme Court that could read the election results. Presidents took to trying to modernize the executive establishment through civil service reform, wrestling with the tariff, and imposing order in industrial relations, as did the Republican Hayes by deploying federal troops in the national railway strike of 1877 and later the Democrat Cleveland doing the same in the Pullman strike of 1894.

The foregoing sketch is meant to be exemplary of ones that might compete with a sketch of the 1890s. The 1870s story, in my judgment, holds up well against the 1890s one, and, as reported above, the statistics for 1876 and 1880 dominate those for 1896. It seems a good bet that if the 1876 election had taken place thirty years after 1860 rather than when it did, we would have heard about it as a realigning election.

PERIODICITY

If the identities of realigning elections are in question, then their periodicity is in question. Above all, it is important not to let periodicity dictate identity. In this regard, it would be in order to take a close look at the election of 1828. Important though that contest was, exactly what justifies its reputation, as compared with other presidential elections perhaps in its vicinity, as a realigning election?

STRESS, TENSIONS, FLASH POINTS, BOILING POINTS

A long buildup of stress ending in explosion is a familiar idea and, sometimes at least, a plausible model of reality. One thinks of, for example, the growing intensity of discontent among African-Americans between the mid-1950s and the mid-1960s, or the anti–Vietnam war cause that accelerated between the mid-1960s and the early 1970s. Instances can be found on the realignments calendar, such as the growing tension between North and South between 1854 and 1860 (although that had evidently happened also between 1844 and 1850 without triggering a realignment or a civil war), and possibly the growing farmer discontent (though the pattern may not have been monotonic) in particularly the drier plains states west of Missouri and Iowa during the decade and a half or so leading up to the Populist movement around 1890.

But a general theory of periodic, thirty-year-long stress buildups seems very dubious. For one thing, if the canonical realignment junctures are respected, it would have to be shown that politically relevant stress, somehow indexed or at least convincingly argued for, was abnormally high in 1892 and 1928. (Any society at any time is under some level of stress or tension.) Those were the years just before the onsets of the devastating and unquestionably stress-inducing depressions of 1893 (Hoffmann 1956) and 1929. Possibly abnormal stress existed in 1892 (even east of the plains and outside the cotton belt), but it is nearly certain that no "stress" case could be made for 1928, when an electorate wafted by record-shattering prosperity made it virtually impossible for Al Smith to gain issue traction. In effect, he had to wage an uphill struggle against burgeoning consumer durables, movie and radio entertainment, and stock prices. We have every reason to believe that, absent the abrupt economic downturn in 1929, voters would have kept on electing presidents like Coolidge and Hoover for quite a while.

At least one serious error lurks in the realignments genre's model of stress buildup — a tendency to elongate political troubles backward in time without warrant. To account for the Republican successes in 1894 and 1896, the 1893 depression is probably sufficient (although the apparently deviating shape of the 1896 result would no doubt have been different without a Bryan insurgency). To account for the Democratic successes in 1930 and 1932, the depression that started in 1929 is enough. In neither of these depression instances is a thirty-year stress buildup required or in evidence.

CONCERN AND TURNOUT

The concept of voter concern, though in principle distinct from turnout, may be intractable. Turnout is measurable. Robert E. Lane (1959:19–20) detected two spans of high turnout in presidential elections during the nineteenth century: 1840–60 (the 1864 and 1868 elections are hard to deal with) and 1876–1900.[1] In the former case, a band of values ranges from 14.5% (1852) to 17.0% (1860) of the total population with high readings also of 16.7% (1856) and 16.5% (1840). In the late nineteenth century, the band ranges from 18.3% (1876 and 1880) through 19.5% (1896) with a high reading also of 19.0% for 1884. Victories, albeit narrow ones, accrue here for the realignments perspective: the highest showings are 1860 and 1896. (As a side note, though, witness the modest levels of all these readings before women became part of the numerator in 1920.)

Yet no one examining a relevant time series for the twentieth century would categorize 1932 as a high-turnout election. It is not a close call (see Lane 1959:19–20; Burnham 1965:11). In the vicinity of 1932, what catches the eye is a nearly monotonic, rather steep rise in turnout between 1920 and 1940. In percentage of the total population voting, 1940 exceeded 1932 by a reported 37.8% to 31.9% (Lane 1959:19); in percentage of eligibles, by a reported 62.5% to 56.9% (U.S. Bureau of the Census 1975, vol. 2, p. 1071). (The 1940 peak is thought-provoking. Was it the imminence of war that brought voters out?)

NEW, LASTING ISSUE OR INTEREST CLEAVAGES

On the subject of the basic issue or ideological stances of the parties during the past two centuries, the most sophisticated and convincing work is by John Gerring (1998), who used about two thousand texts to code rhetoric (including that in party platforms) emanating from candidates and other party figures during presidential campaigns from 1828 through 1992. One result is periodization (though not periodicity), as indicated in Gerring's chapter titles labeling "epochs." For the Whigs and then the Republicans, 1828–1924 was the "National Epoch," which featured emphasis on the work ethic, social harmony, neomercantilism, statism, order, Yankee Protestantism, and nationalism — above all, a quest for order over chaos (Gerring 1998:13–18). Then, at a hinge point in the mid-1920s, much of this assemblage of values gave way. A "Neoliberal Epoch" set in in 1928 that lasted through at least 1992 on the Republican side, featuring emphasis on antistatism, free market capitalism, right-wing populism, and individualism.

For the Democrats, a "Jeffersonian Epoch" lasting from 1828 through 1892 saw an accentuation of white supremacy, antistatism, and civic republicanism. Then, in an abrupt switch in the 1890s, a "Populist Epoch" began that lasted through 1948, bringing emphasis on egalitarianism, majoritarianism, and Christian humanism — above all, a championing of "the people versus the interests." The business sector symbolized by Wall Street (rather than, as earlier, an actually or potentially oppressive state) came to be seen as the chief political menace or enemy. (On this 1890s juncture, see also Huston 1993:1102–5.) Later, for the Democrats, a "Universalist Epoch" began in 1952 that lasted into the 1990s, featuring emphasis on civil rights, social welfare, redistribution, and inclusion. That is, around the middle of the twentieth century, after Harry Truman's "give 'em hell" campaign in 1948, the Democratic party

> discarded its abrasive, class-tinged ethos in favor of a *Universalist* perspective — the extension of rights to all aggrieved claimants and a general rhetoric

of inclusion. Bryan, the evangelical crusader of the Populist era, was traded in for the moderate, ecumenical Lyndon Johnson. Party leaders now praised capitalism without qualification. Arguments for progressive social policies relied on empathy, social responsibility, and impassioned appeals for aid, rather than attacks on privilege and power. Postwar Democrats also reached beyond economic issues to address a wide range of "postmaterialist" concerns. (Gerring 1998:18, italics in original)

(On this mid-twentieth-century juncture, see also Brinkley (1995), who documents the Democratic party elite's abandonment of "anti-monopolyism" as a credible policy stance a bit earlier, in the late 1930s and early 1940s.)

One clear bull's-eye emerges here for the realignment perspective — the Bryanization of the Democratic party in the 1890s — but otherwise there is a complete lack of correspondence between Gerring's coding and the realignments canon. Where are 1860 and 1932 in Gerring's calculations? I suspect that the problem stems at least partly from certain basic properties of electoral politics. Deep-seated, long-lived party issue stances of the sort discussed by Sundquist or documented by Gerring, important as they may be, are a long way from being hegemonic over voter choice. Even in the realm of "issue content," they supply a background to electoral politics but not ordinarily its foreground.

Instead, events, or the management of events, often generate the foreground issues, as in the following examples. In 1844: Should Texas be annexed? In 1854: What should be the reaction to the Kansas-Nebraska Act? In 1860: After John Brown's raid and the rest, what next? In 1864: What should it be — clear-cut military victory with Lincoln or a muddling compromise with McClellan? In 1866: How severe should Reconstruction policy be? In 1890: Have the Republicans gone overboard with their spending and regulatory schemes in the "billion-dollar Congress" under Benjamin Harrison? In 1894: Have the Democrats ruined the economy? In 1920: After two years of economic turmoil, frightening strikes, and international revolution, which party is a better bet for order? In 1932: Who can get the economy humming again? In 1938: After two years of sitdown strikes, Roosevelt's court-packing plan, allegations of Communists in the agencies, and another alarming economic downturn, is it time to curb the New Dealers? In 1952: Is Eisenhower the remedy for "Communism, corruption, and Korea" (the GOP slogan that year)? In 1968: What is the remedy for violence in the cities and a quagmire war? In 1974 and 1976: After Watergate, who can be trusted? In 1994: Can the ambitious domestic policy plans of the Clinton administration be trusted? In 1998: Should Clinton be evicted from office (see Abramowitz 1999)?

There is no way to prevent voters, politicians, or parties from dwelling on event-centered issues like the foregoing. Indeed, any democratic system that tried to do so — imagine a requirement that voters make decisions only by consulting party stances or cleavages of a sort that might last for thirty years — would probably collapse through rendering its elections irrelevant.

In sum, in the realm of long-term issue cleavages, the realignments perspective runs into problems of both validity (is the periodization correct?) and illuminative power (how much of politics and policy making can be accounted for by any kind of long-term issue cleavage?).

IDEOLOGY

Has ideological polarization, levered by the style of the insurgent side, been distinctively characteristic of realignments? Ideology is difficult to define, let alone measure, but let us say it is an ambitious, issue-laden, conflict-generating approach to politics wrapped in abstraction and not weighed down by pragmatism or opportunism. The 1896 election qualifies, as do several elections featuring slavery or Reconstruction issues from the 1840s through the 1870s (it is hard to know which ones to pick out), but how about in the twentieth century? Oddly, none of the New Deal–era presidential elections seems to qualify — certainly not 1928 or 1932. Al Smith's challenge was largely demographic, not ideological. In 1932, it would have been questionable tactics for the Democrats to conduct an ideological campaign, and they did not do so (any more than McKinley had in comparable out-party circumstances during a depression in 1896). There was much criticism of Hoover for not having balanced the budget. Some left-liberal rhetoric did emanate from Roosevelt in 1936, though probably not more than from Truman in 1948. (In actual voting behavior, 1948 was the standout "class cleavage" election between 1936 and 1960: 1936 was average for that time span (see Alford 1963:227).) And with Alf Landon in 1936, the Republicans were already halfway into their quarter-century-long "me-too" mode. In actuality, during the twentieth century, the presidential elections that best fit the "ideological" mold may be those of 1912 with its evangelistic crusade waged by the Theodore Roosevelt Progressives, 1964 with its hard-line conservative Goldwater Republicans, and 1972 with its McGovern Democrats. Possibly the Reagan election of 1980 qualifies.

Still, this is an unsatisfying apprehension of the 1930s, for the midterm elections should be examined also. It was the 1934 midterm that brought Upton Sinclair's "End Poverty in California" campaign, left-wing third-party victories in Wisconsin and Minnesota (the latter was a repeat performance), and, on impressionistic evidence, primary and then November victories by many left-liberal Democrats — for example, Maury Maverick (Democratic representative from Texas) and Joseph Guffey (Democratic senator from Pennsylvania)

— who added a distinctive leftist tone to congressional politics for a few years (see Schlesinger 1960:142–44). A strong nationwide ideological impulse can infuse primary elections, November elections, and the ranks of officeholders without being easily readable off statistics on election results, major-party officeholding, or roll-call voting. That seems to have happened in 1934.

Yet to look beyond presidential contests raises the possibility of ideologized subpresidential elections besides 1934's. If a primary season tilting in one direction counts as indirect evidence of ideologization, consider the Progressive or insurgent victories in the Republican primaries of 1910. If the arrival of a class of particularly aggressive hard-liners in Congress counts as indirect evidence of an ideologized election, then the Republican-edged elections of 1980 and 1994 were arguably ideologized. So was the midterm of 1950 — a kind of opposite bookend to 1934, since it came at the close of a decade and a half when (except during World War II) the questions of a Popular Front, the muscular Congress of Industrial Organizations (CIO) with its many Communist organizers, or the fervent anti-Communism of that era seldom failed to intrude into American elections. Occurring at the height of the Korean War and McCarthyism, the election of 1950 was a disaster for incumbent politicians targetable as left-wingers. Down went Helen Gahagan Douglas in the so-called pink lady campaign in California. Out went, among others, Senator Claude Pepper (then sometimes called "Red Pepper") in Florida's Democratic primary, Senator Frank Graham in North Carolina's Democratic primary, Senator Glen Taylor (Henry Wallace's vice-presidential running mate in 1948) in Idaho's Democratic nominating process, Senator Elbert Thomas in Utah, Senator Millard Tydings in Maryland (Tydings was not a left-winger or even a liberal, but he had got on the wrong side of McCarthy), and the lone American Labor Party congressman, Vito Marcantonio of Manhattan. This 1950 purge — that is what it amounted to — was arguably an exercise of ideology.

It is not clear what to make of the ideological turbulence of the mid-1930s through the early 1950s. Its relation to the Democratic surge election of 1932 is uncertain. Much of Europe exhibited a similiar pattern at the same time (Mayhew 1994). For an American analogy, it may be necessary to look back to the very beginning of national history; between roughly 1793 and 1812, during the height of the French Revolution and its aftermath, much of this country's political elite was comparably caught up in European ideological warfare.

NATIONAL, NOT LOCAL ISSUES

That realignments have been distinctively dominated by national issues could hardly be claimed of elections at the presidential level. Since the presidency has the whole nation as its constituency, all presidential elections offer national issues.[2] But how about House elections? The point is important for Brady (1988:12, 14), who argues that a switch to "national rather than local issues" during realigning elections has generated party mandates enabling Congress to overcome "inertia" and "incrementalism" in the policy realm. But whether House elections actually sort this way is an empirical question — it cannot be settled by assertion or deduction — and, unfortunately, no sure measure exists to supply an answer. However, the case for thus singling out the elections of 1854–60 (Brady 1988:33), 1894 (1988:61–63), and 1932 (1988:91) is far from clear-cut. For one thing, the elections of 1894 and 1932 (and also 1930) were classic "nationwide states of affairs" elections — that is, a poor economy everywhere favored the out party. That situation does make for "national" issues of a sort, yet many other House elections have borne, if in lesser degree, the same profile of a poor economy plus adverse voter reaction. Examples in recent decades include the elections of 1938, 1958, 1974, 1980, and 1982.

Beyond this, if one scans impressionistically for manifest national issue content in past House elections, other elections jut up. In the vicinity of 1894, for example, why should 1894 be said to dominate 1874, which featured Reconstruction issues as well as a poor economy; 1890, which brought an immense national seat swing in reaction to (it has often been casually claimed, although the matter has been understudied) the newly enacted McKinley Tariff; or 1910, with its Progressive insurgency? The evidence is soft, yet the case for the distinctiveness of the canonical realigning junctures is certainly unproven and very likely weak.

POLICY INNOVATIONS

Have electoral realignments ushered in "outpourings of new comprehensive public policies"? (Brady 1988:vii). No one has any doubts about the 1860s and the 1930s, but how about the 1890s? Not then, said Schattschneider, and now Burnham agrees.

This is the third rail of the realignments genre, and Brady was unwise to touch it. In the legislative sphere, policy innovations under McKinley during 1897–1901 probably rank in the bottom quartile of American history. There was the Dingley Tariff of 1897, but the Republicans had a habit of hiking the tariff just after sweeping into power — notably in 1861, 1890, and 1922 as well as 1897. (The Democrats did the opposite in 1894, 1913, and 1934.) There was the Gold Standard Act of 1900, but that came after the inflation issue had lost its punch, and, at any rate, sturdy support for the gold standard had carried down from the Cleveland Democrats (they, not the Bryanites, had been running the country) through the McKinley Republicans. No other legislative policy innovations stand out. In the historical vicinity of the 1890s, Congresses can easily be found that were more innovative than either of McKinley's taken alone or probably together. Under Harrison in 1889–91, the Republicans generated the McKinley Tariff (McKinley was a House member then), naval expansion aimed at making the United States competitive, the Sherman Antitrust Act, the Sherman Silver Purchase Act, and an expansion of Civil War pensions broad enough to help fuel recent discussion about a late-nineteenth-century American welfare state (Skocpol 1992:2). Under Theodore Roosevelt in 1905–7 came a burst of regulatory activity — the Pure Food and Drug Act and the lengthily deliberated Hepburn Act regulating the railroads. Either of Woodrow Wilson's Congresses of 1913–15 and 1915–17 would outscore the 1890s on the "policy innovations" criterion. The McKinley era was not a fertile legislative one (see Mayhew 1996).

Recently, Burnham (1986:269–74) has reached for the business-friendly judiciary, as opposed to the legislative process, as the relevant policy-making arena of the 1894–1937 era. Although that may be justified, the claim at issue here involves change. It would have to be shown that the judiciary had been significantly more hostile to the business community during the generation before the mid-1890s than it was during the generation afterward. Burnham does not say or seem to imply that, and to demonstrate it would be a formidable task.

The 1890s pose a basic interpretive difficulty for the realignments genre. Policy change of turnaround dimensions favoring the business community is not to be found. The problem is the baseline. In the history of the world, when has a governmental environment ever favored private capitalism more than the American environment of the 1860s through the mid-1890s? On offer were high protective tariffs (on balance, they were arguably higher during 1861–96 than during 1897–1930; see Hansen 1990:540), solid property and contract rights, huge free land grants to the railroads, easy availability of an immigrant labor force from Europe, free trade across a continent, low taxes, a stable currency, little government regulation, and, in a pinch, presidents ready to send in federal troops to put down politicizing strikes, as in 1877 and 1894. How much more could be asked?

REDISTRIBUTIVE POLICY

Again, no one would hesitate to associate redistributive policy innovation with the 1860s (consider the Thirteenth Amendment abolishing slavery) or the 1930s. The case for the 1930s seems to become even better as new work appears emphasizing the decade's prodigious relief efforts (Amenta 1998:ch. 4; Amenta et al. 1998; Kennedy 1999:ch. 9) and addressing the likely wealth-equalizing effects of various statutes (Shammas 1993:426–29). But I am not aware of any serious work attributing notable redistributive policy change, in either a progressive or a regressive direction, to the realignment of the 1890s. The tariff aside, there was little policy change of any sort after McKinley's election.

To dwell on alleged past realignments can exact costs — for one, neglect of other past junctures on which a spotlight might productively be flashed. In the redistributive realm, a good candidate would seem to be the immense increase in federal revenue and spending associated with World War II and the Korean War, which proved to be irreversible (Higgs 1987:ch. 2; Schultze 1992; Shammas 1993:426–29).

THE ELECTORATE WEIGHS IN CONSEQUENTIALLY AT REALIGNMENT JUNCTURES ONLY

Burnham (1967:287) claims that "approximately once in a generation" — i.e. at the canonical realignment junctures — "vitally important contributions to American political development" are made (Burnham 1967:287).

This is a large claim, and I believe a mistaken one. It is a basic theoretical error to associate changes in voting alignments, however lasting they may be, with attributes of the electorate's decisions (voter awareness, level of underlying concern, or consequentiality). As long as parties cater to the electorate, or else emanate from it — as do the American parties, with their widely participated-in nominating processes (even before the coming of direct primaries) — any contributions that the electorate wishes to make are likely to intrude into elections regardless of whether those elections feature realigning patterns. Notably, if both major parties accommodate such a contribution, it may come to dominate policy making without disturbing received electoral patterns at all. If, say, in the 1880s, the bulk of Americans had suddenly decided that the country should officially convert to Islam, that idea, if accommodated by both parties in an election campaign, might have come to pass through government action in short order without any electoral realignment. That would have been a major voter contribution. (Sundquist, in a discussion of nonrealignments, pursues this logic (1973:11–18).)

This is not a fanciful idea, perhaps particularly if one looks beyond issues that may last thirty years to ones that, let us say, just come up. Consider the election of 1940. Against a background of France having fallen to the Nazis in May and June and Britain imperiled, the Republicans opted in an open nominating process for a nonisolationist candidate (the surprising Wendell Willkie) without suffering serious defections then or afterward, and the Willkie-versus-Roosevelt November election, despite certain marginal late-season fudging by both sides, was readable as a victory for internationalism. How many election outcomes have been more important than that?

Or take the election of 1948, which generated at least four nontrivial results. An over–90 percent winner, courtesy of Dewey's carrying his party constituency with a "me-too" stance, was the heart of the domestic New Deal. Another bipartisan over–90 percent winner, in its first tryout in national nominating and general election process, was the government's new stance of Cold War internationalism. Given a third-party choice for president—former Vice President Henry Wallace was still a major political property then—voters marginalized Popular Front politics with a devastating zero states and 2.4 percent of the vote. Also offered a choice, voters gave the Dixiecrat candidate Strom Thurmond four deep-southern states and an identical 2.4 percent of the vote—a nonnegligible yet contained showing. All in all, few elections have been more consequential or information-rich than that of 1948, and it would be something of an insult to voters of that time to allege that they could not have been contributing, in Burnham's terms, to American political development just because they neglected to realign themselves. Approached in this way, the elections of 1940 and 1948 and probably many others will stand up against that of 1896.

THE "SYSTEM OF 1896"

Was the American business community, as Burnham (1986) claims, insulated from mass pressures by a "system of 1896" for over a third of a century?

Probably not. First of all, as argued above, there is the problem of contingency. In any reasonably open polity operating in an event-packed world, no election result can program the future to that extent. Republican control of the national government crumbled in 1910 and 1912. Progressive-oriented Democrats came to power under Wilson and proved popular—a development passed over as an off-schedule intrusion by most realignments writers (Sundquist excepted). As of, say, 1916, the most likely electoral future was probably toss-up competition between the two major parties indefinitely. But then came act two for the Democrats, the management of World War I and its aftermath, which seems to have badly damaged them (in Britain, war management destroyed the Liberal party) and brought on their worst defeat ever in 1920. This is contingency. Electorates can key on wars and their aftermaths just as intently as on domestic socioeconomic programs. There is no good reason to credit the old 1896 realignment for the new postwar Republican hegemony that emerged as a "system of 1920" (the label is equally warranted) that lasted through 1930 and 1932. Note that in both the Clubb and colleagues (1980) and Bartels (1998) calculations, 1920 earns a better license as a realigning election than does 1896, and an appealing 1876-like story could be composed about it.

Second, why should it be supposed that the American business community *needed* the alleged insulation after 1896? (The Schattschneider and Burnham "functional" argument is at issue here.) Certainly that community's practitioners had done well enough for themselves during the uninsulated decades of vigorous two-party competition, less accentuated sectionalism, and high (male) voter turnout before the mid-1890s. As for the American economy's presumably high-tension takeoff, that development had occurred, according to W. W. Rostow's schematization (1960:ch. 4), between 1843 and 1860 under Presidents Tyler through Buchanan.

A major defect in the "system of 1896" line of thinking is that it ignores the extraordinary success, at least according to certain relevant indicators, of the American society and economy during the generations both before and after the mid-1890s. It seems not to have needed insulating. Real per capita income nearly tripled between 1870 and 1910; life expectancy rose dramatically (Bruchey 1988:67–69). The American economy grew at an estimated average annual rate of 4.3 percent between 1871 and 1913 (U.S. Bureau of the Census 1975, vol. 1, p. 225). (Another estimate is 4.3 percent between 1973 and the mid-1890s and 5.6 percent between the mid-1890s and 1913; see Coppock 1961:227). Granted, short-term troubles could be severe, as in 1893, and sectors of the agricultural and blue-collar population could and did suffer, but everything we know about electoral behavior suggests that indicator readings like those above bring endorsements of regimes and the parties that manage them. Not least, in what was still dominantly a country of farmers, commercial agriculture grew and flourished. One firewall against Populism in the 1890s seems to have been indifference or antipathy to it among most farmers. Iowa, for example, always an agricultural showcase, stayed with the Republicans in both 1892 and 1896. (On the understandably limited appeal of Populism, see Hughes 1994.) In general, the threatening mass pressures of the "system of 1896" interpretation seem to have been drawn more from tracts than from reality. The best insulation is a 4–5 percent growth rate. As of the early twentieth century, the chief mass pressures of relevance to the United States were probably those associated with Europeans trying to immigrate here.

Did a "system of 1896" impede the development of a major socialist party in the United States? The case may be doubted. As Eric Foner has pointed out, this country did possess, in the early twentieth century, a nascent socialist party that "appeared to rival those in Europe, except the German, in mass

support and prospects for future growth. Around 1910, the American Socialist party had elected more officials than its English counterpart" (1984:60).
But the American party faltered in enrolling immigrant workers, and in World
War I, "apart from the Russian Bolsheviks, the American was the party that
remained most true to socialist principles" (Foner 1984:71–72). That is, it
refused to back its own nation's military cause — a politically suicidal stance
in the United States of 1917–18. Again, contingency associated with World
War I intrudes. In Britain, absent that war, the Labour party might never have
catapulted to competitive status as one of that country's two major parties. On
the subject of America's many nonvoters of the early decades of the twentieth
century — leaving aside whether their nonparticipation had much to do with
the realignment of 1896 — the counterfactual question of how they would
have voted if mobilized is unanswerable. The answer once would have been
"as social democrats," but the full experience of the twentieth century has
supplied too many competing anwers. In various places at various times, widespread voter participation seems also to have helped liberalism, Toryism, nationalism, populism, Christian democracy, Communism, fascism, and racism.

Conclusion

The claims of the realignments genre do not hold up well, and the genre's
illuminative power has not proven to be great. At an analytic level, the genre
has proven vulnerable to at least three counterposing ideas: contingency, strategy, and valence issues.

Electoral politics is strongly influenced by the contingencies of unfolding
events. To the extent that this is true, elections and their underlying causes
are not usefully sortable into generation-long spans. Furthermore, victory-
oriented strategy is plied by candidates and parties, both of which tend to cater
to the electorate as well as emanate from it. (The two ideas are difficult to
disentangle; I am emphasizing the former here.) To the degree that parties and
candidates seek election victories above all else, courting the median voter,
they will often accommodate major impulses from the electorate without tell-
tale signs of realignment appearing in elections. Thus, the size of voter realignments cannot index the importance, innovativeness, and consequentiality of
elections, nor the level of voter concern that underpins them.

If we consider the combination of contingency and victory-oriented strategy, certain results reported by Daniel J. Gans (1985) become understandable.
In the sequence of presidential elections from 1856 through 1980, the distribution of victory "runs" by party (Carter, for example, was a run of one for
the Democrats; Reagan's two victories and George H. W. Bush's one made a

run of three for the Republicans) did not differ significantly from the runs of heads and tails that would be expected from coin flips (Gans 1985:228–30). Also, in the absence of repeat major-party candidates (such as Reagan in 1984 or Bryan in 1900), a presidential election four years ago holds virtually zero predictive value for this year's election — in predicting either this year's victorious party or this year's party shares of the vote (Gans 1985:230–33).

The third idea that poses problems for the realignments genre is that of valence issues. The concept was introduced by Donald J. Stokes (1966) and given major play, at least implicitly, in the sizable econometrics literature gauging the effects of ups and downs in the economy on elections. Unlike position issues, in which one party favors policy X and the other party favors policy Y — the staple kind of cleavage in the realignments genre — valence issues hinge chiefly on government management. Can another party manage the economy or the war, for example, better than the incumbent party has been doing? The more one examines American electoral history, the more it seems to tilt toward valence-issue as opposed to position-issue junctures. More than it did a generation ago, for example, the electoral turmoil of the 1890s seems to implicate the depression of 1893 as much as Bryan's insurgency. A poor economy figured in the critical 1874 midterm, and, according to one recent analysis, a quick nationwide economic downturn was a central ingredient in the Whigs' great victory of 1840 (Holt 1985). Valence issues, which also exemplify contingency and often bring into play opportunistic candidate or party strategies, are not friendly territory for the realignments genre.

It is not a minor matter that contingency, strategy, and valence issues tend to infuse elections. Blindsided by that threesome, for example, were Germany's Social Democrats and Communists in the early 1930s — brought up as they were on a script in which history would eventually favor their interest-based cause and they could simply wait. Politics cannot be about waiting — for electoral realignments or anything else. In the real world, voters are called upon to make judgments, not merely to register enduring interests or preferences — and to make them all the time.

In the ledgers of history and politics, perhaps the chief test for the realignments genre is whether it successfully elevates 1896 to a level with 1860 and 1932. That seems to have been its chief aspiration, both as science (to wit, the alleged periodicity) and as political and historical assertion. The Bryan cause was so terribly important, after all. But it was a lost cause, if an interesting and important one, and as such it is a member of a large universe of not easily analyzable "roads not taken." History moved on, more or less seamlessly, and seamlessness does not easily rival the memorable undertakings of the Civil War and New Deal eras. Between these two eras, if one's concern is electoral turbulence, at least four junctures catch the eye. Choosing which ones to dwell on is largely a matter of policy interest. For race and section, there is the election sequence of 1874 through 1880. For center-periphery relations, there is 1892 through 1896. For Progressive state-building, there is 1910 through 1916. For U.S. international involvement and the ricochet from it, there is 1916 through 1920.

Notes

I am indebted to Bruce Ackerman, Robert Dahl, Alan Gerber, Donald Green, Matthew Green, Rogan Kersh, Joseph LaPalombara, Michael Layton, Harvey Schantz, Ian Shapiro, Steven Skowronek, and Rogers Smith for their helpful comments on this essay. Reprinted, with permission, from *Annual Review of Political Science* 3 (2000), pp. 449–74. © 2000 by Annual Reviews, www.annualreviews.org.

1. Lane (1959) used total population as a denominator, rather than adult eligible voters; for elections prior to the mid-1860s, he considered the total non-slave population. The choice of technique makes little difference in this discussion.

2. Oddly, if the history of presidential contests were seriously searched for elections with localistic aspects, the 1896 one might rank high. That year, a set of geographically concentrated special-interest tails — the silver industry plus cotton and high-plains farmers — managed to wag the huge Democratic dog.

Literature Cited

Abramowitz, A. I. 1999. *It's Monica, stupid: Voting behavior in the 1998 midterm election.* Presented at Annu. Meet. Am. Polit. Sci. Assoc., Atlanta, GA.

Alford, R. R. 1963. *Party and Society.* Chicago: Rand McNally.

Amenta, E. 1998. *Bold Relief: Institutional Politics and the Origins of Modern American Social Policy.* Princeton, NJ: Princeton University Press.

Amenta, E., E. Benoit, C. Bonastia, N. K. Cauthen, and D. Halfmann. 1998. Bring back the WPA: Work, relief, and the origins of American social policy in welfare reform. *Stud. Am. Polit. Dev.* 12(1):1–56.

Bartels, L. M. 1998. Electoral continuity and change, 1868–1996. *Elect. Stud.* 17:301–26.

Blumenthal, S. 1982. *The Permanent Campaign.* New York: Simon & Schuster.

Brady, D. W. 1988. *Critical Elections and Congressional Policy Making.* Stanford, CA: Stanford University Press.

Brinkley, A. 1995. *The End of Reform: New Deal Liberalism in Recession and War.* New York: Knopf.

Bruchey, S. 1988. *The Wealth of the Nation*. New York: Harper & Row.

Burnham, W. D. 1965. The changing shape of the American political universe. *Am. Polit. Sci. Rev.* 59:7–28.

Burnham, W. D. 1967. Party systems and the political process. In *The American Party Systems: Stages of Political Development*, ed. W. N. Chambers, W. D. Burnham, pp. 277–307. New York: Oxford University Press.

Burnham, W. D. 1970. *Critical Elections and the Mainsprings of American Politics*. New York: Norton.

Burnham, W. D. 1981. The system of 1896: An analysis. In *The Evolution of American Electoral Systems*, ed. P. Kleppner, W. D. Burnham, R. P. Formisano, S. P. Hays, R. Jensen, W. G. Shade, pp. 147–202. Westport, CT: Greenwood.

Burnham, W. D. 1986. Periodization schemes and "party systems": The "system of 1896" as a case in point. *Soc. Sci. Hist.* 10:263–314.

Burnham, W. D. 1991. Critical realignment: Dead or alive? In *The End of Realignment? Interpreting American Electoral Eras*, ed. B. Shafer, pp. 101–39. Madison, WI: University of Wisconsin Press.

Clubb, J. M., W. H. Flanigan, N. H. Zingale. 1980. *Partisan Realignment: Voters, Parties, and Government in American History*. Beverly Hills, CA: Sage.

Coppock, D. J. 1961. The causes of the Great Depression, 1873–96. *Manchester School Econ. Soc. Stud.* 29:205–32.

Flanigan, W. H., and N. H. Zingale. 1974. The measurement of electoral change. *Polit. Methodol.* 1(Summer):49–82.

Foner, E. 1984. Why is there no socialism in the United States? *Hist. Workshop* 17 (Spring):57–80.

Gans, D. J. 1985. Persistence of party success in American presidential elections. *J. Interdisc. Hist.* 16:221–37.

Gerring, J. 1998. *Party Ideologies in America, 1828–1996*. New York: Cambridge University Press.

Hansen, J. M. 1990. Taxation and the political economy of the tarrif. *Int. Org.* 44:527–51.

Higgs, R. 1987. *Crisis and Leviathan: Critical Episodes in the Growth of American Government*. New York: Oxford University Press.

Hoffmann, C. 1956. The depression of the nineties. *J. Econ. Hist.* 16:137–64.

Holt, M. F. 1985. The election of 1840, voter mobilization, and the emergence of the second American party system: A reappraisal of Jacksonian voting behavior. In *A Master's Due: Essays in Honor of David Herbert Donald*, ed. W. J. Cooper Jr., M. F. Holt, and J. McCardell, pp. 16–58. Baton Rouge: Louisiana State University Press.

Hughes, J. F. 1994. The Jacksonians, the populists and the governmental habit. *Mid-America* 76(1):5–26.

Huston, J. L. 1993. The American revolutionaries, the political economy of aristocracy, and the American concept of the distribution of wealth, 1765–1900. *Am. Hist. Rev.* 98:1079–105.

Kennedy, D. M. 1999. *Freedom from Fear: The American People in Depression and War, 1929–1945*. New York: Oxford University Press.

Key, V. O. Jr. 1955. A theory of critical elections. *J. Polit.* 17:3–18.

Key, V. O. Jr. 1959. Secular realignment and the party system. *J. Polit.* 21:198–210.

Lane, R. E. 1959. *Political Life: Why People Get Involved in Politics.* Glencoe, IL: Free Press.

Lowi, T. J. 1964. American business, public policy, case-studies, and political theory. *World Polit.* 16:677–715.

Mayhew, D. R. 1994. U.S. policy waves in comparative context. In *New Perspectives on American Politics*, ed. L. C. Dodd and C. Jillson, pp. 325–40. Washington, D.C.: Congressional Quarterly Press.

Mayhew, D. R. 1996. Presidential elections and policy change: How much of a connection is there? In *American Presidential Elections: Process, Policy, and Political Change*, ed. H. Schantz, pp. 157–87.

Nardulli, P. F. 1995. The concept of a critical realignment, electoral behavior, and political change. *Am. Polit. Sci. Rev.* 89:10–22.

Rostow, W. W. 1960. *The Stages of Economic Growth.* New York: Cambridge University Press.

Schantz, H. L. 1998. *Realignment before V.O. Key, Jr.* Presented at Annu. Meet. So. Polit. Sci. Assoc., Atlanta, GA.

Schattschneider, E. E. 1956. United States: The functional approach to party government. In *Modern Political Parties: Approaches to Comparative Politics*, ed. S. Neumann, pp. 194–215. Chicago: University of Chicago Press.

Schattschneider, E. E. 1960. *The Semisovereign People: A Realist's View of Democracy in America.* New York: Holt, Rinehart & Winston.

Schlesinger, A. M. Jr. 1960. *The Politics of Upheaval.* Boston: Houghton Mifflin.

Schultze, C. L. 1992. Is there a bias toward excess in U.S. government budgets or deficits? *J. Econ. Persp.* 6(2):25–43.

Shammas, C. 1993. A new look at long-term trends in wealth inequality in the United States. *Am. Hist. Rev.* 98:412–31.

Skocpol, T. 1992. *Protecting Soldiers and Mothers: The Political Origins of Social Policy in the United States.* Cambridge, MA: Harvard University Press.

Stokes, D. E. 1966. Spatial models of party competition. In *Elections and the Political Order,* ed. A. Campbell, P. E. Converse, W. E. Miller, and D. E. Stokes, pp. 161–79. New York: Wiley.

Sundquist, J. L. 1973. *Dynamics of the Party System: Alignment and Realignment of Political Parties in the United States.* Washington, D.C.: Brookings Inst. Rev. Ed. 1983.

U.S. Bureau of the Census. 1975. *Historical Statistics of the United States, Colonial Times to 1970.* 2 vols. Washington, D.C.: U.S. Government Printing Office.

Woodward, C. V. 1951. *Reunion and Reaction: The Compromise of 1877 and the End of Reconstruction.* Boston: Little, Brown.

Zuczek, R. 1996. The last campaign of the Civil War: South Carolina and the revolution of 1876. *Civil War Hist.* 42:18–31.

10

Actions in the Public Sphere

What do members of the House and Senate do that is particularly conspicuous — that is, what kinds of actions performed by members of Congress are particularly likely to be noticed by the American public? The role of Congress in the American system hinges to a significant degree on the highly visible actions of its members, since actions performed by members in the American public sphere at a high level of prominence ensure a continuing connection between politicians and public.

Members of Congress perform actions beyond just making laws. Yes, Congress is a lawmaking body, but its members take part in the public sphere in an impressive variety of other ways. They investigate. They impeach. They oppose presidential administrations. They run for president themselves. As important as anything, perhaps, they take stands. American political history amounts to, among other things, a more than two-centuries-long sequence of representatives taking highly public stands — from Congressman James Madison (DR-Va.) opposing Alexander Hamilton's banking and credit plans in the late eighteenth century to Senator Edward Kennedy (D-Mass.) opposing President George W. Bush's war in Iraq in the early twenty-first century.

Tracing the conspicuous actions performed by members of Congress in the public sphere over the course of American history can provide a useful perspective on the development of Congress's role in the political system and its contribution to the political process.

Member Actions under George W. Bush

As a preface to a historical analysis of prominent actions by members of Congress, it may help to begin with the concrete and familiar—a brief selection of conspicuous moves by House and Senate members during the 2000 presidential election and the first three years of the George W. Bush administration. The recitation below is for illustrative purposes only, to offer a sense of the range and impact of members' actions. It is not intended as an exhaustive description of American national politics during those years.

- In January 2001, as television zeroed in on the Senate's official counting of electoral votes emanating from the 2000 presidential election, House members Alcee L. Hastings (D-Fla.), Jesse L. Jackson Jr. (D-Ill.), and other African American members of Congress appealed (unavailingly) to the upper chamber not to credit Florida's votes to Bush.[1]
- As the 107th Congress convened, Senate majority leader Trent Lott (R-Miss.), confronted by a new 50–50 party tie in the Senate, worked out what one analyst described as a "sweeping, bold—and risky—power-sharing arrangement" with his Democratic counterpart, Thomas Daschle (D-S.Dak.), for conducting Senate business.[2]
- In May 2001, President Bush's plan for a $1.6 trillion tax cut, assisted by an early endorsement from Democratic senator Zell Miller (D-Ga.), won passage courtesy of Senate Finance Committee leaders Charles Grassley (R-Iowa) and Max Baucus (D-Mont.), who struck a complicated deal for $1.35 trillion. "Rarely has a high-ranking senator provoked more displeasure from his own party colleagues," a commentator from the *Washington Post* observed with respect to Baucus. Daschle had told his fellow Democrat that he was not empowered to reach any deal with Grassley. "I don't have the authority to negotiate?" Baucus is said to have responded, stunned. "That's right," Daschle answered. After reportedly brooding during the night, Baucus struck a deal anyway.[3]
- In May 2001 Senator James Jeffords of Vermont defected from the Republican Party, thus giving control of the Senate to the Democrats for the next year and a half.[4]
- In 2001, Senator Edward Kennedy worked in harness with the White House to craft a major education enactment, the No Child Left Behind program — "a classic piece of horse-trading that provides the Republicans with testing

and accountability in return for more federal money and more generous treatment of poor children." This endeavor continued the Massachusetts senator's record of reaching across party lines to generate new policy programs.[5]

- In the wake of the attack on the World Trade Center on September 11, 2001, Lott, Daschle, House Speaker Dennis Hastert (R-Ill.), and House minority leader Dick Gephardt (D-Mo.) rallied behind the White House and served as a kind of consultative council to Bush for a time.[6]
- At the cost of attracting death threats, Congresswoman Barbara Lee (D-Calif.) cast the only House or Senate vote against the use-of-force resolution enacted on September 18, 2001, to combat terrorism.[7]
- In 2002, campaign finance reform finally succeeded. Under President Bill Clinton, Senators John McCain (R-Ariz.) and Russell Feingold (D-Wis.) had advanced the idea of regulating "soft money" — that is, very large money contributions made by individuals and groups to the American parties during the 1990s in violation of the spirit, if not exactly the letter, of previous rigid ceilings on contributions. In the House, moderate Republican Christopher Shays (R-Conn.) and Democrat Martin Meehan (D-Mass.) had maneuvered a floor victory for that anti-soft-money cause in 1998 on the strength of an aroused C-SPAN audience and a principally Democratic coalition over the opposition of the chamber's Republican-majority leadership. McCain, after his prominent bid for the White House in 2000, had "capitalized on the momentum of his presidential campaign by threatening to tie the Senate in knots if Lott did not accede to his demand for an unfettered debate on campaign finance reform." McCain and Feingold staged "town halls" on the subject around the country. In March 2001 an "unaccustomed spectacle" — a "serious, substantive debate" — did indeed take place in the Republican-led Senate, and a McCain-Feingold bill cleared that body as it had in the House on the basis of largely Democratic votes. McCain's "adept stewardship of the bill surprised many colleagues." In February 2002 Shays and Meehan succeeded again in a Republican-controlled House, staving off a "near-17-hour barrage of rival bills and amendments that Republican leaders had hoped would derail the legislation."[8]
- In the wake of the Enron scandal Senator Paul Sarbanes (D-Md.) is said to have brought unusual knowledge and strategic skill to the crafting of a new bipartisan regulatory blueprint for the accounting industry.[9]
- Congressman Jim McDermott (D-Wash.), during a visit to Baghdad in September 2002 as war loomed, claimed that Saddam Hussein had more credibility than Bush.[10]
- In 2003, Speaker Hastert and House majority leader Tom DeLay won notice for their efficient Republican Party apparatus. The *Washington Post* reported

that they had "systematically changed internal rules to seize greater authority over rank-and-file members," as in the awarding of committee chairmanships. Two years earlier, Hastert had found ways to "inoculate House Republicans against Democratic attacks on [embarrassingly framed] issues by scheduling House floor votes on GOP-flavored legislative remedies," in the words of Richard E. Cohen in the *National Journal.*[11]

- Senate majority leader Daschle, on the other hand, had drawn criticism for allegedly poor agenda planning as the 2002 midterm election approached. Couldn't the Democrats have positioned themselves more coherently on Bush's Iraq resolution in October 2002? Did the authorization of the new Homeland Security Department need to be held up during the last weeks before the election, offering an issue for the Republicans?[12]

- As the war in Iraq proceeded in 2003, Senator Robert Byrd (D-W.Va.), now in his mid-eighties, dean of the chamber, took on a role familiar from Roman times as a senatorial guardian against what a *Wall Street Journal* commentator described as "an increasingly arrogant, wartime White House." Byrd's speeches were posted on the Internet, where especially the younger generation, it is speculated, responded with some 3.7 million hits during March 2003 alone.[13]

- In the legislative realm in 2003, Senator Kennedy helped spark another cross-party enterprise, this time on the question of financing prescription drugs through Medicare: on June 16 the *Wall Street Journal* reported that "at a Democratic luncheon this past week, Mr. Kennedy set off a storm by loudly urging his colleagues to declare victory and embrace [a centrist proposal then being discussed, rather than a purely liberal one] as their own." The Democratic senators did that, more or less, to their and Kennedy's later regret as the agreement paved the way to a successful Republican-flavored enactment in November 2003 that they strongly opposed. This enactment, which is said to have called for the biggest changes in Medicare since its creation in 1965, cleared the House in a riveting 220–215 vote, for which Hastert's leadership team kept the count open for a record-setting three hours during the middle of the night in order to badger and inveigle the needed support.[14]

- In 2003, six Democratic members of Congress ran for the presidency — Senators Joseph Lieberman (D-Conn.), Bob Graham (D-Fla.), John Edwards (D-N.C.), and John Kerry (D-Mass.), and House members Gephardt and Dennis Kucinich (D-Ohio). On the Iraq resolution of October 2002 giving the White House authority to wage war, all of the six except Graham and Kucinich voted yes. On the later measure of October 2003 appropriating $87 billion to fund the war and its aftermath, all but Lieberman and Gephardt voted no.

- As the war ensued, Senator Kennedy took an unusually strong oppositional stance, accusing the White House of "fraud" in staging the intervention.[15]
- In 2003, House majority leader DeLay reached into the politics of his home state to maneuver a mid-decade gerrymander of Texas's congressional districts aimed at converting a Democratic majority of 17–15 into a Republican majority as large as 22–10.[16] (In fact, a Republican edge of 21–11 accrued from the subsequent election of November 2004).

Aspects of High-Profile Member Actions

The various moves by House and Senate members listed above were all performed at a particularly high level of conspicuousness. At least four points can be made about them.

First, to dwell on the conspicuousness, on exhibit here is the public face of Congress and its members. Insofar as the American public watches, takes note of, monitors, audits, is influenced by, or is induced to react to the congressional realm, the odds are that it does so substantially because of high-profile activity by members. The moves cited above were probably noted by millions of people, many by tens of millions, some even possibly by more than a hundred million.

Second, these member actions were important. More specifically, to give that idea some empirical grounding, credible reason very likely existed among the relevant audiences taking note of these actions to size them up as consequential, potentially consequential, or otherwise in some fashion significant. Especially for the African American population, the appeal on the Florida vote dramatized an alleged injustice and spotlighted the absence of blacks at that time in the Senate (not one of the hundred senators took up the appeal).[17] It was a statement. Probably the Lott-Daschle power-sharing agreement made a difference. Possibly Zell Miller's early endorsement of the Bush tax cut made a difference. Many infuriated Democrats thought that Max Baucus's maneuvering on that measure made a difference. Senator Jeffords's defection made a difference (even if it stopped well short of radically switching control of the Senate for policy purposes from a typical conservative Republican stance to a typical liberal Democratic stance).[18] It was consequential for the American population that Senator Kennedy helped along both the education measure and, to his regret, the Medicare prescription drugs measure. For both domestic and foreign audiences, it was an important signal that the leaders of the congressional parties formed their consultative foursome after September 11. Barbara Lee's nay vote was a statement, a kind of footnote to the 9/11 crisis. In the cases of McCain, Feingold, Shays, and Meehan on campaign finance, recalling the role played by James Stewart in *Mr. Smith Goes to Washington,* here is a classic instance of members of Congress whipping up public support to enact a reform over the resistance of a congressional majority party. It was probably important that Speaker Hastert led the House the way he did, possibly important that Majority Leader Daschle led the Senate the way he did (trying to herd senators is no bargain for any leader). It would likely be a mistake to underrate Senator Byrd's speeches. The Texas redistricting plan engendered by Tom DeLay, it was speculated, could help keep the House in Republican hands for a decade or more. As usual, for the party not holding the White House, Congress supplied much of the talent for the presidential nominating season in 2003–4. The roll-call positions that Kerry, Lieberman, Edwards, Gephardt, and Kucinich had taken on the key Iraq questions supplied much of the discussion material for that season.

Third, the members who undertook the actions highlighted above did so with an appreciable degree of personal autonomy. True, the actions were typically *influenced,* it is fair to say, by states of affairs or considerations outside their control. Typically, bands of political feasibility existed within which the politicians crafted their moves. It would be highly unlikely that a representative from Tom DeLay's conservative district in the Houston suburbs would have protested the Florida count or voted nay on the use-of-force resolution along with Barbara Lee. Montana, Max Baucus's home state, had scored a 25 percent edge for Bush in the election of November 2000. Lott, Daschle, Hastert, and Gephardt after September 11 were representing the public of the United States, not that of, say, Syria. On balance, Speaker Hastert's largely united Republican caucus was pleased to give him some leadership leeway. With the upcoming Democratic primaries and the November 2004 election in mind, those congressional representatives aiming for the White House had to think very carefully about these different contexts when positioning themselves on the Iraq questions.

All this is true. Yet it does not add up to anything like a case that external cosiderations *determined* these representatives' actions. Trent Lott would have surprised no one by organizing the Senate in its customary partisan fashion even with a wafer-thin 51–50 majority, relying on Vice President Dick Cheney to break ties. Senator Baucus could have brooded himself into a different decision on the tax cut (the Democratic senators from neighboring, even more decisively pro-Bush, North Dakota opposed the cut).[19] Senator Jeffords could have stayed put (as most senators who are miffed at their parties do). Senator Kennedy could have passed up his education and prescription-drugs endeavors (as most Democrats would have done). McCain and Feingold could have given up on campaign finance reform—consigning their cause to the historical dustbin alongside many other legislative drives of the past like those for a school-prayer amendment and a federal consumer-protection agency. Senator Byrd could have orated less. Absent Senator Sarbanes's efforts, the accounting reform could have ended up less effective (like some other regulatory reforms). Speaker Hastert could have run the House in a more relaxed way in the style of, perhaps, Speaker Tom Foley (D-Wash.) in the early 1990s. Senator Kerry could have joined his home-state partner Kennedy to vote nay on the joint resolution authorizing the use of force against Iraq in October 2002. Barbara Lee would have caused little surprise by joining her customary allies on the left such as Maxine Waters (D-Calif.), José Serrano (D-N.Y.), and Jan Schakowsky (D-Ill.) to vote yes on the use-of-force resolution in 2001. On Iraq, Kennedy could have looked for a term other than *fraud*. Certainly Tom DeLay could have refrained from the mid-decade Texas redistricting.

An additional consideration bears on member autonomy. During 2001–3, what did the members *not* do that they might have done? What are the plausible counterfactuals? Where human autonomy is involved, it is a great mistake to accept whatever happened as an exhaustive universe of the possible. Why didn't the conservative Zell Miller, who later endorsed President Bush for reelection, defect to the Republicans in 2001 to counter Jeffords? While controlling the Senate during 2002, why didn't the Democratic leadership mount a harder-hitting investigation of pre–September 11 intelligence failures? (Consider the explosive investigations of the intelligence agencies in 1975–76.) After September 11, why didn't some enterprising committee chair conduct a flashy probe of alleged domestic terrorist elements? Imagine Islamic fundamentalists appearing before cameras. Why didn't some Democrat market an appealing argument against the repeal of the estate tax (labeled shrewdly the "death tax" by Republicans)?[20] Where were the deficit hawks? Why didn't Senator Pete Domenici (R-N.M.), a power on budget questions, blanch at Bush's deficits the way he had blanched at Reagan's? Why didn't some Republican committee chair probe into allegations of dubious activities in Senator Daschle's very narrow reelection in South Dakota in 2002? Why wasn't any senator available to craft a deal with the White House on energy the way Kennedy did on education? Couldn't some innovative Democratic members of Congress have devised a more gripping domestic program for the party? Where were the Democratic equivalents of Newt Gingrich (R-Ga.) and Gingrich's Contract with America? Why didn't House minority leader Nancy Pelosi (D-Calif.) try to counter Tom DeLay by pressing for a mid-decade redistricting in, say, Illinois, where the Democratic Party came to control the entire state government as a consequence of the 2002 election? None of these moves would have been highly implausible during 2001–3, but no one made the relevant moves.

The Realm of Public Affairs

The fourth point about the actions of members of Congress such as those highlighted above is that they do not enjoy much of a place in social science, even if they rate high with journalists, traditional historians, and alert citizens. As a theoretical matter, social scientists tend to see Congress as a place where externally determined views or interests — that is, those of the society's classes, interest groups, electorates, and the like — are *registered*. Causal arrows are aimed at Capitol Hill, and they hit. That is virtually all that happens.[21] Also, as a conceptual matter, the making of laws tends to be the only activity worth addressing. And as an empirical matter, roll-call voting in the service of lawmaking is virtually the only evidence worth examining.

This is a caricature of contemporary congressional studies as undertaken by social scientists, but not by much. Certainly the current emphasis leaves out too much and also gets certain essentials wrong. For one thing, "registering" preferences or interests on Capitol Hill, given that they can be said to exist, is more problematic than it might seem. Members of Congress actually have to *do* things in order to advance their various aims, and they might or might not perform. Talent and drive need to be applied.[22]

For another thing, on many kinds of matters it is a precarious assumption that preferences or interests really do exist out there in society in anything like a pristine form to be congressionally "registered." The content of public life is complicated. In politics as opposed to, say, personal tastes in ice-cream flavors or a desire to earn fifteen dollars an hour as opposed to ten dollars an hour, a high degree of influence external to individual human beings is often brought to bear in the crafting of personal preferences or self-perceived interests. It is a good bet that members of Congress, along with presidents and many other political actors in society, to be sure, figure significantly in the crafting. Political products can be invented and merchandised, hence such causes as the "Contract with America," "family leave," "unfunded mandates," "campaign finance reform," the "death tax," and the "patients' bill of rights," all of which have been shaped by elite actors and found appreciative audiences in recent times. Elite influence over individual preferences bears on congressional roll-call studies, too. To array members of Congress from most liberal to most conservative on a summary roll-call measure, a popular simplifying device, is to say little about the substantive content of that dimension. The ingredients of the content need to be invented day after day, year after year, generation after generation, by enterprising politicians and others. They do not exist "naturally."

There is much to be said for the intuitions of journalists, historians, and alert citizens. Legislators' "actions" can take on a major role, and the relations between the public and the government can take on a rich, complicated, and interesting form if one abandons — at least as anything like axiomatic or exhaustive — the idea that Capitol Hill life consists merely of carrying out or catering to preferences or interests that exist coherently outside the legislative realm, waiting to be carried out or catered to. Once past this notion, relations between the public and elective officials can be seen as interactive rather than just one-way. Members of Congress are not simply the targets of society's vectors. Opinion formation can be viewed as internal to political processes rather than somehow executed externally. Members of Congress and other elite actors can be hypothesized to *shape* opinion as well as to react to it. In their various undertakings, veteran representatives such as Kennedy, McCain, and DeLay can be seen as effective cue-givers to a nationwide audience, owing to their long built-up "policy reputations." In lawmaking and otherwise, members can take on a role familiar in the private market economy as "entrepreneurs."[23]

More generally, the realm of "public affairs" or the "public sphere" can supersede the registering of preferences or interests as a model of political reality. If members of Congress enjoy a significant degree of autonomy, the American realm of public affairs can be seen as a stream of collective consciousness in which certain actions by individuals, including members of Congress, come to be noticed and remembered. Individuals' actions seem to reach this standing if they are widely thought to be consequential, potentially consequential, or otherwise significant. They are observed by politically aware citizens trying to size up events in their environment. They afford a kind of connection. They are worth noticing. Baucus's support of the Bush tax cut signaled a nationwide audience that significant Democratic support existed for the measure, thus possibly helping to legitimize it. McCain's drive for campaign finance reform defined a problem and helped shape a nationwide constituency for that reform measure. Lee's negative vote on the use-of-force resolution post-9/11 signaled a nationwide audience, in particular African Americans, that misgivings were possible about that solidly backed move. Kennedy's cry of "fraud" on the Iraq War advised a nationwide liberal constituency what they should be thinking, or at least considering thinking. In the American system, public affairs is "a busy timestream of events featuring uncertainty, open deliberation and discussion, opinion formation, strutting and ambition, surprises, endless public moves and countermoves by politicians and other actors, rising and falling issues, and an attentive and sometimes participating audience of large numbers of citizens."[24]

Members of Congress are in the thick of this activity, which, given the country's constitutional contours, may entail members' actions of several varieties beyond lawmaking. With the member's job goes a license to persuade, connive, hatch ideas, propagandize, assail enemies, vote, build coalitions, shepherd coalitions, and in general cut a figure in public affairs. A legislature can be a decision machine, a forum, an arena, a stage, or a springboard.[25] Some members may craft bills — in the long reach of American history, consider Senator Robert F. Wagner (D-N.Y.), the author of the landmark National Labor Relations Act (the Wagner Act) of 1935. Some may conduct investigations — consider Senator Joseph McCarthy (R-Wis.), the anticommunist investigator of the 1950s. Some may undertake issue crusades — consider Senator Huey Long (D-La.) and his "Share Our Wealth" crusade of the 1930s. Some may run for president — consider Senators Barry Goldwater (R-Ariz.) and John F. Kennedy (D-Mass.) of the 1950s and 1960s.

Actions That Gain Public Notice

With public affairs or the public sphere as a conceptual template, one can analyze the *kinds* of activities that win members of Congress significant public notice. What kinds of things do legislators do that people actually pay attention to? In principle, this is an empirical question whose answers should feed back into a theoretical illumination of the public sphere. If a kind of activity is reasonably widely noticed, then the very noticing of it might say something about the connection between the elected officials and the public — or at least an alert sector of the public. In principle, this is a view of representative relations in which the public itself has a large role in choosing the sorts of things it sees fit to monitor. The following discussion will cover a selection of the more important categories analyzed in my study, *America's Congress: Actions in the Public Sphere, James Madison through Newt Gingrich*, published by Yale University Press in 2000. Categories covered in the study but *not* taken up here include member moves in regard to processing presidential nominations, taking appointments (as when a member of Congress moves to the cabinet), revising congressional rules, impeaching executive or judicial officials, censuring other members of Congress, running for president or vice president, or serving as party leaders.

Approached as a serious empirical enterprise, determining the kinds of member action that get "noticed" raises considerable problems of evidence.

Rather than ransacking newspapers over many generations, I resorted to a fallback data source in *America's Congress.*[26] The study covers American national history from the beginning. It utilizes a selection of thirty-eight works of "public affairs history" — a genre in which the historians, whatever else they do, try to gather and transmit a past collective understanding, at least among the politically aware public at relevant past times, of what was going on in the public sphere. "Noticing" by the public is in principle captured. These are standard, well-known books on such subjects as "the Jacksonian era" and "the New Deal era." They tell us that Henry Clay (W-Ky.) did this, George Norris (R, Ind.-Neb.) did this, and Robert A. Taft (R-Ohio) did that. Many difficulties arise in using a data source like this, not the least of which is that serious tracking of representatives' actions is not possible beyond 1988. That is because adequate history books do not yet exist that would allow it. The result is a data collection that covers exactly two centuries, 1789 through 1988. Recorded were the historians' mentions of actions of all kinds engaged in by individuals serving as members of Congress. The result was 2,304 member actions in all. Each one was sorted into a category or categories according to its *kind.* An action might be multiply coded, for example, as both "legislate" and "big speech." The issue area of "foreign policy" had its own category.

Patterns of member actions as they have accumulated across two centuries can serve as a useful window into the American regime. Presented below are the main data displays from *America's Congress,* supplemented by suitable, albeit unsystematically collected, information for more recent years. The traditional roles of several kinds of congressional action in the American system are discussed, followed by a speculative analysis of how those roles may be upheld or attenuated during the twenty-first century, keeping in mind the following questions: What is the future of conspicuous action by members of Congress? What is necessary for its sustenance? Why should the citizenry care?

LEGISLATING

The obvious story about legislatures is that they legislate. *Legislate* is coded here as any sort of rhetorical, coalition building, or formal parliamentary move by a member of Congress (whether or not it was successful) aimed at enacting, amending, or blocking a congressional measure.[27] At the least, member actions in the legislative process can tip off an alert sector of the public about the issue content, prospects, and coalitional underpinnings of lawmaking drives. Monitoring and appraisal by the public are assisted. At the most, member actions can help to shape those drives — as in Senator McCain's definition of the issue and mobilization of nationwide support in the cause of campaign finance reform.

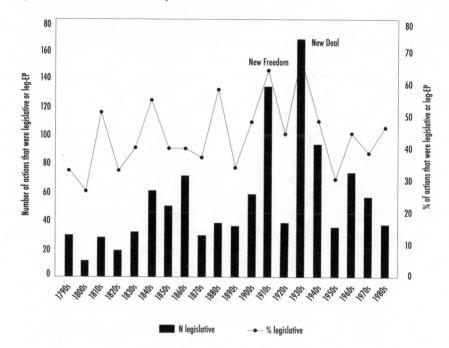

Figure 10.1. Legislative actions. *Source:* Thirty-eight "public affairs" history books listed in David R. Mayhew, *America's Congress: Actions in the Public Sphere, James Madison through Newt Gingrich* (New Haven: Yale University Press, 2000), pp. 34–35.

In the 2000 study, the coding scheme for "legislate" picked up 1,079 items from 1789 through 1988. For their frequency by decade, see the vertical bars in Figure 10.1.[28] For the percentage of member actions of all kinds that they comprised during each decade, see the connected line in that figure. Not surprisingly, the 1910s and the 1930s stand out. In the former era, many members of Congress figured prominently in the Democrats' New Freedom legislative drive under Woodrow Wilson, as did also Senator Henry Cabot Lodge (R-Mass.) and others in thwarting the president's campaign to ratify the Versailles Treaty with its League of Nations commitment a few years later. In the uniquely busy 1930s, Senator Wagner, perhaps the leading designer of the American welfare state, joined many other members in prominently advancing or impeding the many legislative enterprises of the New Deal era. In the decades after World War II, the main exhibits of congressional action were the historic drives to enact the Civil Rights Act of 1964 — fifteen actions, including the orchestration by Senator Richard Russell (D-Ga.) of a seemingly endless although losing filibuster; and Reagan's tax and expenditure cuts in 1981 —

ten actions, including some adept maneuvering by Congressman Phil Gramm (D-Tex.), a key White House ally at that time although not yet a Republican.

An appropriate continuation of Figure 10.1 beyond 1988 might generate vertical bars about as high as those of the 1970s or 1980s. Legislating on a New Deal scale has not been seen in this period, although there have been moments. Likely among the highlights, for example, would be several member actions during President Clinton's unproductive drive for health care reform in 1993–94 — skillful though uphill committee work by Congressmen John Dingell (D-Mich.) and Daniel Rostenkowski (D-Ill.), critical comments dropped by Capitol Hill's unconvinced leading intellectual on the subject, Senator Daniel Patrick Moynihan (D-N.Y.), energetic leadership by Senate majority leader George Mitchell (D-Maine), temporizing but then tough opposition by Senate minority leader Bob Dole (R-Kans.). In the Congress of 1995–96, Speaker Newt Gingrich (R-Ga.) certainly made a public mark as a legislative entrepreneur. His Contract with America foundered after winning passage in the House, as did the Gingrich-Dole budget that provoked a showdown with the Clinton White House over shutting down the government, yet the failure was not complete in either case — and it is true that American high politics was largely structured for a while by these endeavors. There were other promising items under George H. W. Bush and Clinton, such as the framing of banking reform by Senator Gramm (R-Tex.) in 1999. High-profile legislative actions under George W. Bush have already been discussed. In general, members' legislative actions since 1988 if suitably documented would probably approximate the two-century norm in volume as well as texture — nothing special.[29]

To go back to the main data set, however, perhaps the most interesting aspect of the "legislate" realm of member action is that it constituted only 47 percent of the items during 1789 through 1988 — 1,079 of the total 2,304. Clearly, members of Congress do other kinds of things that win notice.

INVESTIGATING

One of the things members of Congress do to gain attention is *investigate*, a category that accommodated 114 member actions, or 5 percent of the data set, from 1789 through 1988. That is, a member of Congress called for, took part in, or was otherwise associated with a congressional investigation or hearing on any subject for any purpose — and won the requisite notice for it.[30] Since seventeenth-century England, a basic prerogative of free legislative bodies has been the right to investigate — if necessary through use of the subpoena power. Transparency in the conduct of executive branches has been one end often served; illumination of problems in society has been another. The investigative role is by nature high profile with regard to member action, since personal initiative is called for (investigations do not happen naturally; someone has to spark and carry them), and dramatic exposure tactics that draw attention and shape opinion are often key to the art.

Figure 10.2 shows the two-century American "investigate" data display. High-publicity investigating has always been an avenue for members' entrepreneurialism, but, perhaps surprisingly, such activity did not fully blossom until the twentieth century. From the vantage point of today, the 1910s through the 1970s looks like a long age of congressional exposure. Entrepreneurs serving on House and Senate committees forged techniques of day-by-day, week-by-week revelation to rivet public attention on various alleged malperformance or misbehavior in the society or the government. The effects were often pronounced. There seem to have been three phases. From roughly 1913 through 1937, the Progressive left on Capitol Hill supplied the energy and inventiveness. Private corporations became a choice target: for example, Senator Thomas Walsh (D-Mont.) pursued (in fact, largely created) the Teapot Dome scandal involving relations between oil companies and the administration of President Warren G. Harding in the mid-1920s, and Senator Robert La Follette Jr. (Ind.-Wis.) hammered various firms for their labor practices in a consequential locale-by-locale exposé that dovetailed with the national organizing drive of the Congress of Industrial Organizations (CIO) in 1936–37. Then the conservative side took the lead. Congressman Martin Dies (D-Tex.) pioneered the investigation of un-American activities ("naming names" on the witness stand arose as a technique) starting in 1938, Congressman Howard Smith (D-Va.) harried several New Deal and war agencies around 1940, Senator McCarthy pursued alleged Communists in the State Department and the army in 1953–54, and Senator John McClellan (D-Ark.) exposed certain culpable practices of labor unions in the late 1950s. Then the initiative went back to the left. The cold war "imperial presidency" came under fire as Senator J. William Fulbright (D-Ark.) staged damaging hearings on the Vietnam War starting in 1966, Senator Sam Ervin (D-N.C.) brought a folksy charm to the televised Watergate probe that crippled the Nixon administration in 1973, and Senator Frank Church (D-Idaho) exposed certain practices of the intelligence agencies in 1975.

That is a formidable record. It exhibits the power and potential of members' investigative action. In Figure 10.2, the reading for the 1980s is modest by comparison. Is this an indication of slippage in the investigative domain? It would seem so, notwithstanding such eye-catching enterprises of recent times as the probe led by Senator Fred Thompson (R-Tenn.) in 1997 into the Clinton

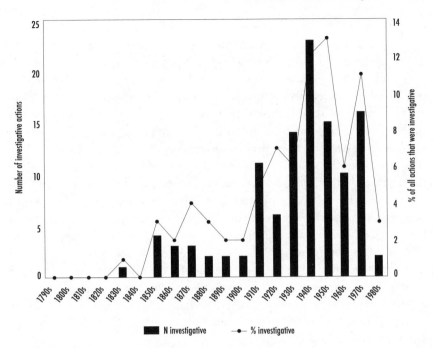

Figure 10.2. Investigative actions. *Source:* See Figure 10.1.

administration's campaign finance practices (the alleged sale of the Lincoln bedroom, the White House coffees, the Buddhist nuns as alleged donors, and the rest), and the House Judiciary Committee hearings chaired by Henry Hyde (R-Ill.) in 1998, ending in Clinton's impeachment.[31] Here is the point. Since the mid-1970s, the process of day-by-day exposure has largely moved elsewhere. Investigative journalism came into its own with Watergate. Special commissions have been set up to study the *Challenger* disaster, the September 11 intelligence failure, and other events of recent decades. Independent counsels entered the scene in the 1970s. Note that by the time the House Judiciary Committee inherited the Clinton imbroglio in mid-1998, there was virtually nothing left to reveal or expose. An independent counsel's office plus the media had already performed the labor. In earlier decades, members of Congress as diverse as Walsh, Dies, McCarthy, Fulbright, and Church might have been taking the lead. It is a difficult question whether today's relative eclipse of member investigative action, if that is what is being witnessed, has left the country better off. For one thing, camera-seeking senators versus runaway independent counsels is not an easy choice.

TAKING STANDS

Taking stands is one of the fundamental activities that members of Congress engage in.[32] Looked at one way, politics is an unending sequence of contributions to a national conversation—an often cranky and contentious one, to be sure. Members of Congress, validated as they are by having won elections and gifted with formal powers that can back up speech, are in a privileged position to make contributions that can swerve or more along that conversation. Many of them perform accordingly, often with consequence.

As a conceptual or coding matter, "taking stands" has blurrier boundaries than, say, legislating or investigating, which are linked reasonably clearly to formal procedures. In principle, taking stands simply means registering a position on some matter before some audience. The reelection drive can animate it, but so can other aims including trying to shape national opinion. For the latter purpose, being a member of Congress supplies an effective platform and some members have famously used it—for example, Congressman James Madison in propagandizing for a new Jeffersonian Republican party in the 1790s; Senator Charles Sumner (D-Free Soil, then R-Mass.) through his antislavery speeches in the 1850s; and Senator Gerald P. Nye (R-N.D.) in conducting his isolationist crusade in the 1930s.

In this study, taking stands could overlap other kinds of member activity, and it often did—notably legislating. An action counted as both "legislating" and "taking a stand" if a member of Congress was documented as making some parliamentary move but also expressing a view—as did Senator Russell, for example, in both formally impeding and rhetorically assailing the civil rights measure in 1964. Altogether, a total of 1,081 of the 2,304 member-action items from 1789 through 1988 qualified as "taking a stand." Of these, 427 or 40 percent were also coded as "legislating." In the residual 60 percent of these items emerges an inventive variety of techniques and venues used by members to get their points across. Table 10.1 presents a selection of those nonlegislative expressions exhibiting their variety. Much of the prominent public history of the two centuries surfaces in this list.

In recent years, congressional stand-taking has continued alive and well. An update of Table 10.1 might include the following: In 1991, Congresswoman Barbara Boxer (D-Calif.) led a march by women House members to the Senate to protest the way the hearings to confirm Clarence Thomas as a Supreme Court justice were being conducted (controversial testimony by Anita Hill was involved). In 1993 Senator Sam Nunn (D-Ga.) threw cold water on the Clinton administration's gays-in-the-military policy. At a critical moment in 1994, Senator Moynihan called for an independent counsel to investigate the

Table 10.1 *Selected Instances of Nonlegislative MC Stand-taking*

1798	Matthew Lyon (DR-VT)	H	spits in the eye of ideological foe Roger Griswold (F-CT)
1801	Theodore Sedgwick (F-MA)	H	boycotts Jefferson's inauguration as Federalist gesture
1814	Timothy Pickering (F-MA)	S	promotes secessionist Northern Confederacy
1825	George Kremer (D-PA)	H	charges (in newspaper) corrupt deal between H. Clay & J. Q. Adams
1831	John Quincy Adams (NR-MA)	H	introduces his first antislavery petition to House
1856	Preston Brooks (D-SC)	H	canes Charles Sumner on the Senate floor after Kansas speech
1858	Stephen A. Douglas (D-IL)	S	takes part in Lincoln-Douglas debates
1858	William Seward (R-NY)	S	delivers his "irrepressible conflict" speech in Rochester, NY
1860	Robert Toombs (D-GA)	S	issues a secession manifesto
1861	Clement Vallandigham (D-OH)	H	as "Copperhead," backs obstruction of northern war effort
1867	William D. Kelley (R-PA)	H	tours South to carry GOP doctrine to freedmen audiences
1868	Benjamin Butler (R-MA)	H	waves a bloody shirt (literally) as Johnson impeachment manager
1872	Charles Sumner (R-MA)	S	backs Democrat Greeley over Republican Grant for president
1874	Lucius Q. C. Lamar (D-MS)	H	eulogizes deceased Sumner in North–South reconciliation speech
1881	Roscoe Conkling (R-NY)	S	resigns Senate seat in a huff over Garfield's patronage turndowns
1889	Henry Cabot Lodge (R-MA)	H	writes *North American Review* piece backing House rules reform
1892	William B. Cockran (D-NY)	H	delivers anti-Cleveland oration at Demo. national convention
1896	David B. Hill (D-NY)	S	boycotts New York City speech of pres. candidate W. J. Bryan

Table 10.1 Continued

1901	Benjamin Tillman (D-SC)	S	assails Theodore Roosevelt for inviting blacks to the White House
1910	Nelson W. Aldrich (R-RI)	S	moves to fund orthodox GOP congressional candidates
1910	Jonathan Dolliver (R-IA)	S	dares Taft to try to expel Progressives from GOP
1917	Henry Cabot Lodge (R-MA)	S	runs to shake Wilson's hand after presidential speech proposing war
1920	Andrew J. Volstead (R-MN)	H	co-leads a church service to celebrate Prohibition
1922	Robert La Follette, Sr. (R-WI)	S	calls national conference of Progressives
1926	Fiorello La Guardia (R-NY)	H	stages news conference to mix an (anti-Prohibition) illegal drink
1934–35	Huey Long (D-LA)	S	promotes his Share Our Wealth program nationwide
1936	Ellison D. Smith (D-SC)	S	walks out of Democratic convention as black preacher speaks
1937	Josiah W. Bailey (D-NC)	S	co-drafts anti-FDR Conservative Manifesto
1940	Gerald P. Nye (R-ND)	S	helps found America First movement
1944	Alben Barkley (D-KY)	S	resigns Democratic leadership post in tiff with FDR over taxes
1943	Arthur Vandenberg (R-MI)	S	presses anti-isolationist resolution at GOP Mackinac Island meeting
1950	William Jenner (R-IN)	S	denounces General Marshall as a front man for traitors
1951	Joseph Martin (R-MA)	H	assails Truman administration after General MacArthur firing
1952	Henry Cabot Lodge, Jr. (R-MA)	S	promotes pro-Ike "fair play" reso. at GOP national convention
1952	Wayne Morse (R-OR)	S	defects from GOP over McCarthyism
1956	Albert Gore (D-TN)	S	won't sign segregationist Southern Manifesto

Table 10.1 Continued

1956	Adam Clayton Powell (D-NY)	H	endorses Republican Eisenhower for reelection
1957	Eugene McCarthy (D-MN)	H	takes lead in founding liberal Democratic Study Group
1962	Barry Goldwater (R-AZ)	S	authors foreign policy work *Why Not Victory?*
1962	Kenneth Keating (R-NY)	S	charges JFK administration with tolerating Soviet missiles in Cuba
1964	Kenneth Keating (R-NY)	S	leads walkout of moderates from GOP national convention
1968	Robert F. Kennedy (D-NY)	S	celebrates Easter mass with labor organizer Cesar Chavez
1968	Eugene McCarthy (D-MN)	S	won't back Humphrey after Democratic convention in Chicago
1970	Gaylord Nelson (D-WI)	S	suggests celebration of Earth Day (and it happens)
1973	Lowell Weicker (R-CT)	S	assails Nixon administration in Watergate hearings
1974	Hugh Scott (R-PA)	S	as leader of Senate GOP, calls Nixon tapes disgusting
1975	Bob Carr (D-MI)	H	puts Vietnam $ cutoff reso. through House Democratic Caucus
1978	Edward Kennedy (D-MA)	S	attacks Carter admin. from the left at midterm Dem. conference
1983	Phil Gramm (D-TX)	H	switches to GOP, resigns House seat, and is reelected
1984	Barry Goldwater (R-AZ)	S	fumes at CIA mining of Nicaragua harbors
1984	Jesse Helms (R-NC)	S	backs right-wing El Salvador leader D'Aubuisson
1987	Edward Kennedy (D-MA)	S	leads fight against Bork nomination to Supreme Court

Source: Mayhew, *America's Congress*, pp. 93–95.

Clintons' Whitewater entanglement. In 1995 came the Contract with America. Two years later, the Republican Revolution having wound down, Congressman Lindsey Graham (R-S.C.) led an abortive coup against Speaker Gingrich. That same year, Congressman Bob Barr (R-Ga.) called for the impeachment of President Clinton, and Senator Jesse Helms (R-N.C.) defiantly blocked the nomination of Governor William F. Weld (R-Mass.) as ambassador to Mexico. Also, Senator Lieberman publicly chastised the president after the Monica Lewinsky revelations broke. In 1999 Senator McCain emerged as the leading proponent of all-out American military intervention in Kosovo to ward off Serbian genocide there.[33] Instances of prominent stand-taking for the George W. Bush years have already been mentioned, including Senator Kennedy's cry of fraud on the Iraq War. For a good instance of membership in Congress as an avenue to a national audience, consider Congressman Kucinich's propagation of his many views during the Democrats' presidential nominating season of 2003–4.

FOREIGN POLICY

Congress is ordinarily seen as a domestic institution, yet a healthy share of member action has gone to foreign policy — defined here as all items pertaining in any way to the conduct of U.S. foreign or defense policy. The share is 23 percent, with 539 items from 1789 through 1988. Figure 10.3 gives the time series. The highlights are the 1790s and 1800s, at least in a relative sense since foreign policy dominated a lean congressional agenda back then, and the two decades of the world wars, yet also the run-up to World War II and the time span of the Vietnam War. Perhaps this foreign policy emphasis is surprising. It stems from not seeing Congress as just a lawmaking body. Some two-fifths of the foreign policy actions also code as "legislate" (as in treaty ratifications), but more than that proportion also code as "take stand" and many also code as "investigate."[34] It is impossible to appreciate the place of members of Congress in foreign policy history without considering these non-lawmaking roles. In the investigative realm, for example, Senator Nye's high-publicity probe of munitions-makers in the mid-1930s probably delayed an acceleration of American involvement in World War II, and Senator Fulbright's televised hearings in the 1960s probably hastened a deceleration of the Vietnam War. Even without chairing committees, aggressive congressional stand-takers can help to crystallize opinion constituencies — as in the cases of isolationist senators such as William E. Borah (R-Idaho) and Burton K. Wheeler (D-Mont.) around 1940 and dovish senators such as George McGovern (D-S.D.), Eugene McCarthy (D-Minn.), and Robert F. Kennedy (D-N.Y.) in the late 1960s.

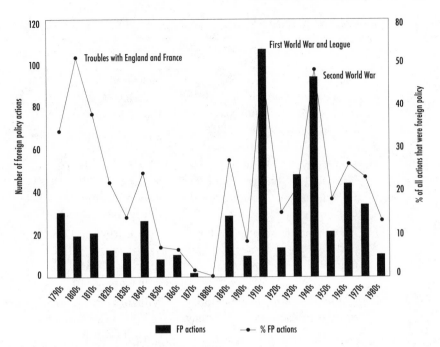

Figure 10.3. Foreign policy actions. *Source:* See Figure 10.1.

Foreign policy went into eclipse after the close of the cold war, but it has resurged, and stand-taking by members of Congress has helped shape the contexts of the recent White House–led wars in Yugoslavia, Afghanistan, and Iraq. On Yugoslavia, Senator McCain pressed the Clinton administration from the hawkish side. On Iraq, Senators Kennedy, Kerry, Edwards, Daschle, and others pressed the Bush administration from the dovish side in 2002–3 as Senator Lieberman and Congressman Gephardt assisted from the center. All this is standard congressional action.

IDEOLOGICAL IMPULSES

Additional kinds of member action have inhered in specific processes or contexts — for example, moves to impeach presidents or to run for the presidency oneself (as with the six Democratic candidates in 2003–4). Yet two categories of a more omnibus quality may be worth dwelling on. The first is *ideological impulses*. This category covers just the twentieth century, since the overall "action" counts needed to motor it were considerably more numerous than in the nineteenth century. In principle, any kind of standard move by a member of Congress could be coded additionally as "ideological impulse" — legislate, investigate, take stand, and the rest. Isolated in this study were

Table 10.2 Major MC Ideological Impulses in the Twentieth Century

Years	N	Ideological Impulse	Notable Participants
1901–10	37	Old Guard domestic conservatism under Theodore Roosevelt and Taft (on currency and tariff legislation, regulation of RRs, etc.)	Nelson W. Aldrich (R-RI), Joseph G. Cannon (R-IL), John C. Spooner (R-WI)
1905–12	34	Progressive insurgency under late TR, Taft (on tariff duties, RR regulation, Cannon's Speakership, etc.)	Albert Beveridge (R-IN), Jonathan Dolliver (R-IA), Robert La Follette (R-WI), George Norris (R-NE)
1912–17	41	New Freedom domestic reform under Wilson (plus warmup for it in 1912–13)	Claude Kitchin (D-NC), Robert La Follette (R-WI), Oscar Underwood (D-AL), many single-shot actors
1917–20	32	Antiwar and anti-League opposition to Wilson's foreign policy	William Borah (R-ID), Robert La Follette (R-WI), Henry Cabot Lodge (R-MA)
1921–31	41	Promotion of Progressive causes under Harding, Coolidge, and early Hoover	Robert La Follette (R-WI), George Norris (R-NE), Thomas J. Walsh (D-MT), Burton Wheeler (D-MT)
1931–37	73	New Deal domestic reform under FDR (and warmup under late Hoover admin.)	Edward Costigan (D-CO), R. La Follette, Jr. (I-WI), David J. Lewis (D-MD), Robert F. Wagner (D-NY)
1933–38	39	Left-populist challenge to New Deal: more inflation, nationalization, relief, wealth-taxes or antimonopoly than FDR wanted	Hugo Black (D-AL), Huey Long (D-LA), Elmer Thomas (D-OK), Burton K. Wheeler (D-MT), William Lemke (R-ND)
1934–39	36	Right opposition to New Deal (incl. court-packing & govt. reorganization)	Josiah Bailey (D-NC), John J. O'Connor (D-NY), Burton K. Wheeler (D-MT) after 1936
1933–41	28	Isolationist opposition to U.S. involvement in internat'l. orgs. and European affairs	William E. Borah (R-ID), Hiram Johnson (R-CA), Gerald P. Nye (R-ND), Burton K. Wheeler (D-MT)

Table 10.2 Continued

1945–54	30	Foreign-policy internationalism under late FDR, Truman, Eisenhower (pro UN, Marshall Plan, NATO, vs. McCarthyism)	Thomas Connally (D-TX), Arthur Vandenberg (R-MI)
1947–54	40	Isolationism, Asia-Firstism, and disloyalty hunting under Truman and early Ike admin.	Patrick McCarran (D-NV), Joseph McCarthy (R-WI), Richard E. Nixon (R-CA), Robert A. Taft (R-OH)
1961–68	29	Domestic reform under JFK and LBJ (civil rights, Medicare, etc.)	Hubert Humphrey (D-MN), Mike Mansfield (D-MT), Wilbur Mills (D-AR), Edmund Muskie (D-ME)
1961–68	26	Conservative opposition to domestic reforms of the 1960s	Harry F. Byrd (D-VA), Barry Goldwater (R-AZ), Richard Russell (D-GA), Howard Smith (D-VA)
1964–75	36	Opposition to the Vietnam War and the national security establishment that conducted it	Frank Church (D-ID), J. W. Fulbright (D-AR), Robert F. Kennedy (D-NY), Eugene McCarthy (D-MN), Geo. McGovern (D-SD)
1981–88	34	Pursuit of Democratic foreign and domestic policies under Reagan	Edward Boland (D-MA), Patrick Moynihan (D-NY), Thomas P. O'Neill (D-MA), Claude Pepper (D-FL), Daniel Rostenkowski (D-IL)

Source: Mayhew, *America's Congress*, pp. 200–201.

subsets of twenty-five or more temporally clustered member actions in which members pursued the same policy goals or ideological cause.[35] The goal here was to accommodate major political impulses that have surged in importance at particular junctures and that have extended beyond single issues to embody something like passionately expressed belief systems. The Progressivism of the early twentieth century is an example, or New Deal liberalism, or the isolationism of the 1930s (the foreign policy area can generate passionate belief systems, too), or the Great Society liberalism of the 1960s, or the Contract with American conservatism of the mid-1990s.

The fifteen clusters that met the criteria are listed in Table 10.2. Chronologically, they range from the old guard conservatism promoted by Senator Nelson W. Aldrich (R-R.I.) and Speaker Joseph G. Cannon (R-Ill.) at the beginning of the century through the Democratic liberalism championed by Speaker Thomas P. O'Neill (D-Mass.) and others in the 1980s. In ideological direction, the clusters range from the Aldrich-Cannon conservatism and the "Asia first" anticommunism expressed by Senators Joseph McCarthy, Patrick McCarran (D-Nev.), and others around 1950 through, say, the Progressive insurgency spearheaded by Senator Robert La Follette (R-Wis.) around 1910 and the left-populist challenge to the New Deal staged by Senators Huey Long, Burton K. Wheeler, Elmer Thomas (D-Okla.) and others in the early to mid-1930s. In generational terms, some of the "impulses" centered in high-seniority congressional veterans — the Aldrich-Cannon conservatism, the O'Neill liberalism, the cross-party opposition to the liberal domestic reforms of the 1960s. Some of them centered in feisty newcomers — the Progressive insurgency around 1910, the Asia-first anticommunism around 1950, the opposition to the Vietnam War around 1970. Occasionally, one impulse countered another — as with the Aldrich-Cannon conservatism versus the La Follette Progressivism.

In substantive terms, these impulses could entail either domestic or foreign policy, and they varied accordingly. Five of the fifteen were dominantly the latter. Finally, in process terms the impulses could accommodate lawmaking as their chief content, but they were not limited to that. Ample place is given here to the energetic legislating of the 1910s, 1930s, and 1960s carrying out the Democrats' domestic programs of those items (the congressional side of the New Deal leads the list with seventy-three member actions). But there is room also for impulses tilted toward investigating or taking stands — for example, those embodying the opposition to the Vietnam War or the outburst of Asia-first anticommunism. In a rich and variegated action mix, the former impulse also included antiwar bids for the presidency — by Democratic senators Eugene McCarthy, Robert F. Kennedy, and George McGovern. The America-first anticommunist drive is a choice instance of a dominantly *non*-domestic-policy and *non*-lawmaking ideological impulse. Witness its action ingredients in Table 10.3.[36]

Much of the cut and thrust of twentieth-century public affairs is incorporated in these fifteen ideological impulses. Where did they come from? To a large degree, to be sure, they have been emanations of public sentiment or accommodations to moves by the White House, yet, in line with the central argument here, they are also partly an accomplishment of congressional entrepreneurialism. The causation needs to be shared. It is a good bet that American opinion has been shaped by these clusters of congressional moves as well as embodied in them. A better advertisement for that idea could scarcely be

Table 10.3 The Isolationist, Asia-First, Anti-disloyalty Impulse of 1947–54

Year	Member	Age	Cong. Term	H/S	Action
1947	Walter Judd (R-MN)	49	3	H	claims State Department sold out China
1947	John Rankin (D-MS)	65	14	H	plays role in HUAC investigation of Hollywood
1947	Robert A. Taft (R-OH)	58	5	S	has reservations about Truman Doctrine
1948–49	William Knowland (R-CA)	40	2	S	notable Asia Firster
1948	Karl Mundt (R-SD)	48	5	H	Mundt-Nixon bill re internal security
1948	Richard M. Nixon (R-CA)	35	1	H	Mundt-Nixon bill re internal security
1948	Ricard M. Nixon (R-CA)	35	1	H	pursues Alger Hiss in HUAC investigation
1948	J. Parnell Thomas (R-NJ)	53	6	H	chairs HUAC probe of espionage
1948	Robert A. Taft (R-OH)	59	5	S	chief congressional critic of Marshall Plan
1949	Karl Mundt (R-SD)	49	6	S	spokesman for "China lobby"
1949	Robert A. Taft (R-OH)	60	6	S	argues against NATO treaty
1950	Styles Bridges (R-NH)	52	7	S	backs McCarthy's anti-Communist drive
1950	Homer Capehart (R-IN)	53	3	S	makes key speech about internal subversion
1950	William Jenner (R-IN)	42	3	S	an emerging McCarthyite leader
1950	William Jenner (R-IN)	42	3	S	says Gen. Marshall is front man for traitors
1950	Patrick McCarran (D-NV)	74	9	S	McCarran Internal Security Act

Table 10.3 Continued

1950	Joseph McCarthy (R-WI)	42	2	S	his Wheeling speech launches McCarthyism
1950	Joseph McCarthy (R-WI)	42	2	S	makes accusations before Tydings Committee
1950	Joseph McCarthy (R-WI)	42	2	S	intrudes into CT and MD Senate elections
1950	Richard M. Nixon (R-CA)	37	2	H	runs "pink lady" campaign vs. H. G. Douglas
1950	Robert A. Taft (R-OH)	61	6	S	backs McCarthy's anti-Communist drive
1950	Robert A. Taft (R-OH)	61	6	S	favors lower military spending
1950	Robert A. Taft (R-OH)	61	6	S	demands Cong. role in Korean War policy
1950–51	Robert A. Taft (R-OH)	61	6	S	takes part in major debate re foreign policy
1950	Kenneth Wherry (R-NE)	58	4	S	backs McCarthy's anti-Communist drive
1951	Joseph Martin (R-MA)	67	14	H	leaks MacArthur anti-Truman letter re Korea
1951	Joseph Martin (R-MA)	67	14	H	attacks Truman admin. after MacArthur firing
1951–52	Joseph McCarthy (R-WI)	43	3	S	attacks Marshall, Acheson, others
1951–52	Richard M. Nixon (R-CA)	38	2	S	attacks Acheson, others
1952	Patrick McCarran (D-NV)	76	10	S	McCarran-Walter Immigration Act
1952	Karl Mundt (R-SD)	52	7	S	his "Korea/Communism/corruption" slogan
1952	Francis Walter (D-PA)	58	10	H	McCarran-Walter Immigration Act
1953–54	John Bricker (R-OH)	60	4	S	Bricker Amdt. to restrict pres. treatymaking

Table 10.3 Continued

1953–54	William Knowland (R-CA)	46	5	S	hardline anti-coexistence foreign policy
1953	Joseph McCarthy (R-WI)	45	4	S	opposes Chas. Bohlen as ambassador to USSR
1953	Joseph McCarthy (R-WI)	45	4	S	gets Greek shipowners to stop China trade
1953	Joseph McCarthy (R-WI)	45	4	S	hunts Communists in State Department
1954	John F. Kennedy (D-MA)	37	4	S	only Demo. senator silent on McCarthy censure
1954	Joseph McCarthy (R-WI)	46	4	S	chairs Army-McCarthy hearings
1954	Joseph McCarthy (R-WI)	46	4	S	is censured by Senate

Source: Mayhew, *America's Congress*, pp. 205–6.

imagined than the conservative "revolution" led by Newt Gingrich on Capitol Hill in the mid-1990s. Probably this has been the only post-1988 cluster of member actions, given an appropriate search for evidence, that would merit an entry in an updated Table 10.2. The excitement of Gingrich conservatism radiated out from Washington, D.C. It even seems to have spilled over into the province of Ontario, affecting an election and a government there.[37] It was probably the twentieth century's sixteenth and last "ideological impulse." Its successors of the twenty-first century will no doubt materialize sooner or later.

OPPOSITIONS

The second omnibus category is *opposition.* Notwithstanding the importance of Congress, the presidency is ordinarily the center of power, energy, initiative, and attention in the American system. Few would disagree with that reading. Accordingly, the White House draws opposition year in and year out, and Congress has historically been the chief supplier of it. Coded here as "opposition" was "any effort by a member of Congress to thwart the aims or impair the standing of a presidential administration." That came to 511 member actions, or 22 percent of the data set, from 1789 through 1988. All these items were also coded more basically as legislate, investigate, take stand, or something else directly behavioral.[38] In a separation-of-powers system like the American one, this definition of opposition is generous yet realistic. It accommodates major legislative disagreements yet also verbal assaults, hostile investigations, and even moves to impeach. It is true that "opposition" as defined here is not quite the same thing as "the loyal opposition" of a kind found in British-style parliamentary regimes—that is, leadership formations of the party out of power that perform in parliament as something like full alternative governments. In contrast, American congressional oppositions can be more fragmentary, inconstant, and reckless—but they can also be more versatile and variegated, and often they can cause a change of policy without a change of government.[39]

To put some familiar meat onto this framework, just over half of the 511 opposition items could be sorted into clusters. The criterion was that the historical works that were consulted treated certain items as ingredients of a single, interrelated, time-specific effort. The resulting eighteen clusters, which can be said to document eighteen distinct congressional "oppositions," to use a plural formulation, are listed in Table 10.4.[40] They sprawl across the two centuries—from James Madison's pioneering use of the House as an opposition site in the 1790s and Henry Clay's similar use of the Senate in the 1830s through the familiar institutional clashes since World War II. Once again, foreign policy surfaces as a motif. It dominates five clusters and enters into another four—including, during the twentieth century, every entry from the isolationism of the late 1930s through the Watergate crisis of the 1970s. Note that some of these eighteen oppositions mattered a great deal more than others, even if all of them can be said to have met a plausible threshold of prominence. In Table 10.4, that variation is signaled through a designation of magnitude that resembles a restaurant rating system. Roughly, the number of asterisks accompanying an opposition indexes its volume of member actions. In the four- or five-asterisk range are the Reconstruction opposition to Andrew Johnson in the 1860s, the antiwar and anti–League of Nations opposition to Wilson in the 1910s, the isolationist, Asia-first anticommunist opposition to Truman and Eisenhower around 1950, and the anti–Vietnam War opposition to Lyndon Johnson and Nixon in the 1960s and 1970s.[41] These are the historical high points. Still, it was unpleasant for a president to experience even a one-asterisk member challenge like those of the La Follette Progressives to Taft around 1910 or Huey Long to FDR in the 1930s.

For Congress's place in the American regime, possibly nothing has been more important than these exercises of opposition. Often they have been consequential—consider the policy aggressiveness directed against the White House during the Reconstruction era, the senators' mobilization of public

Table 10.4 Clusters of Opposition Actions

Years	Leading Actors	Cause	Magnitude
1790–93	James Madison (DR-VA)	vs. Hamilton's Treasury program	**
1793–96	James Madison (DR-VA)	vs. Washington admin.'s pro-England foreign policy	**
1803–08	John Randolph (DR-VA) Nathaniel Macon (DR-NC)	"Quid" opposition to Jefferson's policies	*
1832–36	Henry Clay (W-KY) Daniel Webster (W-MA) John C. Calhoun (W-SC)	Whig opposition to Jackson administration	***
1857–60	Stephen A. Douglas (D-IL)	vs. Buchanan admin.'s pro-South slavery policies	*
1864–68	Thaddeus Stevens (R-PA) Charles Sumner (R-MA) Benjamin F. Wade (R-OH)	congressional vs. presidential Reconstruction policy; impeachment of Andrew Johnson	*****
1869–72	Charles Sumner (R-MA) Carl Schurz (R-MO) Lyman Trumbull (R-IL)	Liberal Republican opposition to Grant administration	**
1877–81	Roscoe Conkling (R-NY)	patronage showdowns with Hayes & Garfield admins.	*
1906–12	Robert La Follette, Sr. (R-WI) Jonathan Dolliver (R-IA)	Progressive insurgency	*

Table 10.4 Continued

Years	Leading Actors	Cause	Magnitude
1917–20	Robert La Follette, Sr. (R-WI) Henry Cabot Lodge (R-MA) William E. Borah (R-ID)	antiwar opposition in 1917 blends into anti-League opposition led by Lodge in 1919	****
1922–24	Robert La Follette, Sr. (R-WI) George Norris (R-NE) Thomas J. Walsh (D-MT)	Progressive opp. to Harding and Coolidge admins.; Teapot Dome probe	**
1934–35	Huey Long (D-LA)	populist "Share Our Wealth" challenge to FDR	*
1937–38	Josiah W. Bailey (D-NC) Burton K. Wheeler (D-MT) John J. O'Connor (D-NY)	break with FDR over court-packing, executive reorganization, unions, minimum wage; the "Conservative Manifesto"	***
1939–41	Gerald P. Nye (R-ND) Arthur Vandenberg (R-MI) Burton K. Wheeler (D-MT)	isolationist opposition to involvement in Europe	**
1938–44	Martin Dies (D-TX) Howard Smith (D-VA) Harry F. Byrd (D-VA) Kenneth McKellar (D-TN)	conservative assault on New Deal and war agencies; many investigations	**

Table 10.4 Continued

Years	Leading Actors	Cause	Magnitude
1947–54	Joseph McCarthy (R-WI) William Knowland (R-CA) William Jenner (R-IN) Patrick McCarran (D-NV)	anti-Communist loyalty probes blended with Asia First policy critique; "Who lost China?" "Who promoted Peress?"	* * * * *
1964–72	J. William Fulbright (D-AR) Eugene McCarthy (D-MN) George McGovern (D-SD)	vs. Vietnam War and national security establishment; the government's "credibility gap"	* * * *
1972–74	Samuel Ervin (D-NC)	Watergate	* * *

Source: Mayhew, *America's Congress*, pp. 111–12.

sentiment against FDR's Court-packing plan in 1937, and a later generation of senators' mobilization of public sentiment against the Vietnam War. Oppositions like these have offered the regime a kind of flexibility: It has been possible to push presidents to the wall not just during elections, and not just by members of the non–White House party. Voters were assisted to draw the inference that more than normal party-versus-party scrapping was at issue when, for example, Senator Stephen A. Douglas (D-Ill.) broke ranks with President Buchanan, a fellow Democrat, over Kansas statehood with its slavery implications in 1857, Senator Wheeler broke with fellow Democrat FDR over packing the Supreme Court in 1937, Senator Fulbright broke with fellow Democrat LBJ over Vietnam in 1966, and Senator Barry Goldwater (R-Az.) informed the Watergate-beleaguered Nixon that it was time to quit in 1974. All these were devastating moves.

As for recent years, the Republican assault against the Clinton administration during 1994–98 qualifies as a full-blown opposition cluster. That would be the nineteenth in American history.[42] Uncommon intensity and energy went into opposing the Clinton White House. It was a time of high-publicity moves by members of Congress involving lawmaking, taking of stands, investigations, and finally impeachment. Gingrich, Dole, and other members such as

Table 10.5 Members of Congress Who Performed Ten or More "Actions"

N Actions	Member	Chamber	Action Career
40	Henry Clay (DR, W-KY)	H,S	1811–1850
37	Henry Cabot Lodge (R-MA)	H,S	1890–1921
30	Robert A. Taft (R-OH)	S	1939–1953
27	William E. Borah (R-ID)	S	1917–1939
27	Robert La Follette, Sr. (R-WI)	S	1906–1924
27	Charles Sumner (D/FS, R-MA)	S	1851–1872
24	George Norris (R, I-NE)	H,S	1909–1940
23	John Sherman (R-OH)	H,S	1856–1897
22	Stephen A. Douglas (D-IL)	S	1845–1861
21	Nelson W. Aldrich (R-RI)	S	1899–1910
21	Daniel Webster (DR, W-NH, MA)	H,S	1813–1850
20	Robert F. Wagner (D-NY)	S	1927–1949
19	James Madison (DR-VA)	H	1789–1796
17	Samuel Rayburn (D-TX)	H	1914–1961
17	Arthur Vandenberg (R-MI)	S	1933–1948
16	John C. Calhoun (DR, W, D-SC)	H,S	1811–1850
16	Lyndon B. Johnson (D-TX)	S	1953–1960
16	Thomas P. O'Neill (D-MA)	H	1967–1985
15	William Seward (W, R-NY)	S	1849–1861
15	Thaddeus Stevens (R-PA)	H	1861–1868
14	John Randolph (DR-VA)	H,S	1800–1826
14	Burton K. Wheeler (D-MT)	S	1923–1941
13	James G. Blaine (R-OH)	H,S	1872–1881
13	Barry Goldwater (R-AZ)	S	1960–1984
13	Matthew Quay (R-PA)	S	1887–1902
12	J. William Fulbright (D-AR)	H,S	1943–1968
12	Hiram Johnson (R-CA)	S	1919–1945
12	Lyman Trumbull (R-IL)	S	1861–1872
11	John Quincy Adams (F, DR, NR, W-MA)	H,S	1803–1842
11	Thomas Hart Benton (D-MO)	S	1829–1848
11	Harry F. Byrd (D, I-VA)	S	1937–1964
11	Arthur P. Gorman (D-MD)	S	1881–1904
11	Henry Jackson (D-WA)	S	1957–1976
11	Edward Kennedy (D-MA)	S	1968–1987+
11	Robert La Follette, Jr. (R, I-WI)	S	1928–1939
11	Mike Mansfield (D-MT)	S	1962–1973
11	Edmund Muskie (D-ME)	S	1963–1980

Table 10.5 Continued

N Actions	Member	Chamber	Action Career
11	Thomas B. Reed (R-ME)	H	1889–1897
11	Benjamin F. Wade (R-OH)	S	1851–1868
10	Hubert H. Humphrey (D-MN)	S	1949–1977
10	Huey Long (D-LA)	S	1932–1935
10	Wilbur Mills (D-AR)	H	1960–1972
10	Richard Russell (D-GA)	S	1948–1970
10	Samuel Smith (DR-MD)	H,S	1800–1827

Source: Mayhew, *America's Congress,* pp. 170–71.

Henry Hyde became household names. Afterward, the early years of the George W. Bush administration brought single-shot opposition moves of significance — as in Kennedy crying fraud on the war — but probably not enough to form a cluster. Even so, like ideological impulses, opposition clusters probably have a future in the twenty-first century.

High Performers

The continual mention of Senator Edward Kennedy herein signals that some members of Congress have produced more actions than others. That is overwhelmingly true. In the action realm, radical inequality among members has been one of the first facts of congressional life.[43] Consider Table 10.5, which lists all of the forty-four members of Congress who performed ten or more actions between 1789 and 1988. (An "action career" in the last column supplies the dates of a member's first and last actions on Capitol Hill.) All told, almost a third of the data set's 2,304 items involved just these forty-four individuals. In order, they range from Henry Clay with forty items down through a handful of chiefly twentieth-century members with ten apiece. The thrusts of the various high performers have varied in kind — some as lawmakers, some as opinion leaders, some as all-around politicians whose careers included White House bids. Notably, as with American presidents, everyone on the list is a white male (more about this in a moment), and virtually all the surnames are northwestern European — Senator Edmund Muskie (D-Maine) seems to be the only exception.

Since 1988, the best candidates for congressional high performers (all white males still) would seem to be Senator Kennedy, who already appears in Table 10.5, Speaker Gingrich, and Senator McCain. Kennedy, in the wake of mounting a damaging challenge to President Carter from the left-liberal side of the Democratic Party in the late 1970s, stage-managing the defeat of Robert Bork for a Supreme Court justiceship in 1987, and many other early and mid-career moves, has kept it up. He has effectively maneuvered across party lines to help advance the Americans with Disabilities Act in 1990, the Kassebaum-Kennedy health portability insurance act of 1996, a measure providing health care for children in 1997, the No Child Left Behind Act, and (to his regret) the Medicare prescription drugs measures under George W. Bush, and he has regularly taken prominent positions, as on Iraq.

Gingrich, in a House career spanning a decade and a half, launched the Conservative Opportunity Society (a House Republican activist group of the 1980s), made use of C-SPAN inventively (along with Robert Walker, R-Penn.) to reach out to a small but engaged national audience, stirred up damaging media exposure of Speaker Jim Wright's (D-Tex.) finances in 1989 (Wright reacted by resigning from the House), wrecked a cross-party deal for a George H. W. Bush administration budget in 1990, drummed up candidates and money for the Republican takeover of the House in 1994, coauthored and marketed the Contract with America, presided over House enactment of that program in 1995, shook up the House leadership structure in 1995, confronted Clinton over the budget in the winter of 1995–96, and championed the president's impeachment in 1998. That is a considerable résumé. Senator McCain has, among other things, pressed the case for war in Yugoslavia, shepherded an ambitious tobacco deal in 1998 (it didn't quite win), bid for the presidency himself in 2000, helped maneuver a patients' bill of rights bill through the Senate in 2001, and guided campaign finance reform to completion.[44]

Member Actions in the Twenty-first Century

Enough of data displays and anecdotes: In the end, why is the realm of member action important? Certainly it is a major aspect of the only political system the United States has had or is ever likely to have. It has helped encase the country's basic separation-of-powers arrangements in a kind of public sphere that has been central to the functioning and stability of those arrangements.[45] The roots of these relationships seem to go back to Stuart and Tudor times: There is the instance of William Pym using his House of Commons office to mobilize the English public against the Crown in the 1640s. Granted, it is possible that the U.S. Constitution was a wrong historical turn. Parliamentary government as it evolved in Britain might have been a better option.[46]

As a practical matter, however, that seems to be an irrelevant consideration at this time. American presidents, senators, and House members, legitimized as they are by direct popular choice at all points of nomination and election, are very likely here to stay. Moreover, as indicated in a national survey of public opinion conducted in 2004 by Annenberg's Institutions of American Democracy project, the contemporary American public strongly endorses Congress's place in the system. In answer to the question: "When it comes to making important policy decisions, do you think that decisions should be made by the Congress or by the president?" the response was 59.4 percent by Congress, 20.5 percent by the president, 13.9 percent by both. (An unsurprising partisan tilt emerged in these results, with Republican respondents leaning more toward the president, who was George W. Bush at the time, but pluralities of both Republican and Democratic respondents opted for Congress.) In addition, the public emphatically endorsed the idea of checks and balances — as least as it is indexed in the following survey question: "Which view is closer to yours — legislative checks are good, or legislative checks cause gridlock and inaction?" Favoring "checks are good" were 69.9 percent of the public; favoring "cause gridlock and inaction" only 19.8 percent. Furthermore, there is a healthy, perhaps surprising, appreciation of the non-niceties of the legislative process. In answer to the question: "Which one do you agree with most? A) Conflict is a natural part of the legislative process, or B) Members create conflict where there need not be any," 62.7 percent of respondents chose option A; only 31.5 percent chose option B. These various results speak well for continuing public appreciation of the role of Congress. For all its problems, the American separation-of-powers system is a tough, durable one that anybody living under might as well sign on to and try to make the best of.

Tough as it may be, and improvable though it may be in certain ways, the system also needs to be tended and maintained. Not least, as the twenty-first century gets under way, the realm of legislator action could use some tending and maintaining — or at least some thoughtful examination. Is it in decent enough shape? What are the threats to it? Note that the place of legislative branches in public life is not guaranteed. A theme of twentieth-century scholarship is that they, after all, tend to decline. Legislatures can fail to attract talented members. They can come to be ignored by the media. Regardless of constitutional provisions, they can hemorrhage power to executive branches and as a consequence fall from public attention. All of these things can happen. Consider the apparent trajectory of city councils in America's big cities during the twentieth century. For the twenty-first century, a good bet for the chief menace to the American institutional mix is the White House's continuing flexing of military muscle in imperial enterprises abroad. On the record, that kind of activity, however well-advised on policy grounds, is not auspicious for a balanced constitution.[47] Congress, the courts, and popular rule all tend to pale before it. A dismal scenario for the year 2100, even lacking any formal constitutional changes, would be a U.S. Congress bereft of member actions as they have been described here — a body diminishing to city-council status, deprived of talent, media coverage, public attention, and real power as the executive branch expands to conduct an imperial role.

With the future trajectory of member action in mind, at least four areas of concern may be worth broaching — media connections, academic culture, congressional membership diversity, and second-order institutions. In the area of *media connections,* a decent supply of information flow from officials to citizens is obviously needed to keep a public sphere going. In particular, media coverage is crucial. Yet in today's environment there are problems. Coverage of Congress seems to have grown scantier in recent times. On network television, at least, there is less of it. Going by testimony supplied by Capitol Hill staff members in a survey conducted by Annenberg's Institutions of American Democracy project in 2004, that falloff in coverage seems to have affected the House of Representatives more than it has the Senate. Asked whether they agreed that "The reduced coverage of public affairs in the news media has made it harder for members of Congress to get media attention for their politically important activities," 63.7 percent of House aides agreed and 34.3 percent disagreed, although Senate aides divided evenly on the question. That is not good news for "the people's body" — the traditional designation of the House given its constitutional design. Beyond questions of volume, media coverage of Congress has also grown more negative. In general, in an environment of channel specialization and proliferation, it is hard for ample, coherent coverage of public affairs to materialize and have reach. For these reasons, and no doubt many others, today's young people, according to survey data, "are more withdrawn from public affairs than earlier birth cohorts were when they were young."[48]

On the brighter side, it is also true that no stable golden age of media connections has ever existed. From 1789 onward, members of Congress have continually needed to invent new ways to get themselves across as media technologies have relentlessly evolved.[49] In recent times, the members' moves have included C-SPAN, talk-show appearances, and the Internet (note Senator Byrd's website). Perhaps such catching up will keep occurring, but this is a front worth constant monitoring.

As for *academic culture,* the chief problem here is that the country's long tradition of writing American public affairs history has fallen on hard times. In general, historians in today's academic departments have shifted their tastes elsewhere. Figures of previous generations such as John Morton Blum and

William E. Leuchtenburg are not being replaced. One gets the sense that the history profession has largely given up on the idea of the United States as a self-governing republic whose relations between public and government need to be investigated and recorded. Certainly elected officials as consequential actors, presidents aside, have gone into eclipse. Formal processes are out, protest and other emphases are in.

History texts for elementary and secondary schools have followed the trend. The *National Standards for United States History,* offered by leading historians in 1994 as a guideline for teaching American history in grades five through twelve, was officially censured in the U.S. Senate by a vote of 99–1 in 1995 (possibly partly as a statement of institutional self-regard). It is a 246-page document awash in the names of historical personages. To be sure, it lacks the detail that the actual history books have. It is suitably workmanlike on major events. But its emphasis, or rather the lack of it, comes through. Huey Long is the only member of Congress mentioned in connection with the New Deal era; there is no sign of Senator Wagner. Senators Blanche Bruce and Hiram Revels, the African American Republicans from Mississippi, are the only members mentioned in connection with Reconstruction; there is no sign of Charles Sumner or Thaddeus Stevens (R-Penn.). Overall for the two centuries, Senator Joseph McCarthy receives by far the most attention of any member of Congress. There is no sign of Daniel Webster (W-Mass.), John Quincy Adams (W-Mass.) in his antislavery phase as a House member, Stephen Douglas, John Sherman (R-Ohio), Robert La Follette, George Norris, Martin Dies, Robert Taft, Arthur Vandenberg (R-Mich.), Sam Rayburn (D-Tex.), Adam Clayton Powell Jr. (D-N.Y.), J. William Fulbright, Edmund Muskie, Eugene McCarthy, or Edward Kennedy. At issue is the following: How much grasp of public affairs history do American students require in order to become watchful citizens? Fortunately, academic fashions come and go.[50] Perhaps a new generation of historians will compensate.

Still, it is well to appreciate one reason for this laundering of the past. It is dead white males who are being laundered out through, to be sure, a standard exercise of political correctness by academics. But on this topic the academics may be acting as a kind of soured proxy for American society, or at least for substantial parts of it. One threat to the future of congressional member action is Congress's lack of *membership diversity.* American society has changed a great deal in recent times, as has the electorate. In the 1990s, for example, Americans voting in presidential elections hit an all-time peak as a fraction of the resident U.S. population (regardless of age or citizenship), and that participatory achievement probably also indexed a peak in voter diversity, variously considered.[51] But Congress has changed less. Women members of

Congress constitute only some 15 percent of the House and Senate. Owing partly to demographics and the accidents of state boundaries, there were no Hispanics or African Americans in the Senate at the beginning of the twenty-first century, although Barack Obama (D-Ill.), Mel Martinez (R-Fla.), and Ken Salazar (D-Colo.) joined the chamber in January 2005. A lag on these fronts is probably diminishing the public sphere. The legitimacy of, regard for, and attention accorded to Congress and its members may be suffering. What can be done? For one thing, a surge in women representatives in the Congress, not to mention women members taking the lead in future "ideological impulses" and "oppositions," might do wonders for the realm of member action. Nancy Pelosi is a start. So would statehood for the District of Columbia, by no doubt fostering the election of two African Americans to the Senate. Arguably, an important missing voice in that body during the 1980s and 1990s was the Reverend Jesse Jackson.

The last rubric is *second-order institutions,* by which is meant institutions and procedures that are important yet fall short of constitutional standing. This is a tricky subject, but here are two ideas. First, exceptionally strong political parties are probably not good news for the realm of member action. For the American public sphere to function as it has traditionally done, in the context of the nation's complicated presidential system, members of Congress need to be able to perform as individuals, and the public needs to be able to witness them performing as individuals. In recent times, partisanship has reached one of its all-time extremes on Capitol Hill, and that development should give pause. On the House side in particular, staff members of that body reported in the Institutions of American Democracy project survey: "The increased influence of the party leaders has made it harder for other members of Congress to undertake politically important activities." Agreeing with this judgment were 67.2 percent of the aides, disagreeing 32.2 percent.[52] A caution signal to high-minded advocates of strong parties might be: Beware of getting what you wish for. From the standpoint of a healthy realm of legislator action, an appealing feature of the McCain-Feingold campaign-finance reform, however that measure might be evolving since passage, is that it aimed to weaken the parties. "Soft money" wielded by centralized parties was coming to look like a threat to member individualism. For a century, an underappreciated — and important — feature of campaign-finance regulation in the United States is that it has channeled money to individual candidates, not parties.

Second, getting rid of the Senate filibuster would arguably be bad news for the American public sphere. How can this be? The familiar mathematical case indicts the filibuster, or the stiff cloture requirement underlying it, as an impediment to majoritarian democracy. For better or worse, these practices can *block* public opinion. But this assumes that public opinion is structured in some primordial fashion external to the actions of politicians, which often it is not. In the operation of the U.S. Senate, legislative delays of weeks, months, even years can also assist the *formation* of public opinion as political actors inside and outside Congress make their cases before the public. On this reckoning, the important aspect is the delay, not the roll-call arithmetic. An example is the gradual mobilization of opposition to FDR's court-packing plan in 1937. Actions by individual members of Congress seem to have played a major role.[53] Even in the instances of the great civil rights enactments of the mid-1960s, the lengthy Senate debates probably helped ease the white South's acceptance, more or less, of the results.[54] In the American system, the likeliest beneficiary of strict, quick majority rule in both houses of Congress would be the White House. Presidents would find it easier to plead emergency or mandate and get what they want, quickly and without much discussion.

These concerns having been expressed, there is no sign that public awareness of members of Congress has been decreasing during the past half century. In various spot-checks of national public awareness or knowledge of members of Congress (the survey questions vary), representatives registering below 25 percent though well above zero have included Senator Henry Jackson (D-Wash.) in the immediate postwar decades, Congressman Jack Kemp (R-N.Y.) around 1980, and Senator Richard Lugar (R-Ind.) and the unflamboyant Speaker Foley in more recent times. Scorers in the 25 to 50 percent range have included Senator Harry F. Byrd (D-Va.), Senator Fulbright, and Speaker Carl Albert (D-Okla.) before 1980 and Speaker Jim Wright and Senator Jesse Helms since then. Scorers above 50 percent have included Senators Taft and John Bricker (R-Ohio) in the 1940s, Senators Joseph McCarthy and Estes Kefauver (D-Tenn.) in the 1950s, Senator Goldwater in 1963, Speaker O'Neill in the 1980s, Senators Orrin Hatch (R-Utah), Joseph Biden (D-Del.), Arlen Specter (R-Penn.), Alan Simpson (R-Wyo.), and other participants in the Thomas hearings in 1991, as well as Newt Gingrich, Henry Hyde, Bob Dole, and Dick Gephardt later in the 1990s.[55] A range of plausible and reassuring recognition rates emanated from the survey of national opinion conducted by the Institutions of American Democracy project in 2004 — Edward Kennedy at 95 percent, John McCain at 84 percent, Orrin Hatch at 56 percent, and Congressman Barney Frank (D-Mass.) at 36 percent. Again, newspaper sources could be used to flesh out information like this, at least by inference, throughout American history.

A final bit of evidence regarding public opinion and legislator action. In a national survey in April 1995, respondents exhibited a deft sense of causation that extended to a counterfactual: "If Newt Gingrich had not been Speaker of the House, do you think the Republicans would have been able to pass as many bills as they did, or don't you think so?" This was just after the Contract with America zoomed through the House. The answers were: Yes, would have, 19 percent. No, would not, 60 percent. No opinion, 11 percent.[56] That judgment seems about right.

Notes

I am indebted to Matthew Glassman, Paul Quirk, and Charles Stewart for their helpful comments on this essay, which was originally published as chap. 3 in Paul J. Quirk and Sarah A. Binder (eds.), *The Legislative Branch* (New York: Oxford University Press, 2004). Reprinted by permission of Oxford University Press, Inc.

1. Edward Walsh and Juliet Eilperin, "Gore Presides as Congress Tallies Votes Electing Bush; Black Caucus Members Object as Fla. Numbers Are Accepted," *Washington Post,* January 7, 2001.

2. Kirk Victor, "Lott's Big Gamble," *National Journal* (January 20, 2001), 170–73, quotation at 171.

3. David E. Rosenbaum, "Georgia Democratic Senator Unapologetic in Aiding Bush," *New York Times,* January 23, 2001; David E. Rosenbaum, "Two Leaders of Tax Panel Agree on a Bill," *New York Times,* May 12, 2001; Helen Dewar, "Baucus Deal on Tax Cut Upsets Senate Democrats," *Washington Post,* May 12, 2001; John F. Harris and Dan Balz, "Delicate Moves Led to Tax Cut," *Washington Post,* May 26, 2001.

4. Mike Allen and Ruth Marcus, "GOP Missteps, Jeffords's Feelings about Agenda Led toward Exit," *Washington Post,* May 24, 2001.

5. Lexington, "King of the Hill," *Economist* (January 12, 2002), 33. See also James A. Barnes, "Action versus Inaction," *National Journal* (March 9, 2002), 688–92. The vote was 381–41 in the House and 87–10 in the Senate. On Kennedy's general record: Albert R. Hunt, "The Liberal Lion Roars Louder Than Ever," *Wall Street Journal,* February 19, 1998; "Sen. Kennedy Thrives in Opposition," *New York Times,* January 30, 2001.

6. Richard L. Berke, "A Flurry of Hugs for 'Gang of Five' in Capital," *New York Times,* October 23, 2001.

7. Peter Carlson, "The Solitary Vote of Barbara Lee," *Washington Post,* September 19, 2001; "Congresswoman Lee: Hero of the Left."

8. Paul Alexander, *Man of the People: The Life of John McCain* (Hoboken, N.J.: Wiley, 2003), 182–84, 200–201. On Shays and Meehan: Mary Leonard, "After Months, a Triumph for Meehan," *Boston Globe,* August 4, 1998; Bob Hohler, "Shays Feels GOP Heat over Campaign Bill," *Boston Globe,* July 22, 1998. On McCain and the debate: John Lancaster, "Campaign Bill Unearths a Senate Relic: Debate," *Washington Post,* March 23, 2001. On the town halls: Alexander, *Man of the People,* 340. On McCain's stewardship: John Lancaster and Helen Dewar, "Luck, or Fate, Helped Guide Campaign

Bill," *Washington Post,* March 31, 2001. On House passage: Alison Mitchell, "House Backs Broad Change in Financing of Campaigns: Fast Senate Action Sought," *New York Times,* February 15, 2002.

9. Spenser S. Hsu and Kathleen Day, "Senate Vote Spotlights Audit Reform and Sarbanes," *Washington Post,* July 15, 2002. See also David S. Hilzenrath and Jonathan Weisman, "How Congress Rode a 'Storm' to Corporate Reform," *Washington Post,* July 28, 2002.

10. Michael Barone, with Richard E. Cohen and Grant Ujifusa, *The Almanac of American Politics 2004* (Washington, D.C.: National Journal, 2003), 1701.

11. Jim VanderHei and Juliet Eilperin, "GOP Leaders Tighten Hold in the House," *Washington Post,* January 13, 2003; Richard E. Cohen, "Hastert's Hidden Hand," *National Journal* (January 20, 2001), 174–77, quotation at 176.

12. Tom Daschle with Michael D'Orso, *Like No Other Time: The 107th Congress and the Two Years That Changed America Forever* (New York: Crown, 2003), 10.

13. David Firestone, "For Homeland Security Bill, a Brakeman," *New York Times,* July 31, 2002; David Rogers, "Byrd Unleashes Oratorical Fury," *Wall Street Journal,* May 21, 2003.

14. David Rogers, "Medicare Proposal Yields an Odd Couple: Bush and Sen. Kennedy Back the Plan, But with Opposite Views and Expectations," *Wall Street Journal,* June 16, 2003. See also Carl Hulse, "Kennedy's Stance on Medicare Angers Allies," *New York Times,* June 22, 2003. On the Hastert count: David S. Broder, "Time Was GOP's Ally on the Vote," *Washington Post,* November 23, 2003. See also Robert Pear and Robin Toner, "Sharply Split, House Passes Broad Medicare Overhaul," *New York Times,* November 23, 2003; R. Jeffrey Smith, "GOP's Pressing Question on Medicare Vote," *Washington Post,* December 23, 2003.

15. Andrew Miga, "Ted K Rips Bush for 'Selective' Intelligence," *Boston Globe,* November 17, 2003. See also Helen Dewar, "Kennedy Hits Bush on War," *Washington Post,* January 15, 2004.

16. Editorial, "Tom DeLay's Down-Home Muscle," *New York Times,* July 17, 2003. The mid-decade location of this Texas gerrymander was novel, although in ambition, ruthlessness, and possible implications for long-term party control of the House, DeLay's move resembled that of a previous House leader, Philip Burton (D-Calif.), who had brought off an inventive gerrymander of California's congressional map in the early 1970s. On Burton: Michael Barone and Grant Ujifusa, *The Almanac of Politics 1996* (Washington, D.C.: National Journal, 1995).

17. Four years later, in January 2005, during the counting of the electoral votes cast in 2004, Senator Barbara Boxer (D-Calif.) would take the initiative to advance a similar appeal. By this time, the Senate had come to have one African American member— Barack Obama (D-Ill.).

18. In general, the typical, or median in an ideological sense, stances of the congressional parties do not have that kind of influence. A majority party can suffer defections of its centrist members to the opposition side on particular issues. See the argument in Keith Krehbiel, *Pivotal Politics: A Theory of U.S. Lawmaking* (Chicago: University of Chicago Press, 1998).

19. See Matthew Yglesias, "Bad Max: It's a Tempting Story Line That Sen. Max Baucus

Has to Cast All Those Pro-Bush Votes because of Pressure Back Home in Montana. It's Just Not True," *American Prospect* (February 2004), 11–13.

20. On this question, see Michael Graetz and Ian Shapiro, *Death by a Thousand Cuts: The Fight over Taxing Inherited Wealth* (Princeton, N.J.: Princeton University Press, 2005).

21. Agenda manipulation is said to make a difference. But in theory, that ordinarily takes place in a context of ready-made, exogenously determined distributions of ideal points.

22. Terry M. Moe and Scott A. Wilson have written, "The transaction costs of moving a bill through the entire legislative process are enormous. . . . The best prediction is that, for most issues most of the time, there will be no affirmative action on the part of Congress at all. The ideal points [of the members of Congress] may logically support a given outcome, but in reality *nothing will happen.*" ("Presidents and the Politics of Structure," *Law and Contemporary Problems* 57 [1994], 26–27).

23. On interactive rather than one-way: Richard F. Fenno Jr., *Home Style: House Members in Their Districts* (New York: Longman repr., 2003). On not just targets of vectors: In terms offered by Jane Mansbridge, the balance tilts away from "promissory representation" toward "anticipatory" and "gyroscopic" representation. ("Rethinking Representation," *American Political Science Review* 97 [2003], 515–28.) On shaping opinion: Lawrence R. Jacobs, Eric D. Lawrence, Robert Y. Shapiro, and Steven S. Smith, "Congressional Leadership of Public Opinion," *Political Science Quarterly* 113 (1998): 21–41. On policy reputations: Edward G. Carmines and James H. Kuklinski, "Incentives, Opportunities, and the Logic of Public Opinion in American Political Representation," chap. 10 in *Information and Democratic Processes,* edited by John A. Ferejohn and James H. Kuklinski (Urbana: University of Illinois Press, 1990), 252–56. On entrepreneurs: Joseph A. Schumpeter, *Capitalism, Socialism, and Democracy* (New York: Harper and Brothers, 1950), 252–64.

24. David. R. Mayhew, *America's Congress: Actions in the Public Sphere, James Madison through Newt Gingrich* (New Haven, Conn.: Yale University Press, 2000).

25. Ibid., 9.

26. See the discussion of the data source in Mayhew, *America's Congress,* chap. 2. The resulting data set is available at http://pantheon.yale.edu/~dmayhew/data4.html.

27. Here, for coding purposes, it can also mean becoming memorialized in an eponymous bill title such as the Wilmot Proviso or the Taft-Hartley Act. Such items account for about 10 percent of the "legislate" items in the data set. See Mayhew, *America's Congress,* 78–81.

28. Each of these twenty decades except the first and last accommodates five Congresses elected in years ending in 0, 2, 4, 6, and 8. That is out of respect for the common-sense meaning of "decade." But an embarrassment consequently arises. The initial decade here actually accommodates the six Congresses meeting from 1789 through 1801, the last decade just the four Congresses meeting from 1981 through 1988. "Leg-EP" in the vertical axis of Figure 10.1 refers to the eponymous entries such as Taft and Hartley in the Taft-Hartley Act.

29. On Clinton's drive for health care reform, see Haynes Johnson and David S. Broder, *The System: An American Way of Politics at the Breaking Point* (Boston: Little, Brown,

1996). On Senator Gramm's role in banking reform, see Kirk Victor, "Loan Star Phil," *National Journal,* October 30, 1999.

30. See Mayhew, *America's Congress,* 81–90.

31. On Thompson: Francis X. Clines, "Money and Politics: Capitol Sketchbook — The Scene; Partisan Maneuvering for Hearing's Spotlight," *New York Times,* July 9, 1997. On Hyde's role, see Peter Baker et al., "The Train That Wouldn't Stop: Key Players Thwarted Attempts to Derail Process," *Washington Post,* February 14, 1999.

32. See Mayhew, *America's Congress,* 90–102.

33. On Boxer: Maureen Dowd, "7 Congresswomen March to Senate to Demand Delay in Thomas Vote," *New York Times,* October 9, 1991. On Nunn: Michael Wines, "This Time, Nunn Tests a Democrat," *New York Times,* January 30, 1993. On Moynihan: Gwen Ifill, "Moynihan Urges Prosecutor to Study Clinton Land Deal," *New York Times,* January 9, 1994. On Graham: Jim VandeHei and Francesca Contiguglia, "A Year Later, Rebels' Work Isn't Done: On Anniversary of Coup, Conservatives Say They've Matured," *Roll Call* (July 13, 1998), 1, 30. On Barr: "Clinton Critic Requests Inquiry for Impeachment," *Quincy (Mass.) Patriot Ledger,* March 15, 1997. On Helms: Donna Cassatta, "Helms Lashes Back at Critics, Holds Firm in Blocking Weld," *Congressional Quarterly Weekly* (September 17, 1997), 2159–60. (This was a formal parliamentary move as well as a stand.) On Lieberman: Chris Black, "Lieberman, in Senate, Denounces President," *Boston Globe,* September 4, 1998. On McCain: Alison Mitchell, "McCain Presses His Case for Sending Ground Troops," *New York Times,* April 4, 1999.

34. For the coding of the "foreign policy" category, see Mayhew, *America's Congress,* 103–6. The items thus coded are all parasitic. That is to say, all of them are also coded as something more concretely behavioral — legislate, investigate, take stand, run for president, etc. The 23 percent share figure of the "foreign policy" category rises to 34 percent if items associated with the Civil War and military occupation of the South (6 percent) and those for tariffs and other foreign trade policies (4 percent) are added in. Note that there is possible overlap among the various code categories. For example, an item might code plurally as foreign policy, take stand, and investigate.

35. See Mayhew, *America's Congress,* 197–211. Like "foreign policy," the category of ideological impulse is parasitic. Each of its items had to have a primary anchor in a behavioral category like legislate or investigate. No item could be coded as *only* "ideological impulse." An especially useful guide for much of the century is David A. Horowitz, *Beyond Left and Right: Insurgency and the Establishment* (Urbana: University of Illinois Press, 1977).

36. For each relevant member-of-Congress action, Table 10.2 supplies the year in which it occurred, the member who performed it, the age of the member at the time, the number of Congresses the member had served in at the time (whether in the House or Senate), whether the individual was a House or Senate member at the time, and the gist of the action.

37. On the Gingrich-led impulse of the mid-1990s, see Dan Balz and Ronald Brownstein, *Storming the Gates: Protest Politics and the Republican Revival* (Boston: Little, Brown, 1996). On the possible Ontario connection, see W. Bilal Syed, "Ontario's Elite Still Can't Smell the Coffee," *Wall Street Journal,* June 16, 1995; Allan Fotheringham, "Score One for the Angry White Guys," *Maclean's* (June 19, 1995), 64.

38. For this category, see Mayhew, *America's Congress,* 106–22. The "opposition" category is parasitic like those for "foreign policy" and "ideological impulse." Quotation on the coding, 107.

39. Still, it is possible for British MPs to oppose their government in a non–"loyal opposition" way. American-style versatility is available in a parliamentary system also. During the twentieth century in Britain, possibly no exercise of parliamentary opposition, by any definition of that term, was more important than back-bencher Winston Churchill's searing criticism of Prime Minister Neville Chamberlain's policy of appeasing Nazi Germany in the late 1930s. Both Chamberlain and Churchill were Tories at the time.

40. There is an overlap in certain particulars between the oppositions presented here and the ideological impulses presented earlier, yet note that the oppositions range over two centuries rather than just one, much of the action content of the ideological impulses would not qualify as oppositional, and in general the standards for selection of items differ. In principle, oppositions had to be indicated reasonably clearly by the relevant historians in order for them to be denominated as an opposition cluster in Mayhew, *America's Congress,* whereas I used my own judgment in drawing the lines around the ideological clusters.

41. For readers wishing to follow this rating system to ground, here is the procedure. In table 3.3 on pages 111–12 of *America's Congress,* any A item was counted as 5, any B item as 3, and any C item as 1. This allowed a weighted score for each opposition. Then the eighteen oppositions were ranked according to their scores and divided into categories at plausible junctures. If the two Madison-led oppositions of the 1790s are joined to compose one, which they could be (this is a matter of judgment), there is a respectable case on the evidence for awarding four asterisks to the joint product.

42. It should be noted that the data set is a bit ragged for the 1980s, as is discussed in *America's Congress.* That is owing to the diminishing utility of history books as sources for times after the 1970s.

43. See Mayhew, *America's Congress,* 169–76.

44. On Kennedy and Bork: Linda Greenhouse, "Senators' Remarks Portend a Bitter Debate over Bork," *New York Times,* July 2, 1987. On Kennedy in general: "Sen. Kennedy Thrives in Opposition." On Gingrich through 1995: Balz and Brownstein, *Storming the Gates,* chaps. 1, 3. On restructuring the House in 1995: David Rogers, "GOP's Rare Year Owes Much to How Gingrich Disciplined the House," *Wall Street Journal,* December 18, 1995. On the showdown over the budget: Michael Weisskopf and David Maraniss, "Endgame: The Revolution Stalls," *Washington Post National Weekly Edition,* January 29–February 4, 1996. On McCain and tobacco: Alexander, *Man of the People,* 184–87. On McCain and the patients' rights bill: Helen Dewar and Amy Goldstein, "Senate Passes Patients' Rights Bill," *Washington Post,* June 30, 2001.

45. On the contribution to stability, see Mayhew, *American's Congress,* 216–24.

46. On the Stuart era: Mayhew, *America's Congress,* 123–28. On the Tudor era: Samuel P. Huntington, "Political Modernization: America vs. Europe," *World Politics* 18 (1966): 378–414. For a thoughtful recent critique of certain provisions of the U.S. Constitution, see Robert A. Dahl, *How Democratic Is the American Constitution?* (New Haven, Conn.: Yale University Press, 2003). Notwithstanding the U.S.-U.K. dissimilarities in institutions, it is worth noting that a well-functioning parliamentary system has

its own important brand of individual "MP action." In the politics surrounding the Iraq intervention during 2002 and 2003, alert Americans became acquainted with many British MPs: Tony Blair, the prime minister; Jack Straw, the foreign secretary; Geoffrey Hoon, the defense secretary; Gordon Brown, the second-ranking Laborite who occasionally threw his weight around in Blair's interest; Clare Short and Robin Cook, the antiwar defectors from the party cause; George Galloway, the Laborite MP accused of consorting with the Saddam Hussein regime, and others. For a Briton, watching and reacting to what these various people were doing and saying was central to being a citizen during the Iraq affair.

47. On this point, see Hugh Heclo, "What Has Happened to the Separation of Powers?" in *Separation of Powers and Good Government,* edited by Bradford P. Wilson and Peter W. Schramm (Lanham, Md.: Rowman & Littlefield, 1994), at 153–64.

48. On the decline of television coverage of Congress: Greg Schneiders, "The 90-Second Handicap: Why TV Coverage of Legislation Falls Short," *Washington Journalism Review* (June 1985): 44–46; S. Robert Lichter and Daniel R. Amundson, "Less News Is Worse News: Television News Coverage of Congress, 1972–1992," in *Congress, the Press, and the Public,* edited by Thomas E. Mann and Norman J. Ornstein (Washington, D.C.: American Enterprise Institute and Brookings Institution, 1994), 133–35; Stephen Hess, "The Decline and Fall of Congressional News," in *Congress, the Press, and the Public,* edited by Mann and Ornstein, chap. 6. On the increasing negativity of coverage: Lichter and Amundson, "Less News Is Worse News," 137–39; Mark J. Rozell, "Press Coverage of Congress, 1946–1992," in *Congress, the Press, and the Public,* edited by Mann and Ornstein, 109–10; John R. Hibbing and Elizabeth Theiss-Morse, "The Media's Role in Public Negativity toward Congress: Distinguishing Emotional Reactions and Cognitive Evaluations," *American Journal of Political Science,* 42 (1998): 481–84. "In this post-Woodward-and-Bernstein era, rewards seem to flow toward reporters or accentuate 'scandal and sloth.' " John R. Hibbing and Elizabeth Theiss-Morse, *Congress as Public Enemy: Public Attitudes toward American Political Institutions* (New York: Cambridge University Press, 1995), 62, and more generally chaps. 4, 5. On young people withdrawing: Stephen Earl Bennett, "Young Americans' Indifference to Media Coverage of Public Affairs," *PS: Political Science and Politics* 31 (1998): 535–41, quotation at 535.

49. See the discussion in Mayhew, *America's Congress,* 228–32.

50. The study: *National Standards for United States History: Exploring the American Experience* (Grades 5–12 Expanded Edition) (University of California at Los Angeles: National Center for History in the Schools, 1994). In all, I counted mentions of thirty-one members of Congress in the *National Standards.* Twelve are eponymous, as in cases of the McCarran-Walter Act of 1952 and the Dawes Severalty Act of 1887. Eighteen instances are pre-1900, thirteen post-1900. Only two are post-1960: the Ervin committee in 1973 and Thomas O'Neill's opposition speakership of the early 1980s. On history texts following the trend: Diane Ravitch, *The Language Police* (New York: Knopf, 2003), 135. On the Senate censure: Ravitch, 137. On changing academic fashions: Frances FitzGerald, *America Revised* (New York: Vintage, 1980).

51. The high point was 1992, the year of Clinton's first victory, where 42 percent of the resident population voted. (Possibly the 2004 election has now edged out that of 1992.) Figures for the nineteenth century when white males aged twenty-one largely exhausted

the voter roles are low by comparison — 19.5 percent, for example, in 1896. See Charles A. Kromkowski, "Electoral Participation and Democracy in Comparative-Historical and Cross-National Perspective: A New Conceptualization and Evaluation of Voting in Advanced and Developing Democrats, 1776–2002," paper presented at the annual meeting of the American Political Science Association, Philadelphia, August 31, 2003, 28.

52. Here is an interesting historical question: In what era has party discipline peaked on Capitol Hill as an effective override to congressional representatives' personal or constituency preferences? Nobody really knows, but the answer may be the 1850s, when White House patronage maneuvering seems to have had a quite surprising influence over congressional copartisans. It is difficult otherwise to explain the votes of northern Democrats for the inflammatory Kansas-Nebraska Act. Why didn't the northerners block it?

53. See David R. Mayhew, "Supermajority Rule in the Senate," *P.S.: Political Science and Politics* 39 (2003), 31–36.

54. So far as is known, civil rights enactments were never enforceable in the Deep South at any time before the 1960s absent military occupation. Even in the fringe South, it took federal troops to integrate the Little Rock schools in 1957. Earlier, military occupation had ceased being a live option for northern opinion in the 1870s.

55. The sources are: Michael X. Delli Carpini, *What Americans Know about Politics and Why It Matters* (New Haven, Conn.: Yale University Press, 1996), 73–79, 311–17; *Gallup Poll Monthly,* #313 (October 1991), 27; #352 (January 1995), 24; #353 (February 1995), 25; #397 (October 1998), 34–35.

56. *Gallup Poll Monthly,* #355 (April 1995), 12.

11

Supermajority Rule in the U.S. Senate

Fond as James Madison was of checks and balances, one feature of today's institutional life would have surprised him and might have distressed him. That feature is supermajority rule in the U.S. Senate—the need to win more than a simple majority of senators to pass laws.

In the early twenty-first century, filibusters, threatened filibusters, and the three-fifths cloture requirement, except on budgeting and a few other matters, dog the legislative process. The 60-votes barrier has become hard contextual fact for the press, as in *Washington Post* coverage of recent efforts to repeal the inheritance tax and enact anti-cloning legislation: "The vote on the president's proposal was 54 to 44, six short of the 60 required for passage" (Dewar and Eilperin 2002); "Neither side appeared to have the 60 Senate votes needed to prevail" (Dewar 2002). Any observer of recent Congresses can recite instances of cloture-rule casualties—for example, during the Democratic Congress of 1993–94 under Clinton, measures in the areas of campaign finance reform, lobbying reform, product liability, striker replacement, and stimulating the economy (Binder and Smith 1997, 135; Fisk and Chemerinsky 1997, 182; Mayhew 1998, 274).[1] In political science, Keith Krehbiel (1998) has addressed the current 60-votes Senate regime elegantly and convincingly in terms of a "filibuster pivot."

Automatic failure for bills not reaching the 60 mark: That is the current

Senate practice, and in my view it has aroused surprisingly little interest or concern among the public or even in political science.[2] It is treated as matter-of-fact. One might ask: What ever happened to the value of majority rule? This is a complicated question, but I would guess that one reason for the lack of interest or concern is an impression of the past. If majority rule is in principle the preferred standard, conditions may be bad in the Senate today but weren't they even worse in the past? After all, the cloture rule called for an even higher two-thirds vote between 1917 and 1975 (that would mean 67 senators today, not 60). Some political scientists are hypothesizing the existence of a decisive two-thirds "filibuster pivot" during that long middle half of the twentieth century (Young and Heitshusen 2002; Sala 2002). Back before 1917, when there was no cloture rule at all, how did the Senate manage to enact any legislation at all? In the face of this stylized history, the current judgment probably is: If Senate floor majorities have it rough today, they used to have it, if anything, rougher. Why worry?

But was the past really like that? I for one doubt it. This is a general impression. Across a wide range of issues, I doubt that the Senate of past generations had any anti-majoritarian barrier as concrete, as decisive, or as consequential as today's rule of 60. If anything, floor majorities seem to have had it easier. Consider off the top, for example, the big tariff bills that often fired party passions and dominated congressional politics from the 1820s through the 1930s. Often, those bills cleared the Senate by sliver-small majorities, and there does not seem to be much sign that policy minorities enjoyed muscular options on them in the Senate that they lacked in the House (Wawro and Schickler 2006, ch. 6).

This is an extremely difficult subject on both logic and evidence grounds. It raises considerations of anticipated reactions, threatened as well as staged filibusters, modification as well as blocking of bills, not to mention two centuries of congressional history. There are various ways of attacking it. (For some, see Wawro and Schickler 2006). But it is at least an empirical subject. Reading the rules of the Senate to deduce what happened in the past is not enough. My course here is to probe into the Senate record of *one* particular past Congress with an eye for the strategies and actions of floor majorities and floor minorities. If rules are significant, they should leave traces in evidence about strategies.

The 75th Congress of 1937–38 is my choice for examination. This is for three reasons. First, the majority party's legislative aspirations during that Congress were unusually high. Possibly no party's have ever been higher. Franklin Roosevelt had won a landslide reelection, the New Dealers entertained a commensurate agenda, and the Republican congressional minority had been reduced to 16 senators and 89 House members — lows for a major party during the twentieth century. In all of American history, this may have been the left's main chance for a policy breakthrough. Second, it was widely believed, as the Congress began, that if any of the elective institutions was to block the New Dealers' initiatives during 1937–38, it had to be the Senate. The House Democratic party entirely elected on a ticket with FDR in 1936 was thought to be in his pocket. (As it happened, this proved not to be true.) Third, notwithstanding its immense Democratic majorities, the 75th Congress earned a place in history for blocking bills. Concerted opposition in that Congress is not a null topic (Mayhew 2000, 110–13, 219–22).

Here, I examine three lengthy, controversial, and well-publicized legislative drives of that Congress — all of which failed. They are FDR's proposal to pack the Supreme Court, FDR's proposal to reorganize the executive branch, and a major anti-lynching measure. The first two of these initiatives were top White House priorities in early 1937. Structural reform of the courts and agencies had to come first, the White House view was, if New Deal ambitions in various policy areas were to succeed. The anti-lynching measure was *not* a White House or Democratic party priority, although it was advanced by congressional liberals. Obviously, the civil rights area is an exception to any general speculation that Senate floor majorities may have had it easy in earlier times (Wolfinger 1971). Accordingly, the inclusion of the anti-lynching drive here, merited in any case on grounds of its historical importance, will afford some useful empirical and theoretical contrast.

I present sketches of the three legislative drives, and then go on to offer three theoretical arguments regarding the strategies pursued by the relevant political actors in these various drives and the contexts in which they were pursued.

Anti-Lynching

This sketch can be very brief, since it bears out everybody's image of civil rights legislating during earlier times. There are no surprises. Aided by some gruesome southern lynchings, a nationwide campaign to enact an anti-lynching bill gained strength in the 1930s peaking in 1937–38 (Sitkoff 1978, ch. 11). The House passed a bill in 1937, FDR said he would sign it, and it reached the Senate in January 1938 with some 70 senators said to favor it (*Time*, Jan. 24, 1938, p. 10). But the southern Democratic senators, spotting a threat to their region's system of white supremacy, expressed "determination to prevent the bill ever reaching a vote." Many lengthy speeches ensued, as in the report: "[Allen] Ellender [D-LA] Speaks 4 Days and Goes On." Leadership efforts to break the filibuster were lax: "Such rules as might be inconvenient for filibusters were not enforced; all-night or even long-continued sessions were not employed" (Burdette 1965, 198–99). After two weeks, some 20 northern Democrats nominally favoring the bill signaled that it was time to move on as there was "little likelihood of breaking the filibuster." In late January and mid-February, successive cloture motions failed. The southerners continued to obstruct. After seven weeks, the Senate voted 58–22 to lay the measure aside. That concluded the anti-lynching drive of 1937–38.[3]

Court-packing

In early 1937, President Roosevelt, exasperated by Supreme Court strike-downs of several key New Deal enactments during 1935–36 and worried about more such strike-downs, proposed a bill to authorize the appointment of one additional justice for any current justice over the age of 70. As of 1937, this would have expanded the Court to 15 members by adding six FDR nominees. One of the major controversies of American political history ensued (Alsop and Catledge 1938; Baker 1967).

Congressional handling of the Court-packing proposal was lengthy and complicated. There were three phases. In February and March, the bill was taken up in the Senate[4] where a vehement cross-party opposition led by the veteran Progressive Burton K. Wheeler (D-MT) devised a steering committee and a whipping system and joined an anti-FDR media campaign (Alsop and Catledge 1938, 80–105; Patterson 1967, ch. 3). Soon, radio listeners across the country could tune in to hear such senators as Wheeler, Josiah Bailey (D-NC), Carter Glass (D-VA), Henry Cabot Lodge (R-MA), and Arthur Vandenberg (R-MI) inveigh against the president's plan (Baker 1967, ch. 6; Moore 1968, ch. 8; Wheeler 1962, ch. 15). In the Senate, individual senators took to announcing their positions one by one. The press offered horse-race coverage centering on which side could reach a Senate majority — that is, 49 votes. The bet was on FDR — the president would probably get his Court-packing plan if he really wanted it — but the Senate statistics languished along at roughly one-third yes, one-third no, and one-third undecided.[5]

During April and May (phase two), the Supreme Court, evidently reacting to its threatening political environment, handed down landmark decisions approving the Wagner Act of 1935, the Social Security Act of 1935, and other previous liberal or New Deal enactments. "Who needs a Court-packing plan anymore?" came to be asked on Capitol Hill. Considerable steam went out of the White House legislative drive, which fell below the likely majority mark in the Senate (Alsop and Catledge 1938, 135–216).[6]

But then in June and July (phase three), Roosevelt stubbornly insisted on a

Court-expansion measure anyway, this time settling for one incremental justice per year (rather than six all at once). On this revised measure the New
Deal forces, led by Majority Leader Joseph Robinson (D-AR), seemed to have
a slim Senate majority. That was the informed reading (Alsop and Catledge
1938, 217–43; Baker 1967, 231–34). It was showdown time. For the still
adamant Senate opposition, any tampering at all with the size of the Supreme
Court was poison. A vigorous filibuster loomed (Alsop and Catledge 1938,
248–50). Available for participation, according to Senator Wheeler, were 43
senators "ready to fight to the end — in seven speaking teams of five each and
with eight senators in reserve" (*New York Herald Tribune*, July 3, 1937, p. 1).
The ringleaders of this coalition, according to one account, "constituted themselves a sort of battalion of death" (Alsop and Catledge 1938, 248). That gives
a sense of the opposition's determination.[7]

Given the two-thirds cloture rule, shouldn't that have been the end of it? In
fact, it wasn't. Majority Leader Robinson moved to crack down on obstructive activity, and the Senate's presiding officer, Key Pittman (D-NV), contributed some procedural rulings favorable to the White House cause.[8] It
was not clear what the outcome would be. "The President told me he thought
there were enough votes to put the Court program across," Interior Secretary
Harold Ickes entered in his diary" (1954, 166). Senator Wheeler met with
FDR but no compromise emerged: "Roosevelt believed his men had the Senate
votes to pass the Court bill. Wheeler believed he had the strength, by means of
a filibuster, to prevent a vote from being taken" (Baker 1967, 239). Many
prognostications ignored or downplayed the cloture rule. In the *New York
Herald Tribune* (July 6, 1937, p. 9): "Veterans are inclined to agree that no
filibuster really succeeds except at the end of a session." In another newspaper:
"General opinion is the substitute will pass, and sooner than expected, since
votes enough to pass it seem apparent, and the opposition cannot filibuster
forever" (Leuchtenburg 1995, 149). In the *New York Times* (July 2, 1937,
p. 5): "As time marches on and they [the obstructing senators] see their local
bills dying of attrition, it is confidently expected by administration chiefs that
they will have a change of heart and let the compromise come to a vote." As of
early July, according to Alsop and Catledge (1938, 244), "The two sides were
so evenly matched and placed that none could tell how the fight would end."

In the end, fate intruded. Senator Robinson, the respected and, by some,
beloved Democratic leader, died of a heart attack in mid-July as a likely result
of overexertion in the Court-packing cause, and that was that. Because of, or
at least concurrent with, Robinson's death any Senate floor majority for the
substitute measure disappeared and the bill was sent back to committee for
burial (Alsop and Catledge 1938, 266–94). Interestingly, the House may have

also lost its floor majority for the proposal at roughly this time, although no vote was taken (Baker 1967, 243; *New York Times*, July 14, 1937, p. 1).

Executive Reorganization

In many ways, the controversy over executive reorganization during the 75th Congress was a replay of the Court-packing struggle. It reached decision time a year later. In the reorganization case also, the president requested in early 1937, by way of a legislative proposal, vastly more leeway vis-à-vis another branch of government. In this case that leeway involved, among other things, authority to reorganize according to presidential taste any element of the executive branch though *without* the legislative veto power over specific plans that Congress did successfully insist on in the well-known reorganization bill enacted later in 1939 (Polenberg 1966, chs. 1, 2). Not surprisingly, many came to see the reorganization plan as a dangerous White House power grab. The House acted first and favorably. But as the plan reached the Senate floor in March 1938, an opposition coalition of some 40 senators coalesced under the leadership of, again, Senator Wheeler (*New York Times,* March 9, 1938, p. 4). The stakes were thought to be high. Under the headline "Wheeler Warns Senate Against Dictatorship," one report told of "heated interchanges which were reminiscent of the days when Senator Wheeler led the coalition fight on the President's court plan" (*New York Herald Tribune,* March 9, 1938, pp. 1, 10). Senator David I. Walsh (D-MA) saw in the reorganization plan a "plunging of a dagger into the very heart of democracy" (Davis 1993, 213). The Senate debated for several weeks amid well-publicized maneuvering by both sides (Polenberg 1966, ch. 6).

But the opposition's strategy was thoroughly majoritarian. It was to offer several appealing uppercut amendments in the hope that one or more would attract a floor majority. Success nearly came with a "Wheeler Amendment" that lost in a tense 43 to 39 showdown. As for obstruction, or rather its lack, the opposition twice signed on to unanimous consent agreements that guaranteed a final up-or-down Senate decision (Altman 1938, 1111–12), which came in a favorable vote of 49 to 42 in late March.[9] Yet a surprise was in store. Tens of thousands of anti-reorganization protest telegrams, inspired by the Gannett newspaper chain and its spinoff National Committee to Uphold Constitutional Government, flooded into the Capitol in late March and early April. The public seemed to be alarmed. That helped along a dramatic result in the House, where the reorganization plan, back for a second round of decision, was voted down by 204 to 196 on April 8 in an astounding defeat for the Roosevelt presidency (Polenberg 1966, ch. 8). Executive reorganization was finally killed in 1938, but a publicity campaign and the House did it, not the Senate. So much for the Senate as the blocking institution of last resort.

Explaining the Patterns

Those are the three sketches. All three bills ran up against sizable committed minorities. All three bills failed on Capitol Hill, somehow. But what we do *not* see is anything like an automatic application of the two-thirds pivot logic in the Senate. Indeed, the one measure that certifiably did fall to a filibuster, the anti-lynching bill, drew an opposition on the merits, so far as one can tell, of *fewer* than the 33 senators (that is, one-third plus one of the membership) required to work the pivot. The Court-packing and reorganization bills drew spirited minority oppositions of considerably *more* than 33 senators, but obstructive filibustering might or might not have worked in the former case — no one will ever know for sure — and was not tried in the latter.

What can be said that might illuminate these various results and the strategies that underpinned them? To me, a good deal of mystery remains, but I came away from the records with three general ideas or conjectures that might help. Each of them involves relaxing an assumption often made in studying congressional behavior.

1. THE SENATE, WITH ITS RULES THAT ALLOW SLOWDOWNS, IS UNUSUALLY GOOD AT ACCOMMODATING DIFFERENCES IN INTENSITY

The Senate is probably better in this regard than the formally majoritarian U.S. House, although as Buchanan and Tullock pointed out years ago (1962), legislatures in general are pretty good at accommodating differences in intensity. That is one reason for having legislatures. For purposes here, the assumption that needs relaxing is one that is surprisingly commonly embedded, without thinking about it very much, in legislative research — that members have equal intensities on any issue and across all issues. They do not, and the fact that they do not helps to promote continual vote-trading among members and across issues in the form of explicit or implicit logrolling (Stearns 1994, 1277–80). In the particular case of the U.S. Senate, the rules of that body that allow slowdowns give, in effect, extra stacks of trading chips to intense minorities that face not-so-intense majorities.

Perhaps this argument about the Senate is obvious, but the disparate outcomes I have pointed to during the 75th Congress place it in relief. For an intensity differential on Capitol Hill, at least in the realm of reasonably broad issues, possibly nothing in American history has matched civil rights from the

1890s through the 1950s.[10] That helps account for the Senate's distinctive zero-outcome record on civil rights during that time. Anti–civil rights southerners representing their region's dominant white caste cared a lot; pro–civil rights northerners representing few blacks and largely indifferent whites cared little. As a plausible indicator of intensity — which is always difficult to measure — the southern senators were willing to talk forever and stay up all night. This commitment seems to be have been electorally induced, in the sense that the southerners could have gotten themselves into political trouble back home by *not* filibustering against civil rights bills.[11] The effect was a kind of electorally induced weighted voting.[12]

Northern senators, on the other hand, tended to eye the opportunity costs of trying to match the southerners' commitment of time and energy and say no. Other agenda items beckoned. One way to size up intensity in the Senate is to watch the circumstances in which members will favor folding one legislative drive so as to move to another. In the civil rights area, in the face of southern obstruction, such procedural switching was once a signature move for many northerners. In 1890–91, the Federal Elections Bill gave way to pressing tariff and silver issues (Welch 1965). The anti-lynching cause had to give way to "the New Deal's 1935 program" or, for Senator George Norris (Ind-NE), "important economic legislation," in 1935 (Sitkoff 1978, 288; Greenbaum, 1967, 83); to "many other important measures" including a $250 million relief bill in 1938 (*New York Times*, January 25, 1938, p. 6; Sitkoff 1978, 294); to defense and foreign policy considerations in 1940 (Sitkoff 1978, 295).[13] As a practical matter, costs beyond foregone agenda items could arise for northern senators choosing to combat these southern talkathons. Those might include lost family time, impaired health, and even, as Senator Robinson found in the stressful conflict of the summer of 1937, their lives.

For the analysis here, the main point is a contrast. The Court-packing and executive reorganization drives of 1937–38, unlike the anti-lynching drive, did *not* feature an intensity differential between the two sides. Yes, this claim needs defense: Questions of evidence arise, distributions of views as well as coalition medians need to be considered, and, on the Court-packing matter, an intensity gap had indeed quite possibly opened up by mid-July of 1937. But the claim will probably stand. That raises the general question: Given a condition of approximately equal intensities, was it possible for Senate minorities to block Senate majorities back then? That is possibly the $64,000 question. Let me restate it more particularly and pose it as a historical question covering in principle the entire century and a half of American experience before World War II. Given a condition of roughly equal intensities on measures pressed as high priorities by presidents or congressional majority parties, given probably also the background environment of a non-lame-duck Congress (in the old lame-duck Congresses, obstruction was easier because of the March 3 closing deadlines),[14] was it possible for Senate minorities to block the legislative drives of Senate majorities back then? In fact, there seems to be precious little evidence that it was — either before or after the 1917 cloture reform (see Wawro and Schickler 2006; Burdette 1965; Binder and Smith 1997, 135). What are the instances?[15] If this conjecture about the history is, for whatever reasons, correct, that should reduce our surprise that the leaders of the Court-packing drive thought they could just bull their bill through in 1937 or that the opponents of executive reorganization did not even try to obstruct in 1938. There was solid warrant for both strategies.

2. THE RULES ENVIRONMENT IN THE SENATE CAN BE UNCLEAR

A two-thirds rule is a two-thirds rule, is it not? Not so fast! Words on paper are one thing, but the hardheaded expectations of politicians about how the Senate will actually operate are another. In fact, in the case of the Court-packing bill of 1937, it was not clear to the politicians or the Washington press corps what would happen if one-third plus one of the senators tried to block it. This was at least because no one could be certain what a determined floor majority, in league with a friendly Senate presiding officer, would do in a pinch.

For analytic purposes, the assumption that needs relaxing here is that of fixed rules. One theme in contemporary political science is that legislative rules can be *manipulated* (Riker 1986). But legislative rules can also be *changed,* which seems to be a distinctly different matter.[16] As of the 1930s, the history of Anglo-American legislatures had been, among other things, a record of majoritarian coups. Minorities enjoyed procedural prerogatives yesterday that they suddenly lost today. Shut down on the spot in such fashion had been Federalists in the U.S. House in 1811 (Adams 1986, 244–46), Irish Nationalists in the British House of Commons in 1881 (Jennings 1969, 127–30), Democratic victims of the "Reed Rules" in the U.S. House in 1890 (Schickler 2001, 32–43), and Progressive obstructors of a currency bill in the U.S. Senate in 1908 (Burdette 1965, 83–91). Although perhaps short of the coup category, common-law-type rulings from the chair, of which the Senate had seen many, could in effect change the rules and thus hobble or inconvenience obstructive minorities. That had happened as recently as 1935 (Burdette 1965, 185), and indeed it happened during the Court-packing debate itself in July 1937 as Senator Pittman, acting in complicity with Majority Leader Robinson, handed down restrictive rulings that won standing as Senate precedents — one involving the meaning of "legislative day" (*New York Times,* July 9, 1937, pp. 1, 5; Riddick 1974, 436–38).

According to a contemporary political scientist's account: "A plethora of points of order and parliamentary inquiries, though time-consuming, failed to upset the chair's constrictive rulings. . . . For several days the deadlocked sides jockeyed for position, not only in the Senate but before the bar of public opinion. Senator Robinson's death, however, suddenly destroyed his majority and ended the drama. In the failure to complete this experiment in defeating a filibuster by a novel interpretation of the regular Senate rules, it is possible that a valuable precedent for the future was lost" (Altman 1937, 1079).

One way to put it is that the Senate's two-thirds cloture rule back then seemed to lack the sureness of that body's other familiar two-thirds hurdles involving veto overrides and treaty ratifications. It was less sure at least because it was less exogenous. In this circumstance, it was risky for a determined opposition to place anything like all its eggs in the cloture-rule basket — perhaps especially on an issue so explosive as Court-packing. An alternative course of action was more prudent, as see below.

3. OFTEN, ON A HIGHLY PROMINENT ISSUE, THE BEST BLOCKING STRATEGY FOR A SIZABLE SENATE MINORITY IS TO TRY TO SHAPE PUBLIC OPINION

To say this is to relax an assumption that the public, or politicians responsive to it, possess fixed views on public issues. Very often they do not. Rarely is any congressional proposal an exact duplicate of a previous one. Some proposals, such as Court-packing and executive reorganization in 1937–38, are brand-new. Even where legislative proposals come to map onto the country's dominant ideological dimension, as many, perhaps most, do, members of Congress and others routinely move to shape public and elite opinion so as to affect the correlation of any such mapping and its cut point. There is a good case for endogenizing such shaping activity into analysis of congressional context and strategy (see Jacobs and Shapiro 2000; Mayhew 2000).

All this was obvious to the Wheeler-led opponents of Court-packing in 1937. They did not say: "We have the requisite 33 nay votes [which in fact they very quickly did have] so don't try to roll over us." Rather, they headed for the radio and the local speech circuits around the country to make their case. This strategy, aided to be sure by anti-FDR opinion leaders outside the Senate and by the Supreme Court's own retreat from its previous rulings, was evidently a brilliant success. "Rather than being the ally of the Court bill's successful passage, time was the enemy. Time permitted the opponents to gain strength, extend their propaganda, augment their forces" (Baker 1967, 152). Over the months, public support for the president's plan tailed off (Caldeira 1987,

1147). It is a good bet that declining public support came to influence the positions of many senators on the Court-packing plan, as well as their intensities. By July 1937, the legislative drive seemed to be sliding into an adverse intensities gap where the chances of successful minority obstruction seem to maximize, but we will never know if it had slid far enough.[17]

In the argument here, the importance of strategies aimed at shaping opinion is as follows. To the extent that such strategies are employed, the cloture rule and other congressional procedures can recede into a faint role or no role at all. Something else taking place in the realm of strategy can be important, even determinative. Moreover, as a comparative matter, similar exercises of opinion leadership undertaken in different eras can make legislative drives of those eras look surprisingly similar. In this regard, I recommend back-to-back reading of Alsop and Catledge (1938) on the Court-packing saga of 1937 and Johnson and Broder (1996) on Clinton's health-care reform drive in 1993–94. There is considerable commonality in opinion dynamics, and one does not come away with a judgment that the Senate cloture rule played much of a role in either outcome.[18]

In sum, to try to get a handle on Senate supermajority politics of earlier times — specifically here, the Congress of 1937–38 — it may make sense to consider three theoretical moves.[19] First, look to intensity differences. That is, relax the assumption of equal member intensities. Second, look to the potential on-the-spot creation of new rules. That is, relax the assumption of fixed rules. Third, look to the shaping of public opinion. That is, relax the assumption of fixed public (and induced fixed member) views. An implication of the analysis is that Senate floor majorities, the classic and major exception of civil rights issues aside, may not have had it worse back then. If anything, given the evident hardness of today's 60-vote rule, they may even have had it easier.

Notes

I would like to thank Alan Gerber and Eric Schickler for their help on this work. A useful clarifying point came from Morris Fiorina. Matthew Glassman helped with the references. This essay was originally published in *PS: Political Science and Politics* 36:1 (January 2003), pp. 31–36. Copyright © 2003 by the American Political Science Association. Reprinted with the permission of Cambridge University Press.

1. Although evidently not Clinton's health-care reform measure, which never commanded 218 votes in the House. See Johnson and Broder 1996, 509.

2. Although see Gilmour 1994.

3. Most of this chronology is from the *New York Times* of 1938; January 9, p. 1 (first quotation); January 19, p. 4 (second quotation); January 22, p. 5 (the northern Democrats); January 23, p. 5; January 27, p. 6; February 17, p. 12; February 22, p. 1.

4. White House strategists bypassed the House at this stage because of the stern upfront opposition of Hatton Sumners (D-TX), chairman of the Judiciary Committee. Still, it was assumed that the House would swing into line eventually. See Alsop and Catledge 1938, 51; *New York Times,* February 8, 1937, p. 6.

5. Most of this chronology is from the *New York Times* of 1937. The initial situation: February 7, p. 1; 8, p. 1. The horse-race coverage: February 10, p. 1; 14, p. 28; 15, p. 1; 17, p. 2; 22, p. 1; 24, p. 1; 25, p. 1. The opposition: February 10, pp. 1, 15; 12, p. 1; 19, p. 1; 23, p. 4. For horse-race coverage see also *Time*, February 22, 1937, 11–13; March 1, 1937, 10–13.

6. There was an interesting sideline wrinkle in June. The Senate Judiciary Committee voted by 10 to 8 to disapprove the Court-packing measure but sent it to the floor anyway. So much for committees as automatic blockers of measures they do not like. The verdict of the committee majority was not wishy-washy: "It is a measure which should be so emphatically rejected that its parallel will never again be presented to the free representatives of the free people of America." Alsop and Catledge 1938, 233.

7. For the looming filibuster, see also *New York Times,* 1938: June 6, p. 37; June 16, p. 16; June 27, p. 1; June 28, p. 4; July 2, pp. 1, 5; July 3, p. 1; July 6, pp. 1, 20; July 14, p. 1.

8. *New York Times,* 1938: July 6, pp. 1, 20; 7, p. 1; 9, pp. 1, 5; 11, p. 1; 13, pp. 1, 8; 14, p. 1.

9. For these events, see *New York Times,* 1938: March 10, p. 1 (majoritarian strategy); March 19, p. 1 (Wheeler Amendment); March 28, p. 1 (unanimous consent); March 29, p. 1 (final passage).

10. During the past half century, the best candidate for an intensity differential may be labor-management relations, on which congressional Democrats often seem to have shallow commitments to unions and Republican deep commitments to business. Striker replacement legislation easily lost out to Senate obstruction in 1993–94, and overhaul of the Taft-Hartley Act suffered that fate in 1965–66.

11. Such back-home trouble in primaries or general elections might serve as an indirect evidential guide to member intensity.

12. A similar effect of something like societally, if not exactly electorally, induced weighted voting appears in Hall's (1996) study of interest group influence in congressional committees.

13. A generation later, a similar logic involving intensities and trading obtained in the drive to pass the Civil Rights Act of 1957. The times had changed, and the southern senators could not completely block this bill, but they could take steps to modify it. Famously, they made a deal with relatively indifferent westerners—support for the Hells Canyon Dam in exchange for dilution of the civil rights measures. See Caro 2002, ch. 38. By the time of the civil rights enactments of 1964 and 1965, the southern versus northern intensities had probably more or less equalized.

14. There were two other reasons why obstruction might have been more successfully

prosecuted during lame-duck Congresses. The Congresses still considering laws had hemorrhaged legitimacy because new elections had chosen their successors, and congressional minority parties, not trusting presidents to run the country by themselves from March through November, occasionally tried to block legislation before March 4 so as to force the calling of special congressional sessions.

15. To be sure, presidents or parties may sometimes refrain from proposing measures that they see will be blocked. But we shouldn't become immobilized by this consideration. Political actors may advance proposals anyway if they see them to be necessary, right, popular generally, popular with key minorities, or possibly merchandisable.

16. Riker takes up Speaker Reed's rules changes of 1890 in his work on "heresthetics" (1986), but this incident fits oddly into a book that is otherwise largely about manipulation of existent rules.

17. At the cusp of successful obstruction, a complicating factor can be that some senators may choose to diversify their position-taking portfolios. That is, a senator can at once oppose a measure and oppose obstruction against it. Senator Gordon Smith (R-OR) did that at a critical moment on the McCain-Feingold campaign-finance reform bill in early 2002.

18. In a Gallup poll in April 1994, "by a two-to-one margin [respondents] thought quality of care would decline and they would be worse off" if the Clinton plan became law (Johnson and Broder 1996, 371). With numbers like these, not much room remains for a procedurally obstructive opposition.

19. It should go without saying that this is not an exhaustive list of possibly useful moves. I have not taken up Oppenheimer's (1985) case that ample Senate debate time owing to much slimmer issue agendas made effective obstruction a chancier proposition in earlier times.

References

Adams, Henry. 1986. *History of the United States During the First Administration of James Madison, 1809–1813*. New York: Library of America.

Alsop, Joseph, and Turner Catledge. 1938. *The 168 Days*. Garden City, NY: Doubleday, Doran.

Altman, O. R. 1937. "First Session of the Seventy-Fifth Congress, January 5, 1937, to August 21, 1937." *American Political Science Review* 31 (December): 1071–93.

Altman, O. R. 1938. "Second and Third Sessions of the Seventy-fifth Congress, 1937–38." *American Political Science Review* 32 (December): 1099–123.

Baker, Leonard. 1967. *Back to Back: The Duel between FDR and the Supreme Court*. New York: Macmillan.

Binder, Sarah A., and Steven S. Smith. 1997. *Politics or Principle? Filibustering in the United States Senate*. Washington, DC: Brookings Institution Press.

Buchanan, James M., and Gordon Tullock. 1962. *The Calculus of Consent*. Ann Arbor: University of Michigan Press.

Burdette, Franklin L. 1965. *Filibustering in the Senate*. New York: Russell & Russell.

Caldeira, Gregory A. 1987. "Public Opinion and the U.S. Supreme Court: FDR's Court-Packing Plan." *American Political Science Review* 81 (December): 1139–53.

Caro, Robert A. 2002. *Master of the Senate: The Years of Lyndon Johnson.* New York: Alfred A. Knopf.

Davis, Kenneth S. 1993. *FDR: Into the Storm, 1937–1940.* New York: Random House.

Dewar, Helen. 2002. "Anti-Cloning Bills Stall in the Senate; Vote Unlikely Soon," *Washington Post,* June 14, A4.

Dewar, Helen, and Juliet Eilperin. 2002. "Senate Votes Down Permanent Repeal of Inheritance Taxes," *Washington Post,* June 13, A5.

Fisk, Catherine, and Erwin Chemerinsky. 1997. "The Filibuster." *Stanford Law Review* 49 (January): 181–254.

Gilmour, John R. 1994. "It's Time to Curb the Filibuster." *Public Affairs Report* (September), 14–15.

Greenbaum, Fred. 1967. "The Anti-Lynching Bill of 1935: The Irony of 'Equal Justice — Under Law.'" *Journal of Human Relations* 15(3):72–85.

Hall, Richard L. 1996. *Participation in Congress.* New Haven: Yale University Press.

Ickes, Harold L. 1954. *The Secretary Diary of Harold L. Ickes,* vol II, *The Inside Struggle, 1936–1939.* New York: Simon and Schuster.

Jacobs, Lawrence R., and Robert Y. Shapiro. 2000. *Politicians Don't Pander: Political Manipulation and the Loss of Democratic Responsiveness.* Chicago: University of Chicago Press.

Jennings, Ivor. 1969. *Parliament.* 2nd edition. Cambridge: Cambridge University Press.

Johnson, Haynes, and David S. Broder. 1996. *The System: The American Way of Politics at the Breaking Point.* Boston: Little, Brown.

Krehbiel, Keith. 1998. *Pivotal Politics: A Theory of U.S. Lawmaking.* Chicago: University of Chicago Press.

Leuchtenburg, William E. 1995. *The Supreme Court Reborn: The Constitutional Revolution in the Age of Roosevelt.* New York: Oxford University Press.

Mayhew, David R. 1998. "Clinton, the 103d Congress, and Unified Party Control: What Are the Lessons?" In *Politicians and Party Politics,* ed. John G. Geer. Baltimore: Johns Hopkins University Press.

Mayhew, David R. 2000. *America's Congress: Actions in the Public Sphere, James Madison Through Newt Gingrich.* New Haven: Yale University Press.

Moore, John Robert. 1968. *Senator Josiah William Bailey of North Carolina: A Political Biography.* Durham, NC: Duke University Press.

Oppenheimer, Bruce I. 1985. "Changing Time Constraints on Congress: Historical Perspectives on the Use of Cloture." In *Congress Reconsidered,* eds. Lawrence C. Dodd and Bruce I. Oppenheimer. 3rd edition. Washington, DC: Congressional Quarterly.

Patterson, James T. 1967. *Congressional Conservatism and the New Deal.* Lexington: University of Kentucky Press.

Polenberg, Richard. 1966. *Reorganizing Roosevelt's Government: The Controversy Over Executive Reorganization, 1936–1939.* Cambridge: Harvard University Press.

Riddick, Floyd M. 1974. *Senate Procedure: Precedents and Practices.* 93rd Cong., 1st sess., S. Doc. 93–21. Washington, DC: U.S. Government Printing Office.

Riker, William H. 1986. *The Art of Political Manipulation.* New Haven: Yale University Press.

Sala, Brian R. 2002. "Time for a Change: Pivotal Politics and the 1935 Wagner Act." Presented at the annual meeting of the Midwest Political Science Association, Chicago.

Schickler, Eric. 2001. *Disjointed Pluralism: Institutional Innovation and the Development of the U.S. Congress.* Princeton, NJ: Princeton University Press.

Sitkoff, Harvard. 1978. *A New Deal for Blacks: The Emergence of Civil Rights as a National Issue,* vol. 1, *The Depression Decade.* New York: Oxford University Press.

Stearns, Maxwell L. 1994. "The Misguided Renaissance of Social Choice." *Yale Law Journal* 103 (March): 1219–93.

Wawro, Gregory J., and Eric Schickler. 2006. *Filibuster: Obstruction and Lawmaking in the U.S. Senate.* Princeton, NJ: Princeton University Press, chap. 4.

Welch, Robert E., Jr. 1965. "The Federal Elections Bill of 1890: Postscripts and Prelude." *Journal of American History* 52 (December): 511–26.

Wheeler, Burton K. 1962. *Yankee from the West.* Garden City, NY: Doubleday.

Wolfinger, Raymond E. 1971. "Filibusters: Majority Rule, Presidential Leadership and Senate Norms." In *Readings on Congress,* ed. Raymond E. Wolfinger. Englewood Cliffs, NJ: Prentice-Hall.

Young, Garry, and Valerie Heitshusen. 2002. "Testing Competing Theories of Policy Production, 1874–1946." Presented at the annual meeting of the Midwest Political Science Association, Chicago.

Wars and American Politics

Since its founding in 1789, the United States government has conducted hot wars for some 38 years,[1] occupied the South militarily for a decade, waged the cold war for several decades, and staged countless smaller actions against Indian tribes or foreign powers. The effects of these activities on American society (to say nothing of the rest of the world) have been immense.

Yet, in general, political scientists who study American domestic politics have underappreciated these effects. That is true of "American political development" specialists as well as others.[2] In general, the study of elections, parties, issues, programs, ideologies, and policy making has centered on peacetime narratives and causation. Leaving aside the Civil War, a domestic event in its own right, American wars have ordinarily been treated as interrupting distractions after which politics could revert to its normal course. One source of this domesticizing thrust is an entrenched view about the fundamentals of politics: over the long haul, the enduring, chiefly economic, interests of voters infuse into public affairs through the mobilizing activities of parties and movements and then affect policy-making processes. Accordingly, the job of an explainer of politics or political history is to canvass the evolving interests of farmers, laborers, businesspeople, women, minority groups, and so on. The rest of the story is largely arithmetic. In general, this is a peacetime script.[3]

At a conceptual level, John Kingdon has offered a refreshing amendment to the above account, at least in the sphere of policy making, through the metaphor of "windows" of opportunity during which policy change becomes possible. Even if an eager candidate, senator, interest group, or bureaucrat—or perhaps a Socialist Party platform a century ago—has promoted a policy idea, that advocacy is irrelevant unless the idea comes to enjoy the joint good fortune of a favorable political environment (such as an election result) *and* a perceived public "problem" (such as inflation, railroad insolvency, or terrorism). Happenstance rules, at least partly. If the conditions are fortuitously satisfied, a "window" may open. In particular, in Kingdon's view, the explanatory balance tilts away from a long-term interest-based determinism toward a jerky timestream of "problem perception."[4]

Enter wars. Unsurpassed as producers of problems, wars may offer the best case imaginable for a conceptual tilt toward the idea of windows that are opened up by problems. For some decisive instances, consider the passage of the Freedmen's Bureau Act of 1865, the Current Tax Payment Act of 1943 (which began the now routine government practice of withholding income-tax payments paycheck by paycheck),[5] or the USA Patriot Act of 2001. These enactments were triggered by problems that were triggered by wars. I will depend on Kingdon's central insight throughout this essay. Yet the effects of wars cut even deeper. Wars seem to be capable of generating whole new political universes. They can generate new problems and open up policy windows, thus often fostering new policies, but they can also generate new ideas, issues, programs, preferences, and ideologies and refashion old electoral coalitions—thus permanently altering the demand side of politics. Certainly, by strengthening the national state, wars can alter the supply side of politics.

These are strong claims. I will try to substantiate them by documenting certain effects of five major American wars from 1789 through 1945—the War of 1812, the War with Mexico, the Civil War, World War I, and World War II. This omits the obviously consequential, although distantly so by 1789, Revolutionary War. It omits the Spanish-American War, which was brief (ten weeks), required little mobilization, and seems to have affected domestic politics little.[6] It omits the cold war, which would require its own kind of project and is at any rate proximate and familiar; there would be few surprises. Also, it omits the two hot wars in Korea and Vietnam that spliced into the cold war and thus neither followed nor preceded full peace. There are three justifications for focusing on the five hot wars examined here. First, as a general matter, I try to demonstrate what the domestic effects of a major, hot, free-standing war *can be*—in principle in the United States of the past, present, and future yet also in any other country fighting a war. Second, I suggest certain reinterpretations of American political development. Third, I believe that I unearth some surprises, or at least some surprising emphases — not especially in the case of the Civil War, whose story is familiar, but at least elsewhere.

I would guess that the kinds of arguments I make, and the kinds of conclusions I arrive at, in this essay will not be especially surprising to historians (including economic historians), who tend to be at home with events and contingency. The overall patterns I argue for might engage that audience. Yet the chief audience I am aiming for here is political scientists, who have tended to underplay events and contingency — and notably wars — in addressing American history.

By the effects of wars I mean, more precisely, the effects of wars *and* their immediate induced aftermaths. If a war causes a runaway inflation for a year or two after it ends, and the society reacts to the inflation, then that reaction counts as a war effect. The effects of demobilizations can count. This aftermath license needs to be used with caution. For example, it is probably best to steer clear of anything to do with the cold war as an effect of World War II; there is a time gap, and too many additional ingredients had gotten poured into the mix by 1947.

For evidence of causal relations I rely on expert testimony by historians, economists, and political scientists that includes, where possible and appropriate, the presentation of a plausible causal logic. By that term I mean a causal account featuring intuitively plausible reasons why an effect may have come about.[7] In principle, I use "cause" in the following overall sense: an X (that is, a war or its immediate aftermath) was the cause of a Y (that is, a relevant effect) if it was a major contributory cause, and at least a necessary cause, of Y happening at least during the time frame it did and possibly at all. These requirements are not trivial: "necessary" means exactly that,[8] and "major contributory" follows the conventional practice of historians in assigning relative importance to causes.[9] But the requirements are perhaps modest in the sense that they allow ample room for additional, non-war-related causes. Note that the requirements accommodate a range of preexisting conditions. Some of the effects analyzed here — the provision of veterans' benefits, to take a clear case — had causes located virtually entirely within the wars themselves. Yet many others have shared a causal basis with generative ideas, schemes, campaigns, programs, or movements that predated the wars. Often, in the spirit of Kingdon, the equivalent of an *interaction term* is at work on the right-hand, explanatory side. To cite a non-American example, how do we explain the coming to power of the Soviet regime in Russia? On the one hand, it required the Bolshevik movement, which had laid the ground-work for revolution over several decades. On the other hand, it required the turmoil of World War I — absent which the Bolsheviks would very likely come down to us today in a footnote status as just one more failed political movement. In this instance, World War I was a necessary, major ingredient in a joint causal mix. In the American case too, wars have sometimes given parties, movements, or ideologues a chance to achieve what they wanted to achieve anyway, war or no war, and that they might never have achieved otherwise.

In this article I investigate four kinds of effects. First, there can be *policy changes,* including changes in rules, institutional structure, and national boundaries as well as in ongoing administered policies. I am interested in changes that proved to be long-lasting, that is, changes extending at least a decade yet in most cases a generation or longer beyond the wars themselves. Not to be considered are such short-term policy initiatives as price controls or the Fair Employment Practices Committee during World War II or the temporary income tax of the Civil War era.[10] Second, there can be *new issue regimes.* By this I mean new, long-lasting, highly public controversies within specified issue areas. In any era, issue regimes are answers of a sort to the question. What is politics about? During the 1990s, for example, it is plausible to say that the United States experienced issue regimes in at least the areas of foreign trade, taxation levels, campaign finance reform, and health financing. Some issue regimes result in policy changes; some just peter out. In certain past circumstances, issue regimes have bundled into packages that might be called "program regimes," as will be discussed. I have relied on stylized evidence for what qualifies as a policy change or a new issue regime worth addressing, that is, accounts in conventional history texts such as those of the *New American Nation* series as well as, in the case of the policy changes, specialized policy literatures.

A word is in order about the connection between the policy changes and the new issue regimes. They are distinct in principle and ordinarily unrelated in practice. Over two-thirds of the policy changes identified here were *not* followed by long-lasting postwar contestation about whether the changes in question should have been made in the first place. Basic policy questions were settled — in the sense (to cite a non-war-related instance) that the Louisiana Purchase was not followed by a quarter century of debate about whether to sell the territory back to France. Also, most of the new issue regimes identified here were *not* continuing arguments about the advisability of already achieved war-driven policy changes. Rather, they came about somehow otherwise through war-related circumstances. Nevertheless, there is an overlap. In some instances, an actual policy change blended into a new issue regime. That is, a war-induced policy change occurred in a specified policy area, yet a new highly public controversy (perhaps accompanying more change) persisted regarding the advisability of the already achieved policy change for a considerable time also. In such instances, a relevant policy area can be listed here under both the "policy change" and "new issue regime" rubrics. The boundaries around these matters are perhaps blurry but I hope workable.

A third kind of effect can be *shakeups in electoral coalitions.* By this I mean substantial changes in patterns of party voting in presidential elections that persisted for a considerable time — a decade or a generation rather than just a few years. Fourth, there can be *major changes in party ideologies.* With this rubric, I draw particular attention to the twentieth century.

These four categories of war effects are not exhaustive. Wars can be cataclysms. In a general sense, their effects can obviously be horrific and astounding as were, for example, those of World War I in Europe: "It is hard now to appreciate how overwhelming an event and how crushing in its aftermath the conflict must have seemed."[11] For Americans, the Civil War had these dimensions. Here, I am bypassing this larger picture. I am also bypassing a range of additional particular effects that might be taken up. American wars, for example, have produced military heroes who became president, as is widely known. They have fostered nationwide membership organizations, as Theda Skocpol has demonstrated.[12] Possibly they have spurred American "civic engagement": That phenomenon, which in Robert D. Putnam's account has declined in recent times, seems to have declined from a height that the mobilization of society associated with World War II initially raised it to.[13] Perhaps wars have spurred or shaped "public moods." But in this essay I stop with the four effects introduced above.

First, I jointly consider policy changes and new issue regimes war by war. I then evaluate electoral shakeups for all five wars and party ideological changes for the twentieth-century wars. This is a somewhat dissonant plan, but the joint treatment of the first two effects is probably justified by their frequent overlap of issue terrain. To cover the territory outlined above, I need to proceed by way of sketches that are brief to the point of being telegraphic. Also, I have made choices of emphasis. That is a what, when, and why analysis and centrally *not* a who and how analysis. I take it as given that in many, if not all, the historical instances cited below, political entrepreneurs did imaginative work through resourceful use of processes. But most of those stories will not be told here. It is true that a why analysis is incomplete without taking account of entrepreneurs, but the why analysis I undertake here centers on the circumstances in which the entrepreneurs might have operated. My main aim is to place the whats and whens in relief and point to plausible causal logics.

Policy Changes and New Issue Regimes
THE WAR OF 1812

The War of 1812 could serve as a model for the case that wars can have major effects. Two major policy changes emerged quickly after the armistice. Congress established the Second Bank of the United States — a reaction to the near-bankruptcy, currency disorder, and debt brought on by the war[14] — and a high new protective tariff designed to shield American industries nourished during the war, notably cotton textiles, that in peacetime became vulnerable to British competition.[15] Evident here are two good examples of plausible causal logics. Both of these new policies prevailed for a decade and a half. Yet controversy over them persisted, and they figured in new issue regimes that absorbed energy and attention for a quarter of a century starting in 1815. A third new issue regime centering on "internal improvements" followed the same trajectory — although without ever emanating in much actual policy change. In this third case, the War of 1812, which among other things "demonstrated in a particularly forceful manner the need of better facilities for transportation," raised to high issue standing a set of proposals that had been broached years earlier but had not made much of a mark before the war.[16] Bundling occurred across the three issue areas. The bank, the tariff, and internal improvements came to form the chief ingredients of Henry Clay's "American System" — a policy agenda that was seen to be comprehensive and interlocking and that remained prominent, although without ever winning success permanently or on all points, during the postwar quarter of a century.[17] Hence the possible utility of referring to an overall program regime during those years rather than just a collection of issue regimes. Andrew Jackson's well-known veto of the renewal of the Second Bank in 1832 can be seen as a moment in this American System program regime. I emphasize here the War of 1812 as a generative force: "The end of the war marked the beginning of a new era."[18] Analysts agree that a burst of war-induced nationalism animated and justified the new issues and policies. The country's vulnerability had been shown. The American System promised a stronger postwar political economy backed up by a stronger state. Into obsolescence went an earlier generation's contentious concerns, such as fears of aristocracy and monarchy.[19] After the war, "Public opinion found its focus on the domestic issues of currency, banking, tariffs, transportation, public lands, and western migration."[20]

THE WAR WITH MEXICO

The war with Mexico of the 1840s brought one striking policy change — the acquisition of today's American Southwest, extending from Texas through California (in geographic terms, an area larger than today's Britain, France, Italy, Germany, and Spain combined).[21] Yet no less striking was the new issue regime that quickly ensued. What did the new territories imply for the future of slavery? The balance between slave and free states was suddenly at stake. In August 1846 Congressman David Wilmot, an alarmed free-soil Democrat from Pennsylvania, introduced the Wilmot Proviso, barring slavery from any previously free territory acquired from Mexico.[22] This move and its repercussions would prove to "realign the structure of American politics."[23] According to one interpretation, the virtually immediate postwar controversy between Northerners and Southerners over the disposition of the new territories "marked the beginning of sectional strife which for a quarter of a century [that is, all the way through the Civil War and the peak of Reconstruction] would subject American nationalism to its severest testing."[24]

THE CIVIL WAR

The broad effects of the Civil War are well known. Beyond its changes in race policies, the war brought "a spirit of national economic activism unprecedented in the antebellum years," engendering "what might be called the birth of the modern American state."[25] In particular, the major policy changes included:

- *Extension of rights to African Americans.* This was legislated through the Emancipation Proclamation; the Thirteenth Amendment, abolishing slavery; the Fourteenth Amendment, nationalizing rights in general; and the Fifteenth Amendment, extending the suffrage.[26]
- *A high protective tariff.* Originating — at least in large part — as an emergency revenue source, "the so-called war tariff became permanent, both in the statute books and in the minds of the public and of the protected industries."[27] This is a leading instance of a party — the Republicans — getting a chance to do what they would have wanted to do anyway. Suddenly in 1861, tariff revenue emerged as a solution to a problem — a desperate shortage of government revenue as war loomed. Once in place, through the usual operations of path dependence, revenue streams tend to stay in place. (Of course, it is quite possible that a ruling Republican Party would have generated a high protective tariff somehow at some point anyway without the stimulus of the war. But that is speculation. We do

not know what a ruling Republican Party would have amounted to, or whether one could have existed in any stable sense, absent the Civil War and Reconstruction.)

- *Taxes on alcohol, tobacco, and certain luxuries.* As of the early twentieth century, over a third of federal revenue came from these sources.[28]
- *Nationwide banking.* "The beginning of a nationwide banking system," was enabled by passage of the National Banking Act of 1864.[29] The war economy needed better organization.
- *Congressional redesign.* Creation of the House and Senate Appropriations Committees in 1865 and 1867, a major innovation in governmental structure, resulted from "pressures spawned by economic burdens produced by the long years of war."[30]
- *A transcontinental railroad.* The Pacific Railway Act of 1862 and the following two initiatives, the kinds of policy moves once favored by Whigs and now by Republicans, were made possible by the absence from Capitol Hill of Southerners opposed to the policies — a coalitional distortion brought on by the war. The railroad also had a military rationale: "The Far West had to be defended."[31]
- *Aid to higher education.* The Land Grant College Act of 1862 benefited from coalitional distortions and may have also been helped by a war-related rationale: "The land-grant colleges would offer military training."[32]
- *Free Western homesteading.* Through the Homestead Act of 1862.[33]

The Civil War also deposited a number of new long-lived issue regimes. Again, under scrutiny is the content of highly public issue controversy during the ensuing decades. It is not clear what to list, but the following four entries seem plausible. They did not exhaust the agenda of public controversy during the late 1860s, 1870s, and 1880s (other chronic issues of that era, such as civil service reform and regulation of the railroads, did *not* have Civil War origins), but they contributed to it. The relevant new regimes centered on:

- *Civil rights and Reconstruction.* These issues of the late 1860s and 1870s persisted, albeit sporadically, into the early 1890s.
- *The Republican high-tariff system.* The system stirred controversy for several ensuing generations.[34]
- *Currency.* In the wake of the Legal Tender Act of 1862, currency issues remained prominent through the close of the nineteenth century.[35]
- *Veterans' pensions.* Amid chronic controversy, Civil War pensions started small, but grew into a major version of a welfare-state program during succeeding decades.[36]

WORLD WAR I

At least eight major long-lasting policy changes can be credited to World War I:

- *Progressive taxation.* World War I brought "a shock to government finances that dramatically and permanently affected the internal revenue system"[37] as well as "a vast expansion of the Treasury's administrative capacity."[38] Through the Revenue Act of 1916, a stiff preparedness measure enacted in uneasy awareness of the then two-year-old European war, the government "broke the dominion of the tariff over the federal revenue system, transformed the experimental income tax [enacted initially during peacetime in 1913] into the primary instrument of federal taxation, introduced federal estate taxation [now under siege in the twenty-first century],[39] initiated the first significant taxation of corporate incomes, and contributed [along with the Revenue Acts of 1917 and 1918] to the nation's most dramatic departure toward progressive redistributional taxation."[40] As one indicator, the personal income-tax rate paid by the highest income bracket rose from 7 percent in 1913 to 77 percent in 1918 and has not fallen below 25 percent since. This overall progressive shift was not inevitable. A Progressive-oriented left wing ascendant on Capitol Hill during the Wilson administration insisted on it as a condition of funding preparedness and then the war. In the judgment of tax historian W. Elliot Brownlee, "Without the wartime crisis, the growth of the federal government almost certainly would have been slower and reliant on some combination of tariff revenues, sales taxes, and low-rate taxation of personal and corporate incomes or spending."[41]
- *A record high protective tariff.* As in 1815, an "intense nationalistic feeling" abetted a drive to shield industries nourished during the war, this time notably a new chemical industry.[42] Also, metals and ores were now seen to need protection for defense reasons. A new universe of war-kindled trade associations ready with proposals existed in the national capital. Farm interests signed on as postwar conditions ruined crop prices. These pressures ensured passage of the Emergency Tariff Act of 1921 and the Fordney-McCumber Tariff of 1922. In general, despite spirited wrangling over particulars in the legislative process of the early 1920s, "the necessity of protection was hardly challenged."[43]
- *A national budgeting system.* The Budget and Accounting Act of 1921 and a centralization of congressional appropriations sought to accommodate officials who had found themselves "ill-equipped to address the budgetary problems that stemmed from the war."[44]

- *Prohibition.* It is true that the dry cause was advancing on its own in the early to mid-1910s, but the Eighteenth Amendment and the Volstead Act might never have succeeded absent the war. New justifications arose. According to one account, "The entry of the United States into World War I, which was accompanied by a spirit of patriotic self-denial and the reviling of all things German, including beer and schnapps, swelled the dry ranks."[45] "Most important," according to another account, "[the war] brought into the movement such non-prohibitionists as Theodore Roosevelt and Herbert Hoover, who advocated Prohibition to save grain."[46] Another account maintains that "[w]hile the years of antidrink agitation had paved the way, it was the politics of wartime mobilization that provided the impetus for the speedy approval of the [Eighteenth] amendment by the states."[47]

- *Women's suffrage.* No doubt this reform, effected by the Nineteenth Amendment, would have succeeded sooner or later, but energetic contributions by women to wartime mobilization seem to have brought the proximate winning argument. Suffrage extension was "necessary to the successful prosecution of the war,"[48] President Wilson argued; "We have made partners of the women in this war."[49] The United States was not alone. Women won the vote in many other countries during World War I or its near aftermath, evidently through a logic of wartime contribution or various other democratizing impulses associated with war. The instances include Britain (for women over thirty), Canada, Germany, Austria, Poland, Czechoslovakia, Sweden, Belgium, and the Netherlands. Women in France, Italy, Hungary, and Japan had to wait until the close of World War II, when a comparable logic seems to have obtained.[50]

- *Immigration restriction.* After failing for decades, this cause now triumphed through a literacy test and other barriers imposed in 1917. The war atmosphere brought a fear of radicals, pressure for Americanization, and a discrediting of powerful anti-restrictionist nationality groups — notably the German-American Alliance. After the war and its ensuing politicized strikes, Red Scare, and deportations of alleged radicals during 1919–20, a resort to national-origins quotas in 1921 and 1924 bolstered the move of 1917.[51]

- *Domestic intelligence.* In the wake of the Espionage Act of 1917 and the Sedition Act of 1918, the Federal Bureau of Investigation created a General Intelligence Division that functioned during the Red Scare of 1919–20. J. Edgar Hoover started the compiling of files on individuals in 1919, a practice that he continued into the Nixon administration.[52]

- *Cartelization of the railroads under tight government management.* By way of direct government control during the war and the Transportation Act of 1920, a prominent issue regime centering on railroad regulation that dated to the 1880s ended. Henceforth, the rail corporations more or less dropped out of American public life as powerful or controversial entities.[53]

Beyond these policy changes, World War I was a fertile source of new issue regimes. Five of them, in addition to the chronic tariff issue (which figured prominently both before and after the war), came close to exhausting the public agenda during the 1920s:

- *Enforcement of Prohibition* — a perennial subject of dispute until 1933.
- *Cuts in the corporate and individual income taxes established during the war.*   Led by Secretary of the Treasury Andrew Mellon, the Republicans pursued this cause for most of a decade.[54]
- *Hydroelectric power.*   The government had operated a power plant at Muscle Shoals, Alabama, during the war. The question of how to dispose of it stirred a chronic controversy that culminated in the creation of the Tennessee Valley Authority (TVA) in 1933.[55]
- *Agricultural crop supports.*   The war had brought government support of crop prices, prosperity on the farms, and a crystallization of new agricultural interest groups. Once the postwar prices plummeted as they did in 1921, "the experience of price supports was there to be appealed to." In short order, the so-called McNary-Haugen plan for crop supports came to preoccupy public attention and Capitol Hill and to incur vetoes by Coolidge and Hoover. The way was paved for a somewhat different crop-support plan, the Agricultural Adjustment Act of 1933. Nothing like either of these government-centered plans had had any prominence before World War I.[56]
- *Veterans' bonuses.*   Accompanied by chronic commotion, at least five veterans' bonus bills became law over Coolidge, Hoover, and Roosevelt vetoes. Surprisingly, those of 1931 and 1936 are good candidates for the most effective countercyclical spending moves by the government during the Depression years.[57]

WORLD WAR II

As in the locution "postwar era," we still regard World War II as a dividing line, and that makes sense in domestic as well as in foreign affairs. At least nine substantial policy changes can plausibly be credited to the war:

- *Mass-based progressive taxation.*   For lasting effects on the federal revenue structure, nothing has ever surpassed the financing of World War II. The personal income tax was "dramatically expanded" through widening its reach (the share of the workforce paying taxes rose from 7 percent before the war to 64 percent afterward), raising marginal rates (the top-bracket rate peaked at 94 percent and stayed high), and pay-as-you-go withholding.[58] Before the war, revenue from the personal income tax never exceeded 1.5 percent of GNP; since the war, it has dipped only once (around 1950) below 7 percent.[59] Corporate taxes mushroomed also. "The country emerged from the war with a completely different revenue structure."[60] In general, the government has lived off World War II's lucrative tax design for the six ensuing decades. For a while, at any rate, there seems to have been a progressive redistributive effect, as was argued by Douglass C. North in 1966: "It is not at all clear that New Deal measures provided any significant redistribution of income. . . . The really significant fall [in income inequality] is clearly related to the high progressive tax rates imposed during World War II."[61]

- *Fiscal policy to stabilize the economy and ensure full employment.* These policy desiderata were expressed in the Employment Act of 1946 and the creation of the Council of Economic Advisors. According to Herbert Stein, "The great weight assigned to full employment as a postwar goal certainly resulted from the achievement of full employment during the war against the background of ten years of depression."[62] For one thing, the war showed that deficits could work; in the words of Brownlee, it "institutionalized structural Keynesianism."[63]

- *Curbs on labor unions.* Repeated, crippling strikes during the war and its ensuing demobilization phase soured public opinion on unions. An "almost hysterical hostility toward unions" greeted a rail walkout in 1946, for example.[64] For many, John L. Lewis, of the United Mine Workers, became a national villain. Hence the promanagement revisions of labor law by way of the Smith-Connally Act of 1943 and the Taft-Hartley Act of 1947. The latter has remained largely in effect ever since.[65]

- *Progress in voting rights for southern African Americans.* The Soldier Voting Act of 1942 and a Supreme Court ban of the white primary (a move that is said to have indexed the country's opinion change regarding race during the war) in 1944 made possible small but real progress in this area. According to Alexander Keyssar, "The equilibrium in voting laws was decisively disrupted by World War II."[66]

- *Science policy.* The war provided the transforming event from which the modern research system emerged."[67] The idea of government support for basic research in universities through peer review was in place by 1945, as were corresponding practices and connections to industry, although it took until 1950 to establish the National Science Foundation (NSF).[68]

- *Atomic energy policy.* Wartime development of the atomic bomb and the Atomic Energy Act of 1946 necessitated this new policy area.[69]

- *Curbs on the executive branch.* Policies limiting executive power were manifested in the Administrative Procedure Act of 1946, regulating bureau-cratic practices; the Legislative Reorganization Act of 1946, strengthening the congressional committee system for, among other things, executive oversight; and the Twenty-Second Amendment, sent by Congress to the states in 1947, establishing a two-term limit for presidents. World War II, coming as it did on top of the New Deal, stirred considerable nervousness about executive power.[70]

- *A new national security structure.* Reflecting a new "doctrine of national security" developed during the war, the National Security Act of 1947 inte-grated the military services (thus providing a suitable housing for the Joint Chiefs of Staff created in 1942) and established the Central Intelligence Agency (a successor to the wartime Office of Strategic Services).[71]
- *GI Bill of Rights.* The program funded higher education for over two million returning veterans as well as home mortgages and other benefits. According to one assessment, "The transition toward a prosperous, middle-class society was accelerated by decades."[72]

As in the cases of earlier wars, World War II brought about policy changes but also transformed the national policy agenda. Four major issue regimes lasting into the 1960s seem to have stemmed from the war:

- *Civil rights.* If the term "New Deal" is restricted to the 1930s, civil rights — entailing voting rights, fair employment, and access to public accommoda-tions — was not a New Deal issue.[73] It emerged in 1943 and 1944. On the home front, the war's crusade against Nazism is said to have "eroded the moral and intellectual respectability of the claim for racial supremacy." In general, a pronounced spirit of democracy is said to have set in. For their part, African Americans aiding the war effort demanded better treatment, not least as assertive returning veterans. President Truman embraced the cause of civil rights in 1946, inaugurating a long-running controversy that bore fruit in the 1960s, yet has persisted since that time.[74]
- *General aid to education.* Across-the-board subsidies to elementary and secondary schools was not a New Deal issue. It emerged in 1943 as word of failed draft exams circulated, and the implications of halted school con-struction hit home. A postwar teacher shortage loomed. Senate Republican leader Robert A. Taft signed on to the cause in 1945. In general, "World War II proved to be the major force propelling education into the national political arena as a major issue." It stayed there for two decades.[75]
- *National health insurance.* This was another non–New Deal issue that emerged in 1943. The poor health of the draft pool was noted. Britain's Beveridge Report of 1942, itself a product of the war, drew attention and

praise. Senator Robert F. Wagner and others introduced an unprecedentedly ambitious bill. Presidents Roosevelt and Truman signed on to the cause (Roosevelt had not taken any such stand before the war). Thus was launched an issue regime that, with certain detours and discontinuities, emanated in Medicare in 1965.[76]

• *Public housing and slum renewal.* This (public housing, at least) had been briefly and secondarily a New Deal issue, but the cause came into its own in 1944 and 1945. "The war acted as a catalyst . . . and produced a widespread, conscious interest in postwar housing." Construction had largely halted. An immense postwar housing shortage loomed. Taft and Truman signed on. Thus began a durable issue regime that would see the enactment of significant statutes in 1949, 1954, 1961, 1965, 1966, and 1968.[77]

Note that another bundling pattern appears here. Civil rights, education, housing, and health insurance, along with a full-employment thrust, formed the core of what we remember as Truman's "Fair Deal" program.[78] There is a resemblance to Henry Clay's American System. Both of these enterprises were comprehensive, long-running, largely war-stimulated endeavors that can be said to have figured in overall program regimes, that is, not just individual issue regimes. It is anachronistic to read the Fair Deal back so easily into the New Deal, as is commonly done.[79] Of all the conclusions I came to in conducting this project, none surprised me more than this one: the Fair Deal largely stood on its own base. This judgment jumped out of the factual material in the secondary sources — even if some of those sources offered in principle a familiar kind of New Deal continuity narrative. In the final analysis, it is an empirical question whether or not issue regimes came to exist in the 1940s, as is the question of what may have actually triggered their existence. To understand the generative political environment of 1943–45, it is not enough to show that certain New Dealers entertained some not very widely propagated ideas during the late 1930s. As a last point, consider that the Great Society of the 1960s, with its ambitious civil rights, education, health insurance, and housing moves, seems to have been chiefly a fulfillment of the Fair Deal, not the New Deal.

IN GENERAL

See Table 12.1 for a summary of the foregoing material. At least four observations or reflections seem warranted. First, the Civil War and the two world wars obviously outpaced the two earlier wars in generating entries to the table. No doubt one reason is the scale of the three large wars — the cost in money, mobilization, and lives. In particular, the War with Mexico pales in comparison as a cheaper, easier, one-sided contest more akin to the Spanish-American War. Another likely reason is that the federal government in its early decades was functionally specialized: it was not designed to undertake programs of domestic policy initiatives in good times or bad, and on balance it did not.[80]

Even so, it is well to realize that certain entries in Table 12.1 are more important than others. In particular, an unweighted entry count underrates the War with Mexico. Few policy moves have ever exceeded the annexation of the American Southwest in importance. Possibly no American issue regime has ever exceeded the free-soil versus slavery-expansion controversy of the late 1840s and 1850s in intensity, public engagement, and eventual policy effects. Also, Americans have lost a sense of the War of 1812. The casualties may have been low, but even so—the British invasion of the Detroit area and Maine? The American invasion of Ontario? The battles of New Orleans and Baltimore? The American seizure of Indian territories? The burning of the White House? A secession move in New England? Near national bankruptcy? Perhaps we underrate both the war's amplitude and its effects—the latter being a blend of nation building (as seen in the postwar burst of nationalism) as well as state building that is perhaps thinly captured in Table 12.1. Not considered here yet is the war's impact on the party system.

Second, on the evidence here, the country's hot, freestanding wars have left more of a mark in some policy areas than others. What is missing? In the familiar Progressive or New Deal–liberal interpretation of American history, attention centers on adversarial regulation of industry (as in taming the late-nineteenth-century railroads, busting trusts, setting a minimum wage, and policing such areas as occupational safety, securities fraud, consumer affairs, and environmental protection) and on establishing welfare-state entitlements. These topics make at best a faint appearance in the war-related lists of Table 12.1. The only solid exception is veterans' benefits. In general, wartime governments may see fit to make use of industries rather than to confront them, and to allocate their expenditures otherwise. It is not surprising that Progressive and liberal accounts tend to skimp on the wars.

Amply represented in the checklists, by contrast, is a collection of concerns that Alexander Hamilton might feel at home with. The wars have nourished state building and economic management, that is, systems of revenue extraction, the crafting of government institutions, tariff duties for revenue and protection, the banking systems of the nineteenth century, as well as—this seems to fit the pattern—the Keynesian managerial thrust of the mid-1940s. Yet that is not all. Policy moves as diverse as immigration restriction, prohibition of alcohol, curbs on unions, and a transcontinental railroad have

Table 12.1 Lasting Policy Changes and New Issue Regimes in the United States Deriving from Wars

Policy Changes	New Issue Regimes
War of 1812 (1812–15)	
Protective tariff	Protective tariff
Second national bank	Banking policy
	Internal improvements (the "American System")
War with Mexico (1846–48)	
Annexation of Southwest	Free-soil vs. slavery expansion
Civil War (1861–65)	
Rights to African Americans	Civil rights and Reconstruction
High protective tariff	Protective tariff
Excise Taxes	Currency issues
National banking system	Veterans' pensions
Congressional appropriations process	
Transcontinental railroad	
Land-grant colleges	
Free western homesteading	
World War I (1917–18)	
Progressive taxation	Enforcement of Prohibition
Record high protective tariff	Tax cuts
National budgeting system	Public power
Prohibition of alcohol	Agricultural crop supports
Women's suffrage	Veterans' bonuses
Immigration restriction	
Domestic intelligence	
Cartelization of railroads	
World War II (1941–45)	
Mass-based progressive taxation	Civil rights
Full-employment fiscal policy	General aid to education
Curbs on labor unions	National health insurance
Progress on African American suffrage	Public housing and slum renewal (the "Fair Deal")
Science policy	
Atomic energy policy	
Curbs on executive branch	
New national security structure	
G.I. Bill of Rights	

appeared at various times in the mixed bag of war legacies. There are some general patterns. Until the 1960s, the federal government's main efforts to shape higher education drew from wars — the land grant colleges of the 1860s as well as the GI Bill and science policy (including the NSF) deriving from World War II. Three of the hot wars — the War with Mexico, the Civil War, and World War II — revolutionized American race policy, either immediately or by spurring new issue regimes that proved consequential. The Civil War and World War I brought unsurpassed instances, and World War II a lesser but still notable one, of suffrage expansion — for, respectively, blacks, women, and blacks again. (Later, the Vietnam War also left a deposit of teenage voting.)[81] To miss the wars, in short, is to miss a recurrent strain of Hamiltonian construction, yet also, among other things, major developments in education, racial advancement, and electoral democracy.

Third, note the extraordinary power of these wars — all five of them — as agenda setters. The right-hand column of Table 12.1 has the relevant entries. In all five cases, new issue regimes that absent the wars might not have come into existence at all captured public attention that lasted for a generation or more. Why, it seems worthwhile to stand back and ask, did politically aware Americans of the 1850s come to dwell on free-soil versus slavery expansion, their descendants of the 1920s on Prohibition enforcement, tax cuts, and crop-support plans, their descendants of the late 1940s and 1950s on civil rights, federal housing programs, and federal aid to education? War legacies have provided a surprisingly prominent answer to the question, What is American politics about?

A fourth and related point is that one comes to appreciate the sheer non-inevitability of much of American history by sifting through the materials in Table 12.1. This raises the risky topic of counterfactuals, but serious historical explanation does not seem possible without doing that, at least implicitly.[82] A logic of "windows" of opportunity in Kingdon's sense, and then some, pervades the content of Table 12.1. Reverse the close election of 1844, thus possibly skirting the war with Mexico, and who can say what the policies and issue regimes of the 1850s and 1860s would have looked like? Would the Civil War have been averted?[83] Locate World War I in the 1920s, or at least somewhere else if at all, and what would today's federal revenue system amount to? A rather different tax mix could have been chosen as in, say, Sweden.[84] Cancel the world wars and American women might have waited a considerable time for the suffrage — perhaps even until 1971 as in Switzerland. Greatly magnify the American need and shared sacrifice associated with World War II and this country might have reached for national health provision as a consequence then, as did apparently Britain and Japan, despite the cost.[85]

Counterfactual speculation is relatively easy on topics such as veterans' benefits, where one can readily conclude that without a war, there would have been no benefits (although the *shape* of the various veterans' payouts of American history is a complicated matter). Heavier going occurs in areas where a preexisting policy impulse allows a claim that a result might have happened anyway, war or no war. One response here is philosophical: I do not see any reason why in principle a long-term allegedly "underlying" cause of a policy effect should be considered more real, basic, important, interesting, or successfully explanatory than a short-term, contingent cause. This is to step away from, among other things, a commitment that I believe is unwarranted to various social or economic determinisms.

A second response is ad hoc and empirical: There does not seem to be any escape from assessing the causal backgrounds of past phenomena one by one with counterfactual ideas in mind. In general, in apprehending the American past, I would guess that we impute far too much inevitability to what has in fact happened. Our explanations tend to overfit. Of the entries in Table 12.1, which ones were inevitable: war or no war, sooner or later? (This relaxes for the moment any requirement of temporal immediacy—although note that *when* something happens is not necessarily a minor concern; consider the Thirteenth Amendment.) Suffrage for American women was extremely likely, although that judgment does not settle the question of when. Slavery would have come to end, but, absent the Civil War, at what cumulative human cost and when? A transcontinental railroad would almost certainly have been built, although possibly by the states, on private resources, or later or differently. But the near certainties run out quickly. For a century, Whigs, Republicans, and their industrial backers supplied powerful support for high tariffs, but we do not know what would have happened on that policy front absent the wars. After all, it had proven possible for a stable American low-tariff regime of nearly constitutional standing to persist for a full generation leading up to the Civil War.[86] Beginning around 1900, a Progressive or liberal left wing on Capitol Hill set out to bleach the rich through taxation, but they scored their only striking victories during the two world wars.[87] Movements to prohibit alcohol and restrict immigration acquired considerable force in the early twentieth century, but it is a fair bet that neither would have succeeded absent World War I. On immigration, the American policy equilibrium has been to do little or nothing to restrict it, even in the face of widespread public discontent about heavy population intake as was exhibited around 1850, around 1900, and in the 1990s. In this policy area, for complicated reasons, veto politics has normally prevailed.[88] Lacking World War I, it might well have prevailed in the 1910s and 1920s.[89] In the area of labor-management relations, it is obvious that management and its conservative representatives itched after 1935 to roll back the pro-union reforms of the Wagner Act, but it seems no less clear that the unpopular strikes of World War II and its near aftermath made that rollback possible.

The American past is a cemetery of failed impulses and movements. It is news when events assist one to succeed. In general, it is probably a mistake to invest in grand schematic explanations of American history that underplay contingency, and wars are hard to beat as bearers of contingency.

Shakeups of Electoral Coalitions

Policy changes can be popular or unpopular, in a general sense, and they can beget both winners and losers. New issue regimes can crystallize electorates in new ways. Disagreement can mount and last about whether a war should have been fought in the first place. By way of these various routes, all in the realm of "position issues," it is easy to see how wars and their near aftermaths might spur significant, possibly long-lasting, shakeups in electoral coalitions. There is also the route of "valence issues."[90] Little is deadlier for a ruling party than a reputation for incompetent management, and such stigmas can evidently last—as in the case of Herbert Hoover and the Depression-era Republicans. As it happens, nothing tests the managerial capacity of a ruling party more than a war or a turbulent war aftermath, and voters may take notice. As a final consideration, wars can alter the composition of electorates—as through policy changes expanding or contracting the suffrage (Southern whites after the Civil War are an instance of contraction).

This is a jumble of possible causal paths that cannot be sorted out through available historical data. But clues can be sought on the general question of whether wars have been associated with significant and long-lasting electoral change. For this purpose, an apt data set was provided by Jerome Clubb, William Flanigan, and Nancy Zingale in 1980 (although the authors did not emphasize the question of wars in their own analysis).[91] These authors gauge the level of significant, lasting electoral change associated with each presidential election from 1836 through 1964, a span that accommodates four of the five hot wars addressed here. Using an analysis of variance technique, with individual states figuring as statistical units, the authors probe for two distinct kinds of change: "surge" change, where, in a limiting case, all the subsidiary geographic units swing equally toward a specified party in election year B as compared to the previous election year A; and "interactive" change, where, in a limiting case, some states switch one way and some the other way without any net overall change occurring. The authors proceed by analyzing successive election quadruplets (A through D, B through E, and so forth)—the logic being to locate any individual election in a context of both its predecessors and its successors. This is not just a comparison of any given election with its immediate predecessor. The authors' methodology requires them to calculate results separately for each party (owing to third parties, one major party's record is not just the mirror image of the other's). This means that, in principle, any presidential election can generate as many as four kinds of realigning change—Democratic party surge, Democratic party interaction, Republican party surge, and Republican party interaction. Surge change can take a plus or a minus sign, whereas interactive change does not take a sign. The analysis accommodates the Democrats starting in 1836, the Republicans starting in 1868.

For all thirty-three presidential elections of 1836 through 1964, Table 12.2 documents the realignment changes of various kinds that the authors considered ample enough to report.[92] Thus, for example, a high (Democratic) interaction value appears for 1836, when the major parties were still inchoate; the Democrats' pattern of relative state-by-state showings was quite new that year but durable afterward.[93] Thus also, meeting expectations, the Depression election of 1932 registers a durable positive surge of 16.28 percent for the Democrats and a durable negative surge of 11.33 percent for the Republicans.

This is complicated material, but it yields some simple results. After the 1830s, the seven elections associated with the highest change values in Table 12.2 all occurred during or after major crises. Three of them were the first presidential elections to take place after the country's three worst depressions struck—in 1876, after the crash of 1873 (those years also brought a crisis centering on Reconstruction); in 1896, after the crash of 1893; and in 1932, after that of 1929. The other four were the first elections to take place after hot wars ended—and in all four cases volatile war aftermaths had had time to occur and war-induced issue regimes had had time to take hold. Those were the elections of 1848, after the War with Mexico; 1868, after the Civil War; 1920, after World War I; and 1948, after World War II. All four occasions seem to have brought sizable lasting penalties in the 5 to 8 percent range to the incumbent presidential parties (or, more or less the same thing, durable bonuses of that size to the opposition parties). This is in the neighborhood of a recent 4 percent penalty estimated through a different methodology for the Korean War in 1952 and the Vietnam War in 1968.[94]

Lest an ironclad law be spotted here, let it be said that measurement of this sort is not easy and that different techniques can yield different results. One similar analysis has not found such results for 1868 and 1948.[95] In the cases of the elections of 1848, 1868, and 1948, the high shakeup values appearing in

Table 12.2 *Surge and Interactive Realignment in U.S. Presidential Elections, 1836–1964*

	Presidential Candidates[a]		Democratic Vote		Republican Vote[b]	
Year	Democrat	Republican (or Whig)	Surge	Interaction	Surge	Interaction
1836	Van Buren	(3 Whigs)		5.65	*	*
1840	Van Buren	Harrison	-3.61		*	*
1844	Polk	Clay			*	*
1848	Cass	Taylor	-5.59		*	*
1852	Pierce	Scott			*	*
1856	Buchanan	Fremont			*	*
1860	Douglas	Lincoln		2.80	*	*
1864	McClellan	Lincoln		1.65	*	*
1868	Seymour	Grant	+6.09			
1872	Greeley	Grant				
1876	Tilden	Hayes	+1.45		-4.68	
1880	Hancock	Garfield				
1884	Cleveland	Blaine				
1888	Cleveland	Harrison				
1892	Cleveland	Harrison				
1896	Bryan	McKinley			+5.16	
1900	Bryan	McKinley				
1904	Parker	Roosevelt		1.14		
1908	Bryan	Taft				

1912	Wilson	*Taft*				
1916	*Wilson*	Hughes				
1920	*Cox*	Harding		+7.73		−1.77
1924	Davis	*Coolidge*			1.92	
1928	Smith	*Hoover*				
1932	Roosevelt	*Hoover*		−11.33		+16.28
1936	*Roosevelt*	Landon	1.20			
1940	*Roosevelt*	Willkie				
1944	*Roosevelt*	Dewey				
1948	*Truman*	Dewey			1.15	−8.20
1952	*Stevenson*	Eisenhower	1.26	+2.47		
1956	Stevenson	*Eisenhower*				+1.30
1960	Kennedy	*Nixon*		−2.45		
1964	*Johnson*	Goldwater	1.16		2.06	

[a] The candidate of the incumbent party appears in italic type. [b] Values for the Republican Party cannot be calculated before 1868.

Source: Clubb, Flanigan, and Zingale 1980, table 3.1a at 92–93.

Table 12.2 are probably best thought of as suggestive. Perhaps lasting valence judgments did occur. Perhaps the seizure of the Southwest in the 1840s was indeed generally unpopular, given the trouble it brought on. Perhaps the ruling parties in 1868 and 1948 both took permanent hits for their advanced, war-induced positions on civil rights (as the Democrats evidently later did for their advanced albeit non-war-induced position in 1964). But this is speculation.

In one way a striking violation, yet in another way a striking confirmation of the pattern in Table 12.2 is the election of 1816, held in the wake of the War of 1812. Although that election occurred too early to earn a place in mass voting studies, it seems to showcase the idea that wars can bring lasting coalitional change, yet the then-incumbent Democratic-Republican Party reaped a *bonus* in 1816 rather than a penalty. Here is the story. Earlier in 1812, a few months into the war, the Federalist candidate had fallen only one state short of winning that year's presidential election through an able blend of position and valence appeals (the war shouldn't have been fought in the first place; why are the British occupying Detroit?). The Federalists were doing well.[96] But then they dragged their feet on the war effort to the point of near treason, the war closed in a surprising burst of victory and nationalistic enthusiasm, and the discredited Federalists performed dismally in the election of 1816 and never ran a candidate again.[97] They were "the most conspicuous casualty of the War of 1812."[98] A war, in short, can put a party out of business — which is one way to affect coalitional alignments. A similar story involves the Socialist party during World War I. A promising force rivaling the British Labor Party in voter strength as of 1912, the American Socialists opposed their own country's war cause (as did, for example, the Bolsheviks in Russia but *not* the Socialists in France, Britain, or Germany) and as a result hemorrhaged voters, brought on state repression, and were never a serious force again.[99]

World War I, looked at more generally, seems to have affected American voting behavior a good deal.[100] The disastrous defeat suffered by the ruling Democrats in the 1920 election has been underanalyzed. Probably the leading interpretation is a questionable teleological case that the Democrats, that era's natural minority party, *had* to fall from power somehow once the fluky Wilson presidency, the product of an unusual four-way election contest in 1912, was out of the way. But this ignores the landslide Democratic midterm victory of 1910 heralding the Wilson presidency. It ignores the magnitude and durability of the postwar Democratic slide: never otherwise since 1789 has a major American party been bested by consecutive margins of 26, 25, and 17 percent as were the Democrats in 1920, 1924, and 1928.[101] It ignores events. The war itself and its explosive aftermath — strikes, international revolution, the Red Scare, a rocky economy, the League of Nations wrangle — brought a cornucopia of position and valence material for an opposition party to dwell on for a considerable time. And it ignores the corresponding fates of parties or party systems elsewhere in Allied Anglophone countries. In Canada, farmer and labor uprisings in the wake of World War I seem to have permanently broadened that country's party system from two-party to multiparty.[102] In Australia, it is said that the burden associated with managing the war penalized the Labor Party for a quarter century.[103] In Britain, that burden seems to have permanently demoted the Liberal Party from major-party status.[104] It is as if they had been "run over by a bus."[105] It should be no surprise that the American Democrats suffered.[106]

Overall, whatever the precise causal paths may have been, there is a suggestive case on the statistical evidence for the War with Mexico and World War II as electoral levers, a suggestive as well as commonsense case for the Civil War — how could it *not* have made a difference?[107] — and a very good case for the War of 1812 and World War I.

Major Changes in Party Ideologies

A fourth probe into the consequences of wars is made possible by John Gerring's recent work on party ideologies, which is based on a coding of campaign speeches and party platforms of the major American parties from 1828 through 1996.[108] Ideologies are conceived by Gerring to be broader and more basic than issues such as civil rights or than time-specific programs such as the New Deal. In one feature of the study, he looks for hinge-point changes in party ideologies and finds a few (for example, the Democrats' switch to Bryan-style economic populism in the 1890s). The era of the 1810s could not be reached by the study — party platforms were not yet being written then — although perhaps the Democratic-Republicans of that time would be accorded a hinge point following the War of 1812 if they could somehow be coded. That party shifted then to new concerns and a new model of political economy; there was a "liberal [in the classical sense] revision of Republican principles."[109] Also, Gerring does not detect any hinge point associated with the War with Mexico or the Civil War. For my purposes here, I leave the nineteenth century alone. The new issue regimes I have associated with three of that century's hot wars can stand on their own.

Gerring's most interesting and surprising ideological hinge points came in the twentieth century. There were only two. In the mid-1920s, the Republican Party abandoned its century-long stance (in ideological terms, the party is taken to be a continuation of its predecessor, the Whigs) as a party of state building, government activism, reverence for public institutions, and, in

general, authoritative order as a guard against the menaces of disorder, insurrection, and anarchy. The Republicans had been the party of state. Now,
in swept a new emphasis, still abundantly prominent in our own day, on
free-market and anti-statist themes that often flare into populist-style assaults
against Washington, DC.[110] The party's "long-standing and visceral dislike of
big government . . . had its origins in the 1924 and 1928 campaigns."[111] In
Gerring's judgment, this Republican turnaround in the 1920s was "the most
fundamental rethinking of American conservatism since the acceptance of
mass democracy by the New England Federalists."[112]

The Democrats' twentieth-century hinge point came around 1950. Then,
that party shook off its long-standing antimonopoly, anticapitalist, anti–Wall
Street rhetoric well captured in the phrase "the people versus the interests"
that had infused the campaigns of Bryan around 1900 through Wilson, Franklin Roosevelt, and in a last hurrah in 1948, Truman. Out the window went
assaults against capitalism. In swept a new configuration of emphases on civil
rights, social welfare, redistribution, and inclusion. The party "discarded its
abrasive, class-tinged ethos in favor of a *Universalist* perspective — the extension of rights to all aggrieved claimants and a general rhetoric of inclusion." In
general for the Democrats after 1950 or so: "Oppression and injustice were
out; peace, harmony, and community were in. . . . It was a far cry from the
Populist blame game."[113] Since then, the party's appeals to economic populism
have been infrequent as well as unproductive.[114] In effect, an old party theme
switched at that time from dominant to recessive.

The following is speculation. It is not clear why these twentieth-century
hinge points occurred,[115] but the two world wars may have helped them along.
In the first instance, World War I at the hands of a Democratic government in
Washington, DC, brought "an enormous and wholly unprecedented intervention of the federal government in the nation's economic affairs" as the government took over and regulated industries, commandeered plants, allocated a
range of resources, and fixed prices in a pattern of what has been called "war
socialism."[116] Temporary though most of these moves were, it would not be
surprising if they stirred nervousness in the business community, then as now
chiefly Republican, about the implications of central state power. Even more
alarming, it seems, was the revolution in revenue policy. Long-standing tariff
and excise taxes had not troubled the business community, but the new sources
did: "No other single issue aroused as much corporate hostility to the Wilson
administration as did the financing of the war." The wartime tax moves "posed
a long-term threat to the nation's corporations."[117] Among other things, the
new progressive-oriented revenue system "empowered the federal government, as never before, to implement egalitarian ideals."[118] Moreover, a new

towering menace swung into place for Republicans as a by-product of World War I. What is it that American society should be most afraid of? Traditionally for Whigs and Republicans, according to Gerring's analysis, the leading threat to society had been an ensemble of disorder, insurrection, and anarchism (as perhaps now for twenty-first-century Republicans it has become terrorism). But in the wake of World War I, as the Bolshevik regime in the Soviet Union consolidated, international Communism moved into the prime menace niche for Republicans it continued to occupy until around 1990. Here was an entirely new image of state power as threat.[119] All in all, it is understandable that the Republicans shifted ideologically after World War I toward an anti-state stance.

The Democrats' shift around 1950 had a complicated background, but World War II and its aftermath seem to have supplied both a moral jolt and a cognitive jolt. In highlighting the shame of American race relations, the war spurred the Democrats into a new ethic of "rights-based liberalism" that would cascade into multiculturalism in succeeding decades.[120] On the cognitive side, the productiveness of the American economy during World War II proved to be pathbreaking and astounding. The war "quickly and decisively destroyed the economic-maturity thesis [that is, the idea prominent on the left during the Depression era that private capitalism had become obsolete as a productive engine] and, with it, much of the rationale for a highly planned and regulated economy."[121] Also, government experience during the war elevated fiscal policy over the Democrats' traditional "antimonopoly" tonic, which had been more adversarial and intrusive, as an approach to the economy. In addition, in the late 1940s, a dreaded and much theorized-about postwar slump failed to materialize. As during the war, the private economy was humming.[122] It is understandable that the Democrats backed away from their traditional populist-style assaults against capitalism. Lessons seem to have been learned.

Events as Causes

We tend to assume that interests or preferences are the basic building blocks of an analytic political science. That is sensible, yet it risks analysis that is either unhelpfully truistic or unhelpfully abstract. Where do interests or preferences — or the agendas, programs, ideologies, movements, and parties that ordinarily accompany them in the real world of politics — come from? One answer is *events,* of which wars and their aftermaths supply spectacular, although of course not the only, kinds of instances.[123] To take "interests" in the sense of pure economic self-interest, American wars have often generated new configurations for them — for example, the interests of the new citizens of

Texas in the 1840s, the new African American voters of the 1860s, the new textile and chemical industries of the 1810s and 1910s, and the cohorts of veterans always. (A war can also help destroy a configuration of interests, as with slaveholders in the 1860s and the country's liquor industry and German-American infrastructure in the 1910s.) New preferences, whether or not they relate to economic self-interest, are a more complicated topic, but there is little problem discerning them as deposits of American wars. Consider the accentuated nationalism of the mid-1810s, the Northern opposition to a feared runaway Southern slave power in the wake of the War with Mexico, the support for emancipation of slaves spurred by the Civil War, the anti-immigration sentiment of the late 1910s, the thrust toward a sense of gender equality brought by women's participation in World War I, or the apparent cooling toward strike-prone unions but warming toward civil rights for African Americans during World War II.

With both interests and preferences, it is difficult to proceed further without noting that wars can generate new, widely accepted *causal stories*. Such stories supply roadmaps to the achievement of old or new interests or preferences, or else new reasons to adopt new preferences. The new stories derive from the experience of the wars. Consider, for example, a story from the mid-1810s: The best way to shake free of the alarming national vulnerability just experienced is to build a stronger U.S. political economy, and the best route to that is the "American System." From the late 1910s: Immigrants cause destabilizing political trouble. Among farmers after World War I: Government crop supports can cause prosperity. During and after World War II: Expensive scientific research is a key to national strength; racial discrimination at home causes trouble for the United States abroad;[124] Keynesian-style economic management works; a globalist strategy is needed for U.S. defense policy.

Another route to war effects is the engendering of new *organizations* — which often champion new interests or preferences or implement the lessons of new causal stories. Such new units can be directly governmental institutions such as the House and Senate Appropriations Committees, the FBI's General Intelligence Division, the Bureau of the Budget, the Council of Economic Advisors, or the Central Intelligence Agency. They can be units chartered by the government, such as the Second Bank of the United States, or fostered by the government, such as the new universe of trade associations during World War I. New organizations, which, like new statutes, tend toward stickiness, are particularly good at rendering the effects of wars long-lasting. Yet path dependency can apply in the cases of interests, preferences, and causal stories also.[125]

In the realm of primitive building blocks, there is a case for ranking events as the equals of interests and preferences in a seriously explanatory political science.[126] Events—here, wars—can create, shape, crystallize, or institutionalize interests and preferences. Too much seems to be missed by missing this basic fact. There is at least an empirical implication: as a matter of evidence, events are no more problematic than preferences or interests; they can be clocked and studied. There may be a modeling implication. As Robert W. Fogel has shown, it is possible to accommodate events in mathematical models, although the results are complex.[127]

To take events seriously is to aim for longitudinal analysis, but also for comparative analysis. Any specialist of American politics might realize, for example, that most of the country's wars and all of its depressions have been transnational, not just national, events. As a result, cross-national, not just United States–specific, evidence can help to illuminate their causes, characteristics, and effects. Possibly this point is obvious to non-American scholars, but research by Americans about American politics can be insular. In writing this essay, I found the transnational patterns of women winning the vote and certain Allied ruling parties incurring electoral devastation in connection with World War I especially illuminating. I did not come across well-developed comparative literatures on subjects like these. There may be an opening.

Since 2001 the United States has been engaged in a war—or at least warlike circumstances—that could have long-lasting effects. Those might include a durable policy change regarding civil liberties, a new issue regime centering on terrorism, and the Republicans' reversion to their nineteenth-century stance as a state-centered party of order.

Notes

I thank Alan Gerber, Matthew Green, Jacob Hacker, Sonam Henderson, Rogan Kersh, Philip Klinkner, Heinz Kohler, Joseph LaPolombara, Bruce Russett, Abbey Steele, and anonymous reviewers for their helpful comments on this essay, which was originally published in *Perspectives on Politics* 3:3 (September 2005), pp. 473–93. Copyright © 2005 American Political Science Association. Reprinted with the permission of Cambridge University Press.

1. Porter 1994b, 58. Porter's total is thirty-four years as of 1994.

2. Notable recent exceptions to this neglect include Bensel 1990, Sparrow 1996, Klinkner and Smith 1999, Mettler 2002, and Katznelson and Shefter 2002. In the comparative analysis of the effects of wars on state building, Tilly (1975) has of course pioneered.

3. Some work in political science does point to the relative autonomy of sectors of the

American national state, notably Skowronek 1982, but this scholarship does not center on wars.

4. Kingdon 1984.

5. Murphy 1996.

6. In the policy realm, it did help to spur the professionalization of the U.S. Army. See Skowronek 1982, 112–18, 212–16. And it brought the annexation of Puerto Rico and the Philippines and, in a side move, Hawaii. Did the Spanish-American War trigger a new "issue regime" centering on, say, imperialism? Probably not. The American imperialist impulse of that era dates to the early 1890s. It is probably better to see the war as a yield of, or a moment in, an already existent issue regime rather than the cause of a new one.

7. In the instances of several dozen alleged effects, I invite readers to test the soundness of the causal logics by consulting the cited sources, which are referenced in detail. In most cases I have tried to pinpoint short stretches of pages that supply particularly apt documentation.

8. Dray 1964, 19.

9. Ibid., 42–43; Nagel 1961, 582–83.

10. In this analysis, I have skirted one evident ratchet effect of short-term wartime policy moves. In the wake of American wars, military personnel levels and military spending as a share of the federal budget have ordinarily continued on above prewar levels. See Russett 1970, 2–4.

11. Stevenson 2004, 486.

12. Skocpol 2003, chap. 2.

13. See Putnam 2000, 54, 81, 84, 103, 267–76.

14. Rockoff 2000, 647–48; Watts 1987, 278.

15. Bauer, Pool, and Dexter 1963, 13–14; Baxter 1995, chap. 2; Binkley 1962, 101–2.

16. Babcock 1906, 247; Wiltse 1961, 27–28.

17. Wiltse 1961, chap. 3; Baxter 1995, chap. 2.

18. Binkley 1962, 101. See also Schoen 2003, 200; Sylla 2000, 519.

19. Watts 1987, 276.

20. Binkley 1962, 101. The postwar issue terrain is discussed in three parallel chapters on the bank, the tariff, and internal improvements in Babcock 1906, chaps. 13–15.

21. Texas had been annexed just before the war, but it took U.S. military action against Mexico to place the annexation beyond dispute. The rest of the Southwest was a direct prize of the war.

22. That is, all the new territory west of Texas.

23. Potter 1976, 23. See also Foner 1969. It is sometimes argued that the Whigs "played the antislavery card" in the 1840s to steer politics away from economic issues and thus upset the hegemony of the Democrats. See, for example, Riker 1982, chap. 9. But that does not seem to be what happened. David Wilmot, who presented the killer amendment in 1846, was representative of a sizable faction of northern Van Burenite Democrats committed to free-soil doctrine. A generation earlier, another northeastern Democrat had presented the relevant killer antislavery amendment during the brief but intense Missouri controversy.

24. Potter 1976, 17. In general, see Potter 1976, chaps. 1–5; Freehling 1990, chaps. 26–31.

25. Foner 1988, 21, 23. In general, see Bensel 1990.

26. Foner 1988, 1–11, 66–67, 251–61, 444–48.

27. Bauer, Pool, and Dexter 1963, 14–15. See also Sylla 2000, 527; Brownlee 1996, 44–45; Hansen 1990.

28. Brownlee 1996, 44–48. See also Sylla 2000, 527–29; Porter 1994a, 260.

29. North 1966, 25. See also Sylla 2000, 531; Rockoff 2000, 651–52; Porter 1994a, 261.

30. Wander 1982, 25–28, quotation at 27.

31. Sylla 2000, 533; Foner 1988, 21.

32. Ibid.

33. Ibid.

34. Previously, the tariff had not figured as a prominent issue between the mid-1840s and the Civil War.

35. Porter 1994a, 260; Foner 1988, 23.

36. Skocpol 1992, chap. 2; Holcombe 1999.

37. Witte 1985, 79–87, quotation at 87.

38. Brownlee 2000, 1030.

39. Graetz and Shapiro 2005.

40. Brownlee 1985, 173.

41. Brownlee 1996, 60–72, quotation at 71. See also Higgs 1987, chap. 7.

42. Kaplan and Ryley 1994, chap. 5, quotation at 100.

43. Hicks 1960, 57. Eichengreen (1989) does not specifically connect the rise of the trade associations to the 1921 and 1922 enactments (his concern is the later Smoot-Hawley tariff), but he has the groups in place. There is a whiff of corporatism: "The sudden rise to prominence of trade associations was attributable to World War I. The war effort required closer ties between government and industry, but upon attempting to establish them the authorities found it difficult to deal with individual enterprises and requested that associations be formed. If the war occasioned the formation and growth of trade associations, the armistice by no means signaled their demise. Once formed into an association the process of marshalling a constituency was no longer so difficult." A result was "to promote effective representation of industrial interests in Washington" (pp. 4–5).

44. Farrar-Myers, Renka, and Ponder 2000, 1; Wander 1982, 31–35.

45. Kyvig 1996, 218–26, quotation at 224.

46. Ferrell 1985, 188–90, quotation at 189.

47. Kerr 1985, 185. See also Cooper 1990, 307.

48. Kyvig 1996, 226–39, quotation at 234.

49. Keyssar 2000, 214–18, quotation at 216. See also Cooper 1990, 307–8; Wynn 1986, 148–52; Behn 2005.

50. Lewis 2004, plus scattered sources on individual countries. The list for World War I includes neutrals, but there could be spillover effects. As of 1914, women had had the vote in New Zealand, Australia, Finland, Norway, and certain American states.

51. Tichenor 2002, 138–46; LeMay 1987, 70–72.

52. Goldstein 1978, chaps. 4, 5; Ungar 1976, chap. 3.

53. Klein 1990; Higgs 1987, 152–53; Skowronek 1982, 283.

54. Witte 1985, 88–96; Brownlee 1996, 67–72.

55. Leuchtenburg 1969, 66–67.

56. Karl 1983, quotation at 43; Hansen 1991, chap. 2; Olmstead and Rhode 2000, 730; Benedict 1953, chaps. 8–12; Eichengreen 1989, 5.

57. Key 1943; Brown 1956, 863–69; Lee and Passell 1979, 384–86.

58. Wallis 2000, quotation at 73; Murphy 1996; Brownlee 1996, 88–101; Witte 1985, chap. 6; Campbell and Allen 1994.

59. Witte 1985, 124.

60. Wallis 2000, 73.

61. North 1966, 178.

62. Stein 1969, chaps. 8, 9, quotation at 171.

63. Brownlee 2000, 1050. The experience of the war seems to have brought a similar result in Britain: "There must be some doubt if an administrative Keynesian revolution (that is, the adoption of Keynesian goals as well as Keynesian instruments) would have occurred had it not been for the Second World War. . . . The key to the institutionalization of the new paradigm was the shock of war—the decisive factor in forcing the Treasury radically to reappraise its ideas on economic policy." Oliver and Pemberton 2004, 423–24.

64. Patterson 1972, 306.

65. Lee 1966, chaps. 1–3; Amenta and Skocpol 1988, 114–15; Young 1956, 63–67; Sparrow 1996, chap. 3; Wynn 1996, 470. Spirited controversy over the Taft-Hartley Act carried into 1949 but then died down as the Democrats retreated. The question of whether it had been wise to curb the unions proved to be unpromising material for a long-lasting new issue regime, just as continuing opposition to the principles of the Employment Act of 1946 was unpromising terrain for the Republicans. These matters were largely settled.

66. Keyssar 2000, 244–55, quotation at 244. See also Klinkner and Smith 1999, chap. 6.

67. Smith 1990, 34.

68. Ibid., 1–3, 34–52; Polsby 1984, 35–55.

69. Green and Rosenthal 1963, chap. 1; Balogh 1991, chap. 2.

70. Wander 1982, 35–38; Rosenbloom 2001; Brazier 1996; Davidson 1990. The term-limit restriction on presidents was the sixth constitutional amendment evidently stimulated by war conditions. A seventh came with the Twenty-Sixth Amendment providing for teenage voting as the Vietnam War wound down. Little has been written about the Twenty-Second Amendment. One safe conclusion seems to be the following: in the 1940s, President Roosevelt would very likely not have become a third- and fourth-term president absent the imminence of war in 1940 and its continuation in 1944. In that case, no term-limiting drive would have arisen. On the elections of 1940 and 1944, see Divine 1974, chaps. 1–4.

71. Yergin 1977, chap. 8, quotation at 193; Huntington 1964, 429–33.

72. Perrett 1989, 439. See also Olson 1974, chaps. 1–3.

73. Antilynching was a legislative cause of the 1930s, although the White House and the leadership of the Democratic Party took little interest, and the drive failed.

74. Klinkner and Smith 1999, chaps. 6, 7, quotation at 200; Keyssar 2000, 244–53; Hart 2004; Collins 2002.

75. Thomas 1975, 20–22, quotation at 20; Patterson 1972, 320–26. In 1943, "for the first time in over fifty years, a federal aid to education bill was debated and acted upon in the United States Senate" (Munger and Fenno 1962, 8; see also 7–10, 16). Bills had been introduced and won committee assent in previous Congresses, but 1943 brought an attention breakthrough.

76. Starr 1982, 280–81; Hirshfield 1970, chap. 5; Derickson 1994, 1340–42; Hacker 2002, 217, 223; Derthick 1979, 317–19.

77. Davies 1966, xi–xiv, quotation at xiii; Patterson 1972, 315–20; Keith 1973, 13–14, chap. 2.

78. On the Fair Deal in general, see Neustadt 1954.

79. The New Deal era of the 1930s had plenty of issues or causes — relief, recovery, social security, labor-management relations, antimonopoly, banking reform, regulation of various industries, the minimum wage, tariff reduction, fair trade laws, mortgage insurance, reforming the Supreme Court, the TVA, rural electrification, agricultural crop supports. But civil rights (aside from the antilynching cause), federal aid to education, and national health insurance were not on the list, and public housing was not high ranked.

80. Deudney 1995.

81. Keyssar 2000, 277–81.

82. Fearon 1991; Bunzl 2004.

83. Kornblith 2003.

84. Steinmo 1993.

85. Yamagishi 2003; Dryzek and Goodin 1986.

86. Whittington 1999, 93–112.

87. Brownlee 1985; 1996.

88. Tichenor 2002.

89. Exclusion of East Asians beginning in the 1880s has been the other major constraint placed on immigration during American history.

90. On position and valence issues, see Stokes 1966.

91. Clubb, Flanigan, and Zingale 1980, chap. 3. See also the discussion in Mayhew 2002, 44–50.

92. Clubb, Flanigan, and Zingale 1980, table 3.1a at 92–93.

93. This means Democrats and Whigs back then. In 1836 the Democrats refashioned their regional base in nominating Martin Van Buren, a northerner. His party predecessor, Andrew Jackson, a southerner, had run in the three preceding elections, losing once and winning twice.

94. Bartels and Zaller 2001, 16. This is a one-shot penalty for the incumbent party, not a lasting penalty.

95. See Bartels 1998, 313–17, which covers the twenty-seven elections from 1868 through 1972. Still, the Bartels study ranks two war-impacted elections among the top four in long-term realigning consequences — the contests of 1920 after World War I (ranked third) and of 1972 as the Vietnam War wound down (ranked fourth). Ranked first and second are the elections of 1932 and 1880, the latter evidently owing to delayed coalitional changes associated with the end of Reconstrucion.

96. Risjord 1971.

97. Binkley 1962, 94–97; Watts 1987, 282.

98. Turner 1971, 299.

99. Lipset and Marks 2000, 184–92, 244–60; Foner 1984, 60, 71–72.

100. Clubb, Flanigan, and Zingale 1980, 92–93; Bartels 1998, 315.

101. The 1920s is often seen as a replay or continuation of the McKinley era. President McKinley defeated the Democratic candidate in 1896 and 1900 by margins of 4 percent and 6 percent.

102. Creighton 1959, 216–17; McNaught 1970, 230–31.

103. MacIntyre 1986, 190.

104. Butler and Stokes 1974, 172–74; Wilson 1966. Another causal account goes: "Between 1914 and 1921 trade-union membership doubled and between 1918 and 1924 Labour displaced the Liberals as the largest anti-Conservative party, as a consequence of the Asquith-Lloyd George split [that is, the war-induced fracture of the ruling Liberal party], the widening of the franchise in 1918, and the heightened class consciousness of British workers—all factors that could be attributed to the war." Stevenson 2004, 440.

105. Wilson 1966, 18.

106. The costs of World War I mounted far higher for, especially, Britain than for the United States. Still, even leaving aside the U.S. postwar turmoil of 1919–20, the war itself was not a minor undertaking for this country. It brought a government-directed economy, the country's "first real taste of truly large-scale government spending," restrictions on civil liberties more serious than anything experienced since September 2001, repression approaching devastation of German-American culture, five million participants in the armed forces, two million troops (42 divisions) deployed in France, 114,000 war deaths (many through disease), and over 200,000 military wounded. See Cooper 1990, 279–80, 288–91, 297–305, quotation at 291; Stevenson 2004, 405, 442; Luebke 1974. Note also that World War I could affect even resolute neutrals through spillover effects. Swedish politics seems to have been revolutionized in 1918 as the fall of Germany's monarchy sent a democratizing impulse across the Baltic. See Berman 1998, chap. 5.

107. It is difficult to analyze electoral continuity in the 1860s and 1870s, given the Democratic party schism in the 1860 election, the wartime subtraction of the South from the electoral universe, the staggered readmission of the Southern states, and the various moves enfranchising blacks and disfranchising southern whites.

108. Gerring 1998.

109. Watts 1987, 281–82.

110. Gerring 1998, 15–16, chaps. 3, 4.

111. Ibid., 140.

112. Ibid., 158.

113. Ibid., 15–18, chaps. 6, 7, quotations at 17, 18 (italics in original), 247.

114. Ibid., 235, 245–50.

115. Ibid., 157–58, 250–53, 274–75, for Gerring's own speculation on the matter.

116. Higgs 1987, chap. 7, quotation at 123. See also Gerring 1998, 157.

117. One of the most detested moves, an excess-profits tax, was only temporary, but a precedent was set.

118. Brownlee 1996, 63.

119. Gerring 1998, 152–55.

120. See, for example, Brinkley 1995, 170.

121. Ibid., 171.

122. Higgs 1999, 606.

123. On the idea of wars creating interests, see Wood 2000.

124. Hart 2004.

125. As instances of causal stories, consider the lessons drawn from Munich and Pearl Harbor that were carried forward from World War II.

126. An elaboration of this argument appears in Chapter 13 of this book.

127. Fogel 1992.

References

Amenta, Edwin, and Theda Skocpol. 1988. Redefining the New Deal: World War II and the development of social provision in the United States. In *The politics of social policy in the United States,* ed. Margaret Weir, Ann Shola Orloff, and Theda Skocpol, 81–122. Princeton: Princeton University Press.

Babcock, Kendric Charles. 1906. *The rise of American nationality, 1811–1819.* New York: Harper and Brothers.

Balogh, Brian. 1991. *Chain reaction: Expert debate and public participation in American commercial nuclear power, 1945–1975.* New York: Cambridge University Press.

Bartels, Larry M. 1998. Electoral continuity and change, 1868–1996. *Electoral Studies* 17 (3): 301–26.

Bartels, Larry M., and John Zaller. 2001. Presidential vote models: A recount. *PS: Political Science and Politics* 34 (1): 9–20.

Bauer, Raymond A., Ithiel de Sola Pool, and Lewis Anthony Dexter. 1963. *American business and public policy: The politics of foreign trade.* New York: Atherton.

Baxter, Maurice G. 1995. *Henry Clay and the American system.* Lexington: University Press of Kentucky.

Behn, Beth A. 2005. Woodrow Wilson's conversion experience: The president, woman suffrage, and the extent of executive influence. Paper presented at the annual conference of the Midwest Political Science Association, Chicago, April 7–10.

Benedict, Murray R. 1953. *Farm policies of the United States, 1790–1950.* New York: Twentieth Century Fund.

Bensel, Richard Franklin. 1990. *Yankee leviathan: The origins of central state authority in America, 1859–1877.* New York: Cambridge University Press.

Berman, Sheri. 1998. *The social democratic moment: Ideas and politics in the making of interwar Europe.* Cambridge: Harvard University Press.

Binkley, Wilfred E. 1962. *American political parties: Their natural history.* 4th ed. New York: Alfred E. Knopf.

Brazier, James E. 1996. An anti–New Dealer legacy: The administrative procedure act. *Journal of Policy History* 8 (2): 206–26.

Brinkley, Alan. 1995. *The end of reform: New Deal liberalism in recession and war.* New York: Alfred A. Knopf.

Brown, E. Cary. 1956. Fiscal policy in the 'thirties: A reappraisal. *American Economic Review* 46 (5): 857–79.

Brownlee, W. Elliot. 1985. Woodrow Wilson and financing the modern state: The Revenue Act of 1916. *Proceedings of the American Philosophical Society* 129 (2): 173–210.

———. 1996. Tax regimes, national crises, and state-building in America. In *Funding the modern American state, 1941–1995*, ed. Brownlee, 37–104. New York: Cambridge University Press.

———. 2000. The public sector. In *The Cambridge economic history of the United States,* vol. 3, *The twentieth century,* ed. Stanley L. Engerman and Robert E. Gallman, 1013–60. New York: Cambridge University Press.

Bunzl, Martin. 2004. Counterfactual history: A user's guide. *American Historical Review* 109 (3): 845–58.

Butler, David, and Donald Stokes. 1974. *Political change in Britain: The evolution of electoral choice.* London: Macmillan.

Campbell, John L., and Michael Patrick Allen. 1994. The political economy of revenue extraction in the modern state: A time-series analysis of U.S. income taxes, 1916–1986. *Social Forces* 72 (3): 632–69.

Clubb, Jerome M., William H. Flanigan, and Nancy H. Zingale. 1980. *Partisan realignment: Voters, parties, and government in American history.* Beverly Hills: Sage.

Collins, William J. 2002. The political economy of state-level fair employment laws, 1940–1964. *Explorations in Economic History* 40 (1): 24–51.

Cooper, John Milton, Jr. 1990. *Pivotal decades: The United States, 1900–1920.* New York: W. W. Norton.

Creighton, Donald. 1959. *The story of Canada.* Toronto: Faber and Faber.

Davidson, Roger H. 1990. The advent of the modern Congress: The Legislative Reorganization Act of 1946. *Legislative Studies Quarterly* 15 (3): 357–73.

Davies, Richard O. 1966. *Housing reform during the Truman administration.* Columbia: University of Missouri Press.

Derickson, Alan. 1994. Health security for all? Social unionism and universal health insurance, 1935–1958. *Journal of American History* 80 (4): 1333–56.

Derthick, Martha. 1979. *Policymaking for Social Security.* Washington, DC: Brookings.

Deudney, Daniel H. 1995. The Philadelphian system: Sovereignty, arms control, and balance of power in the American states-union, circa 1787–1861. *International Organization* 49 (2): 191–228.

Divine, Robert A. 1974. *Foreign policy and U.S. presidential elections, 1940–1948.* New York: New Viewpoints.

Dray, William H. 1964. *Philosophy of history.* Englewood Cliffs, NJ: Prentice-Hall.

Dryzek, John, and Robert E. Goodin. 1986. Risk-sharing and social justice: The motivational foundations of the post-war welfare state. *British Journal of Political Science* 16 (1): 1–34.

Eichengreen, Barry. 1989. The political economy of the Smoot-Hawley tariff. *Research in Economic History* 12:1–43.

Farrar-Myers, Victoria A., Russell Renka, and Daniel Ponder. 2000. Institutionalization in a critical period: Presidency, Congress, and the development of the executive budget. Paper presented at the annual conference of the American Political Science Association, Washington, DC.

Fearon, James D. 1991. Counterfactuals and hypothesis testing in political science. *World Politics* 43 (2): 169–95.

Ferrell, Robert H. 1985. *Woodrow Wilson and World War I, 1917–1921*. New York: Harper and Row.

Fogel, Robert W. 1992. Problems in modeling complex dynamic interactions: The political realignment of the 1850s. *Economics and Politics* 4 (3): 215–54.

Foner, Eric. 1969. The Wilmot Proviso revisited. *Journal of American History* 56 (2): 262–79.

———. 1984. Why is there no socialism in the United States? *History Workshop* 17 (1): 57–80.

———. 1988. *Reconstruction: America's unfinished revolution, 1863–1877*. New York: Harper and Row.

Freehling, William W. 1990. *The road to disunion*, vol. 1, *Secessionists at bay, 1776–1854*. New York: Oxford University Press.

Gerring, John. 1998. *Party ideologies in America, 1828–1996*. New York: Cambridge University Press.

Goldstein, Robert J. 1978. *Political repression in modern America: From 1870 to the present*. New York: Schenkman.

Graetz, Michael, and Ian Shapiro. 2005. *Death by a thousand cuts: The fight over taxing inherited wealth*. Princeton: Princeton University Press.

Green, Harold P., and Alan Rosenthal. 1963. *Government of the atom: The integration of powers*. New York: Atherton.

Hacker, Jacob S. 2002. *The divided welfare state: The battle over public and private social benefits in the United States*. New York: Cambridge University Press.

Hansen, John Mark. 1990. Taxation and the political economy of the tariff. *International Organization* 44 (4): 527–51.

———. 1991. *Gaining access: Congress and the farm lobby, 1919–1981*. Chicago: University of Chicago Press.

Hart, Justin. 2004. Making democracy safe for the world: Race, propaganda, and the transformation of U.S. foreign policy during World War II. *Pacific Historical Review* 73 (1): 49–84.

Hicks, John D. 1960. *Republican ascendancy, 1921–1933*. New York: Harper and Row.

Higgs, Robert. 1987. *Crisis and leviathan: Critical episodes in the growth of American government*. New York: Oxford University Press.

———. 1999. From central planning to the market: The American transition, 1945–1947. *Journal of Economic History* 59 (3): 600–623.

Hirshfield, Daniel S. 1970. *The lost reform: The campaign for compulsory health insurance in the United States from 1932–1943*. Cambridge: Harvard University Press.

Holcombe, Randall G. 1999. Veteran interests and the transition to government growth: 1870–1915. *Public Choice* 99 (3–4): 311–26.

Huntington, Samuel P. 1964. *The soldier and the state.* New York: Random House.

Kaplan, Edward S., and Thomas W. Ryley. 1994. *Prelude to trade wars: American tariff policy, 1890–1922.* Westport, CT: Greenwood.

Karl, Barry D. 1983. *The uneasy state: The United States from 1915 to 1945.* Chicago: University of Chicago Press.

Katznelson, Ira, and Martin Shefter, eds. 2002. *Shaped by trade and war: International influences on American political development.* Princeton: Princeton University Press.

Keith, Nathaniel S. 1973. *Politics and the housing crisis since 1930.* New York: Universe Books.

Kerr, K. Austin. 1985. *Organized for prohibition: A new history of the Anti-Saloon League.* New Haven: Yale University Press.

Key, V. O., Jr. 1943. The veterans and the House of Representatives: A study of a pressure group and electoral mortality. *Journal of Politics* 5 (1): 27–40.

Keyssar, Alexander. 2000. *The right to vote: The contested history of democracy in the United States.* New York: Basic Books.

Kingdon, John W. 1984. *Agendas, alternatives, and public policies.* Boston: Little, Brown.

Klein, Maury. 1990. Competition and regulation: The railroad model. *Business History Review* 64 (2): 311–25.

Klinkner, Philip A., and Rogers M. Smith. 1999. *The unsteady march: The rise and decline of racial equality in America.* Chicago: University of Chicago Press.

Kornblith, Gary J. 2003. Rethinking the coming of the Civil War: A counterfactual exercise. *Journal of American History* 90 (1): 76–105.

Kyvig, David E. 1996. *Explicit and authentic acts: Amending the U.S. Constitution, 1776–1995.* Lawrence: University Press of Kansas.

Lee, R. Alton. 1966. *Truman and Taft-Hartley: A question of mandate.* Lexington: University of Kentucky Press.

Lee, Susan, and Peter Passell. 1979. *A new economic view of American history.* New York: W. W. Norton.

LeMay, Michael C. 1987. *From open door to Dutch door: An analysis of U.S. immigration policy since 1820.* New York: Praeger.

Leuchtenburg, William E. 1969. The impact of the war on the American political economy. In *The impact of World War I,* ed. Arthur S. Link, 57–70. New York: Harper and Row.

Lewis, Jone Johnson. 2004. Winning the vote: International woman suffrage timeline. http://womenshistory.about.com/library/weekly/aa091600a.htm.

Lipset, Seymour Martin, and Gary Marks. 2000. *It didn't happen here: Why socialism failed in the United States.* New York: W. W. Norton.

Luebke, Frederick C. 1974. *Bonds of loyalty: German-Americans and World War I.* De Kalb: Northern Illinois University Press.

MacIntyre, Stuart. 1986. *The Oxford history of Australia,* vol. 4, *1901–1942: The succeeding age.* New York: Oxford University Press.

Mayhew, David R. 2002. *Electoral realignments: A critique of an American genre.* New Haven: Yale University Press.

McNaught, Kenneth. 1970. *The history of Canada.* New York: Praeger.

Mettler, Suzanne. 2002. Bringing the state back in to civic engagement: Policy feedback effects of the G.I. Bill for World War II veterans. *American Political Science Review* 96 (2): 351–65.

Munger, Frank J., and Richard F. Fenno Jr. 1962. *National politics and federal aid to education.* Syracuse: Syracuse University Press.

Murphy, Kevin. 1996. Child of war: The federal income withholding tax. *Mid-America* 78 (2): 203–29.

Nagel, Ernest. 1961. *The structure of science: Problems in the logic of scientific explanation.* New York: Harcourt, Brace, and World.

Neustadt, Richard E. 1954. Congress and the Fair Deal: A legislative balance sheet. In *Public policy,* vol. 5, ed. Carl J. Friedrich and John Kenneth Galbraith, 351–81. Cambridge: Harvard Graduate School of Public Administration.

North, Douglass C. 1966. *Growth and welfare in the American past: A new economic history.* Englewood Cliffs, NJ: Prentice-Hall.

Oliver, Michael J., and Hugh Pemberton. 2004. Learning and change in 20th-century British economic policy. *Governance* 17 (3): 415–41.

Olmstead, Alan L., and Paul W. Rhode. 2000. The transformation of northern agriculture, 1910–1990. In *The Cambridge economic history of the United States,* vol. 3, *The twentieth century,* ed. Stanley L. Engerman and Robert E. Gallman, 693–742. New York: Cambridge University Press.

Olson, Keith W. 1974. *The G.I. Bill, the veterans, and the colleges.* Lexington: University Press of Kentucky.

Patterson, James T. 1972. *Mr. Republican: A biography of Robert A. Taft.* Boston: Houghton Mifflin.

Perrett, Geoffrey. 1989. *A country made by war: From the Revolution to Vietnam — The story of America's rise to power.* New York: Random House.

Polsby, Nelson W. 1984. *Political innovation in America: The politics of policy initiation.* New Haven: Yale University Press.

Porter, Bruce D. 1994a. *War and the rise of the state: The military foundations of modern politics.* New York: Free Press.

———. 1994b. The warfare state. *American Heritage* 45 (4): 57–69.

Potter, David M. 1976. *The impending crisis, 1848–1861.* New York: Harper and Row.

Putnam, Robert D. 2000. *Bowling alone: The collapse and revival of American community.* New York: Simon and Schuster.

Riker, William H. 1982. *Liberalism against populism: A confrontation between the theory of democracy and the theory of social choice.* Prospect Heights, IL: Waveland.

Risjord, Norman K. 1971. Election of 1812. In *History of American presidential elections, 1789–1968,* vol. 1, ed. Arthur M. Schlesinger Jr., 249–72. New York: McGraw-Hill.

Rockoff, Hugh. 2000. Banking and finance, 1789–1914. In *The Cambridge economic history of the United States,* vol. 2, *The long nineteenth century,* ed. Stanley L. Engerman and Robert E. Gallman, 643–84. New York: Cambridge University Press.

Rosenbloom, David H. 2001. "Whose bureaucracy is this, anyway?" Congress' 1946 answer. *PS: Political Science and Politics* 34 (4): 773–77.

Russett, Bruce M. 1970. *What price vigilance? The burdens of national defense.* New Haven: Yale University Press.

Schoen, Brian. 2003. Calculating the price of union: Republican economic nationalism and the origins of Southern sectionalism, 1790–1828. *Journal of the Early Republic* 23 (2): 173–206.

Skocpol, Theda. 1992. *Protecting soldiers and mothers: The political origins of social policy in the United States.* Cambridge: Harvard University Press.

———. 2003. *Diminished democracy: From membership to management in American civic life.* Norman: University of Oklahoma Press.

Skowronek, Stephen S. 1982. *Building a new American state: The expansion of national administrative capacities, 1877–1920.* New York: Cambridge University Press.

Smith, Bruce L. R. 1990. *American science policy since World War II.* Washington, DC: Brookings.

Sparrow, Bartholomew. 1996. *From the outside in: World War II and the American state.* Princeton: Princeton University Press.

Starr, Paul. 1982. *The social transformation of American medicine.* New York: Basic Books.

Stein, Herbert. 1969. *The fiscal revolution in America.* Chicago: University of Chicago Press.

Steinmo, Sven. 1993. *Taxation and democracy: Swedish, British and American approaches to financing the modern state.* New Haven: Yale University Press.

Stevenson, David. 2004. *Cataclysm: The First World War as political tragedy.* New York: Basic Books.

Stokes, Donald E. 1966. Spatial models of party competition. In *Elections and the political order,* ed. Angus Campbell, Philip E. Converse, Warren E. Miller, and Donald E. Stokes, 161–79. New York: Wiley.

Sylla, Richard. 2000. Experimental federalism: The economics of American government, 1789–1914. In *The Cambridge economic history of the United States,* vol. 2, *The long nineteenth century,* ed. Stanley L. Engerman and Robert E. Gallman, 483–541. New York: Cambridge University Press.

Thomas, Norman C. 1975. *Education in national politics.* New York: David McKay.

Tichenor, Daniel J. 2002. *Dividing lines: The politics of immigration control in America.* Princeton: Princeton University Press.

Tilly, Charles, ed. 1975. *The formation of national states in Western Europe.* Princeton: Princeton University Press.

Turner, Lynn W. 1971. Elections of 1816 and 1820. In *History of American presidential elections, 1789–1968,* vol. 1, ed. Arthur M. Schlesinger Jr., 299–321. New York: McGraw-Hill.

Ungar, Sanford J. 1976. *FBI: An uncensored look behind the walls.* Boston: Little, Brown.

Wallis, John Joseph. 2000. American government finance in the long run: 1790 to 1990. *Journal of Economic Perspectives* 14 (1): 61–82.

Wander, W. Thomas. 1982. Patterns of change in the congressional budget process, 1865–1974. *Congress and the Presidency* 9 (2): 23–49.

Watts, Steven. 1987. *The republic reborn: War and the making of liberal America, 1790–1820.* Baltimore, MD: Johns Hopkins University Press.

Whittington, Keith E. 1999. *Constitutional construction: Divided powers and constitutional meaning.* Cambridge: Harvard University Press.

Wilson, Trevor. 1966. *The downfall of the Liberal Party, 1914–1935.* London: Collins.

Wiltse, Charles M. 1961. *The new nation, 1800–1845.* New York: Hill and Wang.

Witte, John F. 1985. *The politics and development of the federal income tax.* Madison: University of Wisconsin Press.

Wood, Elisabeth Jean. 2000. *Forging democracy from below: Insurgent transitions in South Africa and El Salvador.* New York: Cambridge University Press.

Wynn, Neil A. 1986. *From progressivism to prosperity: World War I and American society.* New York: Holmes and Meier.

———. 1996. The "Good War": The Second World War and postwar American society. *Journal of Contemporary History* 31 (3): 463–82.

Yamagishi, Takakazu. 2003. War and the health of the state: The critical war years for national health insurance in twentieth-century Japan and the United States. Paper presented at the annual conference of the American Political Science Association, Philadelphia.

Yergin, Daniel. 1977. *Shattered peace: The origins of the cold war and the national security state.* Boston: Houghton Mifflin.

Young, Ronald. 1956. *Congressional politics in the Second World War.* New York: Columbia University Press.

13

Events as Causes
The Case of American Politics

In explaining American politics, political scientists tend to follow a path that is normal for social scientists: We reach for causes that are seen to be basic, underlying, or long-term rather than ones that are proximate, contingent, or short-term. Institutions, social forces, and enduring incentives tend to win attention as factors. Thus a good deal of scholarship assigns causal status to such phenomena as economic self-interest,[1] the interests of social classes,[2] party identification,[3] electoral realignment coalitions,[4] the American liberal tradition,[5] long-lasting party ideologies,[6] social capital,[7] political decisions that are said to attain a kind of constitutional standing,[8] congressional folkways,[9] fixed institutions such as congressional rules,[10] long-lived cleavage patterns in congressional roll-call voting,[11] the American separation-of-powers system,[12] political movements that take a long time gaining momentum,[13] political party platforms that carry through many years,[14] and political "moods" that exhibit considerable durability.[15]

The Significance of Events

It would be a foolish political science that did not pursue causal factors like these. Yet as a collective explanatory enterprise, the profession may be underinvesting in factors that are proximate, short-term, or contingent. I make a case here for *events* as such explanatory factors. It may be answered that coverage of this sort of thing should be left to historians (of whom some, although not all, have emphasized short-term or contingent factors; imagine a dimension with A. J. P. Taylor at the short-term or contingent pole, Lewis Namier at the long-term or underlying pole, and Fernand Braudel making an appearance at both poles). Yet arguably the first aim of all of us should be to provide satisfying causal accounts, regardless of our disciplinary locations or their boundaries.

Let me offer an example of blinkered explanation brought on by a focus on underlying or long-term factors. In 1940, Paul F. Lazarsfeld and his associates undertook their voter research that emanated in *The People's Choice*, employing a pioneering panel study that ran from May through November of that year.[16] To be probed were such matters as "cross pressures," an "index of political predisposition," a "reinforcement effect," "socio-economic status" (or "SES"), and "intentions at variance with their [the voters'] social environments" — that is, a variety of embellishments on an underlying theme of social determinism.[17] Then in May of that year the Nazis invaded France, in June they defeated France, and in September they came close to defeating Britain. Here was a chance for the Columbia University researchers to tear up their interview schedule. They could have accommodated head-on one of the richest environments of politically relevant events imaginable. Americans, so far as one can tell from casual evidence (consider the lore about Edward R. Murrow's radio reports) and single-shot commercial surveys, were riveted by the European disasters and their implications for this country. How do events of this nature and magnitude play into an election campaign?

Undeterred, the Columbia researchers carried on to their social-deterministic conclusion, for which *The People's Choice* is well-known. So far as one can tell, they did not ask any direct questions about voter reactions to these ominous events, the government's handling of them, or the candidates' capacity to handle them.[18] These were of course first-rate, serious scholars. They do present an event timeline for the 1940 campaign season, and they offer in passing some fascinating if scanty material: Voters apparently surged to President Roosevelt that year *during June when France was falling* — "mainly on the ground that the European crisis necessitated the continuance of an experienced administration in Washington."[19] But this result is presented as an aside rather than a fundamental finding, and it would probably be hard to find anyone who remembers it. Events are again off-message in the Columbia team's work on the 1948 election, *Voting*, where the authors do not take seriously, for example, the Berlin airlift.[20] That gripping exercise of American triumphalism, which I can recall myself from newsreels showing the big planes taking off and landing, extended through the last months of the 1948 campaign when Truman was apparently gaining his edge. Did it make a difference? In political science, the question is understudied. Rare is the account of the 1948 election that does it justice.[21]

Possibly events have been making a better showing in more recent scholarship than they once did. Wars, for example, have come to figure as dummy variables in time-series analyses of voting behavior.[22] Events during election campaigns and as determinants of public opinion have received attention.[23] Droughts and even shark attacks are said to move voters.[24] Crises and disasters have been broached as motors of policy change.[25] Even so, the case that events are underinvestigated still seems valid.

A conceptual discussion is in order. What is an "event"? To use a very commonsensical formulation, an event is something that happens. Most events are irrelevant to the discussion here. In principle, the relevant events are ones that can change a political context by generating a new sense among publics or policy makers about what is important in public affairs, what problems need to be solved, what relevant causal stories are credible, or simply what should be valued or done. I do not see any clear criterion for deciding how elongated an "event" should be allowed to be. Here, I would like to accommodate, at least in principle, both quick happenings such as assassinations or earthquakes as well as lengthier ones such as wars or depressions that are perhaps better thought of as sets of events.

I will dwell here on "chance events" — that is, ones that are contingent in the sense of being unpredicted or unpredictable.[26] Not all events are chance events. The sun comes up every morning. American national elections, which are events, have been held regularly every two years since 1788. Elections are the obvious exhibit for the case that political scientists *do* study events — over and over again. Although American elections — at least in the sense that they do in fact regularly occur — are not chance events, they bear an interesting relation to chance events. They can take on an aspect of chance events in the sense that their results are often unexpected, even sometimes dramatically unexpected, and this can be interesting and important. For one thing, voters may correct later for an electoral "surprise."[27] For another, it is a good bet that an astonishing result like the Republican takeover of the Senate in 1980 can give a new incumbent party more temporary policy leeway than it might otherwise enjoy based on the bare congressional membership numbers. But even when an election result is more or less foreseen (thus taking the election out of the realm of chance events), voters are of course free to use the occasion of an election to channel their reactions to *earlier* chance events, as did, to cite a classic instance, voters weary of the course of the Great Depression in 1932.

Chance, contingency, and unexpectedness are not unproblematic ideas. Unexpected by whom? The catastrophic earthquakes that roiled the politics of Nicaragua in 1972 and Mexico in 1985 were a surprise to everybody. The attack on Pearl Harbor in 1941 was unexpected by Americans, but not by the Japanese government. Audience needs to be considered. For the most part, I deal here with happenings that came along and surprised the U.S. government, this country's political elite, and most of American society. This is ordinarily the profile of, for example, strikes, domestic violence, and economic depressions. They are unexpected. The attacks on Pearl Harbor in 1941 and the Pentagon and World Trade Center in 2001 were, from the American vantage point, unexpected. But "events" in the broad definition used here are of course themselves caused, like everything else, and the U.S. government can in principle itself be a cause as it was in the invasions of Mexico in 1846 and Iraq in 2003. I want to include American wars as events (or sets of events). In what sense are wars "chance events"? For one thing, all of them probably come as something of a jolt to American society even if the government initiates them. More important, wars have their own dynamics: As they go on, regardless of how they started, they are capable of generating unexpected new problems (as in the uncontrolled looting in Iraq in 2003), new causal stories (as in the idea that George W. Bush and Tony Blair lied their way into the Iraq war), and new preferences (as in the new American antipathy toward the French and vice versa). It is true that other kinds of government action might in principle qualify as "events" as defined here. The passage of the Kansas-Nebraska Act of 1854, for example, was a surprise development (given the expectations of, say, a year earlier) that roiled American society through engendering a new mix of perceived problems, causal stories, and preferences: It smelled of a southern slave-power conspiracy.[28] It rivaled Nicaragua's and Mexico's earthquakes in its political consequences. But in the body of this essay I steer clear of government-induced "events" with the complex and partial exception of wars.

What is a "cause"? In political affairs, a search for conditions that are anything like both necessary and sufficient, as in water boiling at 212 degrees, is probably fruitless. Here, I use the explanatory customs of historians as my chief guide to causation. In principle, the sense of "cause" I try to employ is: An X (that, is a politically relevant event) was a cause of a Y (any of a range of specified states of affairs) if it was a major contributory cause, and at least a necessary cause, of Y happening at least during the time frame it did and possibly at all. These requirements are perhaps modest in the sense that they allow ample room for additional causes. Even if an event was an important cause of a Y, a range of other things, ordinarily some of them "underlying," may have figured importantly or even necessarily in the explanatory mix too.

But these requirements are not trivial: "Necessary" means exactly that,[29] and "major contributory" follows the conventional historians' practice of assigning relative importance to causes.[30]

In a statistical sense, no difficulty seems to arise, at least in principle, in juxtaposing events as causes to "underlying" factors as causes. The economic historian Robert W. Fogel, for example, has presented an interesting model mixing the two kinds of factors.[31] In a philosophical sense, these are of course deep waters. But in a practical sense, it is hard to see how the blend can be avoided. Causal factors that are obviously promising can range from the deeply underlying to the starkly proximate. Take the Spanish election of spring 2004 won by the Socialists. No doubt party identifications tracing back generations and regional antipathies tracing back centuries need to be adduced to explain this electoral pattern and outcome, as do many other considerations, but one factor has to be the election-eve demolition of the Madrid trains by Islamic fundamentalists. For another example, deep-seated party and ideological loyalties were probably fierce in the American North in the mid-1860s, but, so far as one can tell, absent General Sherman's victory in Atlanta in September 1864, the presidential election of November of that year would have gone to the Democrat George B. McClellan and possibly been followed by an immediate armistice that preserved southern slavery. "The impact of this event [the capture of Atlanta] cannot be exaggerated."[32]

Below I offer a discussion of these matters that is suggestive and I hope thought-provoking even if it is selective and short of clinchingly systematic. It is drawn from American history back through 1789. For the most part, it centers on complex and extended events rather than simple and brief ones — the chief exhibits being entire wars (rather than, say, individual battles) and sometimes prolonged economic recessions or depressions. This is not to deny the importance of jolts like the battle of Atlanta. But a jolt-centered treatment covering two centuries might end up unduly anecdotal, at least on current readily available evidence. With larger events it is possible to aim for at least an ingredient of systematicness. Also, in the realm of *effects* I emphasize long-lasting rather than short-term ones (although not to the complete exclusion of the latter). This is on grounds of importance but also, in the case of wars, nonobviousness: It is a dog-bites-man story, for example, that wars cause the raising of troops and the short-term expenditure of immense money.

I pay particular attention here to *long-term electoral effects* (that is, not just the outcomes of single elections) and *long-term policy effects* (that is, ones that have lasted for decades or generations). But I do not want to repeat wholesale certain material appearing in the preceding chapter, "Wars and American Politics." Let me incorporate here by reference the bulk of that chapter's discussion of the pattern of U.S. electoral history reported by Jerome M. Clubb, William H. Flanigan, and Nancy H. Zingale.[33] For the statistical gist of those authors' work, see Chapter 12, Table 12.2. Let me incorporate also that chapter's discussion of the effects of one kind of event — the country's major free-standing wars — on elections. In my judgment, those effects have been huge, but I have presented that argument already.

Long-Term Electoral Effects

In the Clubb, Flanigan, and Zingale calculations, seven presidential elections since the 1830s have stood out as bringing major shakeups in electoral coalitions destined to be long-lasting. All seven elections occurred in the course or wake of calamitous events, or perhaps spans of events — in four instances, wars (the elections of 1848, 1868, 1920, and 1948), but in the other three instances, depressions (the elections of 1876, 1896, and 1932). It was not only in 1932 that a presidential election followed three years of excruciating depression that had allowed an incumbent party to show its governing wares and line up for a prolonged voter penalty. That seems to have happened also — or at least it is a good part of the picture — in 1876 and 1896 following the downturns of 1873 and 1893 — respectively the third and second worst depressions in American history. This American experience has not been unique. The slump of 1929 and also apparently that of 1893 brought electoral hinge points elsewhere in the world.[34]

Depressions and recessions have also shaped the historical profile of congressional midterm elections. In party seat holdings, probably most — two notable exceptions are 1994 and 2006 — of the hinge points in House midterm history have followed on economic slumps. Additional considerations have often figured in these instances, but economics has ranked high. In the wake of the economic crisis of 1857, the midterm of 1858 ushered in sixteen years of Republican control.[35] After the downturn of 1873, the midterm of 1874 ushered in a Democratic majority that prevailed for sixteen of the next twenty years.[36] The depression-ridden midterms of 1894 and 1930 each brought another sixteen-year string of, respectively, Republican and Democratic control[37] — although, in a peculiar detour, the ruling New Deal Democrats lost eighty seats and effective *policy* control of the House in the midterm of 1938 following the sharp economic contraction of 1937–38 — which was "in terms of speed if not duration . . . the most serious in the nation's history."[38] A cross-party conservative coalition ordinarily dominated the House for some sixteen years beginning in 1938. Finally, the midterm of 1958, held during a serious recession, brought major Democratic gains in seat holdings — both Senate and House — that greased that party's lawmaking enterprises later in the 1960s. The pattern in all the instances cited above — both presidential and congressional elections — is of a lasting negative electoral surge penalizing the party holding the presidency.

In the events realm, wars and depressions are not the whole story. In another study of elections associated with long-lasting coalitional change, by Larry M. Bartels, the ordinarily uncelebrated election of 1880 (Garfield versus Hancock) spikes very high.[39] Events, albeit of a different sort, seem to have played a role there too. The crumbling of Reconstruction in the South in the 1870s took the form of, among other things, a sequence of events. The spasms of guerrilla insurrection that undercut federal military occupation of Louisiana in 1874, Mississippi in 1875, and South Carolina in 1876 seem to have transfixed the country and fed into electoral patterns in the midterm of 1874 as well as the presidential elections of 1876 and 1880.[40] A national reaction amounting to Reconstruction fatigue apparently aided the Democrats, and, more directly, the surge to white supremacy in the Deep South affected voting patterns there. Yet at the presidential level the southern lunge toward immense Democratic majorities did not occur until 1880 in Florida, Louisiana, and South Carolina — the southern states where Army-fortified Republicans still controlled the count in 1876 and indeed swung the national result to Hayes that year by way of their counting. As well as possibly a complicated farewell to Reconstruction in general, the 1880 reading in the Bartels analysis picks up these extraordinary southern vote swings between 1876 and 1880. In general as regards that era, guerrilla uprisings could be consequential events, too.

Long-Term Policy Effects

I address both depressions and wars in this section. Material drawn from Chapter 12 reappears in the discussion of wars, but I organize it differently here — by policy area rather than by war.

Any discussion of the effects of depressions on policy making needs to center on the Great Depression of 1929, since no American government before that time had attacked a depression with anything like the policy ambition of the 1930s. The Democrats in power during 1893–94, for example, put strenuous effort into repealing the Sherman Silver Purchase Act of 1890 as an antidepression move, and enacted a new income tax as government revenue plummeted, but did little else.[41] In the case of the Great Depression, a simple and convincing reading is: No depression, no New Deal. Absent the Great Depression, we do not know that anything like the New Deal would ever have happened in American history. A few years ago I attended a conference where the historian of the 1930s William Leuchtenburg speculated that in retrospect, at least in terms of its political economy, the New Deal may have been a "neomercantilist aberration."

For analytic purposes, it may help to sort the policy yield of the New Deal era into three categories.[42] The first category addresses policy innovations that proved to be *temporary* rather than long-term in their effects, but the boundaries here can be blurry and items like these should perhaps be mentioned since they are familiar. A plausible list of major innovations that had temporary effects, all of them relief or recovery moves, might be: the National Industrial Recovery Act of 1933, the Federal Emergency Relief Act (FERA) of 1933, and, in terms of agencies, the Reconstruction Finance Corporation in 1932 during Hoover's presidency, the Public Works Administration in 1933, the Civilian Conservation Corps in 1933, and the Works Progress Administration (WPA) in 1935.

The second category addresses innovations that aimed at economic recovery, relief, the renovation of reeling institutions, or management otherwise of the depression emergency — their adoption would have been most unlikely absent such justifications — but which have stayed in effect permanently (in most cases with revisions) or at least through several succeeding generations after the 1930s. This list would likely include the Agricultural Adjustment Act of 1933 inaugurating government crop supports, the Glass-Steagall Act of 1933 reorganizing the banking industry, the Federal Deposit Insurance Corporation of 1933 insuring bank accounts, the Federal Housing Administration of 1934 insuring home mortgages, the Securities Act of 1933 and the Securities Exchange Act of 1934 regulating the discredited securities industry, the abandonment of the gold standard as documented in the Gold Reserve Act of 1934, and unemployment insurance and "welfare," as it later became known, as provisions of the Social Security Act of 1935. Possibly the list should include the Reciprocal Trade Agreements Act of 1934, this country's decisive shift away from high protective tariffs: "The legislative history shows that the State Department mainly sold the bill as something which would help recovery through the promotion of exports."[43] Also on the list would be major tax hikes of the early 1930s as the federal and state governments desperately strove to balance their budgets in the face of vanishing revenue. At the federal level, that meant the progressive-flavored Revenue Act of 1932 signed by Hoover — the principal federal tax increase of the decade. In the state of California, which has received recent study, it meant an emergency switch to highly elastic sales and personal income taxes that, in an unexpected turn, funded the immense expansion of that state's public sector during succeeding generations.[44]

Included in the third category are policy innovations that proved to be long-lasting but that do not seem to have been chiefly justified by reference to emergency depression conditions — or in fact to owe their adoption to any such justification. They came about mainly for a different reason. A political opening supplied by the depression made them possible. The business community was temporarily delegitimized. A traumatized public opinion was indifferent or amenable. Democratic party ranks soared above 300 in the House and as high as 75 in the Senate. Left-liberal interests and activists took up cherished causes that they would likely have pursued in virtually any economic context, given the chance. Here was the chance. Moves in this category would arguably include the Norris–La Guardia Act of 1932 curbing labor injunctions and outlawing yellow-dog contracts, the Tennessee Valley Authority in 1933, the Wagner Act of 1935 prescribing collective-bargaining procedures in private industry,[45] the familiar pensions component of the Social Security Act of 1935, the Public Utilities Holding Company Act of 1935 breaking up the large utility empires, and the Fair Labor Standards Act of 1938 establishing a minimum wage.

As is well known, the New Deal years generated a formidable array of policy moves that stuck. Those documented here in categories two and three were depression-driven moves, through one causal route or another. So far as one can tell: No depression, no moves. Certainly it is plausible that many of the included moves, or something like them, would have come about at some point since the 1930s somehow anyway. Pensions? Securities regulation? A break for the unions? A break for the farmers? These are good candidates, but we do not know when or in what form, and we really do not know whether.[46]

As for American wars, they seem to be underappreciated by political scientists — although not by economists or historians — as generators of major policy innovations that stuck. Five general policy categories plus certain scattered items are worth mentioning. The first is taxes. The federal revenue system has been overwhelmingly a product of wars. The Civil War brought a high protective tariff — originating as an emergency revenue source in 1861 — as well as duties on alcohol, tobacco, and certain luxuries that saw the government through half a century.[47] World War I brought serious progressive taxation — personal income tax rates in the high brackets that have never fallen anywhere near pre-1916 levels since that war, plus corporate and inheritance taxes.[48] World War II brought mass-based progressive taxation. The personal income tax was "dramatically expanded" in the early 1940s through widening its reach (the share of the workforce paying taxes rose from 7 percent before the war to 64 percent afterward), raising marginal rates (the top-bracket rate rose to 94 percent during the war), and pay-as-you-go withholding. The Current

Tax Payment Act of 1943, which established the pay-as-you-go procedure, must rank as one of the most lastingly consequential statutes ever enacted on any subject.[49] In general, the federal government has lived off World War II's lucrative tax design for the six ensuing decades. For a time, at any rate, there seems to have been a progressive redistributive effect, as was noted by Douglass C. North in 1966: "It is not at all clear that New Deal measures provided any significant redistribution of income. . . . The really significant fall [in income inequality] is clearly related to the high progressive tax rates imposed during World War II."[50] Taking American history as a whole, and leaving aside the special payroll withholding scheme associated with Social Security, which seems to enjoy wide approval as a contributory insurance device, there is little evidence that Americans have ever relished financing anything at the federal level except wars — and the wartime taxes have tended to stick.

A second category is the protective tariff. American trade policy has undergone endless variation, but three major duty-raising junctures involved wars — one at the outset of a war (the long-lived Civil War tariff has been mentioned), the other two in the wakes of wars. In a burst of nationalism following the War of 1812, Congress constructed a new high-tariff regime to shield industries nourished during that war, notably cotton textiles, that now fell vulnerable to British competition.[51] A similar burst of nationalism helped spur a record high tariff in the wake of World War I by way of the Emergency Tariff Act of 1921 and the Fordney-McCumber Tariff of 1922. War-nourished industries needed to be shielded again, this time notably a brand-new chemical industry. Metals and ores were now seen to need protection for defense reasons. A new array of assertive trade associations induced into existence by the government during the war now invested the national capital. Farmers signed on as postwar conditions ruined crop prices. In general, despite a good deal of wrangling over specifics in the legislative process of the early 1920s, "the necessity of protection was hardly challenged."[52]

A third category is suffrage expansion. It is well known that the Civil War paved the way to the Fifteenth Amendment enfranchising African Americans — a policy change that "stuck" in the northern and border states although of course the South was another matter. But there is more to be said. World War II brought another dose of small but real progress for southern blacks by way of the Soldier Voting Act of 1942 and a Supreme Court strikedown of the white primary in 1944 (indexing, it is said, the country's changing opinion on race during the war). In general, "The equilibrium [of black disfranchisement] in voting laws was decisively disrupted by World War II."[53] Later on, the Vietnam War left a deposit of teenage voting.[54] Perhaps least appreciated is the role of World War I in the achievement of women's suffrage in 1920 by way of the Nineteenth Amendment. It is a surefire bet that women's suffrage would have won out in the United States sooner or later. A powerful movement was under way in the 1910s. The time seemed ripe. But movements can falter. Women in Switzerland had to wait until 1971. In fact, energetic contributions by American women to the wartime mobilization seem to have brought the proximate winning argument. Suffrage extension was "necessary to the successful prosecution of the war," President Wilson came to argue; "We have made partners of the women in this war."[55] The United States did not act alone. Women won the vote in many countries during World War I or its near aftermath, evidently through a logic of wartime contribution or various other democratizing impulses associated with war. The instances include Britain (for women over thirty), Canada, Germany, Austria, Czechoslovakia, Belgium, the Netherlands, and Sweden (the last two countries were neutrals, but the war could have spillover effects). Women in France, Italy, Hungary, and Japan had to wait until the close of World War II when apparently the same logics operated.[56] In general in American history, wars have been a major engine of electoral democracy.

Related is a fourth policy category: race relations. In addition to the Fifteenth Amendment, it is of course fundamental that the Civil War levered the Emancipation Proclamation and the Thirteenth Amendment abolishing slavery as well as the Fourteenth Amendment guaranteeing individual rights against the states. World War II seems to have been critical to race policy in a different way. Immediately, it did not produce a great deal of policy change that proved durable (FDR's Committee on Fair Employment Practices, for example, did not survive the postwar environment). As noted earlier, however, the war and its aftermath raised the civil rights issue to prime status, where it stayed and in time proved productive. Feisty returning African American veterans were part of the picture.[57]

The fifth policy category is veterans' benefits—to which one's initial response might be: Well, yes, what else is new? Yet veterans' benefits have played a peculiarly important role in the history of American policy making.[58] In the case of the Civil War, the benefits started small but grew into a large, ornate entitlements program in the late nineteenth century. They became an American version of a welfare state.[59] In the case of World War I, the payouts were also designed later: At least five veterans' bonus bills became law over the vetoes of Coolidge, Hoover, and Roosevelt. Surprisingly, those of 1931 and 1936 are good candidates for the most effective countercyclical spending moves by the government during the depression years.[60] Indeed, they probably merit inclusion as major relief moves along with the FERA and the WPA. In the case of World War II, the G.I. Bill of Rights, which was designed while the

war was still on in 1944, funded higher education for over two million returning veterans as well as home mortgages and other benefits. It brought another
American version of a welfare state. According to one assessment of the G.I.
Bill, "The transition toward a prosperous, middle-class society was accelerated by decades."[61]

In discussing depressions, I emphasized the "political opening" provided by
the Great Depression of the 1930s. That logic can work in the case of wars, too.
There are two particularly interesting instances. In the case of the Civil War, the
enduring policy changes of that era did have, in general, emergency roots. But
obviously, that is not all that was going on. In the realm of political economy,
here was an all-time chance for the Whiggish legislative program that had
lurked for decades without ever being satisfyingly accomplished. Now in 1861,
the generally skeptical Southerners had abandoned Congress. Coalitional opportunities improved. As in the 1930s, core interests and activists could spark
the kinds of innovations they would have wanted anyway, war or no war.
Hence, via at least this one path of the full causal story, the Morrill Tariff of
1861, the Land Grant College Act of 1862, the Pacific Railway Act of 1862 (an
"internal improvement" in nineteenth-century terminology), the Homestead
Act of 1862, and the National Banking Act of 1864.[62] We see here an updated
version of Henry Clay's "American System"—the ambitious program that
itself had come into existence to serve needs exposed by an earlier war, the War
of 1812.[63] The other instance is from World War I. For something like the first
half of the twentieth century, in the wake of the turn-of-the-century consolida-
tion of nationwide U.S. corporations, a Progressive left-wing faction on Capitol Hill, composed of mainly though not solely Democrats, itched to push the
rich to the wall through taxation. They got a chance to do that in the Revenue
Acts of 1916, 1917, and 1918. Fortuitously, Progressive-oriented forces held
key positions in Washington, D.C., when World War I came along, and their
price for financing "preparedness" and then the war was stiff progressive
taxation. In this sense, it was an emergency-driven accident that the modern
American revenue system took on such a progressive cast.[64]

I have not tried to list the durable institutions spurred into existence by the
wars, but there have been many. The Second Bank of the United States, for
example—the one later undone by Andrew Jackson—was an answer to the
near-bankruptcy, the currency disorder, and the debt brought on by the War of
1812.[65] The Bureau of Internal Revenue (the ancestor of the Internal Revenue
Service) originated in the Civil War. The House and Senate Appropriations
Committees, launched in 1865 and 1867, were an answer to the fiscal pressures of the Civil War,[66] as was the Bureau of the Budget in 1921 a response to
those of World War I.[67] In the wake of the Espionage Act of 1917 and the

Sedition Act of 1918, J. Edgar Hoover began compiling files on individuals in the newly created General Intelligence Division of the Federal Bureau of Investigation in 1919.[68] The Central Intelligence Agency grew out of World War II's Office of Strategic Services. The National Science Foundation, although not formally established until 1950, grew from a new World War II–inspired blueprint for supporting basic scientific research.[69] There is a good case for the Council of Economic Advisers, launched in 1946: World War II had "institutionalized structural Keynesianism," showing that well-calculated deficit management could work.[70] Why not have more of it?

Finally, in a miscellaneous category, I found surprisingly good cases for war as a necessary cause of three of the leading *restrictive* innovations of American policy history — federal curbs on alcohol, immigration, and unions. The Prohibition movement was a lively cause in the 1910s, but the Eighteenth Amendment and the Volstead Act might never have happened minus the World War I logics of a need to conserve grain, a "spirit of patriotic self-denial," and an association of alcohol with German American culture.[71]

In general in American history, possibly no policy area has brought a greater mismatch between public opinion and government action than immigration. Not even during the high-intake times around 1850, around 1900, and during the past twenty years, all of which have featured considerable discontent, has immigration been seriously curbed. Immigration has been a classic arena of veto-group politics.[72] The only major exceptions are East Asian exclusion starting in the 1880s and a sweeping cutback that accompanied World War I — by way of a literacy test and other barriers imposed in 1917, and, once those measures failed to produce a satisfying enough postwar cut, the imposition of national-origins quotas in 1921 and 1924. As animating causes, the war and its aftermath brought an intense fear of radicals, pressure for Americanization, and a discrediting of antirestrictionist nationality groups that previously had been hard to beat — notably the German-American Alliance.[73] It is intriguing that the success of both Prohibition and immigration restriction seems to have had something to do with German American culture or influence. A player was subtracted from the policy-making table with the discrediting of the country's prominent German strain during World War I. In a lesser way, to be sure, it was something like the white South going home during 1861–65. Yet, as in the case of women's suffrage, World War I seems to have triggered many countries, not just the United States, to restrict immigration. In Britain, France, Switzerland, and Germany, immigration had remained "essentially uncontrolled" until World War I.[74] Canada, Argentina, Brazil, and Australia, neo-European ex-settler colonies like the United States, cut back on immigration in the 1920s "to prevent a worldwide flood of refugees from war-torn Europe."[75]

Labor unions, high-flying after the government's enabling moves of the mid-1930s, received their comeuppance during and after World War II. Repeated, crippling strikes soured the public. An "almost hysterical hostility toward unions" greeted a rail walkout in 1946, for example. John L. Lewis of the Mine Workers became a national villain. Hence the pro-management revisions of labor law by way of the Smith-Connally Act of 1943 and the Taft-Hartley Act of 1947.[76] The essentials of the latter are still in effect today.

A Word on Assassinations

I have skimped on brief or short-term events, although there is no shortage of supremely important instances. In 1856, for example, crucial to the Republicans' emergence as the country's main opposition party were the so-called Sack of Lawrence [Kansas] by a pro-slavery mob and the caning of Senator Charles Sumner on the Senate floor. "These two acts, one on top of the other, traumatized the nation."[77] In the 1960s, key to the enactment of the Civil Rights Act of 1964 and the Voting Rights Act of 1965 were the Birmingham and Selma confrontations—the police dogs and the rest—that riveted national attention on practices in the Deep South courtesy of the Rev. Martin Luther King Jr. as impresario.[78]

But assassinations may deserve a special word. Not easily subjected to systematic treatment—they are nearly in a category with the Nicaragua and Mexico earthquakes—they have been neglected as causal factors. (Actually, a certain order has characterized them in the sense that many American assassins have *not* been randomly acting lunatics: It is sobering that President Lincoln, President McKinley, President Kennedy, Robert F. Kennedy, and the Reverend King were shot by, respectively, a southern nationalist, an anarchist, a defector to the Soviet Union, an Arab nationalist, and a white supremacist.)[79] I do not want to take up familiar speculations here on the order of: What if Lincoln had served out his full second term? I will stop at addressing two particularly energetic bouts of national policy making—in fact, possibly the two most consequential exercises of American lawmaking since World War II.

One was the "Reagan Revolution" of 1981—that is, the Republicans' program of unprecedented tax and spending cuts enacted that year. A classic political opening prepared the way: The 1979 oil shock, double-digit inflation, and the Iran hostages crisis lofted the Republicans to power in 1980, enabling them to bill as an economic cure-all a program they no doubt would have been happy to pursue anyway. Yet as of March 1981 the plan seemed to be headed for the rocks on Capitol Hill. Then John W. Hinckley Jr. shot and nearly killed President Reagan. That brought on a "display of jaunty courage" by the president (as in his "Honey, I forgot to duck!"), which "turned Reagan into a national hero and immeasurably helped the passage of his fiscal program." His survey ratings soared. "The legislative payoff was dramatic": Moderate and conservative Democrats, hearing messages from home, signed on. The cuts were approved in a series of showdown votes that spring and summer.[80] All this is entirely believable, even if it takes a suspension of deeply held conventional wisdom to appreciate the quite credible evidence. Without the assassination episode: no Reagan Revolution.

The other venture in significant lawmaking was the Great Society — or, more broadly, the extraordinary harvest of legislation enacted by a left-centered coalition on Capitol Hill during calendar year 1964 and in the wake of the 1964 election during 1965. President Kennedy's legislative record had been so-so, but then he was assassinated in November 1963. The impact was enormous. "All that Kennedy had tried to do, all that he stood for, became in some sense sanctified." Lyndon Johnson took over the presidency with a "Let us continue" appeal: "We would be untrue to the trust he reposed in us, if we did not remain true to the tasks he relinquished when God summoned him."[81] As the new president, Johnson "possessed an enormous advantage that liberal predecessors had been denied since the late 1930s: a national mood so eager for strong presidential leadership that even Congress and interest groups had to take heed." That advantage owed chiefly to "the impact of Kennedy's assassination."[82] It helped make 1964 possibly the most productive legislative year since the 1930s.

But that was not all. Calendar year 1965, following the election, was even more productive. An underappreciated structural logic seems to have helped, although of course many other things were going on as always. It is a good bet that the assassination had one more effect — through the medium of augmenting Democratic congressional gains in the 1964 election. Here is the logic. We know from recent comparative work on presidential systems that congressional elections held *within* presidential terms tend to vary in their results according to when they are held. On average, the earlier in the presidential term, the better the presidential party does.[83] In the United States, we see only midterms. But if we had a quarter-term system, so to speak, one in which the interim congressional elections were held after just one year, we would likely have developed a popular and professional lore centering on "quarter-term bonus" rather than "midterm penalty." The effect in 1964 was that the Democrats lucked out. Not only did they enter the election season with a post-Kennedy aura, but the election itself, owing to timing, had the structural cast of a confirming plebiscite one year into the Johnson presidency. In the succeeding midterm of 1966, the Democratic congressional majorities came down with a thud, but by then the Great Society was on the books. All this having been said, it is certainly plausible that, given the strong impulse toward state expansion in the 1960s and 1970s in this country and elsewhere, much of the content of the Great Society would have found its way into American policy sooner or later anyway. But we cannot know how much or when, and quite possibly a good deal of it would not have.

Possible Implications

As a general matter, building on the above, it seems to me that we pay a considerable price as would-be explainers of politics by ignoring the following. First, events as causes: They deserve a place on the palette. Second, contingency: Many events are contingent, and in the real world unexpected happenings are powerful engines of political change. Third, counterfactuals: Once contingency is squarely looked at, alternative courses of political change are nearly impossible to block from one's mind, as many of my accounts above suggest. There is a case for deploying more professional resources into cautious (it is easy to be silly) counterfactual work. A good recent instance is Gary J. Kornblith's work speculating what would have happened if the close Polk-Clay election of 1844 had gone the other way. No War with Mexico? No Civil War? What happens to slavery?[84] Counterfactuals can help frame what *did* happen. Fourth, path dependence: The consequences of contingent events earn a good deal of their interest because, for a multitude of reasons, they tend to stick.[85] Hence, for example, the U.S. federal revenue system. Such stickiness is a powerful thing.

Beyond these general points, I see four implications for the study of American politics that are more particular.

First, it might be good to rethink the general explanatory apparatus of "underlyingness" that sees political change growing out of basic interests, enduring preferences, generation-long party platforms, and the rest. In fact, to employ statistical terminology, a great deal of the sweeping political change of American history has owed to *interaction* between any such "underlying" considerations and certain contingent events, notably depressions and wars, that allowed the "underlying" considerations to prevail. "Political openings" became available, as in the cases of the Whiggish economic program of the 1860s and the left-center New Deal thrust of the 1930s. Granted, it is possible for more or less event-free upwellings of policy change to occur — perhaps the Progressive era qualifies, although that is a complicated subject. Yet it is extremely difficult, given among other things the cast of this country's separation-of-powers system, to shake American policy out of whatever its existent equilibrium is. Party electoral sweeps taken alone have often failed as effective shakers: Consider the shifts to unified party control in 1948, 1952, 1960, 1976, 1992, and 2000 that brought only modest policy change. Events can be wonderful shakers, and the possible *interaction effect* between contingent events and programmatic drives is well known to anyone who participates cannily in political life — consider, to take a best-case non-American example, Lenin idling in Switzerland in 1917. Such interaction has a place in the intellects of many political actors, and it might have more of a place in the explanatory equipment of political science.[86]

Second, in studying policy change we probably pay too much attention to elections. Granted, elections play a vital role. In the case of elections that *precede* policy change, they can often be said to cause it, in a proximate sense, or else, for one thing, to channel impulses or messages stirred by previous events such as economic crises that serve as more convincing distant causes — the medium for these transactions often being partisan electoral shifts. But a great deal happens *between* elections. Events can occur then, too. It is interesting to sift through American lawmaking history for significant enactments resulting from interelection events — that is, instances where it is decisively credible that a successfully enacted measure would *not* have been enacted absent a triggering event that occurred since the last biennial election (even if, yes, it is also true that the shape of the reaction to the event, or whether there was any reaction at all, owed at least partly to the propensities of the set of officeholders now in office yielded by that last election). The list might include the following:

- Alien and Sedition Acts of 1798 (there were troubles with France)
- Embargo Act of 1807 (troubles with England)
- Creation of the Second National Bank in 1816
- Force Bill of 1833 (reining in the South Carolina nullifiers)
- First Reconstruction Act of March 1867 (spurred by events occurring in the South *after* the midterm election of 1866)[87]
- First Ku Klux Klan Act of 1970 (troubles in the South)
- Repeal of the Silver Purchase Act in 1893
- Aldrich-Vreeland Currency Act of 1908 (in the wake of a currency crisis)
- Style-setting Revenue Act of 1916[88]
- Espionage Act of 1917

- Sedition Act of 1918
- Flood Control Act of 1928 (following the great Mississippi flood of 1927)[89]
- Revenue Act of 1932
- Emergency Banking Relief Act of March 1933 (the banking system was collapsing during the months *after* the election of 1932)
- Burke-Wadsworth Selective Service Training Act of 1940 (with the Nazis on the march, an army might be needed)
- Atomic Energy Act of 1946 (what to do with the new energy source?)
- Marshall Plan in 1948 (troubles in Europe)
- McCarran Internal Security Act of 1950 (following the Alger Hiss trials, the exposure of Klaus Fuchs as an atomic spy, and other events)
- National Aeronautics and Space Administration Act of 1958 (after *Sputnik*)
- National Defense Education Act of 1958 (also following *Sputnik*)
- Kefauver-Harris Act of 1962 regulating pharmaceutical drugs (after the thalidomide scare)
- Civil Rights Act of 1964 (after Birmingham)
- Voting Rights Act of 1965 (after Selma)
- Open Housing Act of 1968 (after the shock of Reverend King's assassination)
- Rail Passenger Service Act of 1970 creating AMTRAK (after the Penn Central went bankrupt)
- Federal Election Campaign Act of 1974 (after the Watergate revelations)
- Bailout of New York City in 1975
- Bailout of the Chrysler Corporation in 1979
- Bailout of the savings and loan industry in 1989
- Persian Gulf Resolution of 1991 (Saddam Hussein had invaded Kuwait)
- Use of Force Resolution of 2001 (after September 11)
- USA Patriot Act of 2001
- Corporate Responsibility Act of 2002 (following the collapse of Enron)
- Creation of the Homeland Security Department in 2002

To use the terms presented by Keith Krehbiel in *Pivotal Politics*, it is not just elections that are capable of moving status quo policy outside the Capitol Hill "gridlock interval."[90] Events, too, can shake up a preference distribution among the realm of elected officeholders to the point where presidential vetoes, Senate filibusters, and the rest cease to be a bar to action in some direction. Let me nail this down with an instance. On December 7, 1941, Pearl Harbor was attacked. On December 8, 1941, Congress and the president opted to abandon the American status quo policy of *not* waging war against Japan, and war was declared.

Of course, there is also a role for elections that *succeed* policy change, in which retrospective voter judgments come into play. That role is vital too, but it has limits. Commitments have been made — as with the Marshall Plan in 1948. Vast enactment energy has been expended that is unlikely to be expended again — as with the Civil Rights Act of 1964. Veto-point politics would disallow a policy rollback — as with any number of enactments.[91] Moves have been authorized that cannot be undone — as in the case of the Persian Gulf Resolution of 1991 legitimizing a war. Most important, perhaps, events themselves have engineered new states of affairs that have entailed, as I argued earlier, new perceptions of problems, new causal stories, new ideas about what to do. *That* is where the explanatory focus should often go — on the social construction and management of events rather than on the elections that bracket those events.[92]

A third implication for the study of American politics has to do with congressional studies. Room needs to be allowed for events and their consequences. In today's scholarship, not a great deal of room is allowed by possibly the most influential, and certainly a splendid, achievement in congressional studies of recent times — Keith T. Poole and Howard Rosenthal's charting of congressional roll-call behavior since 1789 along chiefly one master dimension.[93] From the vantage point of events, I see four problems in this construction of history — or in an interpretation that is widely given it. First, events can have *cardinal* as well as ordinal-scale consequences. In 1859, for example, according to David M. Potter: "There was a revolution of opinion in the South within six weeks after [John Brown's raid on] Harpers Ferry."[94] Sectional tension heightened. Civil war loomed. No doubt there were relevant roll calls. An ordinal measure, which the Poole-Rosenthal scale basically is, may not pick up such cardinal widening.[95] Second, an event can instantaneously shift the entire membership of Congress along some important policy dimension — as with the members' change of mind about war with Japan on December 8, 1941, as opposed to on December 6, 1941. That kind of shift cannot be picked up by the Poole-Rosenthal scale. Third, a gripping event may provoke a unanimous or near-unanimous roll call or a voice-vote decision — as with the declaration of war against Japan in 1941 (one negative House vote was the only Capitol Hill opposition), the creation of the National Aeronautics and Space Administration in 1958 (voice-vote passage in both houses after *Sputnik*), the Kefauver-Harris drug regulation act of 1962 (voice-vote passage in both houses after the thalidomide scare), or the Use of Force Resolution in 2001 (the Pearl Harbor pattern was exactly duplicated). Virtually all roll-call analysis, including Poole and Rosenthal's, excludes results that are so one-sided. Yet policies arrived at so one-sidedly are not necessarily unimportant in a substantive sense (consider World War II), and one-sidedness can send its own kind of important signal: In real political life, 51 percent is not always the only verdict that is meaningful or worth aiming for on Capitol Hill. Finally, what does it mean if, as Poole and Rosenthal plausibly find, most congressional roll-call history maps onto a single dimension? It might mean that Congress is forever in the business of cataloguing a timeless distribution of dimensionalized interests or preferences that exists out there somehow naturally in the society. But this is unlikely.[96] There is too much chaos. Reality changes every day. Even if any such timeless distribution existed, we do not have anything like certain rules for mapping it onto a roll-call dimension. In fact, there is a place for events in the *creation* of a long-lasting dimension in roll-call voting. Somebody needs to process the chaos of the world into ideological order by decreeing that, for example, *this* is the left-wing solution to the savings-and-loan crisis or the Somalia mess and *that* is the right-wing solution. In one of its roles, the Capitol Hill community is a kind of collective Madame Defarge, weaving day after day an ideologically ordered tapestry out of whatever material comes in — including events.

For a fourth and last general point, American political science may tilt too much toward legislative politics as opposed to executive politics. Obviously, legislatures react to events, and they can also stage them: Consider the widely publicized Pecora hearings savaging Wall Street in 1932–33 that paved the way to banking and securities reform, or the Army-McCarthy hearings of 1954. But events are dominantly an executive realm. We like to think that we choose presidents to advance party programs, but, in fact, presidents once in office ordinarily focus on managing events. The Kennedy presidency, for example, hinged largely on addressing a series of trouble spots that included Berlin, Laos, Vietnam, Cuba (the Cuban missile crisis), Mississippi, and Alabama. In its historical importance, the Truman presidency was almost entirely an events presidency. I have not emphasized the point in this essay, but chief executives can also obviously *create* events. The discretionary wars waged by both of the Bushes in Iraq and Bill Clinton in Yugoslavia are recent cases in point. Such action is not an idiosyncrasy of the American presidential system: British prime ministers of both parties pursued policies identical to the American ones in all three of these instances. Rather, it reflects the enormous, risky leeway that inheres in executive power. No doubt publics have always known this. For American voters, the presidency has always been the main prize of the system, and that may owe chiefly to voter awareness of a president's power to manage and stage events.

Notes

I am indebted to R. Douglas Arnold, John Ferejohn, Sonam Henderson, and Matthew Glassman for their helpful comments on this essay, which is an adaptation of an essay bearing the same title, published as chap. 4 in Ian Shapiro and Sonu Bedi (eds.), *Political Contingency: Studying the Unexpected, the Accidental, and the Unforeseen* (New York: New York University, 2007).

1. Kramer 1971. This and the entries in succeeding notes to this paragraph are intended as examples.

2. Stonecash 2000.

3. Green, Palmquist, and Schickler 2002.

4. Burnham 1970.

5. Hartz 1955.

6. Gerring 1998.

7. Putnam 2000.

8. Whittington 1999.

9. Matthews 1960.

10. Polsby, Gallaher, and Rundquist 1969; Krehbiel 1998.

11. Poole and Rosenthal 1997.

12. Dahl 2003.

13. Skocpol 1992.

14. Sundquist 1968.

15. Stimson 1999.

16. Lazarsfeld, Berelson, and Gaudet 1968.

17. Ibid., xxviii, xxxiv, 17, 25, 60, 87.

18. There is a treatment of voters' "attitude toward the European war," but that approach has limits as a probe. Ibid., 35.

19. Ibid., 71.

20. Berelson, Lazarsfeld, and McPhee 1954.

21. One good account by a historian is Divine 1974, chs. 6, 7. Divine's summary judgment at p. 275: "The Berlin blockade, as much as the liberal domestic program or any one ethnic group, gave Truman a priceless political asset when day after day he stood firmly against the Communists abroad without involving the nation in war."

22. For example, Bartels and Zaller 2001.

23. See, for example, Shaw 1999; Mueller 1973, ch. 9.

24. Achen and Bartels, 2004.

25. Kingdon 1984, 99–105; Birkland 1997.

26. To use a term from Fogel 1992, 216.

27. Alesina and Rosenthal 1995.

28. On the impact of the passage of the Kansas-Nebraska Act, see for example Brady 1988, 172.

29. For a discussion, see Dray 1964, 19.

30. See Dray 1964, 42–43; Nagel 1961, 582–83. These philosophers of science seem to

scratch their chins about this historians' practice, but then they reflect: Well, that is what historians do.

31. Fogel 1992.

32. McPherson 1988, 770–76, 858, quotation at 774.

33. Clubb, Flanigan, and Zingale 1980, ch. 3, data from table 3.1a at 92–93.

34. See the discussion in Mayhew 2002, 77, 150, 164.

35. Huston 1987, ch. 6. In particular, the Republicans scored dramatic, lasting gains in traditionally Democratic Pennsylvania in 1858. In the circumstance of economic difficulty, workers in the state's nonagricultural sectors seem to have bought into a Republican anti-free-trade ideology. Of course, North versus South issues figured in the late 1850s also.

36. On the depression of 1873: Foner 1988, 512–24 ("The Depression and Its Consequences").

37. In the case of 1894 it seems a reasonable bet, although the history has not been written this way, that many voters in the generation after 1893 saw the Democrats as simply bunglers. Given simultaneous control of the presidency, House, and Senate during 1993–94 for the first time since 1858, the party, it could be surmised, proceeded virtually immediately to ruin the economy.

38. Renshaw 1999, 344.

39. Bartels 1998, 315.

40. Foner 1988, 550–52, 554–55 (on Louisiana), 558–63 (on Mississippi), 570–75 (on South Carolina). On South Carolina in 1876, see Zuczek 1996. On Mississippi, see Lemann 2006.

41. On the repeal of the Sherman Silver Purchase Act: Faulkner 1959, 147–51. On the income tax of 1894 as a remedy for falling revenue in depression circumstances: Gordon 2004, 273–74. The Supreme Court quickly struck down the income tax.

42. Sources on the era: Leuchtenburg 1963, chs. 3, 7, 10, 11; Schwarz 1970, 88–98 and chs. 5, 6, 8.

43. Schlesinger 1959, 257. Still, the RTAA may fit better into category three here. By instinct and belief, the Democrats of that time were of course a low-tariff party.

44. Hartley, Sheffrin, and Vasche 1996. "The fiscal system enacted in California during the 1930s has persisted in its basic structure through today [1996]. These changes have allowed real per capita state expenditure to grow by a factor of approximately 10 from 1929/30 to 1989/90." P. 658. This California revenue switch of the 1930s took place under Republican governors.

45. Yet the Wagner Act had an event-centered side, too. Among other things, the measure was a reaction to nationwide strikes during 1934 that amounted to "social upheavals." See Bernstein 1970, ch. 6, quotation at 217; Plotke 1989, 117.

46. For a discussion weighing short-term as opposed to long-term causes of the enduring policy changes of the New Deal era, see Wallis 1985.

47. Bauer, Pool, and Dexter 1963, 14–15; Brownlee 1996, 44–48; Sylla 2000, 527–29; Porter 1994, 260.

48. Brownlee 1985; Brownlee 1996, 60–72; Brownlee 2000, 1030; Higgs 1987, ch. 7; Witte 1985, ch. 4.

49. Wallis 2000, quotation at 73; Murphy 1996; Brownlee 1996, 88–101; Witte 1985, ch. 6; Campbell and Allen 1994.

50. North 1966, 178–79.

51. Bauer, Pool, and Dexter 1963, 13–14; Baxter 1995, ch. 2; Binkley 1962, 101–2.

52. Hicks 1960, quotation at 57; Kaplan and Ryley 1994, ch. 5; Eichengreen 1989, 3–5.

53. Keyssar 2000, 244–55, quotation at 244; Klinkner and Smith 1999, ch. 6; Zelden 2004, 97–98, 132.

54. Keyssar 2000, 277–81.

55. The case for a causal connection between the war and women's suffrage is available in Kyvig 1996, 226–39, first quotation at 234; Keyssar 2000, 214–18, second quotation at 216; Cooper 1990, 307–8; Wynn 1986, 148–52; Behn 2005.

56. On the cross-national pattern of women's enfranchisement: Lewis 2004, plus scattered sources on individual countries. As of the beginning of World War I, women had had the vote in New Zealand, Australia, Finland, Norway, and certain American states.

57. Klinkner and Smith 1999, chs. 6, 7; Keyssar 2000, 244–53; Hart 2004; Collins 2002; Fleegler 2006.

58. See Campbell 2004.

59. Skocpol 1992, ch. 2; Holcombe 1999.

60. Key 1943; Brown 1956, 863–69; Lee and Passell 1979, 384–86.

61. Perrett 1989, quotation at 439; Olson 1974, chs. 1–3.

62. See, for example, Bensel 1990.

63. Wiltse 1961, ch. 3; Baxter 1995, ch. 2; Binkley 1962, 101.

64. See the accounts in Brownlee 1985; Brownlee 1996, 60–72.

65. Rockoff 2000, 647–48; Watts 1987, 278.

66. Wander 1982, 25–28.

67. Farrar-Myers, Renka, and Ponder 2000, 1; Wander 1982, 31–35.

68. Goldstein 1978, chs. 4, 5; Ungar 1976, ch. 3.

69. Smith 1990, 1–3, 34–52; Polsby 1984, 35–55.

70. Brownlee 2000, 1050–51, quotation at 1050. See also Stein 1969, chs. 8, 9.

71. The causal case is available in Kyvig 1996, 218–26, quotation at 224; Kerr 1985, 185; Cooper 1990, 307; Ferrell 1985, 188–90; Lerner 2007, 13, 29–34, 38–39.

72. See Tichenor 2002.

73. Tichenor 2002, 138–46; LeMay 1987, 70–72.

74. Kaufmann 2004, 56.

75. Graham 2002, 47.

76. Patterson 1972, quotation at 306; Lee 1966, chs. 1–3; Amenta and Skocpol 1988, 114–16; Young 1956, 63–67; Sparrow 1996, ch. 3; Wynn 1996, 470.

77. Gienapp 1987, 295–303; Fogel 1992, 227–29, quotation at 229.

78. Burstein 1985, chs. 3–4, 8; Sitkoff 1981, chs. 5, 6.

79. For an interesting treatment, see Clarke 1981.

80. Unger 2002, 215–17. See also Barone 1990, 613; Brody 1991, 146–47; Brownlee and Steuerle 2003, 160–61. In the latter assessment, the assassination episode "had the effect of increasing popular support for the president and, by extension, whatever program he wanted. Congress found the pressure irresistible."

81. Matusow 1984, 131.

82. Patterson 1996, 530–31.

83. See Shugart 1995, 332–33.

84. Kornblith 2003. On counterfactuals, see also Fearon 1991.

85. See Pierson 2000.

86. An interaction-effect argument of this sort addressing specifically bankruptcy legislation appears in Berglöf and Rosenthal 2004, 6. During the 110 years through 1898, federal bankruptcy laws were enacted only when (a) an economic panic had just occurred, and (b) the Federalists, Whigs, or (post-1860) Republicans enjoyed unified control of the government.

87. See Donald 1965, 56–57; McKitrick 1960, 455–60, 473–85.

88. See Brownlee 1985.

89. Pearcy 2002.

90. Krehbiel 1998.

91. See, for example, Vogel 1993, 260–62, 266–68.

92. Political leaders, for example, in reacting to events, can often "frame" political contexts. See Arnold 1990, 96.

93. Poole and Rosenthal 1997.

94. Potter 1976, 382.

95. For a similar comment, see Krehbiel 1998, 74n.

96. See Converse 1964.

References

Achen, Christopher H., and Larry M. Bartels. 2004. Blind Retrospection: Electoral Responses to Drought, Flu, and Shark Attacks. Paper presented at conference on "Knowledge, Problems, and Political Representation: Can Government Perform Better?" at University of Virginia, November 12–13.

Alesina, Alberto, and Howard Rosenthal. 1995. *Partisan Politics, Divided Government, and the Economy.* New York: Cambridge University Press.

Amenta, Edwin, and Theda Skocpol. 1988. Redefining the New Deal: World War II and the Development of Social Provision in the United States. In *The Politics of Social Policy in the United States*, eds. Margaret Weir, Ann Shola Orloff, and Theda Skocpol. Princeton: Princeton University Press, 81–122.

Arnold, R. Douglas. 1990. *The Logic of Congressional Action.* New Haven: Yale University Press.

Barone, Michael. 1990. *Our Country: The Shaping of America from Roosevelt to Reagan.* New York: Free Press.

Bartels, Larry M. 1998. Electoral Continuity and Change, 1868–1996. *Electoral Studies* 17, 301–26.

——, and John Zaller. 2001. Presidential Vote Models: A Recount. *PS: Political Science and Politics* 34, 9–20.

Bauer, Raymond A., Ithiel de Sola Pool, and Lewis Anthony Dexter. 1963. *American Business and Public Policy: The Politics of Foreign Trade.* Chicago: Aldine Atherton.

Baxter, Maurice G. 1995. *Henry Clay and the American System*. Lexington: University Press of Kentucky.

Behn, Beth A. 2005. Woodrow Wilson's Conversion Experience: The President, Woman Suffrage, and the Extent of Executive Influence. Paper presented at the annual conference of the Midwest Political Science Association.

Bensel, Richard Franklin. 1990. *Yankee Leviathan: The Origins of Central State Authority in America, 1859–1877*. New York: Cambridge University Press.

Berelson, Bernard R., Paul F. Lazarsfeld, and William N. McPhee. 1954. *Voting: A Study of Opinion Formation in Presidential Campaigns*. Chicago: University of Chicago Press.

Berglöf, Erik, and Howard Rosenthal. 2004. "Power Rejected: Congress and Bankruptcy in the Early Republic." Paper presented at History of Congress conference, Stanford University, March 2004, revised September 2004.

Bernstein, Irving. 1970. *Turbulent Years: A History of the American Worker, 1933–1941*. Boston: Houghton Mifflin.

Binkley, Wilfred E. 1962, 4th edition. *American Political Parties: Their Natural History*. New York: Alfred A. Knopf.

Birkland, Thomas A. 1997. *After Disaster: Agenda Setting, Public Policy, and Focusing Events*. Washington, D.C.: Georgetown University Press.

Brady, David W. 1988. *Critical Elections and Congressional Policy Making*. Stanford: Stanford University Press.

Brody, Richard A. 1991. *Assessing the President: The Media, Elite Opinion, and Public Support*. Stanford, Calif.: Stanford University Press.

Brown, E. Cary. 1956. Fiscal Policy in the 'Thirties: A Reappraisal. *American Economic Review* 46, 857–79.

Brownlee, W. Elliot. 1985. Woodrow Wilson and the Financing of the Modern State: The Revenue Act of 1916. *Proceedings of the American Philosophical Society* 129, 173–210.

———. 1996. Tax Regimes, National Crises, and State-Building in America. In *Funding the Modern American State, 1941–1995*, ed. Brownlee. New York: Cambridge University Press, 37–104.

———. 2000. The Public Sector. In *The Cambridge Economic History of the United States*, vol. III, *The Twentieth Century*, eds. Stanley L. Engerman and Robert L. Gallman. New York: Cambridge University Press, 1013–60.

———, and C. Eugene Steuerle. 2003. Taxation. In *The Reagan Presidency: Pragmatic Conservatism and Its Legacies*, eds. W. Elliot Brownlee and Hugh Davis Graham. Lawrence: University Press of Kansas, 155–81.

Burnham, Walter Dean. 1970. *Critical Elections and the Mainsprings of American Politics*. New York: Norton.

Burstein, Paul. 1985. *Discrimination, Jobs, and Politics: The Struggle for Equal Employment Opportunity in the United States since the New Deal*. Chicago: University of Chicago Press.

Campbell, Alec. 2004. The Invisible Welfare State: Establishing the Phenomenon of Twentieth Century Veteran's Benefits. *Journal of Political and Military Sociology* 32, 2004, 249–67.

Campbell, John L., and Michael Patrick Allen. 1994. The Political Economy of Revenue

Extraction in the Modern State: A Time-Series Analysis of U.S. Income Taxes, 1916–1986. *Social Forces* 72, 632–69.

Clarke, James W. 1981. American Assassins: An Alternative Typology. *British Journal of Political Science* 11, 81–104.

Clubb, Jerome M., William H. Flanigan, and Nancy H. Zingale. 1980. *Partisan Realignment: Voters, Parties, and Government in American History.* Beverly Hills, Calif.: Sage.

Collins, William J. 2002. The Political Economy of State-Level Fair Employment Laws, 1940–1964. *Explorations in Economic History* 40 (1): 24–51.

Converse, Philip E. 1964. The Nature of Belief Systems in Mass Publics. In *Ideology and Discontent,* ed. David E. Apter. London: Free Press of Glencoe, 206–61.

Cooper, John Milton, Jr. 1990. *Pivotal Decades: The United States, 1900–1920.* New York: W. W. Norton.

Dahl, Robert A. 2003. *How Democratic Is the American Constitution?* New Haven: Yale University Press.

Divine, Robert A. 1974. *Foreign Policy and U.S. Presidential Elections, 1940–1948.* New York: New Viewpoints.

Donald, David. 1965. *The Politics of Reconstruction, 1863–1867.* Baton Rouge: Louisiana State University Press.

Dray, William H. 1964. *Philosophy of History.* Englewood Cliffs, N.J.: Prentice-Hall.

Eichengreen, Barry. 1989. The Political Economy of the Smoot-Hawley Tariff. *Research in Economic History* 12, 1–43.

Farrar-Myers, Victoria A., Russell Renka, and Daniel Ponder. 2000. Institutionalization in a Critical Period: Presidency, Congress, and the Development of the Executive Budget. Paper presented at the annual conference of the American Political Science Association.

Faulkner, Harold U. 1959. *Politics, Reform and Expansion, 1890–1900.* New York: Harper and Brothers, 1959.

Fearon, James D. 1991. Counterfactuals and Hypothesis Testing in Political Science. *World Politics* 43, 169–95.

Ferrell, Robert H. 1985. *Woodrow Wilson and World War I, 1917–1921.* New York: Harper and Row.

Fleegler, Robert L. 2006. Theodore G. Bilbo and the Decline of Public Racism, 1938–1947. *Journal of Mississippi History* 68, 1–28.

Fogel, Robert W. 1992. Problems in Modeling Complex Dynamic Interactions: The Political Realignment of the 1850s. *Economics and Politics* 4, 215–54.

Foner, Eric. 1988. *Reconstruction: America's Unfinished Revolution, 1863–1877.* New York: Harper and Row.

Gerring, John. 1998. *Party Ideologies in America, 1828–1996.* New York: Cambridge University Press.

Gienapp, William E. 1987. *The Origins of the Republican Party, 1852–1856.* New York: Oxford University Press.

Goldstein, Robert J. 1978. *Political Repression in Modern America: From 1870 to 1976.* Urbana: University of Illinois Press.

Gordon, John Steele. 2004. *An Empire of Wealth: The Epic History of American Economic Power.* New York: HarperCollins.

Graham, Hugh Davis. 2002. *Collision Course: The Strange Convergence of Affirmative Action and Immigration Policy in America.* New York: Oxford University Press.

Green, Donald, Bradley Palmquist, and Eric Schickler. 2002. *Partisan Hearts and Minds: Political Parties and the Social Identities of Voters.* New Haven: Yale University Press.

Hart, Justin. 2004. Making Democracy Safe for the World: Race, Propaganda, and the Transformation of U.S. Foreign Policy during World War II. *Pacific Historical Review* 73 (1): 49–84.

Hartley, James E., Steven M. Sheffrin, and J. David Vasche. 1996. Reform During Crisis: The Transformation of California's Fiscal System During the Great Depression. *Journal of Economic History* 56, 657–78.

Hartz, Louis. 1955. *The Liberal Tradition in America.* New York: Harcourt, Brace.

Hicks, John D. 1960. *Republican Ascendancy, 1921–1933.* New York: Harper and Row.

Higgs, Robert. 1987. *Crisis and Leviathan: Critical Episodes in the Growth of American Government.* New York: Oxford University Press.

Holcombe, Randall G. 1999. Veteran Interests and the Transition to Government Growth: 1870–1915. *Public Choice* 99, 311–26.

Huston, James L. 1987. *The Panic of 1857 and the Coming of the Civil War.* Baton Rouge: Louisiana State University Press.

Kaplan, Edward S., and Thomas W. Ryley. 1994. *Prelude to Trade Wars: American Tariff Policy, 1890–1922.* Westport, Conn.: Greenwood.

Kaufmann, Eric P. 2004. *The Rise and Fall of Anglo-America.* Cambridge: Harvard University Press.

Kerr, K. Austin. 1985. *Organized for Prohibition: A New History of the Anti-Saloon League.* New Haven: Yale University Press.

Key, V. O., Jr. 1943. The Veterans and the House of Representatives: A Study of a Pressure Group and Electoral Mortality. *Journal of Politics* 5, 27–40.

Keyssar, Alexander. 2000. *The Right to Vote: The Contested History of Democracy in the United States.* New York: Basic Books.

Kingdon, John W. 1984. *Agendas, Alternatives, and Public Policies.* Boston: Little, Brown.

Klinkner, Philip A., and Rogers M. Smith. 1999. *The Unsteady March: The Rise and Decline of Racial Equality in America.* Chicago: University of Chicago Press.

Kornblith, Gary J. 2003. Rethinking the Coming of the Civil War: A Counterfactual Exercise. *Journal of American History* 90, 76–105.

Kramer, Gerald H. 1971. Short-Term Fluctuations in U.S. Voting Behavior, 1896–1964. *American Political Science Review* 65, 131–43.

Krehbiel, Keith. 1998. *Pivotal Politics: A Theory of U.S. Lawmaking.* Chicago: University of Chicago Press.

Kyvig, David E. 1996. *Explicit Authentic Acts: Amending the U.S. Constitution, 1776–1995.* Lawrence: University Press of Kansas.

Lazarsfeld, Paul, Bernard Berelson, and Hazel Gaudet. 1968 (3rd edition). *The People's Choice: How the Voter Makes up His Mind in a Presidential Campaign.* New York: Columbia University Press.

Lee, R. Alton. 1966. *Truman and Taft-Hartley: A Question of Mandate.* Lexington: University Press of Kentucky.

Lee, Susan, and Peter Passell. 1979. *A New Economic View of American History.* New York: W.W. Norton.

Lemann, Nicholas. 2006. *Redemption: The Last Battle of the Civil War.* Farrar, Straus and Giroux.

LeMay, Michael C. 1987. *From Open Door to Dutch Door: An Analysis of U.S. Immigration Policy Since 1820.* New York: Praeger.

Lerner, Michael A. 2007. *Dry Manhattan: Prohibition in New York City.* Cambridge: Harvard University Press.

Leuchtenburg, William E. 1963. *Franklin D. Roosevelt and the New Deal, 1932–1940.* New York: Harper and Row.

Lewis, Jone Johnson. 2004. Winning the Vote: International Woman Suffrage Timeline. *http://womenshistory.about.com/library/weekly/aa091600a.htm.*

MacIntyre, Stuart. 1986. *The Oxford History of Australia,* vol. 4, *1901–1942: The Succeeding Age.* New York: Oxford University Press.

Matthews, Donald R. 1960. *U.S. Senators and Their World.* Chapel Hill: University of North Carolina Press.

Matusow, Allen J. 1984. *The Unraveling of America: A History of Liberalism in the 1960s.* New York: Harper and Row.

Mayhew, David R. 2002. *Electoral Realignments: A Critique of an American Genre.* New Haven: Yale University Press.

McKitrick, Eric L. 1960. *Andrew Johnson and Reconstruction.* Chicago: University of Chicago Press.

McPherson, James M. 1988. *Battle Cry of Freedom: The Civil War Era.* New York: Oxford University Press.

Mueller, John E. 1973. *War, Presidents and Public Opinion.* New York: John Wiley and Sons.

Murphy, Kevin. 1996. Child of War: The Federal Income Withholding Tax. *Mid-America* 78, 203–29.

Nagel, Ernest. 1961. *The Structure of Science: Problems in the Logic of Scientific Explanation.* New York: Harcourt, Brace & World.

North, Douglass C. 1966. *Growth and Welfare in the American Past: A New Economic History.* Englewood Cliffs, N.J.: Prentice-Hall.

Olson, Keith W. 1974. *The G.I. Bill, the Veterans, and the Colleges.* Lexington: University Press of Kentucky.

Patterson, James T. 1972. *Mr. Republican: A Biography of Robert A. Taft.* Boston: Houghton Mifflin.

———. 1996. *Grand Expectations: The United States, 1945–1974.* New York: Oxford University Press.

Pearcy, Matthew T. 2002. After the Flood: A History of the 1928 Flood Control Act. *Journal of the Illinois State Historical Society* 95, 172–201.

Perrett, Geoffrey. 1989. *A Country Made by War: From the Revolution to Vietnam—the Story of America's Rise to Power.* New York: Random House.

Pierson, Paul. 2000. Increasing Returns, Path Dependence, and the Study of Politics. *American Political Science Review* 94, 251–67.

Plotke, David. 1989. The Wagner Act, Again: Politics and Labor, 1935–37. *Studies in American Political Development* 3, 105–56.

Polsby, Nelson W. 1984. *Political Innovation in America: The Politics of Policy Innovation.* New Haven: Yale University Press.

——, Miriam Gallaher, and Barry S. Rundquist. 1969. The Growth of the Seniority System in the U.S. House of Representatives. *American Political Science Review* 63, 787–807.

Poole, Keith T., and Howard Rosenthal. 1997. *Congress: A Political-Economic History of Roll Call Voting.* New York: Oxford University Press.

Porter, Bruce D. 1994. *War and the Rise of the State: The Military Foundations of Modern Politics.* New York: Free Press.

Potter, David M. 1976. *The Impending Crisis, 1848–1861.* New York: Harper and Row.

Putnam, Robert D. 2000. *Bowling Alone: The Collapse and Revival of American Community.* New York: Simon and Schuster.

Renshaw, Patrick. 1999. Was There a Keynesian Economy in the USA between 1933 and 1945? *Journal of Contemporary History* 34, 337–64.

Rockoff, Hugh. 2000. Banking and Finance, 1789–1914. In *The Cambridge Economic History of the United States,* vol. II, *The Long Nineteenth Century,* eds. Stanley L. Engerman and Robert E. Gallman. New York: Cambridge University Press, 643–84.

Schlesinger, Arthur M., Jr. 1959. *The Coming of the New Deal.* Boston: Houghton Mifflin.

Schwarz, Jordan A. 1970. *The Interregnum of Despair: Hoover, Congress, and the Depression.* Urbana: University of Illinois Press.

Shaw, Daron R. 1999. A Study of Presidential Campaign Event Effects from 1952 to 1992. *Journal of Politics* 61, 387–422.

Shugart, Matthew Soberg. 1995. The Electoral Cycle and Institutional Sources of Divided Presidential Government. *American Political Science Review,* 89, 327–43.

Sitkoff, Harvard. 1981. *The Struggle for Black Equality, 1954–1980.* New York: Hill and Wang.

Skocpol, Theda. 1992. *Protecting Soldiers and Mothers: The Political Origins of Social Policy in the United States.* Cambridge: Harvard University Press.

Smith, Bruce L. R. 1990. *American Science Policy Since World War II.* Washington, D.C.: Brookings Institution Press.

Sparrow, Bartholomew. 1996. *From the Outside In: World War II and the American State.* Princeton: Princeton University Press.

Stein, Herbert. 1969. *The Fiscal Revolution in America.* Chicago: University of Chicago Press.

Stimson, James A. 1999. *Public Opinion in America: Moods, Cycles, and Swings.* Boulder, Colo.: Westview Press.

Stonecash, Jeffrey M. 2000. *Class and Party in American Politics.* Boulder, Colo.: Westview Press.

Sundquist, James L. 1968. *Politics and Policy: The Eisenhower, Kennedy and Johnson Years.* Washington, D.C.: Brookings Institution Press.

Sylla, Richard. 2000. Experimental Federalism: The Economics of American Government, 1789–1914. In *The Cambridge Economic History of the United States,* vol. II,

The Long Nineteenth Century, eds. Stanley L. Engerman and Robert E. Gallman. New York: Cambridge University Press, 483–541.

Tichenor, Daniel J. 2002. *Dividing Lines: The Politics of Immigration Control in America.* Princeton: Princeton University Press.

Ungar, Sanford J. 1976. *FBI: An Uncensored Look Behind the Walls.* Boston: Little, Brown.

Unger, Irwin. 2002. *Recent America: The United States Since 1945.* Upper Saddle River, N.J.: Prentice-Hall.

Vogel, David. 1993. Representing Diffuse Interests in Environmental Policymaking. In *Do Institutions Matter? Government Capabilities in the United States and Abroad,* eds. R. Kent Weaver and Bert A. Rockman. Washington, D.C.: Brookings Institution Press, 237–71.

Wallis, John Joseph. 1985. Why 1933? The Origins and Timing of National Government Growth, 1933–1940. In *Emergence of the Modern Political Economy,* supplement 4, *Research in Economic History, A Research Annual,* ed. Robert Higgs. Greenwich, Conn.: JAI Press, 1–51.

———. 2000. American Government Finance in the Long Run: 1790 to 1990. *Journal of Economic Perspectives* 14, 61–82.

Wander, W. Thomas. 1982. Patterns of Change in the Congressional Budget Process, 1865–1974. *Congress and the Presidency* 9, 23–49.

Watts, Steven. 1987. *The Republic Reborn: War and the Making of Liberal America, 1790–1820.* Baltimore, Md.: Johns Hopkins University Press.

Whittington, Keith E. 1999. *Constitutional Construction: Divided Powers and Constitutional Meaning.* Cambridge: Harvard University Press.

Wiltse, Charles M. 1961. *The New Nation, 1800–1845.* New York: Hill and Wang.

Witte, John F. 1985. *The Politics and Development of the Federal Income Tax.* Madison: University of Wisconsin Press.

Wynn, Neil A. 1986. *From Progressivism to Prosperity: World War I and American Society.* New York: Holmes and Meier.

———. 1996. The 'Good War': The Second World War and Postwar American Society. *Journal of Contemporary History* 31, 463–82.

Young, Roland. 1956. *Congressional Politics in the Second World War.* New York: Columbia University Press.

Zelden, Charles L. 2004. *The Battle for the Black Ballot: Smith v. Allwright and the Defeat of the Texas All-White Primary.* Lawrence: University Press of Kansas.

Zuczek, Richard. 1996. The Last Campaign of the Civil War: South Carolina and the Revolution of 1876. *Civil War History* 42, 18–31.

14

Incumbency Advantage in U.S. Presidential Elections

The Historical Record

How can we illuminate the pattern of outcomes in American presidential elections? I argue here for *incumbency advantage* as an account, drawing on simple data and electoral history back through 1788. Familiar as it is in the congressional realm, incumbency advantage could perhaps use more emphasis in the presidential realm. It seems to be a major factor there. Plausibly considered, for example, in light of the historical record regarding incumbency and elections, incumbent-free contests like those of 2000 and 2008 loom as even-up propositions in terms of either party's likely success. From the 1790s through 2000, parties holding the American presidency lost it exactly half the time when they did not run incumbent candidates.

Accounts of Presidential Elections

In the accumulated lore of political science, there seem to exist three prominent accounts of presidential elections. In a *realignments* account, stable eras of party dominance are bounded by critical elections that upset coalitional patterns. A specific empirical expectation given this view, it is probably fair to say, would be a punctuated-equilibrium pattern of stability, change, stability, change, and so forth in party electoral success in presidential elections. Yet history has not been kind to this expectation.[1] Daniel J. Gans has shown, for example, that in the sequence of presidential elections from 1856 through 1980, the distribution of victory "runs" by party (Jimmy Carter, for example, was a run of one for the Democrats; Ronald Reagan and George H. W. Bush a run of three for the Republicans) did not differ significantly from what one would expect to get in a distribution of runs of heads and tails through coin flips.[2]

It is true that party success in congressional elections, notably for the House, has been stickier. At the congressional level, eras of party dominance have indeed occurred — often, for one thing, in the wake of economic downturns such as those of 1873, 1893, and 1929 (and also, according to one account, previously in 1857[3]) that badly discredited ruling parties. Following the slump of 1873, for example, the Democrats won control of the House in 1874 and held it for sixteen of the next twenty years. Following the slumps of 1893 and 1929, the Republicans and Democrats won the House in, respectively, 1894 and 1930 and held it in each case for sixteen consecutive years.[4]

Yet at least three reasons come to mind why party-control stickiness might play a larger role in sequences of congressional elections than in presidential ones. First, personal incumbency always figures in the bulk of congressional contests at the district level — no doubt ordinarily to the net benefit of any national majority party that fields most of the incumbents.[5] Second, once past the force of incumbency advantage, distributions of party identification among voters, ordinarily a force for stability, no doubt score more influence at the relatively inconspicuous congressional level than in presidential contests where candidate-centered information about nonincumbent as well as incumbent candidates is so rich.[6] Third, voters may examine credentials differently. Elected legislators are basically position-takers. Elected executives are essentially managers, and voter perceptions of managerial capability may cloud the usual party and ideological factors in elections — a consideration that probably helps explain the election of Republican governors in Rhode Island and Democratic governors in Utah. At any rate, as a matter of historical reality, party-control stickiness has been one thing at the congressional level, quite another at the presidential level. It is a perhaps surprising aspect of presidential elections since World War II that, as of 2004, the in-party had kept control of the office in eight elections yet lost it in seven. This balance could not be evener. (These particular figures have nothing to do with the incidence of incumbent as opposed to nonincumbent candidates.)

A second account of presidential elections is supplied by the conceptual apparatus of *party identification*.[7] Possible voter "deviations" from a "normal vote" keyed to long-lasting distributions of party identification were the account of presidential elections pioneered by the authors of the Michigan election studies in the 1950s and 1960s.[8] Voter deviations could occur, as they did in the Eisenhower elections, yet they were, well, deviations. Vexed though questions of its provenance and stability might be, party identification is undoubtedly a very good guide to behavior by individual voters. It is a less good guide to behavior by the full American electorate—at least on the binary question of which party finally comes out on top in presidential elections. During the twentieth century, for example—this skirts 2004, which seems to have brought exact parity between the parties in numbers of vote-casting party identifiers—the Republican party apparently enjoyed a party-identification advantage among actual voters (that is, nonvoters are omitted) in all contests from 1904 through 1932, and the Democrats an advantage in all contests from 1936 through 2000.[9] Yet in only fourteen of these twenty-five instances did the party that actually won the presidency enjoy a party-identification edge among voters at the time. Coin flips would have brought twelve and a half such victories, barely a worse showing. (I have taken "actually won the presidency" to mean the party that came to occupy the White House. Of course, that raises the complicating matter of the popular vote tilting one way and the electoral vote the other in very close elections. One such outcome during this century-long span was the familiar Bush-Gore contest of 2000. Another was possibly the Kennedy-Nixon contest of 1960.[10])

A third account might be labeled *econometric* after its methodology and in the spirit of the stem "econo-." For ample reasons a leading explanatory genre, this brand of analysis places presidential elections in a time-series perspective and ordinarily emphasizes ups and downs in the economy as independent variables.[11] Often represented too in such analyses are other kinds of variables —for example, the president's Gallup rating or whether wars are going on. In principle, this tradition of analyzing elections econometrically is as capable of accommodating incumbency status as well as anything else. Yet economic variables ordinarily draw the high-gauge measurement techniques and the substantive emphasis. "Political economy" is the disciplinary rubric. Personal incumbency status has been a minor consideration at best.

Incumbency Advantage

By convention, the term "incumbency advantage" has come to refer to an electoral edge enjoyed by in-office persons, not by in-office parties. That much is clear. But otherwise a fundamental ambiguity has inhered in the usage. On the one hand, incumbency advantage can refer to a statistical fact: For whatever reasons, candidates running again as incumbents perform better in elections than would or do candidates not holding that status.[12] On the other hand, the term can refer to an *explanation* of the statistical fact: Here is *why* candidates already holding office run better in elections. It is incumbency advantage! For example, incumbents may gain from distributing pork to constituents, they may raise more campaign money, or they may draw weak challengers.

Confusion can reign if these statistical and explanatory meanings are blended. This essay is chiefly, and in its early sections entirely, an investigation of incumbency advantage in its statistical sense. Yet the essay then proceeds to the explanatory side: If a statistical pattern exists, what might explain it? The latter discussion is designed to be speculative — not anything like conclusive. A misty aspect of it is that certain of the possible explanations of the statistical fact of incumbency advantage seem to deserve by commonsense criteria the label "incumbency advantage," but some do not, and in other cases it is not clear whether they do.

I want to argue here that incumbency advantage in the statistical sense, underpinned by a corresponding mix of at least promising causal factors, is a good candidate for an account of American presidential elections. Other current scholarship has been pointing this way. Herbert F. Weisberg, drawing on a study of pooled individual survey responses for elections from 1952 through 2000, reports that incumbent presidential candidates enjoyed a bonus of 6 percent in the popular vote.[13] Ray C. Fair, using aggregate data for elections from 1916 through 1996, reports a bonus of 4 percent.[14] David Samuels, using aggregate data in an analysis of presidential elections in twenty-three countries including the United States, reports a bonus of over 8 percent.[15] All three of these studies control for economic conditions. Helmut Norpoth, in an analysis of American presidential elections from 1872 through 2000, reports that incumbent candidates have on balance benefited in, strictly speaking, some circumstances although not all: In this data set, a variable for economic conditions produces a sturdy coefficient with the expected sign when an incumbent candidate is running but not in open-seat circumstances. That is, incumbent candidates, but not in-office parties as such, seem to be aided when the economy is humming. Thus, Norpoth remarks of a specific instance, it is no surprise that the upbeat economy of 2000 was no help to Al Gore.[16]

Presidential Elections Back Through 1788

Historical extensiveness is the particular analytic leverage I aim for here. I examine American presidential elections back not just through the mid-twentieth century or the beginning of reliable economic data but through the very first election featuring George Washington in 1788. Probing back beyond the 1830s is an especially unconventional tack. In their farthest penetrations, modern election analysts have tended to start their data sets in that Jacksonian decade when nationally uniform mass voting for the presidential office kicked in. For some purposes, this starting point obviously makes a good deal of sense. But previous U.S. political experience has come to be ignored as if it had taken place on another planet, and it did not.[17] It is true that "selection event" or some such term may fit the choice of presidents better in, say, 1788 and 1792 than the term "election," conjuring up as the latter does images of routinized party competition, hustling politicians, and campaign broadsides.

Yet a vigorous participatory politics could underpin the selection of presidential electors by state legislatures during those early days, as evidently happened in, for example, 1812.[18] Alexander Hamilton himself hustled voters one by one in the streets of Manhattan in 1800.[19] It was an era of open politics. Competition for the presidency could be tough; opposition forces could be mobilized. In certain key respects, that era was not all that different from our own. The first dozen elections of American history brought two incumbent losses (in 1800 and 1828) and, it is probably fair to say, four close finishes (in 1796, 1800, 1812, and 1824).[20] In the lifetimes of many of us, the past dozen elections through 2004 have brought three incumbent losses (in 1976, 1980, and 1992) and five close finishes (in 1960, 1968, 1976, 2000, and 2004).

The pre-1830s evidence I draw on here, I should perhaps say, does not swerve or motor the overall results, but it does help flesh out a complete historical picture. And it helps amass a data set that is both satisfyingly large and, for analytic purposes, nicely divisible. Starting in 1788, the United States has seen through 2004 a total of fifty-five presidential elections of which thirty-one featured incumbent candidates and twenty-four were open-seat contests. Both costs and benefits are afforded by a 216-year-long data set. On the one hand, times and relations among variables can obviously change. That can argue for confining any analysis to shorter time spans. On the other hand, small numbers are a continuing problem in studies of American presidential elections. Even a half century offers only twelve data points, a vulnerability that can spur illusory extrapolations to larger universes such as might attend witnessing three hurricanes during one month in Florida or pairs of Democratic senators from the Dakotas. The utility of the present study's long data series can be judged from its use. On its side is a reflection by Samuel P. Huntington that the United States enjoys "one of the world's more antique polities." Slash-and-burn as the country may be in countless ways, its basic political institutions date to the eighteenth century or earlier: "With a few exceptions, such as a handful of colleges and churches, the oldest institutions in American society are governmental institutions."[21] That can make for an often surprising sameness or continuity in the way these institutions, including the selecting of presidents, operate.

Closeness of Elections

I take up incumbency advantage directly, but before that it may be illuminating to probe a related pattern in the split data set. That is, presidential elections featuring incumbents have tended to be more one-sided than open-seat contests. This pattern is not surprising, but it is quite clear and its shape and details are worth appreciating. See Table 14.1, which accommodates the thirty-one incumbent-featuring elections in its top half and the twenty-four open-seat contests in its bottom half. For any election, in principle, my measure of closeness is popular vote edge — that is, the winning candidate's percentage of the total popular vote minus the runner-up's percentage of the total popular vote.[22]

I say "in principle" because summary popular vote totals for president are nonexistent or worthless before the 1830s. To get around that problem, I have taken a flight of, I hope, warranted fancy here and imputed the earlier totals. A relevant relationship that does exist allows this move: In general, during the century-and-two-thirds of mass-turnout politics starting around 1830, popular vote edges in elections have corresponded significantly if imperfectly to the, magnified to be sure, electoral vote edges in those elections. Accordingly, I have calculated backward, so to speak, the relationship between electoral vote edges (here the X value)[23] and popular vote edges (here the Y value) for elections between 1828 and 2004,[24] then used the values of the resulting equation to simulate popular vote edges for the earlier elections given those elections' actual electoral vote edges.[25] My assumption, which anecdotal material for the earlier elections seems to bear out, is that a vigorous nationally oriented politics of varying closeness was occurring at lower levels during those times and that the electoral vote edges are a useful if clumsy guide to it. At any rate, precision is not needed; it is good enough to locate the simulated values in rather broad categories.

"Incumbent candidates" in Table 14.1 means all candidates who were presidents at the time they ran again notwithstanding how they reached the White House in the first place. That is, the set includes Theodore Roosevelt in 1904, Calvin Coolidge in 1924, Harry S. Truman in 1948, Lyndon B. Johnson in 1964, and Gerald Ford in 1976 — all of whom rose from vice president to president when their elected predecessors died or, in the case of Richard Nixon, resigned. As it happens, these five vice-presidential succeeders were not slouches as candidates. Four of them kept the White House running as

Table 14.1 Popular Vote Edges in Presidential Elections (that is, winner's percent of the total vote minus runner-up's percent of the total vote)

0–4.9%	5–9.9%	10–14.9%	15–19.9%	over 20%
Elections with incumbent candidates running (with winners named, and nonincumbent winners in italic):				
1800[a] —*Jefferson*	1840 —*W. Harrison*	1828 —*Jackson*	1804[a] —Jefferson	1792[a] —Washington
1812[a] —Madison	1900 —McKinley	1864 —Lincoln	1832 —Jackson	1820[a] —Monroe
1888 —*B. Harrison*	1940 —F. D. Roosevelt	1872 —Grant	1904 —T. Roosevelt	1924 —Coolidge
1892 —*Cleveland*	1944 —F. D. Roosevelt	1912 —*Wilson*	1932 —*F. D. Roosevelt*	1936 —F. D. Roosevelt
1916 —Wilson	1980 —*Reagan*		1956 —Eisenhower	1964 —L. B. Johnson
1948 —Truman	1992 —*Clinton*		1984 —Reagan	1972 —Nixon
1976 —*Carter*	1996 —Clinton			
2004 —G. W. Bush				
Open-seat elections (with winners named):				
1796[a] —J. Adams		1816[a] —Monroe	1928 —Hoover	1788[a] —Washington
1808[a] —Madison				

1824[a]	1852	1836	1920
— J. Q. Adams	— Pierce	— Van Buren	— Harding
1844	1868	1856	
— Polk	— Grant	— Buchanan	
1848	1908	1860	
— Taylor	— Taft	— Lincoln	
1876	1988	1952	
— Hayes	— G. H. W. Bush	— Eisenhower	
1880			
— Garfield			
1884			
— Cleveland			
1896			
— McKinley			
1960			
— Kennedy			
1968			
— Nixon			
2000			
— G. W. Bush			

[a] The value for popular vote spread is imputed. Used as a lever is the statistical relation between electoral vote spread and popular vote spread in the elections from 1828 through 2004. *Source: Guide to U.S. Elections* (Washington, D.C.: Congressional Quarterly Press, 5th edition, 2005), Part III.

incumbents, and in terms of popular vote edges three of them — Roosevelt, Coolidge, and Johnson — scored in the top five among the twenty-six incumbents who have faced election since the mid-1820s. "Winners" in Table 14.1 means, as earlier, candidates who actually made it to the White House even if they ran behind in the popular vote as happened in 1824, 1876, 1888, and 2000.[26] Thus the leftmost column in the table, which houses elections in the 0–4.9 percent category of popular vote edges, includes certain readings with slightly negative, in this sense, values. Each election in Table 14.1 is accompanied by the name of its winner. Among the winners, the names of challenger candidates who defeated incumbents — such as the victorious Carter in 1976 — are in italic.

A lesson in passing from Table 14.1 is that the country's early elections probably merit more attention than they have ordinarily received. Of the table's imputed values of the popular vote, perhaps the most interesting is the close reading for 1812. An incumbent candidate was running that year — James Madison — but it was wartime and the War of 1812 was not going well. For one thing, the British had occupied Detroit. In the election campaign, the opposition Federalists broached the kind of blended position and valence appeal that would later afflict Lincoln, Truman, Lyndon B. Johnson, and George W. Bush: This war was a mistake, and anyway it is being conducted badly. Pennsylvania, Ohio, and North Carolina were thought to be in play in 1812. Pennsylvania by itself made the difference as the nationwide electoral vote divided, in percentage terms, 59 to 41.[27] The Federalists fared even better at state legislative and gubernatorial levels. It would likely have taken worse military losses to propel De Witt Clinton to the White House over Madison — the final result within Pennsylvania was not particularly close — but this was a lively, uncertain, volatile, and close-fought politics.[28]

Across the top half of Table 14.1, the elections featuring incumbents have ranged rather evenly from close contests to landslides. Some have been close, as in 1812 and 2004, but most have not. Of course, most of these entries reflect incumbents winning again by comfortable margins — an unsurprising theme. But that does not exhaust the entries. Some incumbents have *lost* by huge margins — Herbert Hoover to Franklin D. Roosevelt in 1932, John Quincy Adams to Andrew Jackson in 1828, William Howard Taft to Woodrow Wilson in 1912 (in fact, Taft trailed the challenger Wilson by an even worse 18 percent than the table suggests, since Theodore Roosevelt, the third-party challenger who finished second in that contest, counts here as the runner-up). Decisive also (beyond a five-point edge) were Martin Van Buren's loss to William Henry Harrison in 1840, Carter's to Reagan in 1980, and George H. W. Bush's to Bill Clinton in 1992. What seems to happen is that being in office gives an *opportunity* for continued electoral success, but that the opportunity can be blown—sometimes spectacularly blown. Bad luck, as with Hoover weighed down by the Great Depression in 1932, is only part of the story. Executives are closely watched. Through certain kinds of behavior they can risk alienating virtually everybody. That may hold for executives of private as well as public institutions. In a category with John Quincy Adams, William Howard Taft, and Jimmy Carter may belong such figures as recalled ex-governor Gray Davis of California and ex-editor-in-chief Howell Raines of the *New York Times* as well as a number of dethroned monarchs and discredited university presidents.

Open-seat presidential contests, however, tend to be close. Roughly half the elections in the bottom half of Table 14.1 were quite close. Absent an incumbent running, the politics tends to flash to fifty-fifty. It seems to take a lot to generate an open-seat landslide—for example, in 1816 the collapse of the Federalists once the War of 1812 had ended in a nationalistic haze; in 1856 the demise of the Whigs; in 1860 the sectional schism among Democrats. As for the two extreme outliers in the southeast quadrant of Table 14.1, one reflects George Washington's near-coronation as the first president in 1788. In 1920, the electorate seems to have cast an overwhelming verdict against the Democrats' conduct of World War I and its tempestuous aftermath.[29]

Incumbency and Party Success

As a window into incumbency advantage, possibly nothing is more illuminating than a simple, binary measure of whether a party running an incumbent candidate excels in winning elections. Hence Table 14.2, which sorts the American presidential contests as earlier into two categories—elections with an incumbent running and open-seat contests—and then, within each category, tracks the success of in-office *parties* in keeping the office. Thus, for example, the in-office Republicans kept the presidency with Reagan in 1984 and George H. W. Bush in 1988, but the in-office Democrats lost it with Carter in 1980 and Al Gore in 2000.

Here, the data set accommodates only fifty-three elections rather than the earlier fifty-five, since in two instances it makes little or no sense to ask whether an in-office party won again. Those are the election of 1788 when the presidency was new, and that of 1824 when all the serious contenders for the office, notwithstanding their pronounced differences, operated inside the then hegemonic Democratic-Republican party—a sure guarantee of party continuity. Judgment calls were needed. I coded the Federalists as the in-office party in 1792 and 1796 even though George Washington may not have adopted exactly

Table 14.2 Has the Party Holding the Presidency Kept It?

Elections with an Incumbent Candidate Running

Yes, Kept the Presidency ($N = 21$)	No, Lost the Presidency ($N = 10$)
1792 — Washington	1800 — J. Adams lost to Jefferson
1804 — Jefferson	1828 — J. Q. Adams lost to Jackson
1812 — Madison	1840 — Van Buren lost to W. H. Harrison
1820 — Monroe	1888 — Cleveland lost to B. Harrison
1832 — Jackson	1892 — B. Harrison lost to Cleveland
1864 — Lincoln	1912 — Taft lost to Wilson
1872 — Grant	1932 — Hoover lost to F. D. Roosevelt
1900 — McKinley	1976 — Ford lost to Carter
1904 — T. Roosevelt	1980 — Carter lost to Reagan
1916 — Wilson	1992 — G. H. W. Bush lost to Clinton
1924 — Coolidge	
1936 — F. D. Roosevelt	
1940 — F. D. Roosevelt	
1944 — F. D. Roosevelt	
1948 — Truman	
1956 — Eisenhower	
1964 — L. B. Johnson	
1972 — Nixon	
1984 — Reagan	
1996 — Clinton	
2004 — G. W. Bush	

Elections without an Incumbent Running (with winners named)

Yes, Kept the Presidency ($N = 11$)	No, Lost the Presidency ($N = 11$)
1796 — J. Adams	1844 — Polk
1808 — Madison	1848 — Taylor
1816 — Monroe	1852 — Pierce
1836 — Van Buren	1860 — Lincoln
1856 — Buchanan	1884 — Cleveland
1868 — Grant	1896 — McKinley
1876 — Hayes	1920 — Harding
1880 — Garfield	1952 — Eisenhower
1908 — Taft	1960 — Kennedy
1928 — Hoover	1968 — Nixon
1988 — G. H. W. Bush	2000 — G. W. Bush

Note: Omitted from the calculations are 1788, when the presidency was new, and 1824, when all the serious contenders for the office were of the same hegemonic party. *Source: Guide to U.S. Elections* (Washington, D.C.: Congressional Quarterly Press, 5th edition, 2005), Part III.

that identity. I coded the Whigs and Republicans as in-office parties in, respectively, 1844 and 1868 on the ground that those parties had won the preceding presidential elections and staffed the resulting presidencies — even though John Tyler and Andrew Johnson, the vice presidents who succeeded to the White House through deaths in the interim, turned out to be far from party regulars.[30] As earlier, Ford — to date the only holder of the presidential office not to have won election on a previous national party ticket as at least vice president — as well as the other vice-presidential succeeders who came to lead their parties' presidential tickets are accommodated in Table 14.2 as generic incumbent candidates. Franklin D. Roosevelt makes three appearances in the table as an incumbent running again.

The pattern in Table 14.2 is clear. Incumbent candidacy makes a difference. When I first compiled these figures in early 2004, the results had a kind of Pythagorean neatness — in-office parties had kept the presidency exactly two-thirds of the time (twenty out of thirty instances) when they ran incumbent candidates, and exactly half the time (eleven out of twenty-two instances) when they did not. The Bush-Kerry outcome in 2004 clouded the two-thirds fraction a bit. As it happens (see the discussion below), Christopher Achen has contributed a theoretical analysis that predicts exactly such a two-thirds result given the deployment of incumbent candidates elected once earlier.[31]

Admittedly, this fifty-three-item data set, especially once it is subdivided, is still too small to permit sure inferences. A roughly one-in-ten probability remains that no relationship at all exists between the two key variables of incumbent candidacy and in-office party electoral success. A suitable test for a conjunction of the 21-10 and 11-11 patterns yields a p-value of 0.103.[32] What happens if certain of the coding decisions are altered? If the pre-mass-turnout elections before 1828 are dropped from the analysis, a conjunction of 17-9 and 8-11 patterns yields a p-value of 0.065. If the popular vote victors as opposed to the electoral vote victors are declared to be the real winners — that is, if the outcomes of the elections of 1876, 1888, and 2000 are reversed — a conjunction of 22-9 and 11-11 patterns yields a p-value of 0.065. If the Kennedy-Nixon election of 1960 is added to these three reversals, a conjunction of 22-9 and 12-10 patterns yields a p-value of 0.117.[33] It is possible to pick and choose among these various values, but they seem like a family. A rather different result obtains if the five elections involving the vice-presidential succeeders are declared to be open-seat elections — a tenable move, as will be seen below, given the impressive Achen analysis as well as certain other alleged underpinnings of incumbency advantage. In this event, a conjunction of 17-9 and 15-12 patterns yields a relatively unimpressive p-value of 0.244. What can be said about this? I am reluctant to banish Theodore Roosevelt, Coolidge, Truman, Lyndon B.

Johnson, and Ford from their status in Table 14.2 as election-facing incumbents. According to certain additional alleged underpinnings of incumbency advantage to be discussed below, not to mention the ordinary lore of politics, it would be bizarre to do so. All in all, it may cut reality at the right joint to leave them there.

In Table 14.2, the pattern of eleven out of twenty-two victories in open-seat circumstances, an exactly 50 percent success rate, is perhaps especially striking. At the presidential level, once unsupplied with incumbent candidates, the American in-office parties seem to enjoy no electoral advantage at all.[34] As another open-seat election — the country's twenty-fifth (counting 1788 and 1824) — loomed in 2008, the best prediction derivable from Table 14.1 was that it would be close and that there was no telling from Table 14.2 which party would win it.[35]

The Why Question

Incumbency advantage in its statistical sense is a fair label for the two-thirds versus one-half disparity shown above. Explaining the disparity, assuming that it is real, is another matter. In the study of congressional elections, the why question regarding incumbency advantage has drawn a good deal of attention and ingenuity cumulating in a plurality of promising ideas and, sometimes, thoughtful lists of usual suspects. Here, with the presidential elections, I will not try to do much better than present a list of plausible suspects.[36] In certain particulars, however, the extensiveness afforded by the 216-year data set seems to allow some leverage.

Listed in Table 14.3 are six categories of explanation that seem to deserve at least a mention. Certain of them are elaborated into subcategories. Some of these ideas, however compelling they may be, will be noted only in passing. Often, not very much useful can be said. I devote special attention to the fifth and sixth categories, not because I believe they promise particularly high payoff — indeed, I believe they do not — but because they are analytically interesting, they warrant attention, and the data set allows it. As for which of these six categories merit the label "incumbency advantage" in its explanatory sense, that is not easy to say. If the term hinges on behavior that an election-seeking incumbent is capable of engaging in as a consequence of holding the presidential office, or of having previously won it, then only the first and second categories clearly qualify. A slightly more generous construction will pick up category three. Category four, strictly speaking, however important it may be, may not qualify. It is difficult to say. The answer is no for category five, and a suspended judgment for category six. It is not important to get these discriminations exactly right — they speak to an inherently ambiguous language use — but it is worthwhile to hammer home the point that the statistical connotation of the term "incumbency advantage" is one thing, the explanatory connotation of it quite another.

Some Why Answers

The first category of Table 14.3 is largely well-grounded common sense. As a consequence of holding the presidential office, incumbents can acquire or win access to skills, resources, and prerogatives. In the line of skills, presidents as they get grayer possibly ordinarily get better — both as executives and as politicians. Consonant with this intuition, at another level of office, is that U.S. House members on average keep improving their percentages election after election until their fifteenth terms.[37] In the line of resources, an incumbent president is not likely to have a hard time, for example, funding a new campaign. In the line of prerogatives, incumbent presidents can choose when and if to make speeches, break ribbons, sign bills, issue executive orders, send off cruise missiles, hand out ice during Florida hurricanes (as George W. Bush did in 2004), and engage in many other kinds of possibly vote-winning behavior. All this is standard. At a more complex level, Tim Groseclose has recently argued that the opportunity enjoyed by incumbents to cater to electorates through "nonpolicy" or "valence" moves such as the above exercises of office — an opportunity lacking to challenger candidates — enables them to position themselves closer to the ideological center in campaigns than do challengers who need to keep catering to their activist bases through fiery issue stands.[38] On balance, centrism in campaigns is probably a help.

Category two in Table 14.2 accommodates an easy, credible claim: Having run and won a presidential campaign last time may be a help to running one this time.[39]

The third category ushers in voters, who may give an edge to incumbent presidents as such for a variety of reasons. Risk-averseness may come into play.[40] At the executive level, this consideration probably implicates managerial style and capacity as much as it does left-right policy predictability. In 1964, Senator Barry Goldwater's comment about "lobbing one into the men's room of the Kremlin" might have hurt him more than anything to do with his left-right voting score. In 1972, the very lurches in Senator George McGovern's own campaign raised questions about management. In general, the devil you know may be a better bet than the one you don't. As regards risk-averseness for the short term, voters may peer ahead to the start-up costs of a new presidency — a plausible worry given, for example, the many months it takes to staff the

Table 14.3 Possible Explanations of the Two-thirds versus One-half Disparity

---

Categories of explanation

1. Incumbent capabilities acquired due to holding office:
   Skills
   Resources
   Prerogatives
   Valence-issue positioning

2. Incumbent capability acquired in waging the preceding election campaign

3. Voter attitudes
   Risk-averseness
   Perceived start-up costs
   Optimal contract
   Inertia

4. Innately superior talent

5. Incumbent-party fatigue

6. Strategic behavior
   The out-of-office party
   The in-office party

---

executive branch. Although the 1960 election was, to be sure, open-seat and thus not directly relevant here although it allows a point, many voters watching President John F. Kennedy in his early phase handle the Bay of Pigs invasion in 1961 might have reflected: Bring back Dwight D. Eisenhower.[41] Another entry for the third category is an "optimal contract" idea: In the long run, it may not pay electorates wishing good service to discard their public servants wantonly or capriciously.[42] Yet another entry is voter inertia. Voters may just stay stuck in their previous decisions. For one thing, in an effort to ward off cognitive dissonance, they may bend upward their appraisals of incumbent officials so as to convince themselves they didn't make a mistake in voting for those officials in the first place.[43]

The fourth category hinges on personal political talent that is innate — or at least acquired somewhere early in life as in the crib or high school. On offer is a "prize fighters" theory — an argument crafted by John Zaller to account for incumbency advantage among members of Congress (MCs). The idea can extend to presidents. It goes: "The reason that incumbent MCs win reelection at very high rates is the same reason that world heavyweight boxing champions win most of their title defenses: owing to their manner of selection, incumbent champions in both professions are simply better competitors than most of the opponents they face." The case continues: "Incumbents, who, in order to become incumbents, must either beat other incumbents or win open-seat contests, are a more selected group than challengers and hence likely to be more-skilled competitors."[44] In short, a selection effect is at work. Incumbents are premium politicians within their contest class. This is an appealing idea. It is not much help with the vice-presidential succeeders who have not won earlier presidential contests on their own, but it can apply to the generality of presidents. Carried out in this view is a probably widespread intuition that many American presidents—Thomas Jefferson, Clinton, Eisenhower, Franklin D. Roosevelt, and others—might have been just plain unbeatable if only the aging process, the two-term norm, or the Twenty-Second Amendment had not intruded. Zaller presents a list of heavyweight boxing victories of which half a page is devoted to Joe Louis,[45] and on reading it one's mind wanders to Franklin D. Roosevelt here in Table 14.2. It is the prize fighters idea that fuels the prediction by Achen, building from a formal analysis, of precisely a two-thirds success rate for incumbents elected once earlier.[46]

Incumbent-Party Fatigue

On exhibit here, strictly speaking, is the disparity between the two-thirds and the one-half fractions of Table 14.2. What might be the causes of that disparity? Possible extraneous or artifactual considerations need to be taken into account—that is, ones that would not likely appear in any commonsense discussion of incumbency advantage in its *explanatory* meaning. One such factor, to use the terminology of Larry M. Bartels and John Zaller, is the fifth category in Table 14.3: incumbent-party fatigue. For whatever reasons, all else equal, a party in control of the American presidency tends to lose one-half a percentage point of the popular vote for each consecutive term it holds that office.[47] For the analysis here, this poses a difficulty. As a matter of fact during American history, a party's typical deployment of an incumbent candidate has come after *one* term of controlling the presidential office. The in-party has just freshly captured the office from the opposition four years ago and is now running its incumbent president again as with Reagan in 1984 or Clinton in 1996. Yet by contrast, owing at least to the two-term norm and the Twenty-Second Amendment, an in-office party's typical exposure to an open-seat election has come after *two* terms of controlling the presidential office— as with the Republicans in 1988 and the Democrats in 2000. The implication is as follows. On average, at least slightly, the possibly basic phenomenon of

Table 14.4 Incumbent-Party Fatigue versus Incumbent Candidacy as Explanations of Popular Vote Share, 1828–2004 (standard errors in parentheses)

	Model A		Model B		Model C	
Constant	0.549^a	(0.017)	0.503^a	(0.014)	0.528^a	(0.023)
N terms party has held presidency	-0.013^b	(0.007)			-0.010	(0.008)
Whether an incumbent candidate			0.033^b	(0.019)	0.025	(0.019)
N	43		43		43	
R squared	0.079		0.073		0.116	
F-value	3.51^b		3.22^b		2.61^b	

Note: The dependent variable is the percent of the major-party popular vote won by the candidate of the party currently holding the presidency, in elections from 1828 through 2004 (omitting 1864 and 1912). [a] Significant at 0.001; [b] significant at 0.10. *Source: Guide to U.S. Elections* (Washington, D.C.: Congressional Quarterly Press, 5th edition, 2005), Part III.

incumbent-party fatigue, which on evidence is less deadly after one term than after two terms, could be contributing to the *statistical* pattern of incumbency advantage exhibited in Table 14.2. The open-seat candidate Gore, to cite a generic example, may have suffered a bit more from it after eight Democratic years in 2000 than did the incumbent candidate Clinton after four Democratic years in 1996.

   A plausible reaction to the above is that incumbent-party fatigue no doubt prevails but that incumbent candidates no doubt also enjoy an edge independent of it. As it happens, that is exactly the finding of Samuels, on both fronts statistically robust, in his study of executive elections in twenty-three presidential democracies.[48] This is the finding of Fair in his study of U.S. presidential elections from 1916 through 1996.[49] For a suggestive investigation of the American experience farther back, see Table 14.4. The dependent variable here is the in-office party's percentage of the major-party popular vote in the forty-three presidential elections from 1828 through 2004 (omitting the party-schism elections of 1860 and 1912). Entered as independent variables are, for each election, the number of terms the in-office party had consecutively held the presidency at that time, and whether the in-office party was running an incumbent candidate. There are three models: The independent variables are entered alone and then simultaneously. The overall fits are poor, and the relevant variables struggle to reach significance, but the results point the same way as Samuels's.[50] Incumbent candidacy does seem to stand on its own bottom. A boost on the order of 2 or 3 percent may stem from it. Also, incumbent-party fatigue seems to stand on its own bottom. An in-office party may hemorrhage on the order of 1 percent per election during a consecutive span of White House control (which is twice the 0.5 percent Bartels and Zaller found with incumbent candidacy not controlled for). For purposes here, it is probably safe to rule out the idea that the disparity between the fractions shown in Table 14.2 is an effect of incumbent-party fatigue.

Strategic Behavior — The Out-Party

A final possible contributor to the disparity between fractions in Table 14.2 is strategic behavior. That might take place in either the out-party or the in-party, which I will take up here in that order. In the study of U.S. House elections, a familiar and very credible case is that the out-party in a district, confronted by a well-anchored incumbent, may through failing to field a "quality candidate" bolster the winning margin and possibly the victory prospect of the incumbent.[51] This is strategic behavior by a party or its potential candidates. Obviously, in any electoral universe, a widespread wimping out by the outs can bolster the fortunes of the ins.

Does the two-thirds success rate of presidential incumbents during American history reflect any such opposition tendency? It seems doubtful.[52] At the presidential level, the stakes are too high. Campaigns can offer too many surprises. The outcomes are not as foregone as in "safe" congressional districts. Resources for a respectable challenge are likely to be available. A politician who aches for the White House probably cannot afford to wait. In fact, contests for even the most unpromising out-party presidential nominations tend to be hard-fought. Also, the rest of the party ticket is at issue. In general, a major party cannot afford to sit out a presidential election. Occasionally we hear stories that an opposition party's A-candidates sat out an unpromising election in favor of its B-candidates, as in the case of Mario Cuomo and others allegedly making way for Clinton in 1992. But those stories are rare and anyway suspect: Energy, determination, and willingness to take risks are nontrivial traits of an A-candidate. Clinton had those traits in 1992 and Cuomo did not.

Possible food for thought on this question is the actual record of American out-parties in fielding presidential candidates in challenger as opposed to open-seat circumstances. Have the candidates differed in quality? See Table 14.5 for a

Table 14.5 Career Backgrounds of Presidential Candidates of the Party not Currently in Possession of the White House, in Challenger and Open-seat Circumstances

Challengers to Incumbent Presidents	Candidates in Open-seat Elections
1800 – Jefferson, secretary of state, vice president	1796 – Jefferson, secretary of state
1804 – Pinckney, diplomat, ex-VP cand.	1808 – Pinckney, diplomat, ex-pres. cand.
1812 – D. Clinton, mayor (NYC), senator (NY)	1816 – King, senator (NY)
1828 – Jackson, general, ex-pres. cand.	1836 – W. Harrison, general
1832 – Clay, senator, Speaker of the House (KY)	1844 – Polk, Speaker of the House (TN)
1840 – W. Harrison, general, ex-pres. cand.	1848 – Taylor, general
1864 – McClellan, general	1852 – Pierce, senator (NH)
1872 – Greeley, newspaper editor	1856 – Fremont, explorer, senator (CA)
1888 – B. Harrison, senator (OH)	1860 – Lincoln, House member (IL)
1892 – Cleveland, president	1868 – Seymour, governor (NY)
1900 – Bryan, ex-pres. cand.	1876 – Tilden, governor (NY)
1904 – Parker, judge (NY)	1880 – Hancock, general
1912 – Wilson, governor (NJ)	1884 – Cleveland, governor (NY)
1912 – T. Roosevelt, president	1896 – McKinley, House member, governor (OH)
1916 – Hughes, governor (NY), S. Ct. justice	1908 – Bryan, ex-pres. cand.
1924 – Davis, House member (WV), diplomat	1920 – Harding, senator (OH)
1932 – F. D. Roosevelt, governor (NY)	1928 – Smith, governor (NY)
1936 – Landon, governor (KS)	1952 – Eisenhower, general
1940 – Willkie, business leader	1960 – Kennedy, senator (MA)
1944 – Dewey, governor (NY)	1968 – Nixon, vice president

1988 – Dukakis, governor (MA)
2000 – G. W. Bush, governor (TX)

1948 – Dewey, governor (NY)
1956 – Stevenson, governor (IL), ex-pres. cand.
1964 – Goldwater, senator (AZ)
1972 – McGovern, senator (SD)
1976 – Carter, governor (GA)
1980 – Reagan, governor (CA)
1984 – Mondale, vice president
1992 – W. J. Clinton, governor (AR)
1996 – Dole, Senate majority leader (KS)
2004 – Kerry, senator (MA)

Note: Exhibited for candidates, as of the dates of the relevant elections, are the highest offices or stations they had at any time previously held or attained to. Previous presidential or vice-presential candidates are designated with an "ex-." Both Wilson and Theodore Roosevelt are listed as challengers for 1912. Omitted are the uncontested elections of 1788, 1792, and 1820 and the all-Democratic-Republican contest of 1824. *Source: Guide to U.S. Elections* (Washington, D.C.: Congressional Quarterly Press, 5th edition, 2005), ch. 19.

list of the relevant candidates and the highlights of their résumés at the times of selection. It is hard to see any difference.[53]

Strategic Behavior — The In-Party

As for in-party strategic behavior, on offer is what might be called the Senator Trible option. In 1988, freshman Republican Senator Paul S. Trible Jr. of Virginia, then forty-one years old, facing likely defeat by a popular Democratic governor, chose to retire to private life rather than run again for the Senate on the apparent ground that retiring was a more appealing prospect than losing. If every incumbent acted that way, assuming access to reasonably accurate information about electoral environments, few incumbent candidates would ever lose elections. In the presidential realm, that would mean a disappearance from the electoral loss column of incumbent candidates like a preemptively retiring Taft in 1912 or a Hoover in 1932. Also, by way of another causal route to the elimination of losses in November elections by incumbent candidates, parties might choose to trade in their weak incumbents for better nominees. In a world of strategic calculations like these, it is easy to see how the two-thirds fraction in Table 14.2 might soar toward the 100 percent mark. In the real world, we have to wonder whether such calculations might have helped loft the two-thirds fraction as high as it is. In the data set of fifty-three presidential elections, it would not have taken a great deal of strategic manipulation to open up the space between the two-thirds fraction and the one-half fraction.

In actual practice, has strategic behavior played any such role? For a stab at an answer, see Table 14.6. Isolated here are thirty presidential elections in which a selection of incumbents in an especially auspicious position to appear as their party's candidates seem apt for a test. This number is small for statistical testing, but an examination of cases is possible. On exhibit here are incumbents of a generic kind and vintage we would particularly expect to have carried their party's flag, and if they did not do so it is worth asking why not. Excluded are all vice-presidential succeeders since the last election. Notwithstanding the success stories among them, these are often a quirky lot, less orthodox and less skilled as politicians than the presidents who reached the White House directly via the ballot, and thus pose too many reasons why they might not have ended up carrying the party flag. For the purpose at hand, it is best to have a clear decision rule and omit them all.[54] Included in principle are all incumbents previously elected once and nearing the end of their first term. These are presidents who, in the American custom set by George Washington, have been decisively expected to appear as their parties' candidates again.

Excluded are all incumbents nearing the end of their *second* term (or beyond that). A strong norm, and then a constitutional amendment, have lodged against reruns by second termers and it is thus not particularly instructive to ask whether they have appeared as candidates again. A few judgment calls were needed. Excluded here are Theodore Roosevelt as of 1908 and Truman as of 1952. These men were nearing the ends of their *second* terms, more or less, having originally succeeded the deceased William McKinley and Franklin D. Roosevelt in 1901 and 1945, respectively, and were thus pretty strongly subject to the two-term norm.[55] Theodore Roosevelt, in fact, ruled out a 1908 rerun in a public statement at the time of his election victory in 1904. Even though Truman was not formally bound by the then-new Twenty-Second Amendment he was a believer in the two-term norm that that amendment reaffirmed, and he ruled out a 1952 rerun in a private memo in 1950 — although he did later flirt with a repeat candidacy in March 1952 once he ran into trouble collaring Adlai Stevenson as a successor nominee.[56] Included here, however, are Coolidge as of 1928 and Lyndon B. Johnson as of 1968. Having each then served a total of five years as president, originally as vice-presidential succeeders before winning elections themselves, these two men were not barred by any norm or rule from running again and were widely expected to do so. They were widely seen as first termers.

As seen in Table 14.6, a sizable twenty-four of the thirty optimally poised incumbents have appeared as their parties' candidates again. That is 80 percent. Running again has been the custom even in many adverse circumstances. What are the six exceptions? Franklin Pierce, sized up by his party in 1856 as a weak reelection prospect, is still the only previously elected president ever denied renomination.[57] His party substituted James Buchanan and kept the White House with a twelve-point election edge. For the argument here, it is not entirely clear what to make of that. James K. Polk pledged himself to one term as apparently the price of his Democratic nomination in 1844; other ambitious candidates or factions in the party wanted the slate clean for 1848.[58] Rutherford B. Hayes pledged himself to one term at the time of being nominated in 1876; that was a high-minded reform stance in those days.[59] As for Buchanan, it is true that both his party and his country were crashing around him as he neared the end of his term in 1859–60. It is hard to envision a scenario that would have kept him in the White House. It also seems true he was worn out: "I am in my 69th year and am heartily tired of my position as president."[60]

That leaves Coolidge in 1928 and Lyndon B. Johnson in 1968. In these two cases, health concerns intrude. In Table 14.6, as a roundabout clue to health fitness at the junctures when the thirty incumbent presidents needed to decide

Table 14.6 First-term Incumbents Appearing or Not Appearing as Their Party's Candidate Again, Ranked According to How Long They Later Lived (those not appearing as candidates again are in italic)

President	Survival Beyond End of First Term		Comments
	Years	Months	
Hoover	31	8	
J. Adams	25	4	
Madison	23	4	
Jefferson	21	4	
Van Buren	21	5	
Nixon	21	3	
Reagan	19	4	
Cleveland	19	4	
J. Q. Adams	19	0	
Taft	17	0	
Pierce	12	7	Dems ditched him, but they won anyway
Grant	12	5	
Jackson	12	3	
Eisenhower	12	2	
Hayes	11	10	Up front he pledged only one term
Monroe	10	4	
F. D. Roosevelt	8	3	
B. Harrison	8	0	
Buchanan	7	3	Only Reagan was older after one term
Washington	6	9	
Wilson	6	11	
L. B. Johnson	4	0	Uncertain health
Coolidge	3	10	Uncertain health
McKinley	0	6	Assassinated in office
Polk	0	3	Up front he pledged only one term
Lincoln	0	1	Assassinated in office
Carter	27 as of January 2008		
G. H. W. Bush	15 as of January 2008		
Clinton	11 as of January 2008		
G. W. Bush	3 as of January 2008		

Note: Listed here are all incumbent presidents coming up to a reelection juncture who (a) had previously been elected president (this excludes never-elected vice-presidential succeeders) and (b) had served as president no more than six years (this accommodates Coolidge in 1928 and Lyndon B. Johnson in 1968 but not Theodore Roosevelt in 1908, Truman in 1952, and Franklin D. Roosevelt in 1940 or 1944). *Source: World Almanac and Book of Facts 2006* (New York: World Almanac Books, 2006), p. 593.

whether to run again, I have ranked them according to how long they lived—regardless of whether they ran again or were elected again—after the closing dates of their first full terms in office. At the extremes (disregarding assassinations), Hoover carried on for nearly a third of a century after March 1933; Polk died three months after leaving office in March 1849. Note the bottom sector of the table. Regarding 1928, it is a near certainty that Coolidge would have won another term if he had gone for it, yet evidently his and his wife's suspicion that something was seriously wrong with him helped drive a decision to retire. He died of coronary thrombosis at age sixty-one in January 1933, two months short of completing what would have been another term.[61] In 1968, of course, the political environment differed starkly. Johnson, with the Vietnam War going badly and his polls down, had abundant reason to reach for a Senator Trible–like exit. But Johnson was also a physical wreck by that time. A heart condition, infection, repeated surgery, and exhaustion had worn him down. He had ordered a secret actuarial study of his own life in 1967. He doubted he could survive another four years in office.[62] Through a twist of causation, as it happens, Johnson might have actually *hastened* his own death by retiring in 1968 and thus casting off certain constraints of office. He took to drinking more, smoking more, and eating rich foods. Whatever the exact causal path, he suffered a coronary setback in March 1970, an incapacitating heart attack in June 1972, and died on January 22, 1973—just two days after an additional term would have ended.[63] In Johnson in 1968 we have an instance of joint or overdetermination. At the least, both very bad political tidings and very bad health drove his decision to retire.[64]

Discussion

To return to the six categories of Table 14.3, I do not believe that category five (incumbent-party fatigue) and category six (strategic behavior) do much to illuminate the disparity between the two-thirds and one-half success rates scored by in-office presidential parties. As regards in-party strategic behavior, accepting the test conditions of Table 14.6, only the cases of Buchanan in 1860 and Lyndon B. Johnson in 1968 seem to nudge in the predicted direction. The case of the seven-year incumbent Truman in 1952, another Democrat who folded in a bad year for that party, is worth pondering. But the withdrawal decisions in all three of these cases were cloudily and multiply determined.

It seems a good bet that the gap between the two-thirds and one-half fractions owes chiefly to some mix of categories one through four—that is, factors that easily draw the term "incumbency advantage" in its explanatory sense plus the innate superior talent (prize fighters) account. Given an immense data universe, these distinctions might be sorted out. Category one (capabilities that come with the office) and most of the voter considerations listed under category three (that is, risk-averseness, perceived start-up costs, and optimal contract) might apply equally to all incumbents running again regardless of how they reached the White House in the first place. Category two (previous campaign experience) and category three's factor of voter inertia might downplay the vice-presidential succeeders. Category four (prize fighters) might predict a cascade of next-time success rates depending on whether incumbents won the presidential office initially by a knockout (as with Jackson in 1828, Reagan in 1980), in more or less a draw (Kennedy in 1960, George W. Bush in 2000),[65] in a multicandidate free-for-all (Abraham Lincoln in 1860, Wilson in 1912), or through vice-presidential succession. But distinctions like these cannot be sorted out on current evidence.[66] The vice-presidential succeeders, for example, have been far too few to allow much leverage.

To restate the basic finding, parties during American history have kept the presidency roughly two-thirds of the time when they have run incumbent candidates but only exactly half the time when they have not. If this disparity is real — in the senses I have been fishing for it to be here — it might bear interpretive implications for the past as well as tidings for the future.

In particular, long eras of rock-solid party hegemony are often discerned in the American past, but they might not have been that. Incumbency advantage might have been at work. Only three times in American history, it is interesting to note, has a party managed to field incumbent presidential candidates two or more times in a row. The last of these instances, Ford's incumbent candidacy in 1976 following on Watergate in 1973–74 and Nixon's incumbent candidacy in 1972, is hardly an advertisement for incumbency advantage. Nixon in 1972 and Ford in 1976 were the two consecutive election-facing incumbents of the same party, and Ford lost. Yet the first instance, the back-to-back candidacies of the incumbents McKinley in 1900 and Theodore Roosevelt in 1904, which are customarily seen to have helped forge a party era, may also show the Republicans, in effect, lucking out.

Most spectacular, of course, has been the sequence of four incumbent candidacies featuring Franklin D. Roosevelt in 1936, 1940, and 1944 and Truman in 1948. Nothing like that sequence, which brought unbroken victory for the in-office Democrats, had ever happened before or is likely to happen again. The last three of these elections raise a particular point. Of all the recipes for an incumbent candidate's office-induced edge, possibly nothing tops that of an experienced commander in chief managing a military crisis. Several motifs of Table 14.3 can come into play: adept uses of executive power (as when Roosevelt upstaged the Republicans by appointing that party's eminences Frank Knox and Henry Stimson to national-security positions in his cabinet in June 1940), accrued incumbent skills, valence-issue positioning, voter risk-averseness, and a perception of start-up costs for a new administration.

That package seems to have been the story of the 1940 election. The spring and summer of 1940, as the Nazis conquered France and menaced Britain, brought an immense security threat to the American state. Previous to this threat, credible testimony suggests, Roosevelt had not leaned toward running again.[67] In the face of it, he thought he ought to, and public support surged in his favor as France fell.[68] It is true that Roosevelt had won a steady, decent job approval rating in the mid-50s to low-60s range during 1939 and early 1940,[69] yet he had ordinarily polled poorly when respondents were asked if they would vote for him for a third term. Now, in May and June of 1940, the third-term difficulty vanished. The answer to the third-term question became yes—by a double-digit edge.[70] Also in May 1940, a chronic single-digit edge that Roosevelt had enjoyed over Thomas E. Dewey, the early Republican favorite for presidential nominee, surged to a twenty-point edge.[71] In June, once the Republicans nominated the practiced executive Wendell Willkie instead of Dewey, Roosevelt assumed a modest edge over Willkie and kept it into November, yet it seems to have been chiefly a foreign-policy edge. In July, for example, a verdict went 54 percent to 27 percent to Roosevelt on the survey question: "Which presidential candidate do you think would handle our country's foreign affairs better, Roosevelt or Willkie?"[72] Yet in October, a verdict went 53 percent to 47 percent to Willkie on the question: "If there were no war in Europe, which presidential candidate would you vote for, Roosevelt or Willkie?"[73]

If Roosevelt had retired in 1940, it seems a plausible conclusion that the election that year would have receded into a toss-up contest.[74] Just before the Democrats did renominate Roosevelt in July, one survey result favored the Republicans by 35.7 percent to 33.7 percent—basically a tie—on the question: "If Roosevelt does not run for reelection, which party do you think you would be most likely to vote for, as you feel now?"[75] As important as anything in 1940, the Democrats had not groomed a plan-B nominee. No one stood out as especially electable. In survey matchups during 1939 and early 1940, the Republican Dewey had dominated Democratic hopefuls James Farley, Harry Hopkins, Henry Wallace, and Paul McNutt and run roughly even against Vice President John Nance Garner and Secretary of State Cordell Hull—until May 1940, that is, when the 68-year-old Hull surged to a ten-point lead during the European crisis for possibly the same in-office reason as Roosevelt.[76] Beyond Roosevelt, the party's prospects were blurry.

Crisis management would not go away. Four years later, the ongoing war dominated the election of 1944. The election of 1948 is often romanticized as a succession of Truman's whistle-stops and give-'em-hell speeches, but in fact it took place during the scary—we have forgotten just how scary—Berlin crisis of that year, which the incumbent president seemed to be managing well.[77] Casually we write of a long continuing New Deal era, but on the political side the 1940s was a good deal dicier than that. Incumbency probably aided the Democrats. There wasn't any long rock-solid hegemonic party era. Tweak the contingencies a bit and we might be writing of an Age of Willkie or an Age of Dewey.

Notes

Thanks to Christopher Achen, Larry Bartels, Robert Dahl, Alan Gerber, Donald Green, Jacob Hacker, Sonam Henderson, Michael F. Holt, Gary Jacobson, Rogan Kersh, John Lapinski, Joel Middleton, William Nordhaus, Joseph Sempolinski, Stephen Skowronek, Jennifer Steen, and anonymous reviewers for their help on this essay, which is published in *Political Science Quarterly* 123:2 (summer 2008).

1. See the argument in David R. Mayhew, *Electoral Realignments: A Critique of an American Genre* (New Haven, CT: Yale University Press, 2002), ch. 4.

2. Daniel J. Gans, "Persistence of Party Success in American Presidential Elections," *Journal of Interdisciplinary History* 16 (Winter 1986): 228–30.

3. James L. Huston, *The Panic of 1857 and the Coming of the Civil War* (Baton Rouge: Louisiana State University Press, 1987), ch. 6. In particular, a Republican surge in the coal and iron areas of Pennsylvania, then the second largest state, following the Panic of 1857 helped loft the party to long-term control of the U.S. House. Of course, slavery was a major nationwide concern in 1858 also.

4. Of course not all congressional takeovers are economy driven, as the elections of 1994 and 2006 attest. The stickiness of party success in the House popular vote is convincingly demonstrated in Helmut Norpoth and Jerrold G. Rusk, "Electoral Myth and Reality: Realignments in American Politics," *Electoral Studies* 26 (June 2007), 392–403. This study, conducted without statistically privileging any canonical ideas about the existence of critical elections or realignment eras, points to the House elections of 1834, 1860, 1874, 1894, 1932, and 1994 as hinge points. Otherwise, closest to the authors' cut point and carrying a p-value of roughly 0.07 is the midterm election of 1938, which to the detriment of the ruling Democrats followed the sharp economic downturn of 1937–38.

5. A leg-up effect for congressional incumbents has been especially prominent since the 1960s, but it does not seem to have been negligible in earlier times. See, for example, Jamie L. Carson and Jason M. Roberts, "Candidate Quality, the Personal Vote, and the Incumbency Advantage in Congress," *American Political Science Review* 101: (May 2007), 289–301.

6. Since the mid-1950s, the percentage of party identifiers *not* voting for the House candidate of their own party if that candidate was an incumbent has averaged well down in single digits, occasionally reaching 10 percent. There is no evidence of trend. On the other hand, the share of identifiers *defecting* from their own party to vote for an *opposite-party* incumbent surged from roughly 15 percent in the mid-1950s to as high as 50 percent in the mid-1970s, then settled down into the 30s percentiles in the 1990s. In general, the picture here is of voters shaken away from their own party identification only by the complex of factors that favors House incumbents. See Gary C. Jacobson, *The Politics of Congressional Elections* (New York: Longman, 2001), 107–10. The period covered in the analysis is 1956–98. Data source: American National Election Studies.

7. For a recent treatment, see Donald P. Green, Bradley Palmquist, and Eric Schickler, *Partisan Hearts and Minds* (New Haven, CT: Yale University Press, 2002).

8. As in, for example, Philip E. Converse, Angus Campbell, Warren E. Miller, and Donald E. Stokes, "Stability and Change in 1960: A Reinstating Election," *American Political Science Review* 55 (June 1961), 269–80.

9. Estimates for 1920 through 1948, based on recall data from national surveys conducted after 1950, are from Kristi Andersen, "Generation, Partisan Shift, and Realignment: A Glance Back to the New Deal," ch. 5 in Norman H. Nie, Sidney Verba, and John R. Petrocik, *The Changing American Voter* (Cambridge, MA: Harvard University Press, 1976), fig. 5.4 at p. 93. The accuracy of such recall-based estimates has been brought into doubt. See, for example, Richard G. Niemi, Richard S. Katz, and David Newman, "Reconstructing Past Partisanship: The Failure of the Party Identification Recall Questions," *American Journal of Political Science* 24 (November 1980), 633–51. Yet the idea of a major change in the balance of party identification during Franklin Roosevelt's first term is generally consistent with evidence on changes in voter registration by party supplied in James L. Sundquist, *Dynamics of the Party System* (Washington, DC: Brookings, 1983), 220–24.

10. Strictly speaking, American party strategists compete for arrays of state-specific pluralities of the popular vote, not for national pluralities of the popular vote. At issue regarding 1960 is the counting of the popular vote in Alabama, which was cast not for the presidential candidates themselves but rather for individual electors, many of them openly anti-Kennedy conservative Democrats, chosen earlier in a hotly contested party primary, who eventually awarded their electoral votes to Senator Harry Byrd of Virginia. In the scholarship on the subject, a case has mounted and now probably stands at somewhere between respectable and compelling that the Alabama popular vote that year should have been recorded by national counters in a fashion that would have yielded Richard Nixon a national popular vote edge over John F. Kennedy. Notably, the Democrats themselves, in preparing for their next national convention in 1964, allocated a delegate total to Alabama on an interpretation of that state's Democratic popular vote in 1960 that would have given Nixon the national edge. See Neal R. Peirce, *The People's President* (New York: Simon and Schuster, 1968), 102–7; Brian J. Gaines, "Popular Myths about Popular Vote-Electoral College Splits," *PS: Political Science and Politics* 34 (March 2001): 71–75; George C. Edwards III, *Why the Electoral College Is Bad for America* (New Haven, CT: Yale University Press, 2004), 48–51. To award the national

vote edge to Kennedy "involves a moderate amount of license," V. O. Key Jr. wrote just after that election in 1961. See Key, "Interpreting the Election Returns," in Paul T. David (ed.), *The Presidential Election and Transition 1960–61* (Washington, DC: Brookings, 1961), 150–75 at 150.

11. Recent examples in the genre include Larry M. Bartels and John Zaller, "Presidential Vote Models: A Recount," *PS: Political Science and Politics* 34 (March 2001): 9–20; Robert S. Erikson, Joseph Bafumi, and Bret Wilson, "Was the 2000 Election Predictable?, *PS: Political Science and Politics* 34 (December 2001): 815–19.

12. This generalization holds for a variety of American public offices. See Stephen Ansolabehere and James M. Snyder Jr., "The Incumbency Advantage in U.S. Elections: An Analysis of State and Federal Offices, 1942–2000," *Election Law Journal* 1:3 (2002), 315–38.

13. Herbert F. Weisberg, "Partisanship and Incumbency in Presidential Elections," *Political Behavior* 24 (December 2002): 339–60.

14. Ray C. Fair, *Predicting Presidential Elections and Other Things* (Stanford, CA: Stanford University Press, 2002), 46–51.

15. David Samuels, "Presidentialism and Accountability for the Economy in Comparative Perspective," *American Political Science Review* 98 (August 2004): 425–36, at 428–29. This analysis is confined to instances where presidential and legislative elections occurred concurrently.

16. Helmut Norpoth, "Bush v. Gore: The Recount of Economic Voting," ch. 3 in Herbert F. Weisberg and Clyde Wilcox, eds., *Models of Voting in Presidential Elections* (Stanford, CA: Stanford University Press, 2004), 60–63.

17. This point may become plainer as Phil Lampi makes available his new data set "A New Nation Votes: American Election Returns, 1787–1825." Gathered over a period of several decades through an examination of early American newspapers, this data set supplies returns for elections to some 60,000 offices. See the discussion in Jill Lepore, "Party Time: Smear Tactics, Skullduggery, and the Debut of American Democracy," *The New Yorker,* September 17, 2007, 94–98, at p. 97. For current access to the Lampi data set, see the website of the Antiquarian Society, http://dca.tufts.edu/features/aas/

18. See Norman K. Risjord, "Election of 1812," pp. 249–72 in Arthur M. Schlesinger Jr., ed., *History of American Presidential Elections, 1789–1968,* vol. I (New York: McGraw-Hill, 1971).

19. Ron Chernow, *Alexander Hamilton* (New York: Penguin Books, 2005), 608. On the contest in New York City in 1800, see also Edward J. Larson, *A Magnificent Catastrophe: The Tumultuous Election of 1800, America's First Presidential Campaign* (New York: Free Press, 2007), ch. 4.

20. In 1800, according to Lepore, "Party Time," the new Lampi data set credits the Jeffersonian Republicans with roughly 52 percent of the major-party vote across a variety of offices. That is in the neighborhood of the percentage won by the Bush Republicans in 2004 for president and U.S. House.

21. Samuel P. Huntington, *Political Order in Changing Societies* (New Haven, CT: Yale University Press, 1968), 129, 133.

22. The runner-up is the second-place finisher in the popular vote, which means Stephen Douglas in 1860 and Theodore Roosevelt in 1912.

23. More specifically, for each election, this is the difference between the winner's and the runner-up's percentage of the total electoral vote.

24. This is a statistical relation although obviously not a causal one. In the cases of elections where popular and electoral vote edges went in different directions, the values for the popular vote edges in these calculations are slightly negative.

25. Omitted from the calculation are the elections of 1860 and 1912, which brought major-party schisms, and that of 1864, for which the relation between popular and electoral vote edges was way out of line owing no doubt to the Civil War and the absence of the Southern states from the electoral universe.

26. This is marshy territory. Not only is the election of 1960 a puzzle, but there is a certain artifactuality to the results of the very close elections of 1884 and 1888. Only a slight relaxing of the intimidation of African American voters in the South — nothing on the order of overturning the Democratic regimes of the decisively black-majority states of Mississippi and South Carolina — would probably have yielded a national popular edge for the Republican James Blaine juxtaposed to an electoral edge for the Democrat Grover Cleveland in 1884, or a joint popular and electoral vote edge for the Republican Benjamin Harrison in 1888. There is also 1880. A rainstorm in the wrong place that year might have washed away the Republican James Garfield's national popular vote edge of fewer than 10,000 votes, although perhaps not his electoral vote edge, thus yielding another split result. At a level more basic than a rainstorm, a small Democratic edge in the 1880 popular vote during this era of dubious counts could also have been plausibly credited to the intimidation of African Americans in the South. Various conflicting reports place the national Garfield margin at 1,898, 7,368, or 9,457 votes. See Kenneth D. Ackerman, *Dark Horse: The Surprise Election and Political Murder of President James A. Garfield* (New York: Carroll & Graf, 2003), 13.

27. That edge approximates those of Truman over Thomas E. Dewey in 1948, Kennedy over Nixon in 1960, and Nixon over Hubert H. Humphrey in 1968.

28. See Risjord, "Election of 1812"; Marshall Smelser, *The Democratic Republic, 1801–1815* (New York: Harper and Row, 1968), 245–48.

29. On the case of 1920, see David R. Mayhew, "Wars and American Politics," *Perspectives on Politics* 3 (September 2005): 473–93, at 484.

30. In 1864, not just for technical reasons, the winning ticket had been labeled Union rather than Republican. Note that to reverse the coding decisions for 1844 and 1868 would not alter the summary figures here, since the victorious Whigs of 1840 *lost* in 1844 whereas the victorious Republicans (Unionists) of 1864 *won* in 1868.

31. Christopher Achen, "A Baseline for Incumbency Effects," manuscript at Department of Politics, Princeton University, September 2007.

32. These and the following results issue from a single-tailed brute-force test suitable for small samples. I owe the calculations to Joel Middleton and Joseph Sempolinski.

33. A variety of patterns can emerge through subdividing the data by eras, and stories can be woven about such patterns, yet, aside from the mid-1820s, it is not clear where to bound the eras, and whatever the boundaries might be, the numbers available for analysis

are small. For example, in-parties kept the presidency eight out of fourteen times before 1900 in open-seat circumstances, but have done so only three out of eight times since 1900 in those circumstances. It would probably be hazardous to discern much meaning in such a disparity.

34. This fifty-fifty result corresponds to a finding by Gans, "Persistence of Party Success," 232. For the presidential elections of 1856 through 1980, using relative sizes of popular vote pluralities (rather than win versus loss) as dependent variable, there is no statistical relation between a party's previous and its current electoral strength once elections featuring repeat candidates (that is, an incumbent running again, or a repeat challenger such as William Jennings Bryan in 1900) are removed from the picture. "When the effect of voter response to candidate personality is removed from the analysis, the short-term persistence of party success declines to levels indistinguishable from zero."

35. Of course, contextual information specific to 2008 could improve the prediction, much as this morning's forecast ordinarily performs better than the *Farmer's Almanac* in predicting the weather.

36. For a helpful discussion of the range of possibilities, see James E. Campbell, *The American Campaign* (College Station: Texas A&M Press, 2000), 40–42, 110–23.

37. See John R. Hibbing, *Congressional Careers* (Chapel Hill: University of North Carolina Press, 1991), 32–35.

38. See Tim Groseclose, "A Model of Candidate Location When One Candidate Has a Valence Advantage," *American Journal of Political Science* 45 (October 2001): 862–86. This model does not address candidates specifically for the presidency.

39. This argument works less well for the nineteenth century when presidential candidates were recessive. But they were not always recessive, and sometimes they had managers who gained experience across campaigns.

40. See, for example, M. Daniel Bernhardt and Daniel E. Ingberman, "Candidate Reputations and the 'Incumbency Effect,'" *Journal of Public Economics* 27 (June 1985): 47–67.

41. On Kennedy, Eisenhower, and the Bay of Pigs, see Philip B. K. Potter, "Does Experience Matter? American Presidential Experience, Age, and International Conflict," *Journal of Conflict Resolution* 51 (June 2007): 351–78, at 355–58.

42. I owe this idea to Alan Gerber.

43. See Sendhil Mullainathan and Ebonya Washington, "Sticking with Your Vote: Cognitive Dissonance and Voting," paper presented at the American Politics Seminar, Yale University, September 5, 2007.

44. John Zaller, "Politicians as Prize Fighters: Electoral Selection and Incumbency Advantage," ch. 6 in John G. Geer, ed., *Politicians and Party Politics* (Baltimore: Johns Hopkins University Press, 1998), quotations at 125, 126.

45. Ibid., 172.

46. See Achen, "A Baseline for Incumbency Effects." From the paper's abstract: "Incumbents would generally be reelected even without the advantages of office, since they are proven winners and thus likely to defeat the average challenger."

47. One reason may be that an out-party gets hungrier, more focused, and more inclined to appease the median voter the longer it keeps losing. For an analysis of incumbent-party fatigue based on the elections of 1948 through 2000, see Bartels and Zaller, "Presidential

Vote Models," 17. Certain forecasting models have also pointed to in-party decay: Alan I. Abramowitz, "When Good Forecasts Go Bad: The Time-for-Change Model and the 2004 Presidential Election," *PS: Political Science and Politics* 37 (October 2004), 745–46; Helmut Norpoth, "From Primary to General Election: A Forecast of the Presidential Vote," *PS: Political Science and Politics* 37 (October 2004), 737–40. In general, a homeostatic tendency toward party equilibrium should be the result of in-party decay, as is suggested in Donald E. Stokes, "On the Existence of Forces Restoring Party Competition," *Public Opinion Quarterly* 26 (Summer 1962), 159–71.

48. Samuels, "Presidentialism and Accountability," 428–29.

49. Fair, *Predicting Presidential Elections,* 46–51.

50. The *F*-value for the equation accommodating the two *X* variables, a test of their joint significance, is 2.61, yielding a *p*-value of 0.0859.

51. See Gary C. Jacobson and Samuel Kernell, *Strategy and Choice in Congressional Elections* (New Haven, CT: Yale University Press, 1983).

52. See the argument in Weisberg, "Partisanship and Incumbency," 342.

53. The Federalists had a weak bench after 1800, but it was weak in all circumstances.

54. Thus omitted are John Tyler in 1844, Millard Fillmore in 1852, Andrew Johnson in 1868, Chester Arthur in 1884, Theodore Roosevelt in 1904, Calvin Coolidge in 1924, Harry Truman in 1948, Lyndon B. Johnson in 1964, and Gerald Ford in 1976.

55. Finally, Theodore Roosevelt served in the presidency all except six months, and Truman all except three months, of a full two terms.

56. Truman wrote in his 1950 memo: "In my opinion eight years as President is enough and sometimes too much for any man to serve in that capacity. There is a lure in power. It can get into a man's blood just as gambling and lust for money have been known to do. This is a Republic. . . . I want this country to continue as a Republic. Cincinnatus and Washington pointed the way. . . . When we forget the examples of such men as Washington, Jefferson, and Andrew Jackson, all of whom could have had a continuation in office, then will we start down the road to dictatorship and ruin. I know I could be elected again and continue to break the old precedent as it was broken by F.D.R. It should not be done." Truman's staff quickly talked him out of his flirtation in 1952. See Harold F. Gosnell, *Truman's Crises* (Westport, CT: Greenwood, 1980), 507–10, quotation at p. 507; Robert H. Ferrell, *Harry S. Truman: A Life* (Columbia: University of Missouri Press, 1994), 376; Cabell Phillips, *The Truman Presidency* (New York: Macmillan, 1966), 414–19; Donald R. McCoy, *The Presidency of Harry S. Truman* (Lawrence: University Press of Kansas, 1984), 300–301.

57. Roy R. Nichols, *Franklin Pierce* (Philadelphia: University of Pennsylvania Press, 1958), 452.

58. Charles Sellers, "Election of 1844," pp. 747–861 in Schlesinger, ed., *History of Elections,* vol. I, 774–75.

59. Ari Hoogenboom, *Rutherford B. Hayes* (Lawrence: University Press of Kansas, 1995), 266–67.

60. Philip S. Klein, *President James Buchanan: A Biography* (University Park: Pennsylvania State University Press, 1962), 332, 340, quotation, which appeared in a letter from Buchanan to the wife of ex-president James K. Polk, at 340. On the subject of presidential service, there is a tradition of treating the immediate antebellum decades as a time apart:

"This was an era of one-term Presidencies and of frequent rejection of the President as party leader. The Whig platform of 1844 advocated a one-term limit. James K. Polk announced that he would not be a candidate for a second term; Franklin Pierce tried for the nomination and failed. James Buchanan found it expedient not to make the effort. The four-year limitation was accepted in principle to the point where Horace Greeley could use it electorally as a substantial argument against the renomination of Abraham Lincoln in 1864. With Abraham Lincoln and Ulysses S. Grant, however, the two-term tradition was restored." Paul T. David, Ralph M. Goldman, and Richard C. Bain, *The Politics of National Party Conventions* (Washington, DC: Brookings, 1960), 13–14. Perhaps a one-term norm did obtain for awhile. On the other hand, these are small numbers. We might not be entertaining any such case if just one domineering politician on the order of Andrew Jackson had come along around 1850.

61. Donald R. McCoy, *Calvin Coolidge: The Quiet President* (Lawrence: University Press of Kansas, 1988), 389–90, 412; Claude M. Fuess, *Calvin Coolidge: The Man from Vermont* (Boston: Little, Brown, 1940), 392–401, 458–64.

62. Robert Dallek, *Flawed Giant: Lyndon Johnson and His Times, 1961–1973* (New York: Oxford University Press, 1998), 519–30 on Johnson's decision whether to run again, 522–23, 526–29 specifically on the health considerations. See also Irwin Unger and Debi Unger, *LBJ: A Life* (New York: Harper and Row, 1999), 439–41, 458–59; Randall B. Woods, *LBJ: Architect of American Ambition* (New York: Free Press, 2006), 767–68, 817. The actuarial study predicted death at age 64. In fact, Johnson died at age 64 and a half.

63. Dallek, *Flawed Giant*, 602, 605, 619–22. See also Woods, *Architect of American Ambition*, 882–84.

64. Coolidge and Johnson in additional terms of office might have collapsed from command as did Woodrow Wilson.

65. There is an additional consideration. Perhaps the electorate can be expected to exact an illegitimacy penalty next time against candidates who won, or more precisely are perceived to have won, the White House via the electoral college though lacking a popular vote edge. In American history, the instances of incumbents running again carrying this baggage have been John Quincy Adams in 1828, Benjamin Harrison in 1892, and George W. Bush in 2004. The instances are suggestive but the number is small.

66. Perhaps an analysis of state governorship elections would offer leverage. Yet caution is advisable. Governors do not conduct wars or manage foreign-policy crises, and they do not command the attention or resources that presidents do. Differences like these might bear on the categories of explanation offered here in Table 14.3. For example, voter risk-averseness might play a different role regarding officials who do not have a nuclear button to press.

67. On FDR's decision, see Kenneth S. Davis, *FDR: Into the Storm, 1937–1940* (New York: Random House, 1993), 532–35, 584–86; Frank Freidel, *Franklin D. Roosevelt: Rendezvous with Destiny* (Boston: Little, Brown, 1990), 327–28, 341, 346. See also Robert E. Sherwood, *Roosevelt and Hopkins* (New York: Harper and Brothers, 1948), 169–73, quotation at 169: "It is safe to say that, if there had been no international crisis, he would not have run."

68. By happenstance, in one contribution of survey testimony, the Columbia research-

ers Paul Lazarsfeld, Bernard Berelson, and Hazel Gaudet were conducting their well-known Erie County panel study for *The People's Choice* (New York: Columbia University Press, 3rd edition, 1968) during 1940. They found (quotation at 71): "The first influence on the changers [that is, voters changing their minds] as a whole came in June, with the fall of France. The repercussions of that turn in the European war were strongly favorable to the Democrats. Of the people who definitely decided their vote in June, two thirds decided for the Democrats, mainly on the ground that the European crisis necessitated the continuance of an experienced administration in Washington."

69. Gallup Poll data available at the Roper Center's iPOLL Databank. FDR's readings during this time span were generally in that range if the denominators are allowed to include "no opinion" responses. For an analysis covering the era, see Matthew A. Baum and Samuel Kernell, "Economic Class and Popular Support for Franklin Roosevelt in War and Peace," *Public Opinion Quarterly* 65 (Summer 2001), 198–229.

70. The third-term time series, which includes chiefly Gallup polls, is available at the Roper Center's iPOLL Databank. Roosevelt's biographer James MacGregor Burns has written: "As the crisis deepened, Roosevelt's popular backing mounted strongly. Millions of Americans forgot their concern for the third-term tradition as they instinctively rallied behind their leader against the trouble outside." See Burns, *Roosevelt: The Lion and the Fox* (New York: Harcourt, Brace and World, 1956), 422. In Roper surveys in August and September of 1940, respectively 47% and 50% of respondents chose the option "While it may not generally be a good idea for a president to serve three terms, there should be no rule preventing him at a time of national crisis," against the options of, essentially, a third-term bar is a silly idea (15% and 16%) or third terms should never be allowed (34% and 30%). Data available at the Roper Center's iPOLL Databank.

71. The Roosevelt versus Dewey time series is from Hadley Cantril, *Public Opinion, 1935–1946* (Princeton, N. J.: Princeton University Press, 1951), p. 650.

72. Ibid., item 62 (OPOR), p. 617.

73. Ibid., item 76 (AIPO), p. 618.

74. See the discussions in Robert A. Divine, *Foreign Policy and U.S. Presidential Elections: 1940, 1948* (New York: New Viewpoints, 1974), chs. 1, 2; Michael Barone, *Our Country: The Shaping of America from Roosevelt to Reagan* (New York: Free Press, 1990), 133–34, 145, 156, 181.

75. Cantril, *Public Opinion,* item 59 (FOR), p. 617. An announced caveat: "Southern Negroes were omitted in this tabulation because their franchise is largely ineffective."

76. Ibid., items 15 (AIPO) at p. 607, 18 (AIPO) at p. 609, 21 (AIPO) at p. 609, 31 (AIPO) at p. 613, 16 (AIPO at p. 608, 17 (AIPO) at p. 608.

77. See Divine, *Foreign Policy,* chs. 5–7.

Index

academic culture, 262–63
accountability, 21–23, 43n15, 78–79
Achen, Christopher, 369, 373, 388n46
actions, 1, 10, chap. 10; coded, 236–37
advertising, 31–32, 40–42, 66–67
agriculture policy: New Deal, 141, 158, 298, 335; post-*1945*, 97, 127, 195; pre–New Deal, 37–38, 157, 298, 304, 314, 337
Alabama, 39, 385n10
America's Congress data set, 268n26
Arnold, R. Douglas, 13n11, 129n9, 351n92
assassinations, 11, 123, 143, 144, 155, 160, 341–43, 380–81
Australia, 140, 142, 146, 311, 340, 350n56

banking and currency policy: through *1900*, 155, 163, 182, 217, 293, 295, 302, 314, 339; post-*1900*, 109, 157, 158–59, 239, 335
Barone, Michael, 50n99, 52n123, 184, 267n10, 391n74
Bartels, Larry M., 199, 209–10, 221, 319n94, 319n95, 334, 373–75
Baucus, Max, 4–5, 228, 232, 235
Boxer, Barbara, 242, 267n17
Brady, David W., 178n32, 199, 203, 204, 217
Britain: parliamentary system, 6, 21–23, 254, 260, 270n46, 281; parties in, 148, 192–93, 222, 310, 311; policies in *1940s*, 88, 300, 304, 318n63; policies post-*1940s*, 144–45, 146, 347; policies pre-*1940*, 139–40, 142, 297, 338, 340; pre-*1900*, 44n29, 148, 192–93, 222, 260, 281, 302; and World War I, 220, 310, 311; and World War II, 12, 270n39, 329, 383
Broder, David S., 102, 115, 116, 268n29, 283, 283n1

393